INFORMATION TECHNOLOGY LAW IN IRELAND

by

Denis Kelleher

BCL, HDip Econ Sc, Barrister-at-Law

and

Karen Murray

BA, LLB, LLM (QUB), Barrister-at-Law and lecturer in law, National College of Industrial Relations

Butterworths

Ireland	Butterworth (Ireland) Ltd, 26 Upper Ormond Quay, DUBLIN 7
United Kingdom	Butterworths a Division of Reed Elsevier (UK) Ltd, Halsbury House, 35 Chancery Lane, LONDON WC2A 1EL and 4 Hill Street, EDINBURGH EH2 3JZ
Australia	Butterworths Pty Ltd, SYDNEY, MELBOURNE, BRISBANE, ADELAIDE, PERTH, CANBERRA and HOBART
Canada	Butterworths Canada Ltd, TORONTO and VANCOUVER
Malaysia	Malayan Law Journal Sdn Bhd, KUALA LUMPUR
New Zealand	Butterworths of New Zealand Ltd, WELLINGTON and AUCKLAND
Puerto Rico	Butterworths of Puerto Rico Inc, SAN JUAN
Singapore	Reed Elsevier (Singapore) Ltd, SINGAPORE
South Africa	Butterworths Legal Publishers (Pty) Ltd, DURBAN
USA	Michie, CHARLOTTESVILLE, Virginia

© Butterworth Ireland Ltd 1997

A CIP Catalogue record for this book is available from the British Library.

ISBN 1 85475 825X

ISBN 1 85475 825X

Printed in Ireland by Microprint, Dublin.

Preface

The information technology industry is now one of the major engines of growth in the Irish economy. The rapid expansion in the use of information technology means that society in general and lawyers in particular can no longer ignore the reality that legal questions and difficulties will arise in this area in the future. IT will greatly affect certain areas of law, one notable example is the difficulty which intellectual property law faces in the protection of computer programs. Another example is the challenge to the traditional right of privacy created by information technology methods such as data mining. At the same time, some sectors of the information technology industry will find that their growth and success will be determined by their ability to enforce their legal rights. Although the technology behind the Internet and the World-Wide-Web is developing rapidly, many aspects of the law and Irish law in particular will have to adapt and be reformed to take account of these developments.

The Internet is a global network on which distance and location are meaningless. As a result, the international aspects of law are highly significant in the IT law context. At present, many of the initiatives in IT law stem from the European Union. The IT industry and the Internet are heavily dominated by the USA and this means that US standards and decisions are more influential on IT law in Ireland than would usually be the case. This influence can be seen in two ways. Firstly, the direct pressure which the American government has put on the European Union to protect American copyright interests, for example the Software Protection Directive and the Semiconductor Chip Directive. Secondly, the USA is the largest user and supplier of information technology and as a result its courts have the greatest experience of dealing with these problems. This means that US court decisions may be read with greater than usual interest by Irish judges faced with similar problems.

This book explains how the law applies to IT. One of the distinctive features of IT law is that it involves virtually all the legal disciplines, a feature which reflects the fact that IT is now commonplace in all sectors of society. As a result, this book analyses the relationship between IT and diverse legal disciplines such as constitutional, criminal and intellectual property law. Such diversity of analysis is essential but to prevent this book becoming a sprawling legal compendium we have been forced to impose limitations upon ourselves. In particular, readers who are not lawyers should realise that tort and contract law are highly complex areas of law, the fact that they do not occupy as large a part of this book as data protection merely reflects the fact that there has been less legislative and judicial consideration of their relationship to date.

We would like to thank the following people for their assistance: The Data Protection Commissioner, Mr Fergus Glavey; Bob Semple of Price Waterhouse; Amanda Murray, software systems developer for her valuable technical advice; the staff of the Law Library; Louise Leavy, Gerard Coakley and the staff of Butterworths; and finally, Pepsi for taking us for walks.

Denis Kelleher & Karen Murray
Law Library
Four Courts
Dublin 7
kellehed@tcd.ie
kmurray@college.ncir.ie
March 1997

Contents

Chapter 11 Patents and Computer Programs

Chapter 12 Competition Law

Chapter 13 Computer Misuse

Chapter 14 Offences under the Criminal Damage Act 1991

Chapter 15 The Investigation and Prosecution of Offences under the Criminal Damage Act 1991

Chapter 16 Defences under the Criminal Damage Act 1991

Chapter 17 Reform of the Criminal Damage Act 1991

Chapter 18 Other Relevant Offences

Chapter 19 The Origins and Scope of Data Protection

Chapter 20 Control of Data Processing

Chapter 21 Rights of the Data Subject

Chapter 22 The Supervision of Data Protection

Chapter 23 The Reality of Data Protection

Chapter 24 Evidence

Chapter 25 Control of Content on the Internet

Chapter 26 Privacy

Chapter 27 Electronic Commerce

Table of Statutes

Table of Cases

P

R

Chapter 1

Introduction

[1.01] It is less than two decades since the first IBM Personal Computer ('PC') was introduced. Since then rapid developments in computer technology have allowed people to manipulate information in ways which would have been unthinkable 25 years ago. The Internet allows people from around the globe to interact and communicate, the World Wide Web makes this process simpler and more user friendly. However, the computer or information technology industry gives rise to a wide variety of legal concerns. Some of these concerns have resulted in the creation of legislation or case law on computer crimes, privacy, data protection and intellectual property law. Other areas of interest include the treatment of computer evidence in court, the control of content such as pornography and the supply of computer goods and services.

WHAT IS A COMPUTER?

[1.02] Arriving at a satisfactory definition of the term 'computer' is difficult. Legislation in both Ireland and the UK avoids giving such a definition. *The Concise Oxford Dictionary* defines a computer as "A usually electronic device for storing and processing data ... according to instructions given to it in a variable program".[1] Although computers may be traced back to Charles Babbage, a nineteenth century mathematician who invented a 'differential engine' which used cogs and wheels to carry out calculations, the modern history of the industry probably begins with the development of the microprocessor. The creation of the first commercial microprocessor (or chip) in 1971 by Intel, both allowed and defined the resulting development of computers. Once the 'computer on a chip' was completed, it was obvious that it would have applications greater than the calculator for which it was initially intended. Soon the original chip was replaced by faster and faster versions. The 4004 chip, made partly of wood, carried 2300 transistors and had a speed of 750 Khz. In contrast, a Pentium Pro contains 5,500,000 transistors and has a speed of 200 Mhz. However as each of these versions was developed it encountered the problem of compatibility with older models. As a result, compromises introduced to deal with problems

---

[1.] 8th Ed (1990).

1

encountered on relatively slow chips such as the 4004 and the 8086 continue to cause problems today long after the chips for which they were created have ceased to be used in PCs.[2] The Intel chip was extremely popular and it was chosen by IBM when it decided to produce a Personal Computer.

[1.03] The manufacture and sale of the first PC by IBM was the most important development for the computer industry in the 1980s. Due to IBM's then dominance of the corporate market for main-frame computers the computer industry swiftly coalesced around this standard. There were other types of small computer in existence at the time, notably those manufactured by Apple, but IBM had a reassuringly dominant presence in the computer market. The IBM PC soon became popular, but IBM had totally underestimated the demand which their machine would create and it made the crucial mistake of not retaining control of crucial elements of the PC. To keep costs down, components such as the microprocessor and the operating system were bought in from outside suppliers, in this case Intel and Microsoft. These companies were to reap the bulk of the benefits from the future development of the PC.

[1.04] The production of the first microprocessor was impressive but it was a mere curiosity without programs to run on it. Computer programs may be divided into two groups, the operating system such as DOS, OS-2 or UNIX, which manages the operation of the computer, and application software which interact with the operating system and allow tasks such as word-processing (Microsoft Word, WordPerfect, Lotus Amipro) or spreadsheets (Microsoft Excel, Lotus 1-2-3).

[1.05] The relationship between the hardware of a computer (the chip, hard drive and so on) and the programs which run on it has caused problems in the past. Glidewell LJ of the English Court of Appeal in *St Albans City and District Council v International Computers Ltd*[3] considered the question of whether software can be said to be goods. He compared a defective computer program contained on a disk to a defective instruction manual on the maintenance and repair of a car. This analogy is probably incorrect, a car may well drive without the owner having a maintenance manual but computer hardware without a program is a useless (and ugly) lump of plastic and circuitry. A preferable explanation of the functions of computer hardware and software is that given by Laddie J in *Fujitsu Ltd's Application*:[4]

---

2. BYTE, December 1996.
3. 15 Tr L 444, *The Times* 14 August 1996.
4. [1996] RPC 511.

"A general purpose computer may be looked upon as a piece of electronic putty. It is moulded into a useful working apparatus by the programs run on it. It may be thought of as the electronic equivalent of a large box of cogs, wheels, cams, nuts and bolts - a Meccano set - ready to be assembled into a variety of different articles."

[1.06] Over-reliance on analogies with physical objects such as these may ultimately cause more problems than it solves. Computers are far more flexible than Meccano sets, they are more capable than anything which may be constructed using putty. The difference between the two might be better explained by taking as a rule of thumb that if some part of a computer is tangible then it is hardware, if it is intangible then it is software. In legal terms hardware will be treated as personal property in much the same way as a television. Software is intellectual property and will be treated in the same way as literary works.[5]

WHAT IS INFORMATION TECHNOLOGY?

[1.07] The use of the term 'computer' tends to focus attention unduly on the physical components which make up a computer system. However these physical parts are only one part of the industry, the programs which run on a system, the human expertise required to run that system and the data which the system will manipulate are all important parts of the industry. As a result it has become common to refer instead to 'information technology' which encompasses all these elements and various others.[6]

HOW DOES THE LAW APPLY TO THESE NEW TECHNOLOGIES?

[1.08] In recent years the law has developed and adapted to take account of these new technologies. In Ireland, these developments have taken the form of legislation such as the Data Protection Act 1988 and the Criminal Damage Act 1991. It is true that information technology promises (or threatens) to facilitate human activities in all areas of life from social relationships to commerce. This means that just about every aspect of law can be shown to have some putative relationship to the Internet or another aspect of information technology. The object of this book is not to catalogue such relationships, whether real or otherwise, *ad nauseam*, instead it

---

5. However both software and hardware may be 'goods' for the purpose of the Sale of Goods Act 1897-1980: see Ch 28.
6. The term 'Information Technology' is defined by the UK Carriage of Goods by Sea Act 1992 which states that the term "includes any computer or other technology by means of which information or other matter may be recorded or communicated without being reduced to documentary form".

concentrates on those areas where a substantive body of law has grown up. The main areas at present are: Intellectual Property Law; Computer Crime Law; and, Privacy and Data Protection.

The Role of Intellectual Property Law

[1.09] Intellectual property law and information technology have a symbiotic relationship with one another. On the one hand information technology has made intellectual property law far more important. Since 1980 the personal computer industry has moved from non-existence to being worth $100 billion a year, a rise which has been described as "fastest legal accumulation of wealth in history".[7] The main wealth of this industry is information, knowledge and know-how, intellectual property law allows this wealth to be exploited. Copyright law was until recently the 'Cinderella subject of intellectual property law',[8] however, the arrival of information technology has moved the subject centre stage. The suggestion that 'information is money' is now accepted wisdom for people who are told that they are (or soon to be) members of an 'Information Society' living in an 'Information Age'. Intellectual property law allows the companies which manufacture computer equipment, programs and other material for the information technology industry to fully exploit their products. The companies who collect and manipulate this information, and the companies who supply the equipment to carry out these processes will all want to make money from it. The initial investments required are huge and it is unrealistic to expect companies to supply these goods for altruistic reasons especially as the market for these goods is becoming increasingly international. Intellectual property law allows these goods to be exploited. Intellectual property rights are fundamentally the right to prevent something being done as opposed to a positive right. So the owner of copyright in a work may prohibit or control the copying or translation of his work. Information technology allows material to be copied with ease and at low cost, which has the advantage to the owner exploiting his work but it also makes it easy for the pirate or others who do not want to pay royalties to copy material.

Privacy and Data Protection

[1.10] Although statistical and other information has always been gathered by private companies and the State, information technology allows this information to be exploited to the full. Calculations which would have taken months, if not years, can now be done swiftly using computers. The storage

---

7. *The Economist*, 25 January 1997.
8. Laddie Prescott and Vittoria, *The Modern Law of Copyright and Designs*, (Butterworths, 1995).

of information using computers allows detailed information to be kept on large groups of people for long periods of time. This has caused concern in Europe and the USA, however questions such as these remain more or less undebated in Ireland. As a result of such foreign concerns, expressed in the Strasbourg Convention of 1981, the Data Protection Act became law in 1988. Although Ireland now has at least a minimum level of protection for the personal data of its citizens, these protections are infrequently used and little understood. Ireland badly needs to debate the impact of information technology on such fundamental rights and other important rights such as freedom of speech and free access to information.

Computer Crime

[1.11] Computers may be abused and misused in a myriad of ways. Until recently attention has mostly focused on crimes such as gaining unauthorised access to computers and to computer data. These are offences where computers or other equipment are deceived into allowing access. However there is now increasing attention being paid to the fact that as more social and commercial transactions are carried out on the Internet, then criminal behaviour of the more traditional sort will follow those transactions. These are crimes such as fraud and deception which have humans as their victims, not machines.

Chapter 2

Copyright Protection of Computer Programs

INTRODUCTION

[2.01] The object of intellectual property law is to promote creativity and invention. Intellectual property law gives the creator a monopoly with which to exploit his creation. It is hoped that by doing this, creation will be encouraged since creators will be able to benefit from their inventiveness and creativity. This relationship is most obvious in patent law where an inventor may receive a monopoly, potentially world wide, for his invention. Authors of books, computer programs and the creators of films and music will be protected by copyright.

[2.02] The position of intellectual property rights under the Irish Constitution has been examined in two cases. In *Phonographic Performance Ltd v Cody and Princes Investments Ltd*[1] Keane J said that:

> "The right of the creator of a literary, dramatic, musical or artistic work not to have his or her creation stolen or plagiarised is a right of private property within the meaning of Articles 40.3.2° and 43.1 of the Constitution, as is the similar right of a person who has employed his or her technical skills and/or capital in the sound recording of a musical work".[2]

Since intellectual property has the same constitutional protections as real or physical property it enjoys greatly enhanced protection. However, this protection may also limit the ability of the State to legislate for intellectual property matters. It is of course easy for the State to enhance the protections afforded to intellectual property, however, it may not be as easy to reduce them.

[2.03] The constitutional position of copyright law was referred to in *The Attorney General for England and Wales v Brandon Book Publishers Ltd*[3] where Carroll J adopted the view that there is a constitutional right to publish information which does not involve a breach of copyright. This right would be based in Article 40.6.1° of the Constitution which guarantees liberty for citizens to express freely their convictions and opinions, subject to public order and morality.

[1.] [1994] 2 ILRM 241.
[2.] *Ibid* at 247.
[3.] [1987] ILRM 135.

[2.04] Prior to the adoption of the Council Directive on the Legal Protection of Computer Programs[4] ('the Directive'), computer programs were not clearly protected in all Member States of the EU and the protection which existed was varied.[5] There was a danger that these varying standards of protection could have serious effects on the functioning of the common market.[6] The Council recognised that while the development of computer programs required the investment of considerable human, technical and financial resources they could be copied at a fraction of the cost invested in their development.[7] They regarded computer programs and technology as being of fundamental importance for industrial development in the EU.[8] As a result, the Council adopted the Directive which uses copyright law to protect computer programs as literary works.[9] This has been implemented in Ireland as the European Communities (Legal Protection of Computer Programs) Regulations 1993[10] ('The Regulations'). The Regulations faithfully reproduce most of the provisions of the Directive. They apply to all computer programs including those which were created before 1 January 1993 without prejudice to any acts concluded or rights acquired before that date.[11] They do not adapt or clarify any of the definitions or provisions contained in the Copyright Act 1963 and this can lead to inconsistencies.

[2.05] The decision to implement the Directive by means of a regulation as opposed to reforming copyright law by statute is unfortunate. The drafters of the Copyright Act 1963 ('the 1963 Act'), never anticipated that their Act would be used to protect computer software. It is conceivable that the 1963 Act might have been stretched to protect computer programs.[12] However,

---

4. Council Directive 91/250 of 14 May 1991 on the Legal Protection of Computer Programs. 1991 OJ L 122/42.
5. Recital 1 to the Directive.
6. Recital 4.
7. Recital 2.
8. Recital 3.
9. Article 1(1) of the Directive.
10. SI 26/1993.
11. Regulation 9(2).
12. Courts in other jurisdictions have held that computer programs are protected by copyright as literary works without specific legislation. See *Apple Computer v Franklin Computer* 714 F2d 1240 (3rd Circuit) 1983, an Amercian decision. See also *Apple Computer v Segimex* [1985] FSR 608, a decision of the French courts and *Re Copying of Computer Programs* [1990] ECC 465 a decision of the Austrian Supreme Court. In contrast, see a decision of the Australian High Court *Computer Edge v Apple Computer* [1986] FSR 537, where it was held that although the source code of a program was protected as an original literary work, the object code was not.

using this outmoded legislation to protect modern technology will inevitably lead to difficulties.

WHAT IS A COMPUTER PROGRAM?

[2.06] In common with other legislation, the Directive and the Regulations avoid defining terms such as 'computer' or 'computer program'. This is to avoid limiting the scope of legislation to current technologies. This approach is not used everywhere. The World Intellectual Property Organisation (WIPO) has published a definition of computer programs as follows:

> A computer program is a set of instructions expressed in words, codes, schemes or in any other form, which is capable, when incorporated in a machine-readable medium, of causing a 'computer' (an electronic or similar device having information-processing capabilities) to perform or achieve a particular task or result.[13]

[2.07] US copyright law defines computer programs as "a set of statements or instructions to be used directly or indirectly in a computer in order to bring about a certain result".[14]

[2.08] Regulation 2(1) states that the term 'computer program' includes all design materials used in the preparation of the program.[15] The nature of the preparatory work must be such that a computer program can result from it at a later stage.[16] Whether this confers any greater protection on preparatory design materials (such as flow charts) than existed prior to the Directive is doubtful. Once the material was written down it would be protected from copying and other infringements by normal copyright law as an original work anyway. It is probable that the copyright in preparatory design materials could be infringed by developing a computer program based on the design materials of others.[17]

[13.] WIPO, preparatory document (BCP/CE/1/2) for the first session of the Committee of Experts on a Possible Protocol to the Berne Convention, 1991, para 19.

[14.] 17 USC s 101 (1988).

[15.] Regulation 2(2) provides that a word or expression that is used in the Regulations and is also used in the Directive, has unless the context otherwise requires, the same meaning in the Regulations as it has in the Directive.

[16.] Recital 7 to the Directive.

[17.] However, it is questionable whether such preparatory materials would be protected under US law. Flow charts and other graphic representations of a program would possibly be characterised under US law as 'graphic works' which would be subject to 115a 'useful article' limitation. See Samuelson, 'Comparing US 115 and EC Copyright Protection for Computer Programs', Journal of Law and Commerce, Vol 13, 1994, p 279.

[2.09] The source and object codes[18] of a computer program are equally protected since the Directive protects computer programs in any form.[19] In *Total Information Processing Systems Ltd v Daman Ltd*,[20] Baker J suggested that because considerable steps are frequently taken to protect the confidentiality of source code, there may be a doubt that taken by itself the source codes can be the subject of copyright. In the subsequent case of *Ibcos Computers Ltd v Barclays Finance Ltd*[21] Jacob J stated that he did not understand this observation which had not been supported by counsel appearing in the case. He suggested that merely because someone keeps material confidential does not mean that it is not protected by copyright. After all, if a person does not want his personal property stolen, then it is better to hide it away than to give thieves easy access to it.

[2.10] The Directive protects computer programs in any form including those which are incorporated into hardware.[22] An example of a software program incorporated into hardware would be the 'smart cards' which were the subject of litigation in *News Datacom Ltd, British Sky Broadcasting and Sky Television plc v David Lyons, t/a Satellite Decoding Systems*.[23]

The Idea/Expression Dichotomy

[2.11] Generally speaking, ideas are contained in the mind of an individual and they cannot be the subject of copyright. It is only when those ideas are written down that they become expressions. As Lardner J said "the requirement that it (the work) be original relates to the expression of matter in writing or print rather than the ideas expressed".[24]

[2.12] Regulation 3(3) states:

---

18. Computer programs are created by writing lines of instructions. These lines together create the 'source code' for a program. Usually source code is written in a high level programming language which resembles English and can be understood by the programmers. The computer itself cannot easily understand these high level languages, such as BASIC, FORTRAN, C++ and so the source code is converted into a machine readable form. This is known as 'object or machine code'. Usually all programs which are sold commercially are sold in the form of object code. This code consists of a string of numbers, which are 1s and 0s. Different combinations of these numbers form commands which instruct the computer to perform certain functions. Even the simplest operation may demand several lines of object code. These lines of code will appear as a continuous stream of 1s and 0s and as such will be incomprehensible to humans.
19. Recital 7.
20. [1992] FSR 171.
21. [1994] FSR 275.
22. Recital 7.
23. [1994] 1 ILRM 450. See para **[4.19]** *et seq.*
24. *Ibid.*

The ideas and principles which underlie any element of a computer program, including those which underlie its interfaces,[25] are not protected by copyright under these Regulations.

Recital 14 to the Directive is more extensive than the Regulation. It provides:

... to the extent that logic, algorithms and programming languages comprise ideas and principles, those ideas and principles are not protected under this Directive.

This does not mean that a programming language or algorithm will automatically be excluded from protection by copyright, only that the ideas and principles which are expressed by that algorithm or programming language will not be protected.

[2.13] Copying a computer program is possible without actually reproducing the lines of code. The structure and layout of a program may be more valuable than the actual codes themselves. The question then arises of whether or not the structure and layout of a program are merely ideas and as such not within the scope of copyright law. A sequence of ideas has been held to be the subject of copyright. For example, an adaptation of a short story as a ballet would qualify as an infringement, even though no words are spoken and so none of the original expression in the short story is used.[26] Similarly, copying all the ideas or the sequence of ideas used in a program might be infringement even though the actual lines of programming were created independently. This view is strengthened by the protection given to any design materials used in the preparation of a program.[27] Often such design materials contain merely the ideas for a program and none of the expression or actual lines of code.[28]

[2.14] In *Ibcos Computers v Barclays Finance*[29] Jacob J cited with approval the statement by Ferris J in *Richardson v Flanders*[30] that "consideration is not restricted to the text of the code". This, he felt, was correct because most literary works involve both literal matter (the code itself) and various levels of abstraction (the general structure of the computer program). Jacob J therefore felt that both the literal features of a program and its program

---

25. Interfaces are discussed at para **[2.18]** *et seq.*
26. *Holland v Vivian Van Damm Productions Ltd* [1936/45] MCC 69.
27. Regulation 2(1).
28. As computer programs have become larger and more complex, the design and layout of a program has become more important than the actual code which is often written by huge teams of programmers.
29. [1994] FSR 275.
30. [1993] FSR 497.

structure and design features were capable of being copied in breach of copyright. He disagreed with the suggestion that if there is only one way of expressing an idea, no copyright can subsist in it.[31] He suggested that the true position is that:

> "where an idea is sufficiently general, then even if an original work embodies it, the mere taking of that 'idea' will not infringe. But if the 'idea' is detailed, then there may be infringement. It is a question of degree."[32]

Deciding where the division lies between ideas and expressions will often be a question of fact to be decided by the court in a particular case. Direct copying of computer codes almost definitely will be an infringement of copyright, provided the copying is substantial. Deciding whether the structure and other elements of a program embody ideas or expressions is more difficult.[33]

Literary Works

[2.15] It has been suggested that computer programs would have been protected prior to the Regulations, under the 1963 Act as literary works.[34] That assumption may be incorrect in view of the decision in *DPP v Noel Irwin*.[35] In that case, Barron J held that the defendant could not be convicted of copying a video because videos were not protected under the Act as 'cinematographical films', since they did not exist in 1963. The Irish court might have been similarly unwilling to extend the definition of literary work to include computer programs. Regulations have clarified the protection available to computer programs and limited that protection in certain ways. Regulation 3(1) states that:

> ... copyright shall subsist in a computer program and the Copyright Acts, 1963 and 1987, shall apply to every original computer program as if it were a literary work and the legal protection so afforded shall apply to the expression in any form of a computer program.

This protection is expressly made subject to the requirement that the work be original. Literary work is not defined by the Act but it includes "any written

---

31. Baker J in *Total Information Processing v Daman* [1992] FSR 171.
32. Jacob J also suggested that the aphorism "there is no copyright in an idea" is likely to lead to confusion of thought.
33. See infringements at para **[4.11]** *et seq*.
34. See Laddie, Prescott, Vitoria, *The Modern Law Of Copyright And Designs*, (2nd Ed, Butterworths) para 20.21, p 807.
35. High Court, unrep, 25 October 1984, Barron J.

table, or compilation".[36] In *RTÉ v Magill TV Guide Ltd (No 2)*,[37] Lardner J stated that:

> "'literary work' cannot in my judgment be confined to work exhibiting literary art or style. Rather it has the broad sense of any written or printed composition".

ORIGINALITY AND COPYING

[2.16] Under the Regulations, a computer program is protected only if it is original. Regulation 3(2) states that:

> ... A computer program shall be protected if it is original in the sense of being the author's own intellectual creation.

There is no definition of what the 'author's own intellectual creation' actually is. It would appear to be similar to the requirements of the 1963 Act where it simply means that the programmer created the program himself and did not copy it from elsewhere:

> "but produced it independently by the expenditure of a substantial amount of his own skill, knowledge, mental labour, taste or judgment. However, the amount of skill, labour etc which is required to establish a copyright is not large and essentially it suffices if it is not insubstantial. It is not necessary that the work should be the expression of inventive thought, because a substantial amount of purely routine mental labour will equally well satisfy the statutory requirement, conversely, however skill, knowledge etc may make up for a paucity of mental labour."[38]

[2.17] Originality does not mean that the program must be unique or novel in any way. Recital 8 of the Directive states that in deciding whether or not a computer program is original, no tests as to the qualitative or aesthetic merits of the program should be applied. It does not matter how good or bad, complex or simple a program is, nor does it matter how much skill a programmer demonstrates or how improved a program is, the program is still protected.[39] The English courts have found that the aesthetic merits of a work are irrelevant in deciding whether or not the work is a literary work. Exam papers were found to be as worthy of protection as any other work in

---

36. CA 1963, s 2(1).
37. [1989] IR 554.
38. See Laddie Prescott Vitoria, *The Modern Law of Copyright and Designs*, (2nd Ed, Butterworths) para 2.56, p 47.
39. However, the qualifications of authors were noted in *The House of Spring Gardens* case where the plaintiff had acquired considerable expertise and the defendants had none, [1984] IR 631-632. See para **[4.14]** *et seq*.

University of London Press v University Tutorial Press Ltd.[40] Peterson J said:

> "The words 'literary work' cover work which is expressed in print or writing, irrespective of the question whether the quality or style is high. The work 'literary' seems to be used in a sense somewhat similar to the use of the word 'literature' in political or electioneering literature and refers to printed matter."

The provision would appear to have been included to deal with a problem particular to German law. The German courts had formulated an 'average programmer' test which required firstly, that the program be compared to other programs to access its distinctive nature and secondly, that the computer programmer had to have exhibited skills beyond that of the average programmer, otherwise the program would not be protected by copyright.[41]

INTERFACES

[2.18] The code which makes up a computer program is very clearly protected by the Directive and Regulations. The position with regard to other elements of a program is not quite as clear, in particular it is not clear what protection is offered to the user interface of a program.[42] The user interface allows the user of a program to interact with the computer by means of the screen displays and menus which are created by the program. This may be distinguished from interfaces which allow programs to work together or to work with hardware.[43]

[2.19] The Regulations make no specific reference to the user interface of a program. The fact that preparatory materials are specifically protected by the Regulations may be important. In the United States such materials may be categorised as the non-literal elements of a computer program, along with

---

40. [1916] 2 Ch 601, at 608.
41. See Hoeren, *Copyright Software Protection in the EC*, Jongen and Meijboom (eds), (Kluwer Law and Taxation Publishers) p 76.
42. Programs are sometimes sub-divided into their 'literal' and 'non-literal' elements. The literal element of a program is the code which makes up the instructions which control the computer. The non-literal elements of a program are all the parts of the program except the code, including the program's structure, sequence or organisation, screen displays, flow charts and menu structures. This an American division and may not be directly applicable here especially as the preparatory materials used to create a program are specifically included in the programs protection in the EU. In the US the preparatory materials would be classified as non-literal elements of the program and so not necessarily protected.
43. An example of a program interfacing with hardware is a printing program which allows documents created by a word processing program to be printed.

the user interface.[44] The fact that the user interface is not specifically protected may mean that it actually has no protection. Furthermore, the Regulations clearly do not intend that the interfaces which operate between computer programs should be protected. If computer interfaces are not readily available, a user may decompile or dissect a computer program to get them.[45] If the interface which operates between two programs is not protected, it is hard to see how the interface which operates between a user and a program can be protected.

[2.20] In *Lotus v Borland*[46] the United States Court of Appeal for the First Circuit was required to decide whether a computer menu command hierarchy is copyrightable subject matter. In particular, it had to decide whether Lotus's copyright in the software Lotus 1-2-3 was infringed when Borland copied the Lotus 1-2-3 menu command hierarchy into its Quattro and Quattro Pro computer spreadsheet programs. Borland did not contest the fact that its program included "a virtually identical copy of the entire 1-2-3 menu tree". Borland did not copy any of Lotus's underlying code; it copied only the words and structure of Lotus's menu command hierarchy. The purpose of doing so was to enable users who were already familiar with Lotus 1-2-3 to switch to the Borland products without having to learn new commands. Borland offered users a 'Lotus Emulation Interface', this allowed Borland users to see a Lotus menu on their screens and use the Borland product as if it were Lotus 1-2-3, albeit without many of the Borland program functions. The question of whether or not Borland had copied the menu commands was not in issue, the only question was whether or not those commands were protected by copyright. The majority of the Federal Appeal Court held that the Lotus menu structure was not protected. The prohibition against protecting 'a method of operation' was invoked. The menus were held to provide "the means by which users control and operate Lotus 1-2-3". The menus were compared to the control buttons on a video recorder. It would be impossible to copyright the play, record or other buttons on a video recorder. Menu commands on a computer performed a similar function.[47] The court noted that to decide otherwise would condemn

44. See Larvick, 'Questioning the Necessity of Copyright Protection for Software Interfaces', University of Illinois Law Review, Vol 1994, p189.
45. See para **[3.16]** *et seq* on decompilation.
46. 49 F 3d 807; 34 USPQ 2D (BNA) 1014. This decision was appealed to the US Supreme Court, whose decision was eagerly anticipated in the USA. The Supreme Court judgment was an anti-climax however as the Court was unable to agree on an opinion and simply affirmed the decision of the Court below.
47. See Ian Lloyd, '*Lotus v Borland*: New Directions in Software Protection', Computers and Law, April/May 1995, p 16.

the user to learn a different way of performing common functions whenever he used a new program.[48] Even if a similar conclusion was not found to be justified under Irish copyright law, it could be justified by reference to competition law. This decision was appealed to the US Supreme Court which was evenly divided, as a result the decision was upheld and no judgment was given.

AUTHORSHIP

[2.21] Under the Directive "protection shall be granted to all natural or legal persons eligible under national copyright legislation as applied to literary works".[49] This means that authorship is decided by the provisions of the 1963 Act. The Regulation makes no specific reference to authorship, however the Directive recognises that:

> the author of a computer program shall be the natural person or group of natural persons who has created the program or, where the legislation of the Member Sates permits, the legal person designated as the rightholder by that legislation. Where collective works are recognised by the legislation of a Member State, the person considered by the legislation of the Member State to have created the work shall be deemed to be its author.[50]

Some EU Member States do not recognise the rights of corporations or the concept of collective authorship. The Council did not wish to compel those Member States to change their laws.

[2.22] Section 10(1) of the 1963 Act states that the author of an original literary work is entitled to any copyright in his work. Copyright subsists in every original literary work which is *unpublished* and of which the author was a qualified person at the time the work was made or for a substantial period of the time during which the work was being made.[51] A 'qualified person' means a person who is an Irish citizen or is domiciled or resident within the State. This includes a body incorporated under the laws of the State.[52] Copyright subsists in every original literary work which is *published*, if it were first published within the State, provided that the author of the work was a qualified person at the time when the work was first published or

---

48. The *Amicus Curiae* of Copyright Law Professors in the *Lotus v Borland* case is reproduced in the Hastings Comm/Ent LJ, Vol 16.657.
49. Article 3.
50. Article 2(1) of Council Directive 91/250.
51. CA 1963, s 8(1).
52. CA 1963, s 7(5).

if the author had died but was a qualified person immediately before his death.

INTERNATIONAL AGREEMENTS

[2.23] Many software programs used in Ireland are written by authors who may be resident outside the State. This may cause problems if the copyright in these programs is to be asserted. The case of *Milltronics Ltd v Hycontrol Ltd*[53] concerned a Canadian company which had acquired the rights to a computer program which had been written by a Canadian citizen. The defendants unsuccessfully argued that the plaintiffs were not entitled to the protection of the UK Copyright (Computer Software) Act 1985 because the author was not a qualified person.

[2.24] Such a defence would also fail in Ireland where the Copyright (Foreign Countries) Order 1996[54] extends the protection of the 1963 Act to literary works (including a computer program) first published (whether before or after the making of the order) in any country of the Berne Union, the Universal Copyright Convention or of the World Trade Organisation.[55] Where the author is not a national of the European Union, the term of protection of his work will expire on whichever of the following is the earlier: the date of expiry of protection under the law of the country of origin of the work or the date of expiry of protection under the 1963 Act.[56]

[2.25] The Irish Government may extend the benefit of the 1963 Act to other countries by making the necessary order. The 1963 Act may be extended to protect works first published elsewhere, and the work of citizens, residents or those domiciled in other countries. An order may vary the protection given from that in the Act. Before making such an order, the Government must be satisfied that adequate protection is given to Irish works by the country to which the order applies.[57] If the Government believes that a particular country is not giving adequate protection to Irish works, or to particular types of works (regardless of whether the inadequacy stems from the type of work or its country of origin), then the Government may make an order 'designating' that particular country. Such an order may provide that the protection of the Act will not be extended to the work of citizens or to particular types of work originating in that country. This may apply to

---

53. [1990] FSR 273.
54. SI 36/1996.
55. Regulation 3(a).
56. Regulation 4.
57. CA 1963, s 43.

citizens and subjects of that country or to bodies incorporated within that country.[58]

WORKS CREATED DURING EMPLOYMENT

[2.26] In the normal course of employment, the employer will be entitled to the ownership of any works created by the employee.[59] Deciding whether or not a person is an employee is of particular importance where a computer program is created. In the US case of *Avtec Systems Inc v Peiffer*[60] Peiffer was employed as a computer programmer by the plaintiffs who were government contractors for space related computer services. He wrote an 'Orbit program' for Avtec. He demonstrated the program to his employers and also to NASA. However, he failed to improve the program as NASA wished. Instead he worked independently to create a version of the 'Orbit program' which could be marketed commercially. This was done by a company known as Kisak-Kisak Inc. In the three years from 1989-1992, the program generated $197,000, half of which went to Peiffer. Avtec sued, arguing that Peiffer had created the program during the course of his employment and therefore they owned the copyright in it. Peiffer claimed that he wrote the program as a 'hobby'. The Federal District Court held that Avtec failed to prove that the program marketed by Kisak-Kisak Inc. was created during the course of his employment. Avtec had not shown that the new program was written "within Avtec authorised time and space limits".[61] This meant that they could not prove that Peiffer had created his program as part of his employment and so they were not entitled to the copyright in the program.

[2.27] Section 10(2) is an exception to this, as where a work is created during the course of employment by the proprietor, a newspaper, magazine or periodical, then the proprietor only retains ownership of the work for the purposes of publication in the journal. Under Regulation 4, this provision does not apply to employees who create computer programs for the proprietors of newspapers, magazines or similar periodicals. These terms may be varied by contract between the parties.[62] Where the government

---

58. CA 1963, s 46.
59. CA 1963, s 10(4).
60. 805 F Supp 1312 (ED Va 1992), aff'd in part, rev'd in part and remanded, Nos. 92-2521, 92-2607, US App. LEXIS 6522 (4th Circuit. 6 April 1994).
61. For a full review of the American law in this area see: Hyde and Hager, 'Promoting the Copyright Act's Creator Favouring Presumption', Denver University Law Review, Vol. 71 No 3, 1994, p 693.
62. CA 1963, s 10(5).

directs or controls the making of a work, then the government is entitled to copyright.[63]

[2.28] Obviously, a detailed discussion of Irish labour law is beyond the scope of this book. In *McAuliffe v The Minister for Social Welfare*[64] it was held by Barr J that in deciding whether a person was engaged as an employee or as an independent contractor, the most important test is the degree of control. Matters such as statutory entitlements, tax obligations and the provision of equipment were taken into account as being indicators of how much control was exercised over the person and thus whether or not a person was employed as an employee or an independent contractor.

[2.29] The contract of employment for computer programmers will obviously be very important. However it is very difficult for employers to claim ownership of work done by an employee during his spare time unless the employer could show that it was done with the employer's equipment or as part of the employee's normal work. This area will be further complicated if Ireland explicitly recognises the moral rights of authors.[65]

JOINT AUTHORS

[2.30] Section 16 of the 1963 Act provides that where two or more people work together to produce a work, then they share the ownership of the copyright. However, if one of them was not a qualified person, then the other will own the copyright. This is identical to Article 2(2) of the Directive which states:

> In respect of a computer program created by a group of natural persons jointly, the exclusive rights shall be owned jointly.

COMPUTER GENERATED WORKS

[2.31] Computers are extremely useful tools for the creation of works. Programs may be written that allow a computer to 'create' its own works.[66] However, this does not mean that a computer will become the author of the work for the purposes of the Copyright Acts. *Express Newspapers v Liverpool Daily Post*[67] concerned tables of random numbers which were

---

[63.] CA 1963, s 51. See also *Hall v Crosbie & Co* 66 ILTR 22.
[64.] [1995] 1 ILRM 189.
[65.] See para **[2.55]**.
[66.] For example, fractal images and various programs for weather forecasting and the creation of complex mathematical models will all create results with a minimum of human intervention. The natural or legal author of these results should usually be identifiable. It may be the company or other body which owns and controls the computer and program with which the model is created or it may be the person who created the program.

selected by a computer for a newspaper competition. It was argued that since there was no human author the numbers drawn by the computer could not be protected by copyright. Whitford J rejected this argument stating that it was as absurd as saying that a pen could be the author of a book.

[2.32] If a court held as fact that a computer was the author of a work, this would cause serious problems. Under the Directive copyright protection will only be granted to natural and legal persons.[68] If a computer could not be brought within the definition of a legal person then the work would not be protected. The ability of computers to create works on their own was not anticipated by Irish copyright legislation. It would not be realistic to recognise the computer itself as the author, although it is true that the 1963 Act[69] already recognises incorporated bodies as qualified persons. The best approach is to recognise the person who enables the computer to generate the work as the author. This is the approach taken in the UK where the Copyright Act 1988 makes specific provisions for these works. Section 9(3) of that Act provides that in the case of a literary, dramatic, musical or artistic work which is computer generated the author shall be taken to be the persons by whom the arrangements necessary for the creation of the work are undertaken. A computer generated work is defined as a work generated by a computer in circumstances such that there is no human author of it.

THE TERM OF COPYRIGHT PROTECTION

[2.33] At present, the length of time within which a computer program is copyright protected is irrelevant. Most computer programs have a lifespan of only a few years. What period of time would give computer programs adequate protection is unclear, it is certain that at present the length of time given is ludicrously long.[70]

[2.34] The 1963 Act stated that the term of copyright runs for 50 years from the death of the author.[71] This has been amended by the European Communities (Term of Protection of Copyright) Regulation 1995[72] which implements Council Directive 93/98.[73] This provides that the term of copyright will run for 70 years from the date of the death of the author,

---

[67.] [1985] 1 WLR 1089.
[68.] Article 3.
[69.] CA 1963, s 7(5).
[70.] The French Software Copyright Act 1985 grants a period of copyright protection of only 25 years.
[71.] CA 1963, s 8(4).
[72.] SI 158/1995.
[73.] 29 October 1993, OJ L290/9.

regardless of whether or not the work is published before his death.[74] Where a work is published under a pseudonym or anonymously, the copyright will exist for 70 years from the end of the year in which it was first published.[75]

New versions

[2.35] Computer programs are being continuously revised and updated. Many programs will have many different versions, for example, MS-DOS is now in its sixth edition. In order to secure copyright in a new edition which is separate from the old, there must be sufficient new work done to the program to make it capable of protection.

[2.36] Under s 20 of the 1963 Act copyright subsists in every published edition of any one or more literary works where the first publication of the edition took place in the State or where the publisher of the edition was a qualified person at the date of the first publication. Section 20(5) prohibits the reproduction of the typographical arrangement of an edition save for purposes of research or private study. Copyright subsisting in a published edition will last 25 years from the end of the year in which the edition is first published. Since many computer programs sold are updated editions of those that went before it is arguable that this section contains the appropriate period of protection for computer programs.

[2.37] Deciding what is a new edition is a matter for the individual court. Under s 20(1) copyright does not subsist in an edition which reproduces the typographical arrangement of a previous edition of the same work. This problem was addressed by Lord Kinloch in *Black v Murray & Son*[76] who stated:

> "I think it is clear that it will not create copyright in a new edition of a work, or which the copyright has expired, merely to make a few emendations of the text, or to add a few unimportant notes. To create a copyright by alterations in the text, these must be extensive and substantial, practically making a new book. With regard to notes, in like manner, they must exhibit an addition to the work which is not superficial or colourable, but imparts to the book a true and real value, over and above that belonging to the text. This value may perhaps be rightly expressed by saying that the book will procure purchasers in the market on special account of these notes".[77]

---

[74]. Regulation 3, *ibid.*
[75]. Regulation 4(1), *ibid.*
[76]. (1870) 9 M 341, IH.
[77]. This judgment was approved by the Privy Council in *Macmillan & Co Ltd v K & J Cooper* (1923) 40 TLR 186.

MULTI-MEDIA

[2.38] Multi-media has become a 'buzz word' or catch phrase in recent years but it is in fact a misnomer. The term is used in a very broad and ill-defined manner, usually to sell computer products. It is not a multitude of media but rather a multitude of contents. These contents or source materials may come in many forms: written text, films, cartoons, paintings and images, music and characters. The concept of multi-media has arisen because once images, text and music are reduced to a digital form they may be manipulated by a computer as the user wishes and the software permits. Multi-media is often used to refer to a wide variety of commercial products from banking services to cable TV channels. In this chapter the term 'multi-media' is used in a far more limited way. It refers to the manipulation of films, images, literary, artistic and musical works using a computer program to combine elements of all these works into a new composition.

[2.39] At present, most multi-media products are bought on CD-ROM, which contains a program that allows the user to manipulate the source materials contained within.[78] Multi-media may be defined as a combination of many different forms of source materials using software. These source materials are stored and manipulated using a computer. For the computer to do this, the source materials must be in digital form. The new composition which results from this manipulation will be the result of the active participation of the user (or interaction).[79]

[2.40] The ability of this technology to alter and adapt images and other materials is demonstrated by the pornographic computer game which was central to the case of *Charleston v News Group Newspapers Ltd*.[80] The plaintiffs were stars of the Australian soap *Neighbours* and the defendant was the *News of the World*. Unnamed third parties had created a pornographic computer game which contained images of the faces of the plaintiffs superimposed on the bodies of models. This game was then made available to fans of the soap. The plaintiff's claim for libel against the paper for publishing one of the images was rejected by the House of Lords.

[78.] For example Microsoft publish a multi-media package called '3D MovieMaker', which allows children to direct and produce their own films on a computer. The "users can construct plots and dialogue, create and animate characters, add soundtracks and even play around with camera angles and special effects." It is also possible to access a wider variety of material over networks such as the Internet.

[79.] *The Computer Dictionary* (Microsoft Press) defines 'multi-media' as "the combination of sounds, graphics, animation and video. In the world of computers, multi-media is a subset of hypermedia, which combines the elements of multi with hypertext, which links the information".

[80.] [1995] 2 All ER 313.

[2.41] A distinction must be made between the computer program which allows the user to manipulate the source materials and the source materials themselves. The computer program will be protected by copyright law as outlined in the previous chapters. The source materials are protected individually by copyright law as artistic,[81] literary, dramatic and musical works.[82] If they are held in a database, this will also be protected.[83] Multi-media does however, creates several difficulties for copyright law. Firstly, the source materials will have to be licensed to allow their incorporation into a new composition. Secondly, when the source materials are combined to create a new multi-media composition, does this composition amount to an original work? Is it possible that the composition is in fact a compilation of works? Finally, if a new work is created, who owns the copyright in this new work?

Copyright and the Source Materials of Multi-Media

[2.42] The main selling point of multi-media programs is that they allow the works of many different authors to be combined by the computer user into his own new composition. This is also the major problem with multi-media systems for copyright law. Multi-media allows many different works to be manipulated in many different ways. Under copyright law, the consent of every author must be obtained for every different type of manipulation of his work. This can be very difficult and it is no coincidence that many multi-media systems only allow the manipulation of works which are in the public domain.

[2.43] It is not clear just how much of a work must be copied in order for a breach of copyright to occur. The Copyright Act 1963 allows for fair dealing in a work for the purposes of criticism and review. It also allows for fair dealing in research or private study. Whether the definition of fair dealing could be extended to include the manipulation of a work which would occur with a multi-media program is doubtful. Copying in 1963, prior to the invention of the photocopier and the tape recorder was a very different concept to copying over 30 years later. It is questionable whether the 1963 definition of fair dealing extends to the wholesale photocopying and home recording of works which occurs at present.[84]

[2.44] The licence or assignment of copyright which is given will have to provide for the type of manipulation which is possible with multi-media

---

[81.] CA 1963, s 9.
[82.] CA 1963, s 8.
[83.] Database Directive, OJ L 77/20 27.3.1996.
[84.] *Jarvis v A & M records* 827 F Supp 282 (DNJ 1993).

systems. It would not be enough that the publisher should have a licence allowing him the film or other rights in the work. Assignments of copyright which do not anticipate future technologies may not be valid for use with those technologies. In *Peggy Lee v Disney Corporation*,[85] Ms Lee had sung a number of songs and helped compose the music for the Disney film 'The Lady and the Tramp' which was produced in 1955. At that time, Peggy Lee sold her rights in the film. It was only in the 1980s that the film became a huge success because of video sales. Peggy Lee received nothing from these sales. She sued successfully as the court accepted that her consent given in 1955 could not extend to media which did not exist at the time. She was awarded $3.8 million by the Supreme Court of California in 1992.

[2.45] The sale of the program for manipulating multi-media may not give rise to a cause of action. In the English decision of *CBS Songs v Amstrad Consumer Electronics plc*[86] the House of Lords held that the sale of twin deck tape recorders did not amount to inciting or authorising the infringement of copyright in the plaintiff's pre-recorded music tapes. This was because the tape recorder could have non-infringing uses such as recording material in which the author owned copyright. Similarly, the user of a multi-media program may use the program to manipulate works in which he owns the copyright, such as home videos or songs he has recorded himself.

[2.46] The moral rights of an author would also have to be considered before using his work in a multi-media system. Moral rights do not transfer at the same time as economic rights. So even if the author has transferred all rights in his work to a third party, the moral rights of the author, in particular the rights of integrity[87] would remain with him. The Italian courts have allowed a film director to object to the insertion of advertising breaks during the broadcast of one of his films on Italian television as the break interfered with the director's moral rights.[88] The mutilation, twisting and adaptation of a work which can be done by a multi-media program would make the effect of an advertising break seem tame. The author of a work also has an attribution right which entitles him to have his work attributed to him. This right would be very hard to vindicate in a new multi-media composition which might contain the work of many different authors.

[85.] Sakkers, 'Licensing and Exploiting Rights in Multimedia Products', 11 CLSR 1995.

[86.] [1987] 3 All ER 151.

[87.] This allows the author to object to any distortions, mutilations or any other modification of, or derogatory action in relation to, his work which would be prejudicial to his honour or reputation.

[88.] See para **[2.55]** *et seq.*

[2.47] Moral rights are not explicitly recognised by Irish law at present. However, it would be advisable to ensure that these rights are transferred, since they will be recognised in the future.

[2.48] Because of the difficulties of protecting copyright works when they are included in a multi-media system, many authors refuse to licence their works for this use.[89] One major concern for authors is that source materials packaged in a multi-media product may be copied and sold. As a result, some authors will only licence their work if the quality of the work is intentionally downgraded.

Is a Multi-Media Composition a Work?

[2.49] Once a multi-media program has performed its functions, a new composition is created. It is not clear whether this has any status as a 'work' within the meaning of the 1963 Act. The file created which contains the composition will not be a program but merely a presentation of sounds, images and text. It cannot be a literary work since it contains images and sounds. Similarly, it cannot be an artistic or musical work it could not be a film. In *DPP v Noel Irwin*,[90] Barron J held that the defendant could not be convicted of copying a video because videos were not the same as films and so were not protected under the 1963 Act. If a video is not a film under the 1963 Act, then it is unlikely that a computer file can be a film either. If the new composition is to receive protection as an individual work it would probably have to be protected as a special category in some future Copyright Act.

[2.50] At present, the best way of protecting the composition may be as a 'compilation'. The composition is a collection of works, all of which have individual copyright protection. It is the labour and the originality of the user that will give the composition as a whole its protection. Any work other than selecting and arranging the original material which the user does such as creating his own music or images will be protected in its own right alongside the protection given to the individual works of others. Under s 2 of the Copyright Act 1963, literary work is defined as including compilations. This presumably would allow the compilation of works contained in the composition to be protected as a literary work. The fact that the information is held in a digital form, in other words a string of ones and zeros, on the computer would also imply that the composition is in fact a literary work.

[89.] Not all authors are so reluctant. The musician Peter Gabriel has brought out a CD-ROM which encourages the user to manipulate Gabriel's work and create their own multi-media compositions.

[90.] High Court, unrep, 25 October 1984, Barron J.

Who is the author?

[2.51] If the composition was found to be a 'work', then the question arises as to who is the author of the work. There are two alternatives, firstly, the creator of the multi-media composition and the authors of the source materials may be treated as joint authors. Section 16(1) of the 1963 Act defines a work of joint authorship as:

> a work produced by the collaboration of two or more authors in which the contribution of each author is not separate from the contribution of the other author or authors.

For a work to be created by joint authors, there must be collaboration of the authors. This implies that the relationship between the two should be reasonably close. At the very least the authors of the original works which are to be manipulated by the multi-media program should have consented to this manipulation and should be aware that it will give rise to a work of joint authorship with persons unknown. The disadvantage with this is that every composition will have many different authors. If the user wishes to exploit his creation in any way, he will only be one of a number of authors and he will have to get the consent of all the others. This will obviously be impractical. The original authors will also find themselves becoming joint authors of innumerable different works, the content of which they very little control over.

[2.52] Secondly, the creator of the composition may be treated as the author of a compilation of works. His labour, skill and originality in selecting and arranging the contents of the compilation will be protected. At the same time, the authors of the source materials of the compilation will still enjoy protection for their individual works. The author of the compilation will be able to exploit his creation but, he will still have to get the consent of the authors of the source materials. As such this may not make the results of multi-media programs any easier to exploit, but it is a 'cleaner' result, since the contributions of the user and the authors of the contents are all recognised separately and individually.

COPYRIGHT AND OTHER PROTECTIONS

[2.53] Regulation 9(1) states that:

> The provisions of this Regulation and the Council Directive shall be without prejudice to any other legal provisions such as those concerning patent rights, trade marks, unfair competition, trade secrets, protection of semi-conductor products or the law of contract.

This means that other forms of protection may run in parallel with copyright protection and if a program is subject to other forms of protection, whether patent, trade marks or otherwise, then this protection will not prejudice the copyright protection of the program.

[2.54] This question was raised in *House of Spring Gardens v Point Blank Ltd.*[91] In that case the defendants argued that when the plaintiffs applied for a patent in the UK for their bullet-proof vests, drawings of their design were published and as a result placed in the public domain. As a result, the defendants claimed that the designs could be used by anyone (of course in the event that the plaintiffs had been granted a patent they would be granted an exclusive monopoly in the designs). The defendants relied on the English decision of *Catnic Components v Hill and Smith,*[92] where Whitford J in the High Court found that by applying for a patent, the applicant abandons all copyright in the patent drawings. Costello J disagreed with this, stating that there was nothing in either the patent code or copyright code which prevented copyright from existing in patent applications. His judgment was upheld by the Supreme Court.

Moral Rights

[2.55] The moral rights of authors are a development of the continental civil law system. Four such moral rights may be identified:

1. The right of paternity. This is the right of the author to attribution of his authorship.

2. The right of integrity. This refers to the right of the author to object to any distortions, mutilations or any other modification of, or derogatory action in relation to, his work which would be prejudicial to his honour or reputation.

3. The right of disclosure. This is the right of an author to publish or withhold his work from publication.

4. The right of non-attribution. The author has the right not to have attributed to his authorship a work of which he was not in fact the author.

Some civil law jurisdictions recognise the right of review or withdrawal.[93] This is the right of the author to withdraw his work after publication if it contains views which he no longer holds. One controversial case in which the moral rights of the author were asserted was the Italian case of *TV*

[91.] [1984] IR 611.
[92.] [1982] RPC 183.
[93.] Eg, France and Germany.

Reteitalia v Director Mr Germi.[94] In that case the court held that advertising breaks in films broadcast on television could violate the author's moral rights because they might damage his reputation.

[2.56] Under Article 6 *bis* of the Berne Convention, signatory States must give an author certain moral rights in addition to his economic rights. The Berne Convention at present recognises the rights of paternity and integrity. These moral rights are independent of the author's economic rights. They remain with the author after he has transferred his economic rights. Moral rights must be maintained by Member States of the Berne Convention until the expiration of economic rights although States which do not recognise the Berne Convention may limit moral rights to the lifetime of the author. The manner in which they are to be protected is determined by the domestic law of Member States, which does not necessarily have to be copyright law.

[2.57] The position of moral rights in Ireland is unclear. There is no explicit provision in the Copyright Acts recognising them. In the UK it was long argued that moral rights were protected by English law, in particular the law of torts and especially torts such as passing off and defamation. However, tort law was unconvincing as an enforcer of moral rights and the UK explicitly recognised them in the Copyright, Designs and Patents Act 1988.[95]

[2.58] If Ireland is to fulfil its obligations under the Berne Convention then it will be necessary to revise the Irish copyright legislation. This position is further complicated by the fact that international copyright law has been further updated. The World Intellectual Property Organisation (WIPO) draft copyright treaty[96] will have the effect (if implemented) of creating a common world system of copyright protection. Notable features of the treaty are that it explicitly protects computer programs as literary works "whatever may be the mode or form of their expression".[97] Authors of computer works may enjoy the exclusive right of authorising commercial rental to the public of the originals or copies of their works.[98] Adequate legal protection must also be provided against the circumvention of effective technological measures that protect such works.[99] The European Union is also becoming more involved in copyright matters, it sees copyright law as providing the basis for the 'Information Society'.[100]

---

94. Court of Appeal of Rome, 30 May 1989. For discussion of this and other caselaw see Franzosi & de Sanctis, 'Moral Rights and New Technology: Are Copyright and Patents Converging?', [1995] 2 EIPR 63.
95. Chapter 4, Copyright, Designs and Patents Act 1988.
96. Submitted at Geneva on 2 to 20 December 1996.
97. Article 4.
98. Article 7.
99. Article 11.
100. Green Paper on Copyright and related rights in the Information Society, COM 95 382 Final 19.07. 1995.

Chapter 3

The Rights of Owners & Users of Computer Programs

[3.01] Copyright is not a positive right, ie it does not give the author the right to exploit his work. Rather it is a negative right, as it allows him to prevent others from copying his work and otherwise infringing his rights.

RIGHTS OF THE OWNER UNDER THE 1963 ACT

[3.02] If it is accepted that computer programs are literary works then the 1963 Act in general gives computer programs ample protection. Section 7(1) of the Act states that copyright means the exclusive right to do or authorise certain acts which would otherwise be restricted. Section 8(6) defines those acts as being the reproduction, publication, performance, broadcast, diffusion or adaptation of the work and doing any of the foregoing in respect of an adaptation of the work. Copyright is infringed by any person who without licence and not being the owner of the copyright does any of these acts. Under the 1963 Act most activities, such as copying or adaptation, which the owners of computer programs object to, are prohibited. Adaptation means the conversion of a literary work into a dramatic work, a translation of the work or a conversion of the work into a series of pictures or a 'comic'. The translation of a work from one computer language to another would presumably be covered by this.

RIGHTS OF THE OWNER UNDER THE REGULATIONS

[3.03] The European Communities (Legal Protection of Computer Programs) Regulations 1993 ('The Regulations')[1] have clarified the rights of the owners and the users of computer programs. On balance, it has probably benefited the users. It is impossible to say how the Irish courts might have interpreted the 1963 Act in this regard, but it is hard to see how decompilation could have been allowed, considering that the adaptation or translation of a literary work was very clearly within the control of the rightholder.[2] The Regulations set out the "exclusive rights of the

---

[1] See para **[2.04]**.
[2] See CA 1963, s s 8(6) and **[3.16]**. Decompilation might have been allowed under the 'fair dealing' provisions contained in s 12. See para **[5.30]**.

rightholder", basically these are identical to those found in the 1963 Act. The rightholder can control the reproduction, translation, adaptation and distribution of computer programs. The Regulations also contain exceptions to these rights: firstly, the user may in limited circumstances decompile computer programs, secondly, he may make back-up copies of computer programs; finally, he may study the functioning of the computer program to determine the ideas and principles which underlie any element of the program.

[3.04] The first exclusive right of the owner is the right to do or authorise the permanent or temporary reproduction of a computer program by any means and in any form, in part or in whole. Insofar as loading, displaying, running, transmission or storage of the computer program necessitate such reproduction, such acts shall be subject to authorisation by the rightholder.[3] This is the most basic right of ownership of copyright. There is one important limitation to this right contained in Regulation 6(2), which states that "the making of a back-up copy by a person having the right to use the computer program may not be prevented by contract in so far as it is necessary for that use".[4]

[3.05] The second right of the copyright owner is to do or authorise the translation, adaptation, arrangement and any other alteration of a computer program and the reproduction of the results, without prejudice to the rights of the person who alters the program.[5] This is a basic principle of copyright protection. The translation of computer codes from one computer language to another and in particular, the translation of code from a computer readable form to a form which can be understood by humans is a serious threat to the creators of programs.

[3.06] Finally, the rightholder has the power to do or authorise any form of distribution to the public, including the rental of the original computer program or of any copies. The first sale in the Community of a copy of a program by the rightholder or with his consent will exhaust the distribution right within the Community of that copy, with the exception of the right to control further rental of the program or a copy.[6] This gives the rightholder the right to control all distribution to the public including renting the program. Once a copy of a program is sold, this exhausts the owner's power to control the distribution of that copy within the EU with the exception of

---

3. Regulation 5(a).
4. See para **[3.11]** *et seq.*
5. Regulation 5(b).
6. Regulation 5(c).

the right to control further rental. The sixteenth recital to the Directive states that rental "means the making available for use, for a limited period of time and for profit making purposes, of a computer program or copy thereof; this term does not include public lending, which accordingly remains outside the scope of this Directive". This would allow anyone who loans a copy of a program or who rents it, but on a non-profit making basis, to claim as a defence that the owner of copyright had no control over their lending.

RIGHTS OF THE USER

(1) Reproduction and adaptation

[3.07] Regulation 6(1) provides:

> Where there are no specific contractual provisions to the contrary, the acts referred to in paragraph (a)[7] and (b)[8] of the Regulation 5 shall not require authorisation by the rightholder where they are necessary for the use of the computer program by the lawful acquirer in accordance with the intended purpose, including for error correction.

Paragraph (a) of Regulation 5 allows the owner to control all forms of reproduction of the computer program. Paragraph (b) allows him to control the translation and adaptation of the program. These rights are conferred on the lawful acquirer, a term which is not used elsewhere. It presumably refers to the licensee, renter, purchaser or anyone authorised to use the program by the foregoing. This Regulation means that the owner must assert his rights. If he fails to do so, then the user may be given free rein to reproduce or adapt the program. Obviously, the owner will try to limit the rights of the user. This may be done in two ways:

(a) imposing 'specific contractual provisions' which would limit the carrying out of any the above actions

[3.08] The Regulations appear to allow the owner to control the use of a program in this way. This is strengthened by Regulation 9(1) which prohibits contractual provisions which prevent the decompilation of programs, the making of backup copies or the observation and testing of a program's functions, but does not prohibit contractual terms which limit other uses of a

---

7. Paragraph (a) of Regulation 5 provides that the owner has the exclusive right to do or authorise "the permanent or temporary reproduction of a computer program by any means and in any form, in part or in whole. Insofar as loading, displaying, running, transmission or storage of the computer program necessitate such reproduction, such acts shall be subject to authorisation by the rightholder".

8. Paragraph (b) provides that he may do or authorise "the translation, adaptation, arrangement and any other alteration of a computer program and the reproduction of the results thereof, without prejudice to the rights of the person who alters the program".

program such as reproduction and adaptation. It has been suggested that owners would be able to limit extensively the use of their programs and in particular to limit the loading and running of the program. Loading and running a program will involve the reproduction of the program several times.[9] However, Recital 18 of the Directive states:

> ... this means that the acts of loading and running necessary for the use of a copy of a program which has been lawfully acquired, and the act of correction of its errors, may not be prohibited by contract ... in the absence of specific contractual provisions, including when a copy of the program has been sold, any other act necessary for the use of the copy of a program may be performed in accordance with its intended purpose by the lawful acquirer of that copy.

This would suggest that the owner cannot limit the loading and running of a program. This contradiction between the Recital and Directive has been ignored by all Member States with the exception of The Netherlands.[10] It should be remembered that under Regulation 2(2) words or expressions such as 'specific contractual provisions' used in the Regulations have the same meaning as those in the Directive.

(b) limiting the use of the program to its 'intended purpose'

[3.09] There is no definition of what constitutes 'intended purpose'. *Czarnota & Hart*[11] have suggested that the 'intended purpose' may be implied from the conditions under which the program is to be used (number of users, terminals and location) and the function which the program is to carry out (eg, word processing). Another commentator[12] has suggested that the 'intended purpose' may be implied from the brochures and other documents, user manuals, the price of the software and the shrink wrap licence. Of course a court could use both methods simultaneously.

[3.10] The 'intended purpose' of a program specifically includes 'error correction'. Although there is no definition offered for this term, if errors in a program are to be detected and corrected then the program will have to be decompiled.[13] As a result, this term is probably redundant as decompilation

---

9.   Loading a program involves its reproduction on the hard drive of a computer. Running a program will require the program's reproduction within the RAM (or temporary memory) of a computer.

10. Meijboom, 'Copyright Software Protection in the EC', Computer Law Series 12, (Kluwer Law and Taxation Publishers), p 13.

11. *Legal Protection of Computer Programs in Europe*, (Butterworths, 1991), p 65.

12. GP Smith, 'Shrink-Wrap Licences in Europe after the EC Software Directive', Computer Law Journal, Vol X, 1992, p 597.

13. See para **[3.16]** *et seq* for discussion on decompilation.

is stringently controlled by Regulation 7. It would be unusual for a user of a program to be expected to correct errors in the program. Errors would usually be dealt with by the owner of copyright who would send out updated versions of a program. This term may have been included to deal with maintenance contracts. Often more expensive programs are sold with conditions that only the vendor can maintain or correct the program. The inclusion of 'error correction' in the 'intended purpose', may mean that these contracts must be decided with reference to contract law and not copyright law. If this is so, courts would be able to interpret maintenance contracts and other such terms with greater ease than if the terms were decided under copyright law.

(2) Back-Up Copy

[3.11] Regulation 6(2) provides that "the making of a back-up copy by a person having the right to use the computer program may not be prevented by contract in so far as it is necessary for that use". This is an exception to the owner's right to control reproduction under Regulation 5(a) and under ss 7 and 8 of the 1963 Act. The question of what exactly a back-up copy is has given rise to some debate.[14] If a computer program is acquired on a floppy disk and then transferred onto the hard disk of a computer, must the user treat the original disk as the back-up copy or can he make a separate back-up copy? This misses the point. It is not the *number* of copies which is important but rather the *purpose* of the copies. A user can only make a copy where it is 'necessary' to protect him from the loss of the computer program. In particular, if a copy of a program is bought for an office, the back-up copy cannot be used to install another copy of the program onto a home computer. In practice, it is impossible to determine what happens to the back-up copy once it is made. It is considered good practice in the computer industry to make a back-up copy. Regulation 9(1) states that the making of a back-up copy cannot be limited by contract and that any provisions purporting to do so will be null and void.

[3.12] In the French case of *Sarl Artware v Groupe D'utilisation Francophone D'Informatique,*[15] the French Supreme Court found that if a purchaser receives from the seller a back-up copy of the software package, even if it is only a single copy and protected from reproduction, his right to a back-up copy has been observed. The right to a back-up copy did not emanate from the Directive, but rather from s 47 of the French Copyright

---

[14.] Meijboom, 'Copyright Software Protection in the EC', Computer Law Series 12, (Kluwer Law and Taxation Publishers), p 14.

[15.] Judgment of the French Supreme Court, 22 May 1991, [1993] FSR 703.

Act 1985 which states that "any reproduction, other than the preparation of a back-up copy by the user shall be liable to ... sanctions".

(3) Reverse Engineering

[3.13] Reverse engineering is the technique of studying a product in order to determine how it was created.[16] It is a common practice in other industries, notably car manufacturing. Reverse engineering a computer program would essentially involve taking the program apart and recreating it. It is divided into two categories: (a) black box analysis and (b) decompilation. Black box analysis involves subjecting a program to certain input conditions and monitoring its output in an attempt to understand how it works. Decompilation is far more intrusive. This involves the conversion of the computer program from the machine readable object code back to source code.[17] In *Milltronics v Hycontrol Ltd*[18] the defendant, a distributor of the plaintiff's computer program, anticipated that he might lose the licence to distribute the program so he 'disassembled' it and substantially reassembled the lines of code in a very similar order but with sections transposed. He was successfully sued for breach of copyright.

'Black box' analysis

[3.14] Regulation 6(3) provides for so called 'black-box' analysis of computer programs. This involves observing the performance of a program in order to ascertain how the program works. For example, one way of finding out how an encryption program operates would be to encrypt a known text using the program and compare the encrypted output with the known input in order to ascertain how the program works. In practice this would be very difficult since modern encryption programs are so sophisticated, but the same techniques may be useful in other areas.

[3.15] The Regulation states:

> The person having a right to use a copy of a computer program shall be entitled, without the authorisation of the rightholder, to observe, study or test the functioning of the program in order to determine the ideas and principles which underlie any element of the program if he does so while performing any of the acts of loading, displaying, running, transmitting or storing the program which he is entitled to do.

---

16. *Kewanee Oil Co v Bicron Corp* 416 US 470, at 476 (1974). It was stated there that reverse engineering includes "starting with the known product and working backward to divine the process which aided in its development".
17. Ehrlich, 'Fair use or Foul play?' Pace Law Review, Vol 13 p 1003, (1994).
18. [1990] FSR 273.

The analysis of the program may only be carried out where the analyst is carrying out acts which he is entitled to do and which do not breach copyright.[19] Regulation 9(1) provides that contractual provisions purporting to limit this right will be null and void.

DECOMPILATION

[3.16] Decompilation has become extremely controversial in the software industry. This is because it is so easy to copy all or part of a program. Even if one car manufacturer understands how another makes a certain car or part, he may not be able to imitate it. Once a program is decompiled the person who decompiles it may be able to replicate easily all the programs' features.

[3.17] Most programs sold commercially are sold in the form of machine or object code. In this form the program cannot be understood by humans. If the program is to be analysed it must be translated into source code, which is the code in which the program was originally written by the computer programmer. The process of creating object code from source code is known as 'compilation'. The opposite process, where the source codes are recreated from the object code is known as 'decompilation'. If someone wishes to understand how a program works, they could not do so by looking at the object code which they would find on the disks they bought. To do this, they would have to retranslate the object code into source code. This process will involve copying the code several times.[20]

[3.18] There are two reasons why someone would want to decompile a program. Firstly, to ensure the compatibility of other programs. This may be done in various ways. If a programmer wished to write a program which would be compatible with an operating system such as DOS, he might decompile DOS to find out how to do this. Secondly, to produce a program to compete with the one that he is decompiling. The programmer may merely wish to examine his competitor's program and see how it works, using that knowledge to improve his own product. Alternatively, he may wish to copy large parts of his competitor's program or indeed all of it. Decompilation for this latter purpose is obviously what copyright owners object to most.

[3.19] Under the Copyright Act 1963, decompilation would have been a breach of copyright. Firstly, it involves the translation of code from one computer language to another which is a restricted act under s 7(1) of the

---

19. Recital 19.
20. The decompilation is carried out by another program designed for this purpose.

1963 Act and is a breach of copyright.[21] Secondly, the source codes which result from decompilation will be 'adaptations' of that program. Adaptation is defined as including a translation of the work from one language to another. The reproduction of the decompiled source codes, or adaptations, in a subsequent program or anywhere else would also be an infringement of copyright. Finally, decompilation involves copying the program. The program must be copied into the computer's memory, translated and the new source codes must be either saved or printed out. The licences to which most programs are subject permit the copying of the program in very limited circumstances. Copying a program for the purposes of decompilation will almost certainly be in breach of the licence. The reproduction of a program without the consent of the owner of the program is a breach of copyright under s 7(1) of the 1963 Act.[22]

[3.20] The Regulations, however, will permit decompilation in certain limited circumstances. Regulation 7(1) provides:

> The authorisation of the rightholder shall not be required where reproduction of the code and translation of its form within the meaning of Regulation 5(a) and (b) are indispensable to obtain the information necessary to achieve the interoperability of an independently created computer program with other programs, provided that the following conditions are met:
>
> (a) these acts are performed by the licensee or by another person having a right to use a copy of a program or on their behalf by a person authorised to do so.
>
> (b) the information necessary to achieve interoperability has not previously been readily available to the persons referred to in subparagraph (a); and
>
> (c) these acts are confined to the parts of the original program which are necessary to achieve interoperability.

Paragraph (a) of Regulation 5 provides for:

> the permanent or temporary reproduction of a computer program by any means and in any form, in part or in whole. Insofar as loading, displaying, running, transmission or storage of the computer program necessitate such reproduction, such acts shall be subject to authorisation by the rightholder.

This permits the copying of a program for the purposes of decompilation. Paragraph (b) provides for:

---

21. CA 1963, s 8(6) includes the adaptation of a work as one of the acts restricted by copyright, adaptation is defined as including a translation of the work in s 8(6).
22. Decompilation might have been permitted under the fair dealing exception contained in s 12 of the Act. However this is far from clear, see para **[5.30]**.

the translation, adaptation, arrangement and any other alteration of a computer program and the reproduction of the results thereof, without prejudice to the rights of the person who alters the program.

This allows the actual decompilation to occur. The circumstances in which decompilation can occur are very limited.

(a) Licensees or other lawful persons

[3.21] The person who carries out the decompilation must be a licensee or have a right to use a copy of the program. Therefore if a copy of the program was stolen or illegally copied, then it would not be permissible to decompile it. For example, in *Atari Games Corp v Nintendo of America Inc*[23] the plaintiffs obtained an unauthorised copy of the defendant's source code from the US Copyright Office by alleging that it was needed for ongoing litigation.

(b) Interoperability

[3.22] The most important limitation is that decompilation can only occur when it is indispensable to obtain the information necessary to achieve the interoperability of an independently created program with other programs. Interoperability can be defined as the ability to exchange information and mutually to use the information which has been exchanged.[24] Anyone who decompiles a program must be able to show that their program needed to operate with others and that the decompilation was essential to accomplish this.[25] A program cannot be decompiled if the information necessary to achieve interoperability has previously been readily available to the licensee or anyone else entitled to use the program.[26] There is a vast amount of information available about many programs as it is in the interests of most manufacturers to ensure that their programs are compatible with as many other programs and systems as is practicable. If a manufacturer wishes to protect his programs against decompilation then he should ensure that all information necessary for interoperability is readily available. If this is done then nobody can legitimately decompile his program. This is especially true as Regulation 7(2)(b) allows information gained from legitimate decompilation to be passed between users, provided it is needed for the interoperability of independently created programs.

---

23. 24 USPQ 2d (BNA) 1015 (9th Cir 1992).
24. Recital 12.
25. If a program is decompiled, the person who does so would need to be able to show that he was creating another program, this would necessitate retaining design materials.
26. Regulation 7(1)(b).

(i) Interoperability of hardware

[3.23] Recital 10 to the Directive provides:

> The function of a computer program is to communicate and work together with other components of a computer systems and with users and for this purpose, a logical and where appropriate physical interconnection and interaction is required to permit all elements of software and hardware to work with other software and hardware and with users in all the ways in which they are intended to function.

It is not clear from the Regulation whether decompilation is permissible to achieve interoperability between software and hardware but the recital suggests that it is. The Recitals certainly make it clear that hardware and software must communicate together and the use of the term 'components' would suggest that physical hardware as well as software is included. Programs do not operate in a vacuum. Every aspect of a program will ultimately be determined by the characteristics of the hardware on which the program runs. It is the hardware which defines the parameters within which the software operates. For example, the development of DOS and Windows software has been greatly defined by the development of the *Intel* chips on which the programs run.

[3.24] However, the provisions of Regulation 7 seem to anticipate that programs will only be decompiled to ensure the interoperability of other programs. It only permits decompilation where it is "indispensable to obtain the information necessary to achieve the interoperability of an independently created computer program with other programs". The possibility that programs might be decompiled in order to develop hardware which would interoperate with the programs, as occurred in *Apple v Franklin*,[27] appears to have been ignored. In that case, Franklin had manufactured an 'Apple compatible' computer. They were prevented from marketing programs which infringed the copyright in Apple's programs, including programs present in the computer's micro-chips.

(ii) Interfaces and Interoperability

[3.25] The Recitals to the Directive provide:

> The part of the program which provide for such interconnection and interaction between elements of software and hardware are generally known as 'interfaces'[28];

[27.] *Apple Computer Inc v Franklin Computer Corpn* 714 F2d 1240 (3rd Cir 1983), *cert. dismissed*, 464 US 1033 (1984).

[28.] Recital 11.

... this functional interconnection and interaction is generally known as 'interoperability' whereas such interoperability can be defined as the ability to exchange information and mutually to use the information which has been exchanged ...[29]

The term 'interface' is not used in Regulation 7. There is no reason to believe that decompilation can only be carried out to gain access to a program's interfaces. If other information is necessary for interoperability, then decompilation may be carried out to get it. The definition of 'interface' in the Recitals may only be for the purposes of Article 1(2) of the Directive[30] which states that ideas and principles including those which underlie a program's interfaces are not protected.

(c) Decompilation is confined to parts of the program

[3.26] It is not permissible to decompile an entire program if the information required for interoperability is contained in a small part of it. Decompilation must be confined to the parts of the original program which are necessary to achieve interoperability.[31] This provision may not be very practical since it may not be possible to state, from looking at a program in object code form, what parts of it are necessary for interoperability.

Limitations on the Use of the Information Gained From Decompilation

[3.27] The Regulations explicitly state that decompilation is permitted to ensure interoperability between different programs.[32] If a programmer wishes to discover how to make his application program interoperate with an operating system such as DOS, then he may decompile it. He may also be able to decompile another application program, which already interoperates with DOS to see how it accomplishes this task.[33] This amounts to decompiling a program in order to develop a new program to compete with it. It is possible to do this but the Regulation places serious limitations on what can be done with information gleaned from decompilation.

[3.28] Regulation 7(2) states that information obtained through decompilation cannot be used for goals other than to achieve the interoperability of the independently created computer program. Therefore if while decompiling a program, information other than that necessary for

---

[29.] Recital 12
[30.] Enacted as Regulation 3(3).
[31.] Regulation 7(1)(c).
[32.] Regulation 7.
[33.] In *Sega Enterprises Ltd v Accolade Inc* 24 USPQ 2d (BNA) 1561 (9th Cir 1992), it is arguable that the games cartridges which Accolade decompiled were in fact application programs which ran on the Sega game machines.

interoperability is discovered, it must be ignored. Those who legitimately decompile programs might be well advised to destroy the decompiled code once the information necessary for interoperability has been extracted. If the decompiled code were to be abused or used for purposes other than interoperability, then the party who originally decompiled it could be held liable for its subsequent use. Information obtained by decompilation cannot be given to others, except when necessary to ensure the interoperability of the independently created computer program.[34]

[3.29] Finally, information obtained by decompilation cannot be used for the development, production or marketing of a computer program substantially similar in its expression, or for any other act which infringes copyright.[35] This limits the use of decompilation in order to produce a new program which would compete with the decompiled one. While programs can be decompiled, they cannot be copied. This provision only prevents the use of information gained from decompilation in programs which are 'substantially' similar. This leaves the possibility open that it might be legitimate to copy insubstantial parts of a program in order to ensure interoperability.

The Copyright Owner's Legitimate Interests

[3.30] Regulation 7(3) provides that in accordance with the provisions of the Berne Convention for the Protection of Literary and Artistic Works, the provisions of the Regulations may not be interpreted in such a way so as to allow its application be used in a manner which unreasonably prejudices the owner's legitimate interests or conflicts with a normal exploitation of the computer program. This means that the courts have an escape clause which will prevent decompilation in circumstances which would be unfair to the owner. Owners of copyright would be well advised to set out what their legitimate interests are and what the normal exploitation of a computer program is in contracts. However their ability to prevent decompilation is still limited by Regulation 9(1) which states that any contractual provisions which purport to limit decompilation for the purposes of interoperability are null and void.

The US Law on Decompilation

[3.31] Several US cases have examined the problem of decompilation. American law is different from European law in this regard. In Europe, a specific law has been enacted which permits decompilation. In the US, decompilation is permitted only if it can be said to be a 'fair use' as defined

---

34. Regulation 7(2)(b).
35. Regulation 7(2)(c)

in the US Copyright Act.[36] There are four factors which must be considered when determining whether a use is fair:

(1) the purpose and character of the use;

(2) the nature of the copyrighted work;

(3) the amount of the work and substantiality of the portion used in relation to the copyrighted work as a whole;

(4) the effect of the use on the potential market for or value of the copyrighted work.[37]

In *NEC v Intel*[38] a Japanese engineer decompiled the microcode for Intel's 8086/88 microprocessors in order to produce a microcode for NEC's microprocessors. This decompilation was found to be permissible as the code ultimately used by the Japanese was not substantially similar to that of Intel. Any similarities were caused by the constraints imposed by the hardware. In *Atari Games Corp v Nintendo of America Inc*,[39] Atari had created game cartridges for the Nintendo entertainment system. Initially, Atari had been unable to fully decompile Nintendo's code, so they purloined a copy of Nintendo's source codes from the US Copyright Office. The Federal Court of Appeal for the Ninth Circuit stated that had Atari not used the purloined copy of Nintendo's source codes, then the decompilation would have been permissible. In *Sega Enterprises Ltd v Accolade Inc*,[40] Accolade bought Sega's games cartridges and decompiled the object codes which they found in them. They then analysed printouts of the decompiled codes and used it for experiments. As a result, Accolade were able to produce a manual which described the requirements of the Sega system and how to develop compatible programs. Accolade used this information to manufacture its own programs for the Sega system. This was held to be permissible. The court stated that where:

> "disassembly (or decompilation) is the only way to gain access to the ideas and functional elements embodied in a copyrighted computer program and where there is a legitimate reason for seeking such access, disassembly or decompilation is a fair use of the copyrighted work as a matter of law".

[36.] This means that decompilation has effectively been regulated by the US courts. This approach has been criticised and statutory provisions suggested by Soobert, 'Legitimising Decompilation of Computer Software under Copyright Law', The John Marshall Law Review, (1994), p 105.

[37.] 17 USCS 107.

[38.] 10 USPQ 2d (BNA)117 (ND Cal 1989).

[39.] 24 USPQ 2d (BNA) 1015 (9th Cir 1992). It should be noted that the Ninth Circuit covers the West Coast of the US including Seattle and California. 28 USC Ch 3, s 41.

[40.] 24 USPQ 2d (BNA) 1561 (9th Cir 1992).

[3.32] The US law would appear to be similar to the European in that they possibly permit decompilation for the purposes of interoperability. However, this is not definite. None of the above cases are Supreme Court decisions. Decisions in this area have got no further than the Court of Appeal on the relevant Federal Circuit. The reason for this may be because the potential losses to both sides are very great should a definitive adverse ruling be given. Instead, the parties prefer to settle cases. This is partly because many software companies which apply for injunctions to prevent others decompiling their software, are simultaneously decompiling the software of third parties. If the Supreme Court was to prevent all decompilation, it would affect every software company.[41] The cases imply that decompilation is permissible in the US to ensure interoperability between hardware, software and operating systems. This is important, the vast majority of computer companies are American in origin. It would be very surprising if more protection were to be given to these companies by European courts than is available in the US legal system.

CONCLUSION

[3.33] There are obviously circumstances involving computer programs which have not been anticipated by the Regulations and the Directive. It is not clear at this stage how the courts will interpret the Regulations but in the absence of any clear definitions it is likely that the courts will assume that they have considerable leeway. One example of a situation not anticipated is that of the authors of anti-virus scanner. A huge number of viruses are written every year, all of which have the potential to cause considerable damage. That they do not do so is mainly due to the fact that several companies produce anti-virus scanners or detectors. These are programs which identify viruses and warn the user of their existence. They will also remove the viruses and try to repair any damage which has been done. In order to write programs which will identify viruses, the authors of the anti-virus scanners must decompile the viruses, which are themselves programs, in order to discover how the virus works and how it may be identified.[42] However, the virus will have been written by someone else and the author of the virus could argue that he had not consented to this decompilation. A legally astute virus author might include a statement in his code to the effect that any decompilation was not permitted by him and was illegal. The decompilation would obviously not be occurring for the purposes of

---

41. Gage, 'Copyright Law and Reverse Engineering', Baylor Law Review, Vol 46:183.
42. See Soloman & Kay, *Dr Soloman's PC Anti-Virus Book*, (Newtech, 1994) at p 64. "Here is how you identify a virus. 1. You disassemble the virus code ...".

interoperability, indeed the purpose of the decompilation would be to prevent the virus interoperating with any other programs at all. While it is unlikely that such a virus author would seek to assert his rights, this might give the authors of anti-virus scanners cause for thought. It is very unlikely but not to say inconceivable that any court would decide that the author of an anti-virus scanner was illegally decompiling viruses. The courts would presumably have to decide that this decompilation was protected as it is so important that effective anti-virus programs be available for the public good.

[3.34] The important point here is that the Regulations are not all-inclusive. In the same way as a court might have to find an exception to allow anti-virus scanner authors to decompile viruses, they may also have to find exceptions to allow decompilation in other situations which are clearly in the public interest. One exception might be for the purpose of litigation. It would be very difficult to establish substantial similarity between computer programs if decompilation of them is not permitted or if the parties do not have discovery of the source codes. Even if one party has a discovery order for the source codes, they may still want to decompile the offending computer program so that they can be sure that they have in fact received the source codes which correlate to the object code in the program which is the subject of their dispute.[43]

---

43. See para **[24.47]** *et seq.*

Chapter 4

Infringement of Copyright

[4.01] Copyright infringement can take many forms. Debate about the Software Directive and the 1993 Regulations has focused on the problem of decompilation. However, the major computer copyright problem in the world at present is the more mundane problem of pirating or direct copying of software. The retail value of business applications software sales lost due to piracy in Europe in 1994 is estimated at $4.8 billion,[1] the annual cost in Ireland is over $44 million.[2]

INFRINGEMENT UNDER THE COPYRIGHT ACT 1963

[4.02] In general, all infringements of copyright are actionable at the suit of the owner.[3] Copyright is infringed by carrying out one of the acts which the copyright owner controls under s 7(1) of the Act. Section 8(6) lists these acts as being:

    (a) reproducing the work in any material form;

    (b) publishing the work;

    (c) performing the work in public;

    (d) broadcasting the work;

    (e) causing the work to be transmitted to subscribers to a diffusion service;

    (f) making any adaptation of the work;

    (g) doing in relation to an adaptation of the work, any of the acts mentioned in paragraphs (a) to (e) above.

The major concern of computer program copyright owners will be the reproduction, publication and adaptation of their works. 'Reproduction' or copying will obviously infringe copyright. The 'adaptation' of a work might occur by decompiling a computer program or translating it for use with a different type of computer language or might occur if a picture or song is digitised and stored on a computer. The definition of 'publication' is more difficult as the Act offers no meaning. Under the Industrial and Commercial

---

[1.] Price Waterhouse, *Contribution of the Packaged Business Software Industry to the European Economies*, September 1995, p 21.

[2.] *The Irish Independent*, 17 June 1996.

[3.] CA 1963, s 22(1).

45

Property Act 1927,[4] publishing was defined as "the issue of copies of the work to the public". Under an identical provision of the Copyright Act 1911,[5] 'the public' was found to be very broadly defined.[6] Public does not mean the general public, it can include people present in a private club[7] or hotel.[8]

[4.03] Performing the work in public, broadcasting the work or causing the work to be transmitted to subscribers to a diffusion service may appear irrelevant with regard to computer programs.[9] Their obvious application is to television programmes and films. However, they may be relevant in the context of networks such as the Internet.[10]

[4.04] Section 11(2) of the 1963 Act provides that copyright is infringed by any person who:

    (a) imports an article (otherwise than for his own private and domestic use), into the State; or

    (b) sells, lets for hire, or by way of trade offers or exposes for sale or hire any article, or

    (c) by way of trade exhibits any article in public.

The person must know that the making of the article was done in breach of copyright or, in the case of an imported article, would have infringed copyright if made in the State. The section applies to the distribution of infringing articles for the purposes of trade or for other purposes which prejudice the owners of copyright.[11] The difference between these infringements and those under s 8(6) is that the person who infringes must have knowledge of the infringement under s 11(2).

INFRINGEMENTS UNDER THE 1993 REGULATIONS

[4.05] Regulation 8(1) of the 1993 Regulations[12] gives the owners of copyright in computer programs several rights which are particular to computer programs alone. Regulation 8 details three situations in which the

---

4. CA 1963, s 154(3).
5. CA 1963, s 1(3).
6. Offering six copies of a book for sale in a book shop, although none of the books were actually sold, was held to amount to publication: *Francis Day and Hunter v Feldman & Co* [1914] 2 Ch 728, CA.
7. *Harmes Inc v Martans Club* [1927] 1 Ch 526.
8. *Performing Rights Society v Hawthornes Hotel (Bournemouth) Ltd* [1933] 1 Ch 855.
9. However they may be relevant in the context of multi-media, see para **[2.42]**.
10. See *Shetland Times Ltd v Wills* discussed at para **[5.43]** below.
11. CA 1963, s 11(3).
12. The European Communities (Legal Protection of Computer Programs) Regulations 1993 (SI 26/1993).

owner may take legal action. These rights are "without prejudice to the provisions of Regulations 5, 6, and 7 of these Regulations and Parts II and IV of the Copyright Act 1963." Regulation 5 deals with the exclusive rights of the owner of the program and Regulations 6 and 7 with decompilation. Part II of the Copyright Act provides for infringements of copyright and Part IV with remedies for those infringements. There are three infringements set out in the Regulations:

> (1) any act of putting into circulation a copy of a computer program knowing, or having reason to believe, that it is an infringing copy.[13]

This is similar to the act of importing, selling, hiring or exhibiting an infringing copy under s 11(2) of the 1963 Act and the distribution of an article under s 11(3). There is no explicit requirement that the copy be put into circulation for commercial purposes. Therefore circulating a computer program amongst friends and colleagues will amount to an infringement.

[4.06] Allowing an infringing copy to be distributed over a network or allowing it to be placed on a bulletin board may be covered. However, the person who places the infringing copy on a bulletin board or the person who maintains that board must actually know or have reason to believe that the copy is an infringing copy. It is difficult for most administrators of such services to be aware of even a small portion of the information which is passed on them. There is no explicit requirement that the copy be put into circulation for commercial purposes. So someone who places a copy on a bulletin board would be liable for damages even though they may not make any financial gain from their actions.

[4.07] The second infringement is:

> (2) the possession, for commercial purposes, of a copy of a computer program knowing or having reason to believe that it is an infringing copy.[14]

Possession of an infringing copy is not specifically made a civil infringement under the 1963 Act. However, it may be a criminal offence under that Act.[15] The copy must be possessed for commercial purposes. An office which buys one copy of a program and copies it onto several computers may be in breach of this regulation. The converse may also be true, that the owner cannot take action against a person who possesses the infringing copy for private or personal use. The operator of a bulletin board

---

13. Regulation 8(a).
14. Regulation 8(b).
15. See [5.22] *et seq* below.

which contains an infringing copy of a program would possess it. However, it is necessary to show that the possession is for commercial purposes which may be implied from subscriptions.

[4.08] The third infringement provided for by the Regulations is:

> (3) any act of putting into circulation, or the possession for commercial purposes of, any means the sole intended purpose of which is to facilitate the unauthorised removal or circumvention of any technical device which may have been applied to protect a computer program.[16]

Technical devices are sometimes used by the makers of programs to protect their intellectual property. A technical device will be supplied with a program which attaches to the ports at the back of a computer. The device will not interfere with the normal use of the computer but if it is removed, then the program with which it is associated will not work. This reduces the likelihood of the program being copied since there is no point in copying a program unless one can copy the device as well, which may be difficult. The disadvantage with these systems is that they are expensive and users dislike them, especially if they lose the device and cannot use their program. Although such devices will protect the intellectual property of the program maker, they may damage his goodwill as consumers resent being treated as potential pirates. This provision would appear to be aimed at the those who produce methods of avoiding these devices. The owner can only take action where a technical device is put into circulation or possessed for commercial purposes. In *Sarl Artware v Groupe D'utilisation Francophone D'Informatique*,[17] the French Supreme Court held that to sell or offer for sale programs which de-seal or remove the anti-piracy devices on computer software, to describe programs as clones of 'legitimate' programs only faster and without the anti-copying devices, and to tell customers that anti-piracy devices are unnecessarily costly and unlawful would amount to an act of unfair competition.

[4.09] At present, such devices are unpopular. Instead, protection embedded in the software, such as ID numbers are preferred. These ID numbers display whenever a program is used and they allow owners to ascertain whether a program is copied and who it was copied from.[18] It is not clear whether these

---

16. Regulation 8(c).
17. 22 May 1991, [1993] FSR 703.
18. Short, 'Combating Software Piracy: Can Felony Penalties for Copyright Infringement Curtail the Copying of Computer Software', Computer and High Technology Law Journal, Vol 10, 226, 1994.

types of protection would be covered by the Regulation as they may not be 'technical devices'. Nor is it clear whether this Regulation would apply to devices such as holograms which are placed on the packaging of software to identify it as original, in an effort to prevent the sale of pirate copies.

[4.10] The use of such technical devices could also conflict with the right to create a back-up copy contained in Regulation 6(2), if the user has to evade a copy protection device in order to make their back-up copy. If a copyright owner wishes to install a copy protection device, he would be well advised to ensure that users have adequate access to back-up copies so as to comply with the Directive.

ESTABLISHING INFRINGEMENT

[4.11] Before the owner of copyright can successfully bring a claim for breach of his copyright, he must prove that he is the owner of the copyright. This may not be as simple as it seems. There are no provisions for the registration of copyright in computer programs and indeed other literary works. A scheme of registration has been advocated for the UK and schemes are in operation in other jurisdictions, such as Portugal, Spain and Italy.[19] Proving ownership may be made more complicated if the author has assigned his copyright or given an exclusive licence to exploit it.[20]

Evidence under the 1963 Act

[4.12] In all actions, copyright is presumed to subsist in a work unless the defendant puts this question in issue. If a court finds that copyright subsists in a work, then the plaintiff is presumed to be the owner of the copyright, provided that he claims ownership and the defendant does not object.[21] If the name of an author appears on a work, then that person is presumed to be the author.[22] Where the work is published in the State and the name of a publisher appears on the work, then copyright is presumed to exist and to belong to the publisher whose name appears on the work.[23] If the author of a work is dead his work is presumed to be original and to have been first published wherever and whenever the plaintiff in an action alleges it was published. If the work is published anonymously or under a pseudonym, then it is treated as if the author were dead.[24]

[19.] Bond, 'Public Registers for Software Programs', 11 CLSR (1995) p 130.
[20.] See Ch 6 on Licences.
[21.] CA 1963, s 26(1).
[22.] CA 1963, s 26(2).
[23.] CA 1963, s 26(4)
[24.] CA 1963, s 26(6) and (7).

Establishing Infringement

[4.13] No matter how similar a work appears to another, it cannot infringe its copyright if it was created independently. Likewise, if a work is inspired by another, there will be no infringement unless it can be shown to be similar to the original or a substantial part of it. The English Court of Appeal has stated that for copyright to be infringed:

> "there must be present two elements: First, there must be sufficient objective similarity between the infringing work and the copyright work, or a substantial part thereof, for the former to be properly described, not necessarily as identical with, but as a reproduction or adaptation or the latter; secondly, the copyright work must be the source from which the infringing work is derived."[25]

House of Spring Gardens Ltd v Point Blank Ltd

[4.14] The Irish Supreme Court considered this question in *House of Spring Gardens Ltd & Ors v Point Blank Ltd & Ors.*[26] This case dealt with originality in designs as opposed to literary works, however, its principles may be applied to literary works. One of the plaintiff's, Michael Sacks, a tailor, had successfully developed a bullet proof vest. William Waite, one of the defendants, had contacts within the Libyan Military and together with other parties they agreed to supply 15,000 of Sack's vests to Libya, a contract worth £5 million. After this contract was signed, relations broke down completely between the parties. Waite and others set up Point Blank Ltd to manufacture the vests in Cork. Sacks heard of this and sued in the English Courts for, inter alia, breach of copyright. The matter was settled and the defendants agreed to pay Sacks royalties in respect of both the initial contract with the Libyan government and any further contracts. The term 'armoured vest' was defined with reference to a sample annexed to the agreement and as "any variation as might be mutually agreed in writing". The defendants paid royalties in respect of the initial contract. Subsequently, they secured a similar contract with the Libyan Government. In order to avoid the payment of royalties, counsel prepared specifications to avoid the payment of royalties. Counsel prepared specifications which were given to Mr Taylor, an independent designer who was instructed to re-design the original vest. It would appear that the manufacturers ignored the re-designed vest and simply copied the original. When the case came before Costello J in the High Court he stated that "it is well established that the plaintiff in an infringement action must show that the defendant has made use, whether

---

[25.] Diplock LJ, *Francis Day and Hunter Ltd v Bron* [1963] 2 All ER 16.
[26.] [1984] IR 611.

directly or indirectly of his work". He cited with approval *King Features Syndicate Inc & Segar v O & M Kleemann Ltd*:[27]

> "There would be no infringement if the respondents had independently produced a similar figure without copying the sketch directly or indirectly. The question is whether there was copying of the actual sketch. Here the only evidence of actual copying, direct or indirect, is similarity with regard to the figure, which is a substantial part of the sketch, between the copyright work and the alleged infringement. I think, however, that, where there is substantial similarity, such similarity is prima facie evidence of copying, which the party charged may refute by evidence that, notwithstanding the similarity, there was no copying, but independent creation".

[4.15] Costello J agreed with Diplock LJ in *Francis Day and Hunter Ltd v Bron*,[28] that there must be a 'causal connection' between the copyright work and the infringing work, but indirect copying will amount to an infringement once the chain of connection between the two has been established. Costello J used the following test laid down by Willmer LJ in that case:

(1) In order to constitute reproduction within the meaning of the Act, there must be (a) a sufficient degree of objective similarity between the two works and (b) some causal connection between the plaintiffs' and the defendants' work.

(2) It is quite irrelevant to enquire whether the defendant was or was not consciously aware of such causal connection.

(3) Where there is a substantial degree of objective similarity, this of itself will afford *prima facie* evidence to show that there is a causal connection between the plaintiffs' and the defendants' work; at least it is a circumstance for which the inference may be drawn.

(4) The fact that the defendant denies that he consciously copied affords some evidence to rebut the inference of causal connection arising from the objective similarity, but is in no way conclusive.[29]

Costello J held that there was *prima facie* evidence that the defendants had infringed the plaintiffs' copyright. He found that the vests and their component parts were 'virtually identical' and that there was a substantial degree of objective similarity between the designs of the vests and their respective components. This conclusion was strengthened by three additional features of the case. Firstly, the defendants could copy the plaintiffs' work with ease having manufactured the vests for the initial

---

27. [1941] 2 All ER 403, at 413.
28. [1963] 2 All ER 16.
29. As quoted in *Copinger on Copyright* (1980) p 178.

contract. This gave them opportunity. They also had a motive as the Libyan Government only wanted vests similar to those manufactured for the initial contract. Secondly, there were many different ways of designing a vest and the function of the vest would not dictate its design and shape. This reduced the likelihood that similarities between the vests resulted from pure coincidence. Finally, the defendants had used photographs of the plaintiffs' vest in a brochure for their 'own' vest. Their conduct suggested that they "had no moral inhibitions against committing further acts of plagiarism if they were necessary to fulfil the second Libyan contract".

[4.16] This established an inference that there was copying of the plaintiffs' vest. To rebut this, the defendant claimed that he had redesigned the vest and produced an independent original design. When Mr Taylor was engaged to carry out this redesign he attended a meeting with counsel at the offices of the plaintiffs' solicitors.[30] After three hours discussion, he realised that very little design was actually required "and that a child could have done it". Furthermore, there was evidence that Mr Taylor's redesign was not used in the manufacture of the new vests[31] and they simply followed the original patterns. The plaintiffs' solicitor sent the specifications to another independent designer and unassisted, she produced a design which "was very different to (the original) and that eventually produced by Mr Taylor".[32]

[4.17] Costello J found that the defendants' vest was not original and was in fact a variation of the plaintiffs' design. He upheld their claim and awarded substantial damages against the defendants. His judgment was upheld unanimously by the Supreme Court.

Infringement in a computer program

[4.18] At its most basic level, copying a computer program involves reproducing the lines of code in a program. However, there are many parts of a program which can be copied and often the individual lines of code may be the least valuable part of the program. When a program is written, the head programmer will decide how the program's aims are to be effected within the parameters set out. The head programmer divides the program into hundreds of subprograms, each to be written separately. Often writing a program will involve numerous programmers working separately. One of the most difficult parts of writing a program is not writing the individual lines of code but rather co-ordinating the work of all the programmers. As programs

---

[30.] Practitioners should note that the conduct of the lawyers involved in this aspect of the case was criticised by the Supreme Court. See McCarthy J at 708.

[31.] Griffin J in the Supreme Court, at 702.

[32.] *Ibid*, at 674.

get longer and more complex, the work of the head programmers becomes more valuable as their task becomes more difficult. The design and layout of a program may be just as valuable as the lines of code which make up the program. Deciding when the design and layout of a program have been copied is obviously far more difficult than proving straightforward plagiarism of individual lines of code.[33]

[4.19] The Irish High Court considered the question of what constitutes copying in *News Datacom Ltd, British Sky Broadcasting and Sky Television plc v David Lyons, t/a Satellite Decoding Systems.*[34] In that case the plaintiffs transmitted their television signals by satellite in a 'scrambled form' so that they could not be received unless the receiver had been fitted with a decoder. This decoder would have to be activated by a 'smart card' which would only be provided by the plaintiffs in return for the appropriate subscription fee. This smart card contained an algorithm as part of a computer program. The plaintiffs were able to alter the algorithm at will. However, to do so they would have to provide each subscriber with a new smart card. In 1993, the defendants began to market and sell in Ireland a smart card which was not produced by or authorised by the plaintiffs but which would decode the scrambled signal with the same ease as the plaintiff's card. As a result, the plaintiffs sought an interlocutory injunction restraining the defendants from infringing the plaintiff's copyright in the software used in the decoders and the cards. The plaintiffs claimed that the defendant's smart card had to contain a copy or at least a part-copy of the algorithm and other components used in the plaintiff's smart card. Their claim was based solely on the premise that their algorithm was so complex that it was not within the bounds of probability that the defendant could have created his smart card without copying the plaintiff's.

[4.20] Flood J rejected the plaintiff's claim and relied on the decision of Megarry V-C in *Thrustcode Ltd v WW Computing Ltd.*[35] In that case the plaintiffs sought to prevent the defendants from copying and selling their computer programs. Megarry V-C noted that "in the normal case", the written or typed words can be seen, compared and discussed. However, with programs:

> *"the results produced by operating the program must not be confused with the program in which copyright is claimed.* [emphasis Flood J] If I may take the absurdly simple example, 2 and 2 make 4. But so does 2 times 2, or 6 minus 2, or 2% of 200, or 6 squared divided by 9 or many other things.

[33.] Gibbs, 'Software's Chronic Crisis', Scientific American, September 1994, p 72.
[34.] [1994] 1 ILRM 450.
[35.] [1983] FSR 502.

Many different processes may produce the same answer and yet remain different processes that have not been copied one from another. For computers, as for other things, what must be compared are the thing said to have been copied and the thing said to be an infringing copy. If these two things are invisible, then normally they must be reproduced in visible form, or in a form that in some way is perceptible, before it can be determined whether on infringes the other.

In some cases, no doubt, it may be possible in some other way to demonstrate that one is a copy of the other, as when there is some evidence or some admission that when one computer was being programmed, someone was watching and was programming a rival computer in the same or a similar way. Normally, however, what will be needed is a print out or other documentary evidence of the program alleged to have been copied, and of the alleged infringing program, or sufficient parts of each. You must look at what the programs are and not at merely what they do or can do."

In *News Datacom Ltd* the plaintiffs tried to infer that because the two programs were able to accomplish the same task, then one must have been copied from the other. Flood J rejected this as the plaintiffs had not offered any scientific basis for their claim. The plaintiffs had simply proffered the opinion of a 'partisan expert' who claimed that the algorithm was so complicated that nothing short of copying could explain the defendant's success. As the plaintiffs had not offered any direct evidence of any similarity in the software itself, he declined to grant the interlocutory relief sought.

[4.21] Flood J noted that the plaintiffs frequently changed their smart cards and the defendants were able to produce their own cards within a relatively short period of time. This, he believed made it highly improbable that the defendants were copying and made it highly probable that the defendants were in no way infringing the plaintiff's software. Since the plaintiffs could not show any substantial similarity between the programs, the question of causal connection did not arise.

US Law

[4.22] The country which has examined this question in the greatest depth is the US. In *Whelan Associates Inc v Jaslow Dental Laboratory Inc*[36] the plaintiff created a program for the defendant which managed the functions of a dental laboratory called 'Dentalab'. Subsequently, Jaslow created a new program, called 'Dentacom PC', which performed the same function as that written by Whelan but did so on a different type of computer and so was

---

[36.] 797 F 2d 1222 (3rd Cir 1986), cert denied, 479 US 1031 (1987). Also reported at [1987] FSR 1.

written in a different language. As a result, the code in the new program was totally different from that of the original. Whelan sued, alleging breach of copyright. Initially, it was held by the Federal District Court that Dentacom PC had infringed the copyright in Dentalab as its "structure and overall organisation were substantially similar'.[37] This decision was controversial as the Dentacom PC program did not copy the source or object codes of Dentalab because they were written in different languages for different computers. The decision was appealed and the Federal Court of Appeal had to consider the question of whether copyright protection applied to the structure of a program (the non-literal elements) or to just the source and object codes (the literal elements). The difficulty for the Court was that by recognising that the structure and sequence of a program could be protected by copyright, it could be extending protection to ideas. This would run counter to the basic law of copyright that ideas cannot be protected.[38] The Court stated:

> "the line between idea and expression may be drawn with reference to the end sought to be achieved by the work in question. In other words, the purpose or function of a utilitarian work would be the work's idea and everything that is not necessary to that purpose or function would be part of the expression of the idea".

The Court concluded that the structure and sequence of a program could be protected. They defined the difference between expression and idea as:

> "where there are various means of achieving the desired purpose, then the particular means chosen is not necessary to the purpose; hence there is expression, not idea". Broadly, the court said that where there is only one way of doing something then that method is an idea. Where there are a number of ways of doing something, selecting one of them will amount to expression and will be protected. The Federal Court of Appeal stated that the expression of the idea of a computer program " is the manner in which the program operates, controls and regulates the computer in receiving, assembling, calculating, retaining, correlating and producing useful information either on a screen, print-out or by audio communication."

[4.23] The Federal Court of Appeal held that copyright infringement could be proved if it could be shown that the defendant had access to the program

---

37. *Ibid* at 1228-1229.
38. *Baker v Selden* 101 US 99 (1879). This case concerned a bookkeeping system. Selden published a book on the system with a series of blank forms for use in the system at the back. A few years later Baker published a book on Selden's system which reproduced the forms. Selden claimed that this was breach of copyright. The court rejected this view as using the forms was essential for the use of the system and to protect them would amount to protecting Selden's idea.

and by demonstrating a substantial similarity between the two works. Clearly, Jaslow had access to the Whelan program. The Court decided that there was substantial similarity between the programs by relying on the evidence of the plaintiff's expert witnesses. The Court found that five of Whelan's sub-routines had been copied by Jaslow. Although these were only a small proportion of the computer program, the court said that the test was qualitative and not quantitative.

[4.24] At present, the accepted test in the US is that used in *Computer Associates International Inc v Altai Inc.*[39] Computer Associates had employed a programmer for five years before he left to join Altai, a rival firm. When he left, he took with him a copy of the source code for one of Computer Associate's programs. At Altai he worked on a project to develop a program to compete with that of Computer Associates and he used the stolen source codes to do so without Altai's knowledge. It was only when they were sued for breach of copyright that Altai realised that this copying had been going on. The programmer was removed from the project and programmers unfamiliar with the Computer Associate's program were assigned to write a new version. Altai admitted that the original version of their program infringed Computer Associate's copyright, however, they contended that the new version did not. The issue before the courts was whether the second version infringed Computer Associate's copyright in their program. Initially, the Federal District Court found that the Computer Associate's program had not been copied and this was upheld on appeal.

[4.25] The Federal Court of Appeal developed the 'abstraction-filtration-comparison test' to establish whether or not any copying had occurred. The purpose of abstraction is to identify the individual elements of the computer program. The court will start with the program's general idea, such as running a dentist's office. Then the court will identify the sub-programs that together make up the program. There may be other parts of the program such as data structures, interfaces and libraries.

[4.26] After doing this, the court will have to 'filter' these elements to decide which parts are ideas and which are expressions. The parts which are ideas are not protected, nor are those which are in the public domain, stock in trade or externally dictated elements.[40] What remains is the expression in the program, which is protectable. Finally, the court has to decide whether the defendant copied any aspect of the protected expression and assess the copied portion's importance to the plaintiff's overall program. The court

---

[39.] 982 F 2d 693 (1992) and 775 F Supp 544 (1991).

[40.] Eg, the programming language used, the type of computer and operating system.

must make a qualitative judgement as to whether the defendant's work copies 'too much' of the protected expression. This judgment will obviously vary from case to case.

[4.27] This test has been criticised. Firstly, it is said that the court failed to explain exactly how to carry out the test, particularly how to carry out abstraction and filtration.[41] Secondly, the court does not consider the program in its entirety, rather it dissects the program. This criticism rests on the fact that to carry out the test requires the evidence of expert witnesses. Modern programs are so complex that judicial independence may be compromised as judges will be forced into total reliance on these witnesses. While this is unfortunate, it is a feature of many modern cases, frequently judges are forced to rely on medical evidence and that of other professionals to a similar degree.[42]

English case-law

Richardson v Flanders and Chemtec Ltd

[4.28] The English courts have also tackled these questions in *Richardson v Flanders and Chemtec Ltd*.[43] Richardson developed a computer program specifically for use by pharmacists. The program would print out labels and assist in stock-taking. Flanders was employed by Richardson as a programmer to design a version of the program for the BBC computer. This was sold in the UK and Ireland. However, the relationship between the two men broke down and Flanders resigned but continued to work as a consultant to the plaintiff. In 1987, the plaintiff negotiated to develop a similar program for the Irish market which would run on IBM computers. These negotiations fell through but the plaintiff suggested that the defendant might be willing to develop the program. These new negotiations were successful. It was agreed that the defendant would get the rights to sell the program in Ireland but that the plaintiff would retain the rights elsewhere. The program was duly written and sold in Ireland as 'Pharm-Assist'. Later the defendant attempted to sell the program in the UK as 'Chemtec'.

---

41. Lowe, 'A Square Peg in a Round Hole: The proper substantial similarity test for non-literal aspects of computer programs', 68 Washington Law Review (1993).

42. Developments in US law are discussed in: Brown, 'Analytical Dissection of Copyrighted Computer Software - Complicating The Simple And Confounding The Complex', Computer Law & Practice, Vol 11, (1995) p 16; Wernick, 'Market Realities In The Analysis Of Copyright Infringement Of Computer Programs', 1995 11 CLSR, p 133. Bigelow, 'United States Software Protection-Recent Developments', Computer Law and Practice, Vol 11, No 2, 1995, p 50.

43. [1993] FSR 497.

[4.29] The plaintiff sued, claiming that the defendant had infringed his copyright in the program for the BBC computer. He alleged that the defendant had reproduced the general scheme of his program and this reproduction included a number of elements particular to his program. The Court adopted the *dicta* of Millet J in *Spectravest Inc v Aperknit Inc*[44] which stated that the Court should be concerned with the points of similarity in a work as opposed to the points of dissimilarity. To decide whether copying had occurred, Ferris J referred to *Computer Associates v Altai* with approval. However, he noted that he had difficulty in applying the abstraction test and in deciding how the process was meant to work. Ferris J held that instead of trying to identify levels of abstraction in the program, the court should conduct a four stage test and try to answer the following questions:

1. Whether the plaintiff's work was protected by copyright?

2. Whether any similarities existed between the plaintiff's and the defendant's programs?

3. Whether the similarities were caused by copying or whether there were any other explanations.

4. If there was copying, whether the elements copied constituted a significant part of the original work.

Ferris J had no difficulty in deciding that the plaintiff's program was protected by copyright. He examined the similarities between the programs by comparing their screen displays and the key sequences used to operate the program. He found that the plaintiff's program had 13 functions involved in the printing of the labels. The program also carried out stock control and had 17 other features. He found that the 'Chemtec' program had 17 points of similarity to the original. He rejected deliberate copying as a reason for these similarities. In total, 6 of the 17 similarities were explained by reasons other than copying. A further 8 could have been copied from the original but they did not amount to a substantial part of the program. This left 3 points of similarity. They related to editing, amendment functions and the use of dose codes. While there were only three such similarities, the resemblance was striking. The editing function in both programs worked in the same erroneous fashion. The dose codes allow the user to enter abbreviations which would print instructions for the use of the medication on the label. Of the 91 codes used in the original, 84 were found to be reproduced in the new program which gave rise to an inference of copying. The plaintiff was successful in establishing that copying had occurred but the judge added that

---

[44.] [1988] FSR 161.

the copying was "a fairly minor infringement in a few limited respects and certainly not slavish copying".

Ibcos Computers Ltd v Barclays Finance Ltd[45]

[4.30] In this case, Poole, a computer programmer employed by the plaintiff, wrote a program, called 'ADS', for the plaintiff. After he left the company he wrote a similar program, called 'Unicorn', which was marketed by Barclays. The plaintiff sued, alleging that Poole had copied ADS when he wrote Unicorn. Jacob J stated that in order to prove copying the plaintiff must point out similarities between the programs and prove that the defendant had an opportunity of copying the work. If the resemblance is sufficiently great, the court will draw an inference of copying, although the defendant may be able to rebut this inference. In particular, he may be able to show that the similarities derive from material in the public domain, or that it arises because of functional necessity. Jacob J then set out the key similarities. The programs had similar spelling mistakes, headings, sub-programs, file records, redundant code and various other matters. He was satisfied that the similarities could only have resulted from disk to disk copying, although he bore in mind the fact that many lines were not the same.[46] He rejected Poole's suggestion that he was merely writing it all from memory as fantastic.

[4.31] To decide whether or not there was copying, Jacob J made reference to the judgment of Ferris J in *Richardson*.[47] He cited Ferris J as support for his view that he should have regard to not only literal similarities between the programs but also program structure and design features. He rejected the view of Baker J in *Total Information Processing Systems v Daman*[48] that copying the divisions or structure of a program could be likened to copying a table of contents. Baker J had suggested that it would be very unusual that the table of contents of a book could be described as a substantial part of it. Jacob J felt that this was a question of degree. Working out a reasonably detailed arrangement of topics, sub-topics and sub-sub-topics is the key to a successful work of non-fiction. He saw no reason why taking this would not amount to an infringement. On the same basis, he felt that the setting up of the divisions of a program might well involve enough skill, labour, and judgment for it to be considered a substantial part of the program as a whole. He found that there was close correspondence between the program structure

---

45. [1994] FSR 275.
46. He also failed to understand why the defendant's experts did not seem to come to the same conclusion. He suggested that they had not focused on this aspect of the case at all.
47. *Op cit.*
48. [1992] FSR 171.

of the two programs and that copyright had been infringed. He also referred to the features of the programs such as their levels of security, methods of creating invoice types and internal sales systems, all of which were common to the two programs. Although he suggested that this probably the result of copying, he regarded them as no more than features of the programs. Even if they were subject to copyright, copying these functions would amount to just the copying of a general idea or scheme and not the infringement of copyright. Jacob J then turned to the sub-programs which he examined on an individual basis where he found substantial similarities in many sub-programs. Jacob J held in favour of the plaintiff.

CONCLUSION

[4.32] In deciding whether copying of a work has occurred, the court must first decide whether there is substantial similarity between the two works and if so whether there is also a causal connection.[49] In deciding whether a program has been copied it is not enough to say that the programs produce the same result.[50]

[4.33] There is no Irish decision on how to compare two computer programs. The US courts have developed an abstraction-filtration-comparison test which requires the dissection of a program, the elimination of all elements not protected by copyright and finally the comparison of what is left to see whether there is copying. This test has been adopted to some degree in the UK.

[4.34] The differences between US, Irish and British cases may be accounted for by the expert evidence which was called before the US courts. Flood J in *News Datacom* was dismissive of the evidence given to him by the plaintiff's expert which did not refer to the codes which made up the programs. In the UK case of *Richardson*, Ferris J did not attempt to compare the two program codes. An expert witness for the plaintiff produced such a comparison but Ferris J found this "extremely difficult to understand". The plaintiff did not take up an invitation to explain this comparison further. In *Ibcos* Jacob J was able to compare the code and structure of the two programs because the plaintiffs' expert witnesses were able to supply him with the material to make this comparison. While it is unfortunate that the courts have to rely on such expert evidence, it is unrealistic to expect judges

---

[49.] *House of Spring Gardens Ltd & Ors v Point Blank Ltd & Ors* [1984] IR 611.
[50.] *News Datacom Ltd, British Sky Broadcasting and Sky Television plc v David Lyons, t/a Satellite Decoding Systems* [1994] 1 ILRM 450.

to acquire the expertise necessary to do so themselves. It is also not their function.

[**4.35**] When the Irish courts come to examine such similarities between programs, they will have to conduct an analysis similar to that in the *Ibcos* case. To merely compare the outputs of two programs is not enough. In *Richardson* Ferris J compared the screen displays and key strokes of the two programs. While this approach worked there, in general all programs are becoming more and more similar to each other. Finding similarities between word processing programs and spreadsheets is remarkably easy and telling the programs apart is difficult. There is nothing wrong with this, making a program layout familiar to new users makes it easier to sell. It is submitted that the approach of Flood J in *News Datacom* was correct. Flood J held that it was not enough to merely to compare the 'results' or output of two programs. In the same way as the output of the Sky decoder was to decode the satellite signal, the output of the pharmaceutical programs was a screen display.

[**4.36**] As writing programs becomes more of a science and less of an art, deciding when copying has occurred will become more difficult for the courts. At present, software may be said to be in something of a crisis as expensive programs fail to function properly. In order to cope with these problems, programmers may have to become less individualistic and abide by standard rules and procedures set by their industry. This will mean that there may be fewer differences between programs. If the industry only recognises one way of achieving a particular result, then it will be impossible to say that the use of this method involved copying from another programmer.

Chapter 5

Remedies for Breach of Copyright

INTRODUCTION

[5.01] The pirating and counterfeiting of software is a profitable business both in Ireland and elsewhere.[1] Over 82% of software used in Ireland is illegally copied,[2] within Europe the level is 52%.[3] In general, people who copy software can be grouped into three broad categories: organised pirates; individual computer users; and employers and employees within companies. Organised pirates copy on a huge scale for profit, they sell their wares over bulletin boards or they may sell copies of the program together with fake packaging and manuals. Individual computer users wish to avoid paying for software and copy from disks received from friends or colleagues. Employees of companies will copy software which is licensed to the company they work for; although maybe not for the number of persons actually using the software.

[5.02] Most efforts at controlling illegal copying of software have been focused at this last type of offender. Such efforts appear to have been successful in the USA anyway at curtailing corporate copying. The Software Publishers Association (SPA) identifies companies which are suspected of using pirated software and then obtains court orders allowing the association to search the company's offices and seize any non-licensed software. Information about suspect companies comes from disgruntled employees who call their hot-line or unsuspecting users of pirated software who call the manufacturer's customer support number.[4] The policy of the SPA has been to settle with such companies once they purchase legitimate copies of the software. Another US organisation, the Business Software Association (BSA) has taken a more robust line and tends to seek criminal prosecutions.

---

1. For example, in July 1993 a US federal indictment was brought against a corporation which was systematically copying and distributing more than twenty thousand copies of copyrighted and trademarked Microsoft MS-DOS and Windows software and manuals: *United States v Prosys Inc* No CR-93-0348-RHS (N D Cal 1993).
2. *The Sunday Business Post*, 26 May 1996.
3. Price Waterhouse, *Contribution of the Packaged Business Software Industry to the European Economies,* September 1995, p 21.
4. Short, 'Combating Software Piracy: Can Felony Penalties for Copyright Infringement Curtail The Copying Of Computer Software', Computer and High Technology Law Journal, Vol 10, 222, 1994.

At present, both Novell[5] and Microsoft[6] are targeting those who illegally copy their software in Ireland.

[5.03] German software owners have taken similar direct action to catch software pirates. In 1992, free demonstration disks were mailed to numerous companies within Germany. The disk provided a demonstration of a program while at the same time it searched the hard drive for illegal copies of software. If the program encountered any illegal copies, a voucher would appear on the user's screen. The voucher told the user to print it off and send it back. If the user did so they would receive a free handbook. The owners duly received some 400 copies of the voucher, and instead of issuing them the handbook, the users were sent a letter from the owner's lawyers.[7]

[5.04] The remedies for infringement of copyright may be divided into civil and criminal. Civil remedies have obvious advantages over criminal remedies: the burden of proof in civil cases is lower; the case may be settled early; the publicity can be limited and owners can obtain compensation. On the other hand, criminal remedies proceed faster and carry stiffer penalties. In the USA prosecutors prefer civil remedies when pursuing an offender who is wealthy and is not likely to flee the jurisdiction. They tend to institute criminal proceedings against those who run "fly-by-night operations with few ties to the community and little money to pay a judgment".[8]

CIVIL REMEDIES

[5.05] The owner of intellectual property has access to the same reliefs as the owner of physical and other forms of property. All reliefs, such as damages, accounts of any profits or injunctions, are available to the owner.[9]

Damages and Account of Profits

[5.06] The onus is placed on the copyright owner to ensure that others are aware of his rights as there is no provision for registration of copyright. Where a court finds that an infringement has occurred but the defendant was not aware and had no reasonable grounds for being aware of the copyright, then the owner is not entitled to any damages. He can still obtain an account

---

5.   *The Irish Independent*, 17 June 1996.
6.   *The Sunday Business Post*, 26 May 1996,
7.   Ian Lloyd, *Information Technology*, (Butterworths, 1993) p 294.
8.   Walker, 'Federal Criminal Remedies for the Theft of Intellectual Property', Hastings Comm/Ent LJ, Vol 16 p 68. Kent Walker is an Assistant United States Attorney in San Francisco specialising in the prosecution of high-technology crime.
9.   CA 1963, s 22(2).

of profits and any other relief.[10] This might occur where the defendant reasonably thought that the literary work was in the public domain.

[5.07] Where a court finds that an infringement has occurred and the owner will not get adequate satisfaction by compensatory damages, the court may award further or punitive damages having regard to the flagrancy of the breach and the benefits received by the defendant.[11] The owner of copyright is also entitled to all the rights in all infringing copies as if he were the owner of every such copy since it was made.[12] The copyright owner cannot obtain any damages if the defendant was not aware and had no reasonable grounds for suspecting that copyright existed in the copied work or else that the defendant believed and had reasonable grounds for believing that the copies were not infringing.[13] Infringing copy means a reproduction of a literary work other than a film.[14]

[5.08] The plaintiffs succeeded in their claim in *House of Spring Gardens v Point Blank Ltd.*[15] The plaintiffs pointed out that they were entitled to damages for conversion, damages for infringement and aggravated damages. These damages were cumulative and not alternative. In this case the damages would have been very high. However, the plaintiffs elected to receive instead an account of profits. In the High Court, it was argued by the plaintiffs that Costello J himself could assess the damages, based on the evidence put before him. Costello J agreed with these submissions and he awarded the plaintiffs the sum of £3,474,570.50. This was the difference between the price of the vests sold to Libya at £5,446,570.50 and the cost of manufacturing the vests at £1,972,000. On appeal to the Supreme Court, the defendants objected, claiming that the sum was grossly excessive and that Costello J should have ordered the taking of an account. This was rejected by the Supreme Court.[16]

Injunctions

[5.09] In Ireland, as in many other jurisdictions, the injunction[17] is the preferred legal method when dealing with a breach of copyright. It offers a

---

10. CA 1963, s 22(3).
11. CA 1963, s 22(5).
12. CA 1963, s 24(1).
13. CA 1963, s 24(3).
14. CA 1963, s 24(4).
15. [1984] IR 611.
16. See also *Allibert SA v O'Connor* [1982] ILRM 40 and *Folens v O'Dubhghaill* [1973] IR 255.
17. A detailed examination of this topic is beyond the scope of this book. For a detailed discussion see Keane, *The Law of Equity and Trusts in the Republic of Ireland*, (Butterworths, 1989), Ch 15.

quick and effective method of preventing potential breaches. An injunction is a discretionary remedy and may be defined as a court order requiring a person to do, or to refrain from doing a particular act. Usually the court will act to restrain or prevent an infringement, but orders may also be made forcing the hand over of infringing copies or even allowing for the search of premises which it is suspected are used for the copying of protected programs or other works.

[5.10] Injunctions may be classified by the effect which they have. 'Prohibitory' injunctions will prevent the defendant from carrying out specified acts. A right which is to be protected by an injunction must be known to law or equity, so mere inconvenience to the plaintiff will not necessitate the grant of an injunction. *'Quia Timet'* injunctions will prevent actions which the plaintiff fears will occur but which have not yet occurred. 'Mandatory' injunctions will force the defendant to carry out specified acts. In *Leisure Data v Bell*,[18] the defendant had agreed to write a program and the plaintiff had agreed to market it. A dispute arose regarding the copyright of the source codes for the programs and the obligation to correct the programs. The plaintiff was successful in obtaining a mandatory interlocutory injunction requiring the defendant to disclose the source codes upon the plaintiff's undertakings as to confidentiality. The order was made because it was necessary to keep the program free of faults and to update it so that it could maintain its value pending the trial of the action.

Interlocutory Injunctions

[5.11] Injunctions may also be classified by the stage of the legal process at which they are granted and the length of time for which they remain in force. 'Perpetual' injunctions can only be granted at the trial of the action. A plaintiff may have to wait several years before a full trial of his action. In the meantime, application can be made for an 'interlocutory' injunction which will remain in force until the full trial of the action.[19] The action is brought by a motion which must be served on the defendant giving four days' notice. Evidence is heard on affidavit. The speed with which the motion is heard is obviously an advantage. However, often an action will effectively be settled by the grant of an interlocutory injunction, so the court and the parties may also decide to have the hearing of the motion treated as the trial of the action. This means that the parties may never get a proper chance to completely argue their cases and many important issues of law are only ever adjudicated at interlocutory proceedings.

---

18. [1988] FSR 367.
19. The order is granted under Order 50 rule 6 of the Rules of the Superior Courts 1986.

[5.12] The Irish law on interlocutory injunctions was stated by the Supreme Court in *Campus Oil Ltd v Minister for Industry and Energy (No 2)*[20] adapting the principles set out by the House of Lords in *American Cyanamid v Ethicon Ltd.*[21] Before granting an injunction, the court must be satisfied that there is a 'serious question' to be tried. There is no need to show that the plaintiff would probably succeed ultimately or that he has a *prima facie* case. If this test is satisfied then the court must decide whether or not the balance of convenience lies with granting the injunction. In deciding this the court must first decide whether or not damages will adequately compensate the plaintiff if they are given at the trial of the action. If they will, then there is no need to grant the injunction. Therefore, to obtain an injunction the plaintiff must satisfy the court that he will suffer irreparable loss in the event that he is refused the interlocutory injunction. Secondly, the court must decide whether or not damages will adequately compensate the defendant for his loss, if the injunction is granted. This process essentially involves the court in deciding which party will suffer more if the injunction is or is not granted. In general, the court will seek to uphold the *status quo*, especially where the balance of convenience does not clearly go one way or the other. If an interlocutory injunction is granted then the plaintiff must give an undertaking as to damages.

[5.13] In *MS Associates Ltd v Power*,[22] the defendant distributed the plaintiff's software. After spending considerable time adapting their products for the needs of an individual customer, he began to sell this adapted version as his own. The plaintiffs sought an injunction to prevent him doing so. At the interlocutory hearing the plaintiffs showed that they had an arguable case. Falconer J stated that he found it difficult to decide where the balance of convenience lay. In refusing the application, he paid attention to a statement in an affidavit of the defendant's marketing director which stated:

> "Computer technology changes so fast that both computers and computer programs are soon obsolete. This causes the market for particular programs to be short-lived. My estimate is that B-tran [the defendant's program] will cease to be in demand in two or three years. This means that if the second defendant is prevented from entering the market now until trial in this action, which I am advised could be as much as two years from now, the demand for the product will have ceased."

---

20. [1983] IR 88.
21. [1975] AC 396.
22. [1988] FSR 242.

Falconer J also took into account the fact that granting the injunction would almost certainly have made the two employees of the defendant unemployed. Similarly, in *Series 5 Software Ltd v Clarke*,[23] the defendants who were ex-employees of the plaintiff software company had left after their pay cheques had not been honoured. They then set up their own rival company. Laddie J accepted that granting an injunction might well have the effect of depriving the defendants of the means to earn a living. He was not impressed by the plaintiff's claim that the defendants were inflicting immediate and serious damage as they had failed to act vigorously and speedily. As the plaintiffs had competitors other than the defendants, allowing the defendants to trade would not significantly affect the *status quo*.

[5.14] If the matter is especially urgent the court may grant an interim injunction. This will run until the hearing of an application for an interlocutory injunction, normally on the next motion day. It will almost invariably be heard *ex parte* and is grounded on affidavit. As a result it is vital that the plaintiff reveal all the relevant facts to the court.

[5.15] An injunction is an equitable remedy. This means that the defendant can rely on all the usual equitable defences such as: delay; acquiescence; the conduct of the plaintiff (known as the requirement that the plaintiff have 'clean hands'); and hardship to the defendant. *Compaq Computer v Dell Computer*[24] concerned advertisements which compared the plaintiff's computers unfavourably with those of the defendant. The defendant unsuccessfully argued that as the plaintiff had engaged in similar advertising it should be denied an injunction.

[5.16] In *News Datacom Ltd, British Sky Broadcasting Ltd and Sky Television plc v David Lyons*[25] Flood J decided that he could not grant an interlocutory injunction to the plaintiffs because they had:

> "failed to show that they have sown the seed which could fructify at the hearing into a stateable case of infringement by copying of a copyright. At most they have merely shown the fruits of the software and not direct evidence of any similarities in the software itself, or if it had been more accurate to say so, they have simply shown the fruits of the respective algorithms used by the respective parties but have not shown direct evidence of any similarities between the algorithms".

---

23. [1996] FSR 273.
24. [1992] FSR 93.
25. [1994] 1 ILRM 450.

Furthermore, he noted that an interlocutory injunction is a discretionary remedy. The mere fact that the conduct of one of the parties is questionable in ethics or morality is not a reason for granting an injunction.

Anton Piller Order

[5.17] If copyright infringement is suspected, then the copyright owner should ensure that evidence of infringement is gathered as soon as possible. An Anton Piller order will allow him to do this by ordering the defendant to allow the plaintiff to enter his premises in order to search for, inspect, and seize any property which infringes the plaintiff's rights. It is an important order in intellectual property cases where speed and secrecy are of the utmost importance to prevent vital evidence being disposed of. This remedy is discussed in more detail in Chapter 24.

Prohibited goods

[5.18] The owner of copyright may restrict the importation of infringing copies under the Copyright Act 1963 by giving notice in writing to the Revenue Commissioners that he owns copyright in a work and requests them to treat any copies of the work as prohibited goods during a period not exceeding five years. This applies to any copy made outside the State which would be an infringing copy if made within the State. However, this may not apply to software as the subsection only applies in "the case of a work, to any printed copy".[26] It is hard to see how a copy of a computer program could be described as printed. The prohibition notice does not apply where articles are imported for an individual's private or domestic use.[27]

THE COUNTERFEIT AND PIRATED GOODS REGULATIONS 1996

[5.19] The Counterfeit and Pirated Goods Regulations 1996[28] were enacted to give effect to an EU Council[29] and Commission Regulation[30] which laid down measures to prohibit the free circulation, export, re-export or entry of counterfeit or pirated goods which may include computer programs. The copyright owner may apply to the Revenue Commissioners requesting them to suspend the release of any counterfeit or pirated goods or to detain them.[31] This suspension will remain in force for three months or such further period as they may decide.[32] Where a trade mark or design right has been registered,

---

26. CA 1963, s 28(a).
27. CA 1963, s 28.
28. SI 48/1996.
29. Council Regulation (EC) No 3295/94 of 22 December 1994. OJ L 341, 30.12.94, p 8.
30. Commission Regulation (EU) No 1367/95 of 16 June 1995. OJ L 133, 17.6.95, p 2.
31. Regulation 4(2).
32. Provided a fee of £400 is paid to the Revenue Commissioners.

the owner must supply the following: a certificate of registration and a statement from the Controller of Patents, Designs and Trademarks giving any information required by the Revenue Commissioners about that right. If the application is made in respect of an unregistered design right, copyright or a neighbouring right then the owner must submit proof of his ownership or authorship.[33] Likewise, if he does not own a right but is entitled to use it, he must supply the document by which he is entitled, in addition to the material outlined above.[34] When the Revenue Commissioners decide how to act on an application they must notify the applicant in writing.[35]

[5.20] The Revenue Commissioners may ask the applicant to examine a sample of goods taken from a consignment if those goods appear to the Revenue Commissioners to correspond to those described in his application. If the goods appear to bear a trade mark indistinguishable from a registered trade mark mentioned in the application, the applicant must, within 24 hours of a request from the Revenue Commissioners, confirm in writing whether or not the goods are counterfeit and giving his reasons.[36] Counterfeit goods which correspond with the description given in an application may not be exported or distributed.[37] An applicant may be required to give the Revenue Commissioners security against all actions, proceedings, claims and demands, costs or expenses which may result from the detention of goods as a result of the application.[38] In all cases, the applicant must indemnify the Revenue Commissioners against all such liability and expense.[39]

[5.21] An application will have no effect or will cease to have effect if the applicant has failed to comply with any of the requirements of the Regulations or if a change has occurred in the ownership or use of the rights specified in the application which is not communicated to the Revenue Commissioners.[40]

CRIMINAL OFFENCES

[5.22] Section 27(1) of the Copyright Act 1963[41] states that:

>   any person who ...

[33.] Regulation 4(4).
[34.] Regulation 4(5).
[35.] Regulation 4(7).
[36.] Regulation 5.
[37.] Regulation 6(1).
[38.] Regulation 7(1).
[39.] Regulation 7(2).
[40.] Regulation 8.
[41.] As amended by C(A)A1987, s 2.

> (a) makes for sale or hire, or
>
> (b) sells or lets for hire, or by way of trade offers or exposes for sale or hire, or for the purposes of trade has in his possession, or
>
> (c) by way of trade exhibits in public, or
>
> (d) imports into the State, otherwise than for his private and domestic use, any article which he knows to be an infringing copy of the work, shall be guilty of an offence.

Any person who distributes an infringing copy for trade or to prejudice the rights of the owner, is guilty of an offence.[42] Any person who knowingly makes or holds a plate is guilty of an offence.[43] A plate is defined as "including a stereotype, stone, block, mould, matrix, transfer, negative or other appliance".[44] It is unclear whether this would include possession of the source codes of a program in order to copy it or the possession of equipment to allow copying to take place. It would be inconsistent to treat some types of software such as source code, as being appliances to bring them within the terms of this section, while elsewhere treating them as literary works. As a result, possessing source codes and other programs or data to infringe another's copyright may not be a criminal offence, since these are used to create the infringing copies but are not themselves sold or distributed.

[5.23] The owner may apply to the District Court and if the District Justice is satisfied that infringing copies are being sold, hired or distributed, he may order the gardaí to seize them, without a warrant and to bring them before the court. If the court is satisfied that they are infringing copies, it may order them to be destroyed or delivered to the owner or otherwise.[45] If the judge is satisfied by an information on oath that an offence is being committed on any premises, he may grant a search warrant authorising a member of the Garda Síochána, accompanied by such other members as are necessary, to enter onto the premises, if necessary by force and seize any film or any work including plates in respect of which he has reasonable grounds for suspecting that an offence under this section is being committed.[46]

[5.24] It would appear that search warrants may only be granted in respect of premises. In *Seamus Roche v DJ Martin and the DPP*[47] a District Justice had granted a search warrant in respect of videos concealed in a vehicle.

---

[42] CA 1963, s 27(2).

[43] CA 1963, s 27(3).

[44] CA 1963, s 24(4)

[45] CA 1963, s 27(4) (as amended by C(A)A1987, s 2).

[46] CA 1963, s 27(5) (as amended by C(A)A1987, s 2).

[47] [1993] ILRM 651.

However, in the High Court Murphy J found that under s 27 of the Copyright Act 1963, the District Justice only had jurisdiction to grant a search warrant in respect of 'any premises'. Therefore the search warrant granted in respect of the vehicle was not valid and the resultant search was unlawful.

[5.25] Any works or plates seized must be brought to the District Court and if proven to be infringing copies or plates must be destroyed, delivered to the owner or otherwise disposed of.[48] The performance of a work in public is an offence if the performer knows that he is infringing copyright by doing so.[49]

Penalties on conviction

[5.26] Anyone summarily convicted of selling, or distributing infringing copies shall be liable to a fine of £100 per infringing copy on his first offence and in any other case, liable to the same fine or to imprisonment for not more than six months. However, the fine cannot exceed £1,000 in total.[50] A person summarily convicted of possessing a plate or performing a work in public is liable to a fine of not more than £1,000 on his first offence or on any subsequent offence to a fine and/or not more than six months imprisonment.[51] Regardless of whether or not anyone is convicted of an offence, the court may order the destruction of any infringing copy or plate.[52] An appeal lies to the Circuit Court from any order of the District Court. There is no provision under the Copyright Act 1963 for offences to be tried on indictment.

[5.27] The leniency of Irish penalties may be contrasted with the situation in the US where the Copyright Felony Act 1992[53] provides that a person who:

> wilfully and for purposes of commercial advantage or financial gain reproduces or distributes within a 180 day period at least 10 unauthorised copies ... of one or more copyrighted works with a collective value of more than $2,500

will face a term of imprisonment of up to five years and a fine of up to $250,000 for a first offence. A second offence may result in imprisonment for up to ten years. The severity of the penalties is increased by further changes to the US sentencing guidelines. These have suggested that copying

---

48. CA 1963, s 27(6)
49. CA 1963, s 27(8) (as amended by C(A)A1987, s 2).
50. CA 1963, s 27(9) (as amended by C(A)A1987, s 2).
51. CA 1963, s 27(10) (as amended by C(A)A1987, s 2).
52. CA 1963, s 27(11).
53. Pub L No 102-561, 106 Stat 4233 (1992).

software should be treated the same as stealing the software when deciding penalties.[54]

[5.28] Penalties in the UK are not as dramatic as in the US. Under s 107 of the UK Copyright, Designs and Patents Act 1988, on summary conviction, a fine not exceeding £5,000 or a term of imprisonment not exceeding six months or both may be imposed. On indictment, an unlimited fine or imprisonment not exceeding two years or both may be imposed.

[5.29] As can be seen, the Irish penalties are more lenient than the British, whilst lagging far behind the US. The greater penalties in the US and UK may be attributed to the lobbying by the influential software industry in those countries. It is only a matter of time before that strength is felt here. Industry representatives have been very successful in obtaining legislation to deal with video piracy.[55]

The Defence of Fair Dealing

[5.30] Section 12(1) of the 1963 Act states that:

> No fair dealing with a literary, dramatic or musical work for purposes of:
>
> > (a) research or private study or
> >
> > (b) criticism or review, whether of that work or another work,
> >   which is accompanied by a sufficient acknowledgement
>
> shall constitute an infringement of the copyright in the work.

There is no definition in the Copyright Act 1963 of what constitutes fair dealing for the purposes specified in s 12 but it is usually taken to permit the making of copies of a work but taking more than one copy of a work is not permitted.[56] The taking of quotations from a work may occur but there must be 'sufficient acknowledgement' of the original. 'Sufficient acknowledgement' means an acknowledgement identifying the work in question by its title or other description and, unless the work is anonymous or the author has previously agreed or required that no acknowledgement of his name should be made, also means identifying the author.[57]

[5.31] Fair dealing is permitted for purposes of research, which presumably includes both private and commercial research. It has been suggested that this would permit the decompilation of computer programs as was permitted under the American 'fair use' provisions. However, fair dealing would

---

[54.] Walker, 'Federal Criminal Remedies for the Theft of Intellectual Property', Hastings Comm/Ent LJ, Vol 16.681.

[55.] Copyright (Amendment) Act 1987.

[56.] *Sillitoe v McGrath-Hill Books (UK) Ltd* [1983] FSR 545.

[57.] CA 1963, s 12(12).

normally involve only the reproduction of a work or part of a work. In practice, decompilation would involve the reproduction, translation and adaptation of the work in its entirety.

COPYRIGHT ON-LINE

[5.32] One of the major components of the Internet and other networks is bulletin board systems. These allow users to post and read messages. Some messages may include software, pictures, music and any other information which may be stored on a computer. In general, the users are not able to delete or alter any of the information on the bulletin board, but they may add to or copy the information. The distribution of infringing copies of various copyright protected works over networks has become a major problem.

Users of bulletin boards

[5.33] The methods of distributing and paying for pirated software or other works over networks are complex. Infringing works may be swapped or even sold using bulletin boards as distribution sites.

[5.34] Placing a message on a bulletin board is referred to as 'uploading', which involves the copying of the message to the bulletin board. If the message contains material which infringes copyright, such as illegally copied software or other infringing works, then the user who places it on the bulletin board may be infringing copyright in several ways. First, he will obviously be 'reproducing' the work, unless he has a licence which permits him to do this. Secondly, he may be 'publishing' the work as he is issuing it to the public. Thirdly, he might have 'imported' the work from outside the State, however, he must know that the work was copied in breach of copyright. Finally, if he were found to be 'selling' the work or 'exposing' it for sale or hire by way of trade, he would be infringing copyright.

[5.35] The user of a bulletin board who reads or 'downloads' a message from the board will be 'reproducing' the message within the meaning of the 1963 Act. It is impossible to read any message on a bulletin board without copying it in some way. Usually, when a message is downloaded from the bulletin board, it is copied to the hard drive of the user's computer. Even if the user can avoid copying the message to the hard drive of his computer, he would still 'reproduce' the message, as it would be replicated in the temporary memory of his computer. Usually, when a message is placed on the bulletin board there is an implied licence permitting other users to copy the contents of the message. However, if the message contains a copy of a work which was made in breach of copyright or if the person who placed the work on the bulletin board did not have a licence to distribute the work in this way, then any person who 'downloads' or copies that work will be breaching copyright.

[5.36] It is very difficult to pursue ordinary users who have either 'downloaded' or 'uploaded' infringing copies of works. This is because users are hard to trace and even having traced them, it would be hard to prove in court that they had copied the works. For this reason, the owners of copyright may prefer to pursue those who operate or control the bulletin board. In addition, this operator is likely to be a better financial mark and proceedings against such a party will probably have a greater effect in terms of preventing continuance of the particular infringement.

Operators of bulletin board systems

[5.37] Bulletin board systems are usually run commercially on a subscription basis. The operators of bulletin boards have been successfully sued in the USA for permitting infringing copies of works to be left on their bulletin board. In *Playboy Enterprises Inc v Frena*[58] the defendant operated a bulletin board service which charged users for access. The bulletin board contained large amounts of pornographic material. Users could access data from and place data on the bulletin board. Frena claimed that one of its users must have placed 170 digitised images derived from the plaintiff's magazine, onto the bulletin board and replaced the plaintiff's name with that of Frena's. The defendant was nevertheless found to have breached the plaintiff's copyright as providing access to the bulletin board was equivalent to 'distributing' and 'displaying' the infringing images. This decision has been criticised for overextending the meanings of 'display' and 'distribution'.[59]

[5.38] In *Sega Enterprises v Maphia*[60] the bulletin board operator, Maphia, allowed users to upload and download video games which were owned by Sega. The court found that although the defendants may not have uploaded or downloaded the games themselves, they were still liable as they were 'contributing' to the infringement by providing "facilities, direction, knowledge and encouragement" to the direct infringers.

[5.39] How Irish courts would treat such cases is unknown. It could be argued that the operator would have been liable under Irish law for 'publishing' the works.[61] Because there is no definition of publication in the

---

58. 839 F Supp 1552 (MD Fla 1993).
59. Dobbins, 'Computer Bulletin Board Operator Liability For Users Infringing Acts', Michigan Law Review, Vol 94 p 217, October 1995.
60. 857 F Supp 679 (ND Cal 1994).
61. CA 1963, s 8(6)(b).

1963 Act, this vagueness might allow this provision to be effective in this instance. If the bulletin board operator is not directly involved in the copying or publication of infringing works, the owner would have to prove that the operator was involved in the distribution of the work. The difficulty here is that for liability to attach to the operator for distributing an infringing work, under s 11 of the 1963 Act, it must be shown that the operator knew that the works were infringing copies. Proving this in any individual case could be very difficult. Although it could be argued that the bulletin board operator was involved in exposing the work for sale, it would be harder to show that the operator was doing so by way of trade. Merely turning a blind eye to the existence of pirate copies on a bulletin board may not amount to exposing the copies for sale or hire by way of trade. Proving anything more than this would be difficult unless it could be shown that the operator was encouraging the distribution of copies over his bulletin board in the hope of increasing the subscribers to his bulletin board or getting some other direct benefit. In both the US cases this would appear to be what occurred.

[5.40] Although a bulletin board may be used for the distribution of infringing copies, it may also have legitimate uses. In *CBS Songs Ltd v Amstrad Consumer Electronics plc*[62] the twin recording tape decks marketed by the defendants were held not to have amounted to authorising or inciting purchasers to infringe copyright in any pre-recorded audio tapes. It was held that because the tape decks had other non-infringing uses, for example where the user taped works in which he owned copyright, and Amstrad had no control over the use to which the tape decks were put, the defendants could not be held liable. The US Supreme Court in *Sony Corporation of America v Universal City Studios Inc*[63] made a similar decision with regard to video recorders. A prudent bulletin board operator would monitor all activities and make it clear that activities that infringe copyright are not welcome or permitted on his bulletin board. At some stage, the copying and distribution of infringing works on a bulletin board might become so blatant that liability could attach to the bulletin board operator.

Places of public entertainment

[5.41] Under s 11(4) of the 1963 Act copyright will be infringed by any person who allows a place of public entertainment to be used for a performance in public of the work, where the performance constitutes an infringement of the copyright. Section 11(6) states that a 'place of public entertainment' includes any premises which are occupied mainly for other

---

62. [1987] 3 All ER 151.
63. 464 US 417 (1984).

purposes, but are from time to time made available for hire to such persons as may desire to hire them for purposes of public entertainment. 'Performance' is defined by s 2 as including "any mode or visual or acoustic presentation including:

> any such presentation by the operation of wireless telegraph apparatus ... or by any other means ... and references to performing a work or an adaptation of a work shall be construed accordingly.

Whether allowing a copy of a computer program to be placed on a bulletin board so that it could be reproduced would amount to a public performance is unclear. Placing a digitised musical work or image might amount to permitting a performance but where is the performance occurring? A work is not performed by broadcasting or transmitting it. The performance is taken to be effected by the operation of the receiving apparatus, and the occupier of the premises, where the apparatus is situated is taken to be the person giving the performance.[64] This would suggest that even if placing a work on a bulletin board could be deemed a performance, it is the user who downloads the work, who is causing the performance and not the bulletin board operator.

[5.42] Section 11(5) provides an exception to the above where the person permitting the place of public entertainment to be used was not aware or the infringement of copyright and had no reasonable grounds for suspecting that the performance would be an infringement. Alternatively, s 11(4) will not apply if the permission was given gratuitously or for a nominal consideration or did not exceed a reasonable estimate of the expenses to be incurred by him in consequence of the use of the place for the performance. This would allow operators of a bulletin board a defence.

Copyright on the World Wide Web

[5.43] A recent Scottish decision examined the protection of copyright materials on the World-Wide-Web. In *Shetland Times Ltd v Dr Jonathan Wills and Another*[65] the plaintiff[66] published a newspaper called *The Shetland Times* and some sections of this paper were also published on its Web site. The defendants provided a news reporting service called *The Shetland News* which also had a Web site. From around 14 October 1996 the defendants included on their Web site a number of headlines which had appeared in recent issues of the plaintiff's newspaper and on its Web site.

[64.] CA 1963, s 2(5).
[65.] Unreported decision of Lord Hamilton of the Court of Session on 24 October 1996: see *Computers and Law*, Vol 7, No 5 December 1996, p 35.
[66.] Known as the pursuer in Scotland.

Users could double click on the headlines on the defendant's Web site and so gain access to the relevant text of the articles as published by the plaintiff. This was done without the user being required to actually view the plaintiff's Web site and this meant that the user would not view any advertising material on that site. The plaintiff objected on the basis that the headlines on the plaintiff's Web site were cable programmes within the meaning of the UK Copyright, Designs and Patents Act 1988.[67] The Court held that the information on the Web site was being 'sent' although the information passively awaits access being made to it by users and that the information was *prima facie* being sent by the plaintiff on whose Web site it had been established. It was held that the incorporation by the defendants of the information provided by the plaintiff was an infringement under the 1988 Act by the inclusion in a cable programme service of protected cable programmes.

[5.44] Although this argument was successful it was somewhat convoluted. The right to control copying is one of the most important rights of the copyright owner. The links created by the defendants meant that they were effectively reproducing the plaintiff's material without its consent. By placing this material on the World Wide Web the plaintiff might be taken to be consenting to the creation of links between their material and other web sites. This does not mean that they had given up the right to object to some links, particularly those which engaged in such wholesale replication of the work. The judge in *Shetland Times Ltd v Dr Jonathan Wills and Another* indicated that it appeared to him that there was at least some infringement of s 17 of the UK 1988 Act which restricts copying.

E-mail

[5.45] Electronic mail (e-mail) refers to messages which are typed on a computer and sent across a network to their destination. Letters are literary works within the meaning of the Copyright Act 1963.[68] Although there are no cases on e-mail, cases relating to traditional letters should also be applicable to e-mail since they are both literary works. The law becomes

---

[67.] A cable programme is defined in s 7 of the 1988 Act as:
   a service which consists wholly or mainly in sending visual images, sounds or other information by means of a telecommunication system otherwise than by wireless telegraphy, for reception:
   (a) at two or more places (whether for simultaneous reception or at different times in response to requests made by different users),
   (b) for presentation to members of the public.
[68.] *British Oxygen Ltd v Liquid Air Ltd* [1925] Ch 383 .

complex once the letter is sent.[69] The recipient of the letter will become the owner of the letter itself[70] but the author retains copyright.[71] There probably is an implied licence which allows a recipient to print a copy of the electronic mail. However, there is no implied licence which allows the recipient to publish a letter.[72] One circumstance which would allow the recipient to publish the letter would be the refutation of allegations made.[73] If the letter is given to a third party, the author may restrain publication by that third party.[74] It is possible to send a traditional letter to a third party without copying but if the recipient of an e-mail sends it on to a third party, this will involve copying the e-mail, which will of course infringe the author's rights.

[69.] See Merkin and Black, *Copyright and Design Law*, Vol 1, s 8.11, (Longman, 1995).

[70.] *Oliver v Oliver* [1861] CBNS 139.

[71.] *Lytton v Devey* [1884] 54 LJ Ch 293; *Philip v Pennell* [1907] 2 Ch 577.

[72.] *Palin v Gathercole* [1844] 1 Coll 565; *Hopkinson v Lord Burghley* [1867] 2 Ch App 447.

[73.] *Lytton v Devey* [1884] 54 LJ Ch 293; *Cookson v Pountney* (1937) 81 Sol Jo 528.

[74.] *Ashburton v Pape* [1913] 2 Ch 469.

Chapter 6

Licences and Assignments of Copyright

INTRODUCTION

[6.01] In general, owning the copyright in a computer program is pointless unless the owner can devise some way of generating income from it. Most owners do this by selling others a licence which allows them to use the software and the vast majority of software is sold subject to a licence. This is unusual as books, cars and other goods are usually bought outright without any conditions. Those conditions which they do have, such as warranties, favour the purchaser over the vendor. Software contracts normally favour the vendor and the purchaser's right to use his program will usually be severely limited.

[6.02] The history of computer licences is complex. As computers developed, the authors of programs wished to sell them to their clients and the public. In the USA in the 1960s it was unclear whether programs were entitled to copyright protection or indeed any protection at all. As a result, lawyers decided that the only way to protect programs was with trade secret protection. A trade secret may be disclosed to others without losing its protected status, as long as the persons to whom it is disclosed agree that they will not themselves disclose it. However, if the initial purchaser should sell his copy of the program on to a third party then there was a danger that the trade secret protection would break down. Under US law, any restraints on resale or alienation would usually be unenforceable. Therefore, lawyers invented the software licence, the aim of which is to seriously limit the rights of the purchaser. In particular, the purchaser will not receive any of the indicia of ownership. Current program licensing provisions have been condemned as 'feudal'.[1]

[6.03] Computer programs are sold to two distinct groups. First, computer programs may be distributed to the general public and sold over the counter in shops or by mail order. These sales will be subject to the usual consumer legislation such as the Sale of Goods Acts 1893-1980. Secondly, there are larger contracts usually made between large commercial organisations.

[1.] Hemnes, 'Restraints On Alienation, Equitable Servitudes And The Feudal Nature Of Computer Software Licensing', Denver University Law Review, Vol 71, part 3, p 577, (1994).

These contracts may involve the same computer programs as are distributed to the general public or they may involve tailormade programs. These contracts are different because of their size and the fact that they will have been carefully negotiated in advance.

DISTINGUISHING ASSIGNMENTS AND LICENCES

[6.04] The owner of copyright in a work may exploit his interest in the work in two ways by either assigning his interest or by granting licences to others to use his work. An assignment is a transfer of the particular copyright rights which are assigned.

[6.05] A licence grants the licensee the permission to use the work in the manner described in the licence. The two may be distinguished in three ways. Firstly, assignment is absolute and allows the assignee to exploit the works in any manner he thinks fit. A licence is a personal contract which limits the use of the work to certain specific acts and any other exploitation of the work must be agreed with the licensor. Secondly, once the copyright is assigned, the assignor has no right to sue for any infringements, whereas the licensor always retains the right to sue. Thirdly, if the copyright is assigned as part of a larger contract (such as a film), then if the larger contract breaks down then the assignment will still be valid unless there is a contrary clause in the contract. If a licence, on the other hand, is granted as part of a larger contract, and it breaks down, then the licence will usually revert back to the licensor.[2]

[6.06] Deciding whether a contract refers to an assignment or licence is usually a matter for the individual court. The use of the words assignment or licence is not decisive. In *Messager v British Broadcasting Co Ltd*,[3] although the contract described the parties as licensor and licensee, the House of Lords found that it was in fact an assignment.

Assignments under the Copyright Act 1963

[6.07] Section 47 of the 1963 Act states that copyright can be transferred by assignment, by testamentary disposition or by operation of law as personal or moveable property.[4] Assignments may be limited in several ways: First, the assignment may be limited in the type of acts which the owner of the copyright has the exclusive right to do. Secondly, it may limit the countries to which it applies. Finally, there may be a time limit on the assignment of

---

2. See Merkin & Black, *Copyright and Designs Law*, Longman Law, Tax and Finance, para 3.31, (October 1993).
3. [1929] AC 151.
4. CA 1963, s 47(1).

the copyright. All of the above are referred to as partial assignments.[5] All assignments must be in writing signed by or on behalf of the assignor. Writing includes any form of notation, whether by hand or by printing, typewriting or other process.[6] This would include e-mail and other forms of telecommunications.

[6.08] Where a program is commissioned from a programmer there is no copyright in that program when the contract is signed since the program has not been written. The 1963 Act anticipates this situation. An owner may assign copyright in a work which does not exist at present, but will do in the future (this is known as future copyright). If the person to whom the future copyright is assigned agrees to assign that future copyright to yet another, then that third person is entitled to have the copyright vested in him. If copyright comes into existence when the person entitled to it has died, then the copyright passes as if the copyright had been created just before his death.[7]

Licences under the Copyright Act 1963

[6.09] Where an owner of copyright grants a licence, then that licence binds every successor in title to the owner's copyright, except a purchaser in good faith for valuable consideration and without notice (actual or constructive) of the licence.[8] This applies to the owners of future copyrights as well as copyrights already in existence.[9]

Exclusive Licences

[6.10] An exclusive licence entitles the licensee to the same rights and remedies as if copyright had been assigned to him. An exclusive licence must be in writing, signed by or on behalf of an owner or prospective owner of copyright, authorising the licensee, to the exclusion of all other persons, including the grantor of the licence, to exercise a right which by virtue of the Act would (apart from the licence) be exercisable exclusively by the owner of the copyright. The rights of the licensee exist concurrently with the rights of the owner. However, the owner cannot assert any rights over copies under a licence which he would not have been entitled to had the licence been an assignment. This means that the owner cannot use a licence to grant himself 'extra' rights which would not normally be available to him.

---

5. CA 1963, s 47(2).
6. CA 1963, s 2.
7. CA 1963, s 49.
8. CA 1963, s 47(4).
9. CA 1963, s 49(3).

[6.11] Where either the licensee or the owner brings an action under s 22, where they both have rights which exist concurrently with each other, then one cannot proceed with the action unless the other is joined either as co-plaintiff or defendant. This does not affect the granting of an interlocutory injunction. If an action is brought by either the licensee or the owner, then the court must take into account any licence payments which the licensee must make and any damages already awarded to either party. The same defences can be raised against the licensee as can be raised against the owner. Where an account of profits is made, the court may apportion the profits between owner and licensee. If the owner or the licensee has obtained a final judgement in an action, then the other party cannot get any judgment or account of profits in respect of that infringement. If the owner joins the exclusive licensee, or *vice versa*, as a defendant to an action, the plaintiff cannot recover costs from that party unless he enters an appearance.[10]

Distribution under the 1993 Regulations

[6.12] The European Communities (Legal Protection of Computer Programs) Regulations 1993[11] impose restrictions on the rights of the copyright owner. There are several provisions which should be limited by a prudent copyright owner when drafting any contracts or licences for the use or sale of his software. These provisions have been extensively discussed in Chapter 3 which are: the owner's right to control distribution[12] and rental[13] of his program; the reproduction or adaptation of a program;[14] decompilation,[15] and the making of back-up programs.[16]

TYPES OF SOFTWARE LICENCES

Shrink-wrap or end-user licences

[6.13] Mass distributed software is invariably sold subject to a licence. The manner of selling is akin to a supermarket or mail order, neither of which allows for the purchaser or vendor to negotiate a licence agreement. The licence may be exposed on the cellophane wrapping of the software packaging stating that tearing the shrink wrapping on the box will constitute acceptance of the terms of the licence. Alternatively, the licence may be inside the box attached to the disks which are sealed. The licence may state

---

10. CA 1963, s 25.
11. SI 26/1993.
12. Regulation 5(c).
13. Recital 16.
14. Regulation 6(1).
15. Regulation 7(1).
16. Regulation 6(2).

that breaking the seal will constitute acceptance of the licence. The disadvantage with this is that there is no guarantee that the purchaser will ever have read the licence agreement prior to purchase and he may not be able to do so. As a result, he may not have notice of its terms and the enforceability of the shrink wrap licences may be open to question.

[6.14] In *Thornton v Shoe Lane Parking Ltd*,[17] the plaintiff used the defendant's car park. The plaintiff was issued with a ticket by an automatic vending machine when he entered the car park which stated that the issue of the ticket was subject to conditions which were displayed within the car park. These stated that the defendant was not liable for the theft of the car, its contents and for any personal injury to the customer. The court held that these conditions were not part of the contract as the contract had been completed when the plaintiff entered the car park.[18] In *Interfoto Picture Library Ltd v Stiletto Visual Programmes Ltd*[19] the defendant had obtained photographs from the plaintiff for use in an advertising campaign. The photographs were supplied with a note which set out conditions of contract in some detail. One term stated that if the photos were not returned after 14 days a fee of £5 per day per photo would be charged. The defendant held onto the photos for an extra 14 days and received a bill for £3,783.50. The Court of Appeal held that this term was not part of the contract as it should have been drawn to the attention of the plaintiff. Dillon LJ said:

> "if one condition in a set of printed conditions is particularly onerous or unusual, the party seeking to enforce it must show that that particular condition was fairly brought to the attention of the other party."[20]

This could mean that any clause of a software licence which attempts to limit the application of the Regulations should be specifically drawn to the purchaser's attention.

[6.15] In *North American Systemshops Ltd v King*,[21] a firm of accountants bought a single copy of a program and copied it onto several computers. The vendor maintained that the accountants were bound by the licence terms contained in the user manual. They claimed that a copyright symbol was visible on the outside of the packaging and this put the purchaser on notice of the existence of the licence. The court disagreed holding that as there was no copyright symbol visible the purchaser had no notice of the existence of

---

17. [1971] 1 All ER 686.
18. Also see *Olley v Marlborough Court Ltd* [1949] 1 KB 532.
19. [1988] 1 All ER 348.
20. *Ibid* at 352.
21. (1989) 68 Alta LR (2d) 145.

the licence. If the purchaser buys a program without any notice of what the vendor intends the purpose of the program to be, it may be difficult to say that vendor and the purchaser were in agreement as to the intended purpose.

[6.16] At present neither the Irish nor the English courts have considered the enforceability of shrink wrap licences. Developments in the US have forced a move away from the traditional type of shrink wrap licence. If the user does not have to indicate acceptance of the licence until he has an opportunity to read it carefully, then it will be easier to enforce. There have been efforts to print the entire licence on the packaging of a computer program but this is impractical. A better method of displaying the licence was examined in *ProCD v Zeidenberg*[22] by the US Court of Appeal for the Seventh Circuit. The plaintiff created a computer database using information from more than three thousand telephone directories at a cost of $10 million. The Court of Appeal assumed that this database was not protected by copyright following the judgement of the US Supreme Court in *Feist*.[23] In order to recover the costs of this development, ProCD had to sell the same product to different customers at different prices. The database could be bought at a cost of $150 for private use, while commercial users had to pay considerably more. To ensure that private purchasers did not use the information commercially, ProCD relied on the contract of sale. The alternative was either to give private users poorer quality information or charge all users the same price which would put the database outside the reach of most private users. Every box containing the ProCD database disk declared that the software was sold subject to restrictions stated on an enclosed licence. The licence was to be found on the disks, the manuals and appeared on the screen every time the database was used. The licence limited the use of the database to private users only when sold for private purposes. The defendant bought a consumer copy of the database and decided to ignore the licence. He formed a company to resell information on the Internet for a price lower than that charged by ProCD.

[6.17] The plaintiff failed at first instance as the terms of its licence did not appear on the outside of the package. The Court of Appeal disagreed, pointing out that if someone buys a radio they will probably not read the warranty inside the packaging until they get home, yet no American State will disregard the terms of the consumer warranties. Similarly, many pharmaceutical products contain vital information inside their packaging such as dosages and side effects which will not be read until the packaging is opened. The court also pointed out that only a minority of American sales of

---

[22.] 86 F 3d; 1996 US App LEXIS 14951.
[23.] See para **[7.05]** *et seq*.

software are made over the counter in shops. Usually a customer will place an order by phone or over the Internet. The software will be delivered by post or increasingly over the Internet itself. Where software is sold over the Internet, there will be no box "only a stream of electrons" which includes data, application programs, instructions and various limitations as well as the terms of sale. The user will purchase a serial number which will activate the software features. The court pointed out that the defendant was effectively arguing that such unboxed sales are unfettered by terms and conditions. If this were true software prices would either be driven through the ceiling or transactions would be returned to "the horse and buggy age". The Court of Appeal held that ProCD had proposed a contract that the buyer would accept the licence after reading the terms of the licence at his leisure. The shrink wrap licence does not appear to have been of the type which states that opening the box or tearing the box indicated acceptance, instead, the software placed the licence on the computer screen and would not let the defendant use the program unless he indicated his acceptance. The court pointed out that this was not a case where consumers opened a package to find a note saying "you owe us an extra $10,000". If the defendant did not wish to be bound by the licence he could have simply returned the database.

[6.18] When Zeidenberg bought his consumer copy of the ProCD database he presumably could have opted for a commercial copy. The Court does not appear have considered the suggestion of whether or not by taking the option he did Zeidenberg indicated acceptance of the term that he would not use his copy for commercial purposes. By allowing ProCD to make their database available to consumers at an affordable price, enforcing the shrink-wrap licence was in the interests of consumers and this fact carried considerable weight with the court. Although universal or customary shrink wrap licence terms do not exist, it is usual to include them in packaged software. Any purchaser will know that as a matter of course any software package will include a licence although he cannot be sure of its terms until he reads it.[24]

[6.19] Where software is distributed by a company separate from the author of the software, there may be a difficulty in enforcing a licence between the author and the user because there may be no privity of contract between these two parties. However, in this case presumably the distributor will be the agent of the author. This point was raised in a Scottish case, *Beta v Adobe*.[25] The defendants ordered software from the plaintiffs who were the distributors of computer software and not the authors. The defendants sought

---

[24.] This was accepted in both the *Beta v Adobe* and *Trumpet v Ozemail cases* discussed below.
[25.] [1996] Scots Law Times 604. It should be noted that Scotland does not have a common law system.

to return the software and the plaintiffs refused to accept it and sued unsuccessfully for non-payment. It was accepted that it was customary to include shrink wrap licences in packaged software.

Shareware Licences

[6.20] Shareware is a form of licensing which allows individual authors of programs and small companies to distribute their wares over the Internet. Users are encouraged to make copies of the programs on a trial basis. If they are satisfied with the program, then they are invited to register with the author which usually entails paying the author a fee. Authors who market their wares in this way are different from the larger firms. They will actively encourage the copying of their products and to this end they will spend time and money placing their programs on various networks and systems. An American firm, McAfee & Associates has took this to extremes by adapting the motto of 'Steal our Software'. Anyone can copy the software but companies which use it must get a licence. Once McAfee learns that the employees of a company are using their products, McAfee will contact the company and request a licence fee.[26] The shareware method is also used to distribute Netscape software which allows users to traverse the World Wide Web. The software was initially given away free, once it dominated the market it started to charge.[27] Shareware relies on the honesty of the users or their fear of litigation to ensure that licence fees are paid.

[6.21] Users who copy shareware should be aware that the programs are subject to certain licences and that their use may be restricted.[28] Some shareware has a time limit imposed. If the program is not upgraded or the user has not paid a licence by a certain date, the program will cease to work. Programs know the date by consulting the hard drive on a computer, as all computers have calendars.

[6.22] The validity of shareware licences was examined by the Australian Federal Court in *Trumpet Software Property Ltd v Ozemail Pty Ltd*.[29] The plaintiff marketed a program 'Trumpet Winsock' which allows users to gain access to the Internet. The defendant wished to distribute 60,000 copies of the program by means of a computer disk which would have been distributed with the magazine, *Australian Personal Computer*. Although the plaintiff had no inherent objection to this, it was concerned that as the

---

26. Short, 'Combating Software Piracy', Computer and High Technology Law Journal, Vol 10, p 221, 1994.
27. *The Economist*, 25 May 1996.
28. Cavazos and Morin, *Cyberspace and the Law* (MIT Press).
29. (1996) 34 IPR 481.

version of its program which the defendant proposed distributing did not have a 'time lock', many personal users would acquire a copy which they could use indefinitely. The time lock would ensure that the program would cease to work after a given period, usually 30 days. If the user wished to use it after that period they would have to pay a fee. The plaintiff therefore told the defendant not to distribute its program unless they could use a version which had a time lock. Unfortunately, the plaintiff was unable to create this version in time. However, the defendant had already told the magazine that it would be able to distribute the program. Fearful that it would be sued by the magazine the defendant decided that the lesser evil was to distribute the plaintiff's software in spite of the terms of the shareware licence. The plaintiff became concerned about the distribution of its software and also about the fact that its software was being distributed without the appropriate disclaimer notice stating the terms of their licence. Furthermore the defendant altered the plaintiff's program, the result of the alterations was that the user would not be informed automatically of the fact that the software was shareware or the conditions of the shareware licence. The program was altered so that instead of directing the user to register with the plaintiff, it focused on encouraging the user to connect to the defendant's system. The defendant would appear to have regarded the Trumpet software as being in the public domain and thus outside the control of the plaintiff. It did not seem to have regarded it as strictly necessary to get the permission of the plaintiff before distribution. In spite of the plaintiff's objections and solicitors' letters, it carried out a second distribution of the program several months later.

[6.23] The plaintiff sued, alleging several breaches by the defendant. It claimed, first, that once it had told the defendant that it should not distribute its software without a 'timelock' the defendant should then have complied. The defence claimed that once the program was distributed as shareware, a licence was created which could not be revoked. This claim was rejected by Heerey J. Secondly it claimed that the defendant had distributed the software without right. It was accepted that the shareware licence conferred a licence to use the software licence for a period of 30 days for the purposes of evaluation. But the plaintiff did not make the terms and conditions of this licence clear. The plaintiff contended that if the licence conferred any rights of distribution on third parties it did so subject to the conditions that the distribution be: (i) without other software; (ii) without modification, addition or deletion; (ii) in its entirety; (iv) without charge and not for commercial gain to enable such third parties to use the software for a period of 30 days for the purposes of evaluation. Although the court heard considerable evidence about the obligations conferred by a shareware licence it was not able to establish any customary rules in this matter. The court was unwilling to imply a condition limiting the ability of the distributor to include the program in a package with other programs or to make a profit from this distribution. However the court found that the defendant had breached an implied condition not to alter the program.

[6.24] Although shareware is distributed free of charge, the owners of programs who opt for this mode of distribution are unwise to ignore the need for clear licencing conditions. The defendant in *Trumpet Software* only acted as it did because there were no clear indications included in the software that it was not entitled to do so. This judgment should not be taken to indicate that the owners of copyright who decide to distribute their software in this way may be blasé as to how their work is treated. Failure to be as careful as the plaintiff in *Trumpet Software* in asserting the rights of the owner may be taken to be acquiescence. In *Film Investors Overseas Services SA v Home Video Channel Ltd*[30] the plaintiff owned, or was exclusive licensee for various films. The defendant operated a satellite transmission service which transmitted all over continental Europe on the Astra Satellite. The defendant had a licence to transmit the films controlled by the plaintiff but only to the UK and Ireland. Access to the channel was controlled by a smart card system.[31] In early 1993 the defendant became aware that its programmes were being watched in Europe by persons using pirated or re-sold cards. As a result, in February 1993 the defendant decided to market its own cards in Europe, the plaintiff continued to supply films until November 1993. The question for the court was whether the plaintiff was precluded by express or implied acquiescence from complaining of the exhibition of its films outside the licensed area. Carnwath J applied the principle enunciated by Oliver J in *Taylor Fashions Ltd v Liverpool Victoria Trustees Co Ltd*[32] that:

> "... It would be unconscionable for a party to be permitted to deny that which, knowing or unknowingly, he has allowed or encouraged another to assume to his detriment ..."

In this case Carnwath J was satisfied that the defence had proved that from mid-1993 that the plaintiff knew or strongly suspected that films were being shown in Europe but deliberately chose to do nothing about it because it suited it to do so (as it was getting royalties for the extra subscribers signed up in Europe). If the plaintiff in *Trumpet Software* had not objected in the way it did to the distribution of its work then it might have similarly been found to have acquiesced in the defendant's use of it.

[30.] *The Times*, 2 December 1996.
[31.] Similar to that which was the subject of *News Datacom v Lyons* [1994] 1 ILRM 450.
[32.] [1981] 1 All ER 897.

Chapter 7

Databases

INTRODUCTION

[7.01] Computer databases are collections of facts or works which can be accessed via a computer. Databases are the same as the traditional library, the difference being that in a library the information is contained in books, in databases the information is held on computer files. It is not the information which is held that makes a database important, rather it is the ease with which it can be accessed on a computer system. Computer databases offer huge advantages over traditional information storage methods, simply because of their speed of access, the comprehensive searches they can undertake and their compact size. At present, databases come in two forms. First, there are on-line databases, for example LEXIS. These databases can be accessed over networks, such as the Internet. They are usually updated continuously. Secondly, there are databases which are supplied on disks. The most popular form of which is CD-ROM, for example the All England Law Reports. The individual CD-ROMs are sold to the user. The disadvantage with CDs is that once the information is placed on the CD-ROM it cannot be updated, unless the user receives a new CD-ROM.

[7.02] The individual contents of a database may be protected in their own right. For example, if a database was created which contained all the works of modern Irish poets, then each individual poem would be protected by copyright. The person who creates this database may have to put in considerable labour in collecting the poems. Most of the problems which arise with compilations relate to the originality of the author's contribution to the compilation. It is arguable that the efforts of such a creator are no more worthy of protection than are the efforts of any traditional librarian. The labour involved in creating a database may be distinguished from that of a traditional librarian in two ways. First, a database is far more valuable. If it is placed on the Internet it may be accessed by scholars from anywhere in the world. Secondly, it may be copied with ease. As a result, databases are felt to be worthy of special protection.

COMPILATIONS BEFORE THE IRISH COURTS

[7.03] Under the Copyright Act 1963, a literary work is defined as including "any written table or compilation". This suggests that databases which are compilations of facts or other material are protected by copyright.

RTE v Magill TV Guide Ltd

[7.04] The case of *RTE v Magill TV Guide Ltd*[1] examined whether compilations such as the *RTE Guide* could be protected by copyright.[2] *Magill* magazine produced a TV guide which gave details of the programs shown by RTE, BBC and ITV. The television companies were successful in obtaining an injunction which prevented *Magill* from publishing these details. It was submitted by the defendant that the weekly television schedule was merely a list of information and did not have the necessary ingredient of compiler's skill to constitute an original literary work and to enable copyright to subsist in it. This was rejected by Lardner J in the High Court, who stated that:

> "A literary work cannot in my judgment be confined to work exhibiting literary art or style. Rather it has the broad sense of any written or printed composition. And the requirement that it be original relates to the expression of matter in writing or print rather than the ideas expressed. Then, in its ordinary sense, a 'compilation' means a literary work formed by a compilation, that is by collecting and putting together materials. If such a printed or written work of compilation is an original composition and involves labour and time and skill on the part of its author in compiling it, he will be entitled to copyright under section 8 and to prevent others from appropriating the fruits of his labour."

Lardner J in essence prescribed a two point test to ensure that a compilation would be protected by copyright.

Labour, time and skill

[7.05] Firstly, the compilation would have to be created with the labour, time and skill of the creator. Lardner J noted the large amounts of labour, time and skill expended in compiling the *RTE Guide* was important. He referred in detail to the planning process required to prepare the Guide, noting that it began up to a year in advance. The amount of effort expended has been held to be irrelevant elsewhere. In the US Supreme Court decision of *Feist Publications Inc v Rural Telephone Service Co*,[3] it was held unanimously

---

1. [1989] IR 554.
2. See also *Private Research v Brosnan* [1995] 1 IR 534 and the Canadian case of *Tele-Direct (Publications) Inc v American Business Information Inc* (1996) 35 IPR 121.
3. (1991) 20 IPR 129.

that the old view that copyright would protect not only the selection and arrangement of facts but the underlying facts themselves, if sufficient 'industrious collection' or 'sweat of the brow' had gone into their accumulation was incorrect. The Rural Telephone Service was a telephone company which served parts of Kansas. Feist Publications brought out a telephone directory which included areas of Kansas served by Rural. Rural objected to Feist copying their phone book. Of Feist's 47,000 listings, 1300 were copied directly from the rural directory including 4 phoney listings inserted to trap copiers such as Feist. Rural sued Feist for copyright infringement and won in the Federal, District and Appeal Courts. The US Supreme Court found in favour of Feist and rejected Rural's claim that its industry and the usefulness of its directories should entitle it to copyright protection, holding instead that originality was the essential criterion.[4]

Originality

[7.06] Secondly, Lardner J held that the compilation would also have to be original in its composition. This originality relates to the expression of the subject matter of the compilation and not to any ideas contained in the compilation. If copyright is being claimed for a compilation then the creator cannot have just copied the selections or the arrangements of another's work. In *RTE v Magill,* the defendant contended that the list of times and titles contained in the *RTE Guide* were simply information and as such subject to copyright protection. Lardner J rejected this, pointing to the selection of programs by RTE which he said involved the exercise of skill and judgement. This information could not be in the public domain as it originated and was created by RTE. Although the information was published, its publication was restricted to ensure that RTE's copyright was sustained. Lardner J did not propose any test to determine originality, but it should be noted that RTE were completely original in their creation of the *RTE Guide*. RTE would have determined both the expression of the original entries into the Guide and their selection and arrangement. This might suggest that the level of originality required is quite high. RTE had complete involvement in every stage of the creation of the *RTE Guide*, from the decision of what television programmes to buy or produce, to the broadcast of the programmes and the actual expression used in the entry in their *Weekly Guide*. As a result, it may be difficult to apply this case to other compilations where the author of the compilation is separate from the author of the individual entries in the compilation.

[4.] See Gorman, 'The Feist case: Reflections on a Pathbreaking Copyright Decision', Rutgers Computer & Technology Law Journal, Vol. 18, p 733, 1992.

Allied Discount Card Ltd v Bord Fáilte Éireann

[7.07] Compilations were also the subject of litigation in *Allied Discount Card Ltd v Bord Fáilte Éireann.*[5] Allied Discount agreed to supply books of vouchers for Bord Fáilte. These vouchers were to be used in a 'Springtime in Ireland' campaign which Bord Fáilte was running in 1986. As a result, Allied Discount canvassed traders throughout Ireland and 95 retailers agreed to submit vouchers. A dispute arose between Allied Discount and Bord Fáilte, resulting in Bord Fáilte producing its own books of vouchers in 1987 and 1988. Allied Discount then sued Bord Fáilte for breach of copyright. Lynch J accepted that copyright existed in the plaintiff's compilation of vouchers.[6] But he added, that this copyright would not prevent Bord Fáilte from contacting the traders for other booklets of vouchers and the fact that Bord Fáilte would arrange the vouchers alphabetically and so end up with a similar booklet would not breach Allied Discount's copyright, provided that Bord Fáilte relied on its own efforts exclusively. Bord Fáilte had contacted not only the original 95 retailers but other traders for inclusion in the 1987 and 1988 campaigns. Unfortunately for Bord Fáilte, many of these traders simply nominated the same wording for their new vouchers as had been used by Allied Discount.

[7.08] Once Bord Fáilte contacted each trader, it would appear that they avoided the copyright which subsisted in the compilation of vouchers that was Allied Discount's booklet. Lynch J awarded damages to Allied Discount where Bord Fáilte infringed their copyright in the wording of the individual vouchers. Where Bord Fáilte contacted traders who had appeared in Allied Discount's booklet but the traders altered the wording of the vouchers which they submitted, Lynch J did not award any damages. Lynch J only awarded damages to Allied Discount in respect of those individual vouchers which were repetitions of the vouchers included in the 1986 booklet. In 1987, 40 of the 57 vouchers produced were held to be infringements of the plaintiff's copyright. In 1988, 30 of the 56 vouchers produced were held to infringe the plaintiff's copyright. This case suggests that the level of originality required in Ireland is very low. Bord Fáilte did nothing new to produce their compilation of vouchers, all that was required was that they expend their own time and labour in producing it. However, originality may not have been an issue simply because it was Bord Fáilte that first approached Allied Discount to produce the vouchers.

---

5. [1991] 2 IR 185. See also *Waterlow Directories Ltd v Reed Information Services Ltd* [1992] FSR 409.
6. He accepted the decision in *RTE v Magill* in this regard.

[7.09] Courts elsewhere have also found that the level of originality required is quite low. In *Feist v Rural Telephone Service Co*[7] discussed above, the court held that what was required was originality in the selection, co-ordination or arrangement of the data. It was stated that:

> "Original, as the term is used in copyright means ... that the work was independently created by the author (as opposed to copied from some works), and that it possesses at least some minimal degree of creativity ... To be sure, the requisite level of creativity is extremely low; even a slight amount will suffice, the vast majority of works make the grade quite easily as they possess some creative spark, 'no matter how crude, humble or obvious it might be'."[8]

It is unclear how much originality is required in Ireland. The difference between the US law and Irish is that *Feist* explicitly rejects the use of labour as a criteria in determining whether a compilation is protected whereas in Ireland the labour expended would appear to be just as important as the originality of the compilation, if not more so.[9]

PROGRAMS AS COMPILATIONS

[7.10] *Ibcos Computers Ltd v Barclays Finance Ltd*[10] concerned a program known as ADS which consisted of 335 program files, 171 layout files and 46 screen layout files. Jacob J held that a compilation of programs such as this would have protection as a compilation. He found that the whole package of the program as well as the individual programs would be protected by copyright. The amount of skill, labour and judgment which went into creating this package was very substantial, well above the threshold of originality accepted in other fields of copyright. Jacob J suggested that producing a selection of games on a disk might be afforded copyright if there was enough originality in the selection. The games might be wholly separated or have linking elements such as a common control program. In Jacob J's view it was a question of degree. He was highly critical of the statement of Baker J in *Total Information Processing Systems v Daman*[11] that to afford a compilation of programs copyright protection would lead to great inconvenience as copyright owners of one of the components could not interface with other programs without a licence from the compiler. Jacob J stated that this was unsupported by any counsel before him and he could not

---

7. (1991) 20 IPR 129.
8. *Ibid*, at 1287.
9. See Strong, 'Database protection after *Feist v Rural Telephone Co.*', Journal, Copyright Society of the USA (1994), p 41.
10. [1994] FSR 275.
11. [1992] FSR 171.

agree with it. One copyright owner can interface his program with those of other programs. He can not force his way into another's original compilation without licence which is the common position with regard to compilations of poems, songs and other works. The compiler only receives the right to prevent another substantially similar compilation which is copied from his from being produced.

[7.11] Jacob J was correct in stating that compilations of programs are protected. The ADS program would appear to be a compilation of sub-programs and as such would be protected as a program in its own right. The main significance of this judgment is that it suggests that 'suites' of programs such as Microsoft Office will be protected as compilations. It also has significance for programs created by object oriented design.

Object Oriented Design

[7.12] Traditionally, computer programs have been created by 'Top-Down Design'. This involves a team of programmers designing and writing a program from top to the bottom. When a program is designed it is divided into hundreds and thousands of sub-programs which are written by different programmers who must all be able to communicate with each other. Unfortunately, during the writing of the program, it may be necessary to change the characteristics of the sub-programs and in particular to change the interfaces which allow the sub-programs to communicate with one another. A single change to the interface of one sub-program will 'ripple' throughout the rest of the program, requiring changes to all the sub-programs which communicate with it. This can be a mammoth task, more importantly, the programmers may not be completely successful in this and the program may not work, which may be embarrassing and expensive.

[7.13] Object-oriented design minimises the interdependence between sub-programs. The code is kept within independent software objects. The result is that sub-programs are not dependant on each other and if changes are made to one sub-program, it will not necessitate changes to all the rest of the program.[12] It is possible to write a large program simply by selecting and arranging these objects of code. Each of the objects will have copyright protection as an individual literary work. The author of the larger program should have protection under the 1993 Regulations[13] but it might be argued that his work was not original as it simply involved the copying of objects created by others and was not an original literary work. In this event, the

---

[12.] See Wilkins, 'Protecting Computer Programs as Compilations', Yale LJ, Vol 104 p 367, (1994).

[13.] European Communities (Legal Protection of Computer Programs) Regulations, 1993.

author could still rely on the protection given to compilations as outlined above.

THE DATABASE DIRECTIVE

[7.14] The Directive on the Legal Protection of Databases[14] was adopted on 11 March 1996. This Directive was inspired by fears that various Member States would introduce their own legislation in this field which would have a detrimental effect on the internal market for databases, in particular that the freedom to provide on-line database services throughout the Community would be affected.[15] The Directive acknowledges that the creation of databases requires the investment of considerable resources whilst databases can be copied or accessed at a fraction of the cost of creating them.[16] There are huge imbalances between the investment in databases in Europe and elsewhere[17] and this investment will only take place if there is a stable and uniform legal regime to protect the databases.[18] The object of the Directive is different to that of the Data Protection Directive[19] and the Data base Directive is without prejudice to data protection legislation.[20]

[7.15] The Directive confers two important rights on the owners of databases. Firstly, a database will be protected by copyright. This protection is separate to any protection which is given to the contents of a database. Secondly, there is a right to prevent unauthorised extraction and re-utilisation of the contents of the database. This applies where the contents are not protected by copyright or other rights and it applies regardless of whether or not the database itself is protected.

Scope of the Directive

[7.16] The Directive concerns the legal protection of databases in any form. A database means a collection of independent works, data or other materials arranged in a systematic or methodical way and individually accessible by electronic or other means.[21] The Directive covers non-electronic databases[22] and is stated to also protect devices such as CD-ROM and CD-i.[23] The Directive states that it protects collections, sometimes called 'compilations'

[14.] 1996/9 OJ L77/20.
[15.] Recital 2.
[16.] Recital 7.
[17.] Recital 11.
[18.] Recital 12.
[19.] 23.11.1995, OJ L 281/31.
[20.] Recital 48.
[21.] Article 1(2).
[22.] Recital 14.
[23.] Recital 22.

of works, data or other materials which are arranged, stored or accessed by electronic, electromagnetic or electro-optical processes or analogous processing.[24] The term 'database' includes literary, artistic, musical or other collections of works or collections of other materials such as text, sound, images, numbers, facts and data. However, it does not cover a recording or an audio-visual, cinematographical literary or musical work.[25] If a database contains audio-visual works, then the Directive will be without prejudice to any rules concerning the broadcasting of audio-visual programmes.[26] The compilation of several recordings of musical performances on a CD will not come within the scope of the Directive.[27] Protection will extend to all systematically or methodically arranged databases and it is not necessary for these to be physically stored in an organised manner.[28] Some databases may be spread out over several different locations for example a database of all the patients in a town might be shared between every hospital in the town.

[7.17] Protections may also apply to the materials necessary for the operation or consultation of certain databases such as a thesaurus and indication system.[29] The Directive does not apply to computer programs used in the making or operation of databases accessible by electronic means.[30]

[7.18] The Directive is stated to apply without prejudice to the legal protection of computer programs, the rental and lending rights and the term of protection of copyright.[31]

THE COPYRIGHT PROTECTION OF DATABASES

[7.19] Databases, which are the author's own intellectual creation, by reason of the selection or arrangement of the contents, will be protected by copyright. No criteria other than these may be used to determine the eligibility of databases for protection.[32] In particular, no aesthetic or qualitative criteria may be applied.[33]

[24.] Recital 13.
[25.] Recital 17.
[26.] Recital 59.
[27.] Recital 19.
[28.] Recital 21.
[29.] Recital 20.
[30.] Article 1(3). Computer programs are already protected by Council Directive 91/250. See Ch 2.
[31.] Article 2.
[32.] Article 3(1).
[33.] Recital 16. The protection extends to the structure of the database: Recital 15.

[7.20] The creation of a database will normally require huge amounts of labour. Therefore, most of them would have no difficulty with the first part of the *Magill* test. Proving the originality of databases may be more problematic. The Database Directive has only one criterion for protection, that it must be the author's own intellectual creation. No other criteria may be applied. This would seem to leave the 'sweat of the brow' test applied in Magill redundant. However, the *sui generis* right protects the author's investment of time and money.[34]

[7.21] Compilations such as the *RTE Guide* and telephone directories are broadly similar to databases. The difference is that one looks up the information in the *RTE Guide* by purchasing a copy and opening it at the appropriate page. The information on a computer database is looked up by means of a computer search program. Decisions on the copyrightability of directories and timetables may be taken to be directly applicable to databases. While this is tempting, it is not necessarily correct. Directories and timetables are collections of facts, such as the times of programmes or the phone number of restaurants which are arranged and collated by their 'authors'. It is this arrangement which allows them to be original and distinguishes one directory of restaurants such as the Golden Pages from another, such as the Michelin Guide. Databases are not like this. They will only be arranged by their creators in a very limited sense. The most useful databases are those which are fully comprehensive, including every possible item of information on their subject matter. Users of the database may tailor their selections to their own needs. So if one was using a database of restaurants one might select them on the basis of price, location, type or owner. In a database the selection will be determined by the user, while in a directory the selection will to a great extent be determined by the creator. A database can be as original as a directory. The difference is that directories are original because their creators exclude information which they feel is unnecessary. Databases are original because their creators include as much information as they possibly can. However, it is harder to show that the creator of a totally comprehensive database of restaurants has applied any originality in the selection of entries to the database. There is no reason why the creator of a database is being any less original than the creator of a directory. It is simply harder to prove.

[7.22] This difficulty arose in the English case of *J Whitaker & Sons Ltd v Publisher's Circular Ltd*[35] which concerned a publishers newsletter which gave weekly details of all new books published. Publishers of books

---

34. Recital 39.
35. 1946-1949 MCC 10.

informed the compiler of all new books. The court held that no discrimination was involved in the creation of the newsletter, but that the comprehensive nature of the list involved more labour in ensuring that it was as complete as possible. The newsletter was held to be the subject of copyright. In *Dun & Bradstreet v Type Setting Facilities*[36] Harman J rejected the submission of the defendant that the plaintiff's computerised database was not a copyright work. He found that there was sufficient to show direction, compilation, distillation and adding of materials to warrant an assertion that the plaintiff had an original copyright work. He suggested that revising and updating a database might create a new work which would have a copyright separate from that of the unrevised and outdated work.

Authorship of Databases

[7.23] The author of a database is the natural person who created the database or the legal person designated as the rightholder by law.[37] Where a database is created by a group of natural persons, the exclusive rights will be owned jointly.[38] The moral rights of the natural person who created the database belong to the author and should be exercised in accordance with the Berne Convention. However, moral rights are outside the scope of the Directive.[39] Member States may legislate for the situation where an employee creates a database during the course of his employment.[40]

Acts Restricted by Copyright

[7.24] The copyright protection of databases does not extend to their contents and is without prejudice to any rights subsisting in those contents themselves.[41] Works protected by copyright or other rights may not be incorporated into or extracted from a database without the permission of the copyright holder in the work.[42]

[7.25] The author has the exclusive right to determine the way in which his work is exploited and by whom. In particular, he should have the right to control the distribution of his work to authorised persons.[43] The copyright protection of databases will include making databases available by means other than the distribution of copies.[44] This would cover on-line databases

---

36. [1992] FSR 320.
37. Article 4(1).
38. Article 4(3).
39. Recital 28.
40. Recital 29. Under CA 1963, s 10, an employer is entitled to the copyright in any works where they are created by an employee during the course of his employment.
41. Article 3(2).
42. Recital 26.
43. Recital 30.

and other databases which are made available to the public over the Internet or by other means. The author of the database will have the exclusive right to carry out or authorise the following acts:

(1) temporary or permanent reproduction by any means and in any form, in whole or in part;[45]

(2) translation, adaptation, arrangement and any other alteration;[46]

(3) any form of distribution to the public of the database or of copies thereof. The first sale in the Community of a copy of the database by the rightholder or with his consent shall exhaust the right to control resale of that copy within the Community;[47] The exhaustion right of distribution does not arise in the case of on-line databases which come within the field of provision of services. This also applies with regard to a material copy of such a database made by the user of such a service with the consent of the rightholder. This is unlike CD-ROM or CD-i where the intellectual property is incorporated in a material medium which is an item of goods. Every on-line service is in fact an act which will have to be subject to authorisation where the copyright so provides.[48]

(4) any communication, display or performance to the public;[49]

(5) any reproduction, distribution, communication, display or performance to the public of the results of any translation, adaptation or arrangement of the database.[50]

Exceptions to the restricted acts

[7.26] A lawful user of a database may perform any of the restricted acts if they are necessary for the purpose of access to the contents of the databases and normal use of them. He will require the authorisation of the author of the database. If the user is authorised to use only part of the database, this provision will apply only to that part.[51] Once the author of the database has chosen to made available a copy of the database to a user, whether by on-line service or by other means of distribution, that lawful user must be able to

---

44. Recital 31.
45. Article 5(a).
46. Article 5(b).
47. Article 5(c).
48. Recital 33.
49. Article 5(d)
50. Article 5(e)
51. Article 6(1).

access and use the database for the purposes and in the way set out in the agreement with the author of the database, even if access and use would necessitate the performance of restricted acts.[52] This means that database owners cannot use the provisions of the Directive to enforce unfair contract terms or practices against their users. Any contractual provisions which are contrary to Article 6(1) will be null and void.[53]

[7.27] Member States have the option of providing for limitations on the restricted acts in the following situations:

(1) Reproduction for private purposes of a non-electronic database;

(2) Illustrations for teaching or scientific research. Scientific research includes both the natural and human sciences.[54] This will only be permitted where the source is indicated and the extent justified by the non-commercial purpose to be achieved;[55]

(3) Where the acts are necessary for the purpose of public security or for the purposes of an administrative or judicial procedure;

(4) Other exceptions to copyright which are traditionally authorised under national law will be allowed.[56] This would permit practices such as the delivery of copies of books to certain libraries under s 56 of the Copyright Act 1963 to continue.

The Directive requires that a list should be drawn up of exceptions to the restricted acts. Member States will have the option of providing for such exceptions in certain cases but these exceptions should only be allowed in accordance with the Berne Convention.[57] Article 10(1) of the Berne Convention is not affected by the Directive.[58] This provides that it is permissible to make quotations from a work which has already been made lawfully to the public, provided that their making is compatible with fair practice and their extent does not exceed that justified by the purpose.

[7.28] Article 6 may not be interpreted in such as way as to allow its application to be used in a manner which unreasonably prejudices the

---

[52.] Recital 34.

[53.] Article 15.

[54.] Recital 36.

[55.] Article 6(2)(b).

[56.] Article 6.

[57.] Recital 35. A distinction should be made between exceptions for private use and exceptions for reproduction for private use. This last provision relates to levies on blank cassette tapes and recording equipment which exist in some Member States.

[58.] Recital 37.

author's legitimate interests or conflicts with the normal exploitation of the database.[59]

SUI GENERIS RIGHT

[7.29] The *sui generis* right is particular to databases. It was created because it was feared that normal copyright law would not be sufficient to protect databases and became some databases would not be protected by copyright. The increased use of digital recording technology exposes a database author to the risk that the contents of his database may be copied and rearranged electronically, without the author's authorisation, to produce a database of identical content which does not infringe any copyright in the arrangement of his database.[60] The Directive tries to safeguard database authors from the misappropriation of the results of the financial and professional investment they have made in obtaining and collecting the contents, by protecting the whole or substantial parts of a database against certain acts by a user or competitor.[61] The object of the *sui generis* right is to protect the author or creator of a database by giving him the option of preventing the unauthorised extraction and re-utilisation of all or a substantial part of the contents of the database. This right will only protect the person who takes the initiative and risk of investing in a database. It will not protect sub-contractors.[62]

[7.30] Member States must provide for a right for the author of a database who shows that there has been a substantial investment in terms of quality or quantity in either the obtaining, verification or presentation of the contents of the database. This right will allow the author to prevent extraction and re-utilisation of the whole or a substantial part of the contents of that database evaluated in terms of quality or quantity.[63] Extraction means the permanent or temporary transfer of all or a substantial part of the contents of a database to another medium by any means or in any form. Re-utilisation means any form of making available to the public all or a substantial part of the contents of a database by the distribution of copies, by renting, on-line or by other forms of transmission. Public lending is not a act of extraction or re-utilisation.[64] This right relates to acts by the user which go beyond his legitimate rights and harm the author's investment. The right relates not only to the manufacture of a parasitic competing product but also to any user

---

59. Article 6(3).
60. Recital 38.
61. Recital 39.
62. Recital 41.
63. Article 7(1).
64. Article 7(2).

who, through his acts, causes significant detriment, evaluated quantitatively or qualitatively, to the investment of the author.[65] This effectively gives the author the right to police the use of his database. Where a database is transmitted on-line, the right to prohibit re-utilisation will not be exhausted by the transmission.[66] If an on-screen display of the contents of a database necessitates the permanent or temporary transfer of all or a substantial part of such contents to another medium, the consent of the author must be obtained.[67] Although the author has the specific right to control the transmission and display of the database, there is no mention of printing out the contents of the database.

[7.31] This right may be transferred, assigned or granted under a contractual licence.[68] The right to prevent extraction and re-utilisation will apply irrespective of the eligibility of that database for copyright protection or any other protections. In addition to this, it will apply irrespective of the eligibility of the contents of that database for protection by copyright or by other rights. This is without prejudice to any rights existing in the contents of the database[69] and will not lead to the creation of a new right in any of the contents of the database.[70] The right does not constitute an extension of copyright protection to mere facts or data.[71]

[7.32] The repeated and systematic extraction or re-utilisation of insubstantial parts of the contents of the database is not permitted where it is inconsistent with the normal exploitation of that database or where it unreasonably prejudices the legitimate interests of the author of the database.[72] A *sui generis* right must not be used to facilitate abuses of a dominant position, in particular, to prevent the creation of new products and services which have an intellectual, documentary, technical, economic or commercial added value.[73]

Exceptions to the Sui Generis Right

[7.33] Member States may stipulate that lawful users of a public database may, without the authorisation of its author, extract or re-utilise a substantial part of its contents in the following circumstances:

[65.] Recital 42.
[66.] Recital 43.
[67.] Recital 44.
[68.] Article 7(3).
[69.] Article 7(4).
[70.] Recital 46.
[71.] Recital 45.
[72.] Article 7(5).
[73.] Recital 47.

(1) Extraction for private purposes of a non-electronic database;[74]

(2) Extraction for the purposes of illustrations for teaching or scientific research.[75] This exception may be limited to certain categories of teaching or scientific research institutions.[76]

(3) Extraction or re-utilisation for the purposes of public security or an administrative or judicial procedure.[77]

If these exceptions are allowed, they must not prejudice the exclusive rights of the author to exploit the database and their purpose must not be commercial.[78]

Users' Rights

[7.34] The author of a database may not prevent a user from extracting or re-utilising insubstantial parts of its contents for any purpose. If the user is only permitted to use a part of the database, then this provision will only apply to that part. A lawful user of a database which is made available to the public may not perform acts which conflict with the normal exploitation of the database or unreasonably prejudice the legitimate interests of the maker of the database. The lawful user may not cause prejudice to the holder of a copyright or related right in respect of the works or subject matter contained in the database.[79] Any contractual provisions which are contrary to Article 8 will be null and void.[80]

Term of Protection

[7.35] The *sui generis* right will exist from the date of completion of the database and will run for 15 years from 1 January of the year following the date of completion of the database. The Council of Europe obviously want to encourage authors of databases to make them available to the public. To this end, if a database is made available to the public in any manner before the end of the 15 years, then the term of protection will expire 15 years from the 1st of January of the year following the date when the database was first made available to the public. Any substantial change, whether qualitative or quantitative, to the content of the database including any substantial change due to the accumulation of successive additions, deletions or alterations which would cause the database to be considered a substantial new

---

74. Article 9(a).
75. Article 9(b).
76. Recital 51.
77. Article 9(c).
78. Recital 50.
79. Article 8.
80. Article 15.

investment will qualify the improved database for a new term of protection.[81] The burden of proving that a substantial modification of the contents of the database is to be granted as a substantial new investment lies with the author of the database resulting from the investment.[82] A substantial new investment may include a substantial verification of the contents of the database.[83]

Beneficiaries of protection under the *sui generis* right

[7.36] The *sui generis* right will apply to authors who are nationals of a Member State or who have their habitual residence within the Community. This will apply to companies and firms who have their registered office, administration or business within the Community. However, if a company has only its registered office within the Community, then its operations must be genuinely linked to the economy of the Member State. The Council may make agreements extending the *sui generis* right to databases made in third countries.[84] The *sui generis* right will apply to nationals of third countries only if the third country offers comparable protection to databases produced by nationals of the EU.[85]

PROVISIONS COMMON TO COPYRIGHT AND SUI GENERIS PROTECTION OF DATABASES

[7.37] Member States must provide appropriate remedies for infringements of the rights of authors of databases,[86] including infringements of the *sui generis* rights as well as copyright.[87] The Directive is without prejudice to other protections. In particular, it does not prejudice copyright, rights relating to copyright, or any other rights subsisting in the data, works or other materials incorporated into the database, patent rights, trade marks, design rights, the protection of national treasures, laws on restrictive practices and unfair competition, trade secrets, security, confidentiality, data protection and privacy, access to public documents, and the law of contract.[88] Other legal provisions relating to the sale and supply of databases and other services will continue to apply in addition to the *sui generis* and copyright protection of databases.[89]

---

81. Article 10.
82. Recital 54.
83. Recital 55.
84. Article 11.
85. Recital 56.
86. Article 12.
87. Recital 57.
88. Article 13.

[7.38] Member States must bring into law the provisions of the Directive before 1 January 1998.[90] Copyright protection under the Directive will be available to databases created prior to the implementation of the Directive which fulfil the copyright requirements of the Directive. If a database does not fulfil these requirements but is protected by the existing copyright legislation in a Member State the Directive will not result in the curtailment of the remaining term of protection given by that legislation. *Sui generis* protection will be available to databases which were completed not less than 15 years before the date of implementation of the Directive and which fulfil the criteria laid down in Article 7 on that date. Copyright and *sui generis* protection is without prejudice to any acts concluded or rights acquired before the date of implementation of the Directive. In the case of a database which was completed not more than 15 years prior to the date of implementation of the Directive, the term of *sui generis* protection will expire 15 years from 1 January following the date of implementation.[91] The burden of proving the date of completion of a database lies with the author.[92]

[7.39] Not later than 1 January 2001, the Commission must submit a report to the European Parliament, Council and the Economic and Social Committee on the application of the Directive. The report will examine in particular the application of the *sui generis* right and whether or not its application has led to an abusive or dominant position or other interference with free competition which might justify appropriate measures being taken including the establishment of non-voluntary licensing arrangements.[93] Compulsory licensing provisions had been included in the draft Directive.[94]

BULLETIN BOARDS AS DATABASES

[7.40] Bulletin board systems allow users to leave their own messages and read messages left by others by accessing a central computer over phone lines. Many web sites have similar functions. A bulletin board system is a computerised version of a physical notice board on which messages are pinned, some of which are intended to be read by anyone, others may be addressed to a named individual. Some messages on the bulletin board may be mundane, such as the time and location of a meeting. Where messages are left, the author will own the copyright. However, the messages together will

---

[89.] Recital 58.
[90.] Article 16(1).
[91.] Article 14.
[92.] Recital 53.
[93.] Article 16(3).
[94.] Article 11(1), COM (93) 464 final - SYN 393. OJ 93/ C 308/01.

form a collection or compilation and the copyright in this collection may be owned by the bulletin board operator. It is suggested that this would only occur where he acts as a moderator or controls the content of the collection. CompuServe, one of the largest on-line services, actively asserts a compilation copyright on user messages as do other on-line services and some bulletin boards.[95] The Database Directive[96] defines a database as a collection of independent works, data or other materials arranged in a systematic or methodical way and individually accessible by electronic or other means.[97] Bulletin boards would come within this definition.

[95.] Cavazos and Morin, *Cyberspace and the Law*, The MIT Press, p 56.
[96.] OJ L 77/20, 27.3.96.
[97.] Article 1.

Chapter 8

Trade Marks, Passing-Off and Digital Signatures

[8.01] The illicit copying of computer programs by so called 'pirates' is already a lucrative business. Obviously, such pirates will want to maximise the profit which they make from every illicit copy. If the illicit copies are sold on their own without manuals, in circumstances where any user would know that the copies were illegal then obviously potential purchasers will not be willing to pay much, if anything at all. However, if the pirate can produce a copy of the program which is indistinguishable from the original, having all the necessary packaging and manuals, then purchasers will be willing to pay considerably more, even the same as for a legitimate copy.

[8.02] Although computer programs are the main victims of such piracy[1] at present, in the future multi-media works and databases will also suffer serious difficulties. If a program is being illegally copied and sold then the rightholder will obviously proceed against the copier using the remedies provided by the Copyright Act 1963. However, aside from copyright protection for the program itself, there are other methods set out below which may be used to protect intellectual property rights. In particular, these remedies may help the owner to restrict the marketing and sale of the infringing copies.

COPYRIGHT IN THE PACKAGING OF COMPUTER PRODUCTS

[8.03] Copying the packaging of a program or other work will infringe the law in several ways. While it has been held that a name *per se* such as 'EXXON' cannot be protected by copyright,[2] any more substantial writings such as explanatory materials will count as literary works and will therefore be protected.[3] Any artistic works included in the packaging will also be protected. Section 9 of the Copyright 1963 Act defines artistic work as "paintings, sculptures, drawings, engravings and photographs, irrespective

---

[1.] Over 82% of software in Ireland is illegally copied, *The Sunday Business Post* 26 May 1996.

[2.] *Exxon Corp v Exxon Insurance Consultants International Ltd* [1981] 3 All ER 241.

[3.] The tort of passing off will also give protection in this situation, see para **[8.22]** below. In *Grange Marketing Ltd v M & Q Plastic Products Ltd* High Court, unrep, 17 June 1976, the defendant was found liable for passing off as its product was marketed in similar packaging to the plaintiff's with an identical slogan.

of their artistic quality". Copyright restricts the reproduction and publication of such artwork without the consent of the rightholder. It will be virtually impossible to reproduce the packaging of a program without infringing these copyrights.

TRADE MARKS

[8.04] At present, one of the most important protections given to the holders of intellectual property rights is that of trade mark protection. This is because trade marks can be registered. If a software company obtains a trade mark registration for its brand name and then places this trade mark on all its software or other works,[4] it is easier for the company to enforce its rights than relying on copyright alone. There is no need to prove substantial similarity between the company's software and that marketed by the pirate or to show a causal link between the works as is required by copyright law. All the software company need do is point to their registered trade mark and prove that their mark, or a confusingly similar mark, has been used or copied by the pirate or counterfeiter. Obviously, some pirates will remove such trade marks but this may be complex and customers may not be willing to pay as much or anything for a program or other work which does not appear to come from a reputable publisher.

The Trade Marks Act 1996

[8.05] If a person does not wish to rely on passing off to protect his goodwill and reputation then he may wish to register as a trade mark, the name of his products or company, or any sign which distinguishes his goods from those being produced or sold by another. Although a trade mark is often in writing, it may consist of something which is capable of being expressed graphically, such as music, eg, the jingle used in an advertisement. Trade mark registration offers several advantages. First, it is protected from the date of registration, with effect backdated to the date of application, regardless of whether or not the trade mark is used. Secondly, registration greatly strengthens the position of the owner in any court litigation. The owner will not have to prove the reputation of his trade mark as he would in a passing off action. Finally, the protection available to the owner of a trade mark is national or in the case of a Community Trade Mark Registration, can extend throughout the entire European Union. It is advisable to conduct a search of current registrations and applications before expending substantial sums on a new brand name. This will greatly reduce the risk of an expensive conflict

---

4. Most software programs will display their trademarked names such as 'MS-DOS' or 'Word for Windows' when they are run on a computer.

with an existing right. The Trade Marks Act 1996 implements the Council Directive Approximating the Laws of the Member States Relating to Trade Marks[5] and it also clarifies and updates the Irish law in other respects. The most important change is that it is now possible to register service marks.[6]

Definition of a Trade Mark

[8.06] 'Trade mark' is defined as any sign capable of being represented graphically which is capable of distinguishing goods or services of one undertaking from those of another. In particular, a trade mark may consist of words (including personal names), designs, letters, numerals or the shape of goods or of their packaging.[7] Signs which do not satisfy these requirements cannot be registered.[8]

[8.07] There are several cases which examined what constituted a trade mark within the meaning of the Trade Mark Act 1963. The definition of trade mark in the 1996 Act is different. However, both Acts have requirements that a trade mark be 'capable of distinguishing' the goods of one trader from another.[9] *Waterford Glass v Controller of Patents Designs and Trade Marks*[10] the Supreme Court held that the mark WATERFORD had achieved 100% factual distinctiveness in relation to the products of Waterford Glass Ltd and that as such the company was entitled to have the mark registered. The court held that the words 'capable of distinguishing' were to be understood in their plain sense.[11] In *Miller Brewing v Controller of Patents, Designs and Trade Marks*[12] the Supreme Court held that the term HIGH LIFE was capable of distinguishing the plaintiff's beer from that of other manufacturers.

---

5. First Council Directive 89/104 of 21 December 1988 to Approximate the Laws of the Member States Relating To Trade Marks; 1989 OJ L 40/1.
6. In *Bank of Ireland v Controller of Patents, Designs and Trade Marks,* High Court, unrep, 31 March 1987 (Costello J) the plaintiff's application to register the word 'PASS' in relation to its bank cards was rejected as the bank was supplying a banking service as opposed to goods. Under the 1963 Act, a trade mark could not be registered unless it could be shown that the user of the mark would be 'trading in' the goods in relation to which the mark was to be used. *Ibid* p 11.
7. TMA 1996, s 6.
8. TMA 1996, s 8(1).
9. TMA 1996, s 18(1) laid down a requirement that a trade mark be capable of distinguishing goods with which the proprietor of the trade mark might be connected from those goods with which no such connection existed.
10. [1984] ILRM 565.
11. The court rejected the view of the House of Lords in *York v Registrar of Trade Marks* [1982] 1 All ER 257 where it was decided that 'capable' meant legally capable rather than capable in fact.
12. [1988] ILRM 258.

The Refusal of Registration of a Trade Mark

[8.08] Trade marks which are devoid of any distinctive character, which serve to designate the kind, quality, quantity, purpose, value, origin, the time of production of the goods or services or trade marks which consist exclusively of signs or indications which have become customary in the trade cannot be registered.[13] Trade marks cannot be registered if they consist exclusively of the shape which results from the nature of the goods, the shape of the goods which is necessary to obtain a technical result or the shape which gives substantial value to the goods.[14] This prevents trade mark registration being used to obtain potentially perpetual protection in respect of designs which are subject to a separate registration system and protected only for a maximum of fifteen years. Shape might be broadly interpreted as including how a computer program appears to a user when displayed on a computer screen such as a graphical user interface used by a word processing program. A trade mark may include a graphical image and if it were possible to trade mark the image of a graphical user interface, this subsection would still limit the application of that trade mark.

[8.09] A trade mark will not be registered if it is contrary to public policy or morality or if it is intended to deceive the public.[15] A trade mark will not be registered if its use is prohibited by law or if the application is made in bad faith.[16] Neither will it be registered if it consists of or contains State emblems or the flag of the State.[17] A trade mark will not be registered if it is identical with an earlier trade mark and the goods or services for which the trade mark is applied for are identical to those for which the earlier trade mark is protected.[18] If there exists a likelihood of confusion on the part of the public about similarities between a trade mark and an earlier registered trade mark, then registration will be refused.[19]

The Benefits of Registration

[8.10] If a trade mark is registered, this gives the owner a property right and the owner of a registered trade mark will have the rights and remedies provided by the Act.[20] If a trade mark is not registered then no proceedings

---

13. TMA 1996, s 8(1).
14. TMA 1996, s 8(2)
15. TMA 1996, s 8(3).
16. TMA 1996, s 8(4).
17. TMA 1996, s 9.
18. TMA 1996, s 10(1), subject to s 12.
19. TMA 1996, s 10(2) subject to s 12.
20. TMA 1996, s 7(1).

will lie to prevent or recover damages for the infringement of it. However, nothing in the Act affects the law relating to passing off.[21]

[8.11] The owner of a registered trade mark has exclusive rights in the trade mark and his rights will be infringed where the trade mark is used in Ireland without his consent in relation to the goods or services covered by the registration.[22] It will be infringed by any person who, in the course of trade, uses a sign which is identical to the trade mark in relation to goods or services which are identical to the goods or services for which the trade mark is registered.[23] A trade mark will also be infringed by the use of a sign which might create confusion in the minds of the public.[24] The mark will be infringed by the use of a sign which is identical or similar to the trade mark and is used in relation to goods or services which are dissimilar to those for which the trade mark is registered if the trade mark has a reputation and the sign takes unfair advantage of or is detriment to that reputation.[25] The use of a sign includes fixing it to goods or packaging, selling goods under the sign, importing or exporting goods under the sign or using the sign on business papers or in advertising.[26] A registered trade mark will not be infringed by the use of a person's name or address, the use of indications concerning the kind, quality, quantity, purpose, value, origin, the time of production of goods or of rendering of the service or other characteristics of goods or services. Neither will the trade mark be infringed by the use of the mark where it is necessary to indicate the intended purpose of a product or service, in particular, as accessories or spare parts.[27]

The Registration Procedure

[8.12] Applications for registration of a trade mark must be made to the Controller of Patents, Designs and Trade Marks. The application must state that the trade mark is being used by or with the consent of the applicant in relation to the goods or services specified in the application or that the applicant has a *bona fide* intention that it should be so used.[28] Goods and services must be classified for registration and every trade mark must be registered in respect of particular goods or services.[29] In *Mercury*

---

21. TMA 1996, s 7(2).
22. TMA 1996, s 13(1).
23. TMA 1996, s 14(1).
24. TMA 1996, s 14(2).
25. TMA 1996, s 14(3).
26. TMA 1996, s 14(4).
27. TMA 1996, s 15(2)
28. TMA 1996, s 37.
29. TMA 1996, s 39.

Communications Ltd v Mercury Interactive (UK),[30] the plaintiff supplied telecommunications services and had registered the trade mark MERCURY. This was stated to apply to 'computer software' in the specification for the trade mark registration. The defendant claimed that the plaintiff's registration of the trade mark MERCURY should only apply to software for the telecommunications industry instead of 'computer programs' in general. Laddie J stated that in his view it was thoroughly undesirable that a trader who is interested in one limited area of computer software should by registration obtain a statutory monopoly of indefinite duration covering all types of software including those which are far removed from his own area of trading interest.

[8.13] The date of filing of the trade mark is the day on which all the requisite documentation is supplied to the Controller.[31] Once the application is made, it must be examined by the Controller. If he is satisfied that the requirements for registration have been met, then he will accept the application[32] and it will be published in the Patents Office Journal. Any person may give notice of opposition to the registration of a trade mark to the Controller in writing.[33] A person may also send in observations to the Controller about a published trade mark.[34] If an application has been accepted and no notices of opposition have been received or all opposition proceedings have been resolved, then the Controller must register the trade mark unless it appears that the application was accepted in error.[35] Once a trade mark is registered, the date of filing of the application for registration will be treated as the date of registration.[36] On the registration of the trade mark the Controller must publish the registration in the Patents Office Journal and issue the applicant with a certificate of registration.[37] The registration of a trade mark may be declared invalid if it was incorrectly registered[38] unless the proprietor of an earlier trade mark or other right has acquiesced for a period of five years.[39] A registered trade mark is personal

---

30. [1995] FSR 850.
31. If there are a number of documents filed on different days, the date of filing is the last of those dates: s 38.
32. TMA 1996, s 42.
33. This occurred in *The Seven-Up Co v Bubble Up Co Inc and the Controller* [1990] ILRM 204 where the High Court found that the term 'bubble-up' could be registered.
34. TMA 1996, s 43.
35. TMA 1996, s 45(1).
36. TMA 1996, s 45(3).
37. TMA 1996, s 45(4).
38. TMA 1996, s 52.
39. TMA 1996, s 53.

property[40] and it may be jointly owned[41] or assigned.[42] A trade mark will be registered for a period of ten years from the date of registration[43] and may be renewed for further periods of ten years.[44] It is an offence to make a fraudulent application for a trade mark[45] and it is also an offence to falsify the Register of Trade Marks[46] or to falsely represent that a trade mark is registered.[47]

Infringement Proceedings

[8.14] Where a registered trade mark is infringed, the infringement will be actionable by the proprietor of the trade mark. In an action for infringement of a registered trade mark the usual reliefs will be available to the proprietor.[48] A court may order any person who has infringed a registered trade mark to cause the offending sign to be erased, removed or obliterated from any infringing goods, materials or articles in his possession, custody or control. If this is not practical the court may order the destruction of the infringing goods, materials or articles. If this order is not complied with, the court may order those goods to be delivered to such person as the court may direct so that the order may be carried out.[49]

[8.15] The proprietor of a registered trade mark may apply to court for an order for the delivery up of any infringing goods which an individual has in his possession, custody or control, in the course of business or other dealings.[50] An order for delivery up of goods cannot be made more than six years from the date on which the trade mark was first attached to the infringing goods, materials or articles. This will not apply if the proprietor was under a disability or prevented by fraud or concealment from discovering the facts.[51]

[8.16] Where infringing goods, materials or articles have been delivered up, s 23 provides that an application may be made to the court for an order that they should be destroyed or forfeited or for a decision that no such order

---

40. TMA 1996, s 26.
41. TMA 1996, s 27.
42. TMA 1996, s 28.
43. TMA 1996, s 47(1).
44. TMA 1996, s 47(2).
45. TMA 1996, s 92.
46. TMA 1996, s 93.
47. TMA 1996, s 94.
48. TMA 1996, s 18.
49. TMA 1996, s 19.
50. TMA 1996, s 20.
51. TMA 1996, s 22.

should be made.[52] In considering whether or not to make such an order the court must consider whether other remedies would be adequate to compensate and protect the interests of the proprietor.[53] If the court decides not to make an order then the person who possessed the goods before they were delivered up is entitled to their return.[54] The District Court may grant search warrants to allow the gardaí to enter premises and seize goods and bring them before the court.[55] If groundless threats of proceedings are made, any person aggrieved may apply to the courts for relief.[56]

The Community Trade Mark

[8.17] The Community Trade Mark Regulation[57] provides for a single registration procedure which will cover all Member States of the European Union as a single territory. The Community Trade Mark Office, officially known as the Office for Harmonisation for the Internal Market (OHIM) is situated at Alicante in Spain. Marks may be registered for a period of ten years which may be renewed for successive ten year periods. OHIM will not search national registers only its own register of Community Trade Marks (CTMs). The owners of earlier trade marks must oppose conflicting applications within three months of publication. This means that there may be a very high level of opposition to CTM applications. The EU Commission estimates that some 80% of applications will be opposed. If a trade mark registered in one Member State conflicts with a later CTM registration, then the application for a CTM may fail or be revoked. OHIM began taking applications on 1 January 1996 with a three month lead in period for the filing of the initial applications. The earliest date attainable therefore is 1 April 1996.

[8.18] Part III of the Trade Marks Act 1996 contains provisions relating to CTMs. The Minister for Enterprise and Employment may make appropriate regulations in connection with the operation of the CTM. Provision has been made for the filing of applications for CTMs through the Irish Patents Office,[58] and may be made in respect of the procedures for determining *a posteriori* the invalidity or liability to revocation of the registration of a trade mark from which a CTM claims seniority and the conversion of a CTM or an application for a CTM into an application for registration under the Trade

---

52. TMA 1996, s 23(1).
53. TMA 1996, s 23(2).
54. TMA 1996, s 23(5).
55. TMA 1996, s 25.
56. TMA 1996, s 24.
57. 20 December 1993; 1994 OJ L11/1.
58. SI 10/1996.

Marks Act 1996. The Minister may also designate which courts in the State have jurisdiction over proceedings relating to CTMs.[59] The Act also contains provisions to allow the implementation of the Madrid Protocol and certain provisions of the Paris Convention.

DOMAIN NAMES

[8.19] A domain name is the electronic address of a person who is connected to the Internet. It is as undesirable for two users to share the same domain name as it is for two telephones to have the same telephone number. To avoid this, domain names are registered. However, in the United States the body which does this, Network Solutions Incorporated, has found that some people will register domain names which others may feel they are not entitled to. For example, Rolex Watches were appalled to discover that Janice Ard of Colorado had registered 'rolex.com'. Some are particularly unprincipled, UNHCR.org does not belong to the United Nations High Commission for Refugees but rather the Refugee Republic Corporation of Nevada, USA.[60] This problem has also affected British Telecom which has found that Ivan Pope, a Londoner, has called himself 'British Telecom' on the Internet. Pope runs a web site which lures in customers of BT expecting information about their services. BT has issued a writ against Pope alleging trade mark infringement.[61]

The Irish rules for registering domain names

[8.20] The rules which apply to registering domain names in Ireland would make it more difficult to register the trade mark or other identification of another as a domain name.[62] Each application for a domain name must contain detailed information about the applicant. A domain name must correspond with reasonable closeness to the name of the applicant or to an abbreviation or trade mark in relation to which the applicant is well known. Where the proposed name is either already in use or appears likely to be claimed by another applicant, another name shall be chosen. Names such as IBM.ie, Dublin.ie, IRFU.ie are protected by this requirement. If the proposed name is likely to lead to confusion in the opinion of the naming

---

59. TMA 1996, s 57.
60. *The Economist*, 8 June 1996.
61. The site contains articles such as "Four things I hate about my BT account manager". Pope began his campaign after his phones failed to work for a week which almost made his business bankrupt. British Telecom is not alone, Microsoft is trying to remove a site in the US called 'Microsnot'. *The Sunday Times*, 9 June 1996.
62. The Register of Domain Names in Ireland is administered at UCD. The rules were first published in June 1995 and revised in May 1996. The relevant information can be found on the Internet at http://www.ucd.ie/hostmaster/ie.dom.html.

authority, another name must be chosen. An application for a domain name may be refused if the applicant already holds one in Ireland. This should prevent the hoarding of domain names.

[8.21] The rules do not include provisions for arbitrating between rival claimants once a domain name is registered. An aggrieved party could request that the authority terminate the registration of the domain name to which they object. In this situation the authority states that it is free to determine which application to honour. If this is not satisfactory, a party may wish to apply to court to protect its rights. If a company were to find that its trade mark had been registered by somebody else as a domain name, it could find it difficult to enforce its rights under trade mark law. This is because s 15 of the Trade Marks Act 1996 provides that a registered trade mark will not be infringed by the use by a person of his own name and address. This presumably applies to electronic addresses as much as postal ones. In this situation the appropriate remedy might be to sue for passing off. Of course, an action could be taken for both trade mark infringement and passing off in appropriate circumstances.[63]

PASSING OFF

[8.22] If a trade mark is not registered (or if it cannot be registered) then a trader may have to rely on the law of passing off to protect the reputation of his product and his goodwill.[64] The common law has provided that an individual who passes off his own products as those of another will be liable for his actions. So, if a company sought to market a software package which is packaged similarly to a well known brand, this could amount to passing-off.[65] In *Jian Tools for Sales Inc v Roderick Manhattan Group Ltd*,[66] the plaintiffs had developed a computer program called BIZPLAN BUILDER which was sold in the USA to enable businesses to produce business plans. The defendants launched their own program called BUSINESSPLAN BUILDER for the UK market in April 1995. The plaintiffs did not market their product in the UK, however, they successfully applied for an injunction restraining the defendants from marketing their software under the name

---

63. The London department store 'Harrods' is reported to have been granted an injunction by the English High Court ordering 'domain-name-highjackers' to return certain domain names to the store?

64. A lengthy discussion of passing off is beyond the scope of this book. The reader is referred to Drysdale & Silverleaf, *Passing Off - Law and Practice*, 2nd Ed (Butterworths, 1995).

65. Any similarity in the contents of the packages is not relevant to the issue of passing off. In *United Biscuits Ltd v Irish Biscuits Ltd* [1971] IR 16, Kenny J stated that because the parties' biscuits were sold in packages, the characteristics of the biscuits were irrelevant.

66. [1995] FSR 924.

BUSINESSPLAN BUILDER. There were two issues in the case. First, whether the plaintiff had goodwill in the UK and secondly whether BIZPLAN BUILDER was an entirely descriptive term. Knox J came to the conclusion that although the plaintiffs had only a very few small number of customers within the UK, it was not so small that the plaintiffs could not be said to have any goodwill there. He did not accept that BIZPLAN BUILDER was exclusively descriptive, particularly as the capital P in the middle of the word BIZPLAN was not descriptive, although he did find that it had a strong descriptive content. He found a further two factors which were likely to lead to confusion and misrepresentation. First, there was significant trade evidence of the probability of confusion and secondly, the fact that the two names have identical meaning.

[8.23] In *Muckross Park Hotel v Randles*[67] the plaintiffs had acquired 'The Muckross Hotel' in 1990, and changed the name to 'The Muckross Park Hotel'. In 1992 the defendants built a hotel which was to be known as 'The Muckross Court Hotel'. It was established that the similarities between these two names had caused considerable confusion. Barron J, in finding for the plaintiffs, held that passing off occurs when it is established that persons are likely to be deceived. It is not necessary that an actual instance of deception should be established. The decision as to whether people are likely to be deceived is a matter entirely for the individual court. It is submitted that these principles would apply to a case where one party's electronic address or domain name (such as rolex.com) was causing confusion with that of another.

[8.24] This decision was applied in *An Post v Irish Permanent plc.*[68] That case concerned saving certificates which were marketed by the plaintiffs for 65 years. However, in 1994 the defendant started marketing its own saving certificates. Kinlen J stated that "the action of passing off has evolved so that it is no longer restricted to a trader representing his own goods as the goods of somebody else". He applied the judgment of the House of Lords in *Warnink v Townend*[69] to the effect that the tort of passing off extends to the deceptive use of a descriptive term in order to protect the goodwill in the descriptive term enjoyed by those entitled to use it.

---

[67]. [1995] 1 IR 130.
[68]. [1995] 1 IR 140.
[69]. *Warnink BV v J Townend & Sons (Hull)* [1979] 2 All ER 927; [1979] AC 731.

DIGITAL SIGNATURES

[8.25] The development of digital works which may be programs, pictures, music or films has created a new challenge for copyright holders. Once a work is digitized, it is easily copied and distributed over the Internet or on some storage medium such as a CD-ROM. Others may claim the work as their own and charge third parties for copies of it. To combat this, various methods have been developed of installing digital signatures or identifiers in digital works. One method developed under the auspices of the European Information Technology for Information Science (EURITIS) initiative of the European Commission is the Copyright in Transmitted Electronic Documents (CITED). The object of this project is to research a mechanism for copyright protection in a digital environment and to monitor the use of copyrighted material. CITED software tries to produce an integrated package to protect all aspects of a copyright in a work. It includes billing, auditing, licensing and identification functions. A work containing CITED (a CITEDised) work cannot be displayed until it finds itself in a trusted environment. The work is encrypted and it will not respond to a user unless he provides personal identification or satisfies other requirements which may be defined by the sender. The system allows the rightholder to control the access to and use of their works. However, once a work is opened the system cannot control its further use. To deal with this problem the system has to include an invisible yet retrievable label. This is a digital fingerprint.

[8.26] Digital fingerprints may be based on mathematical formulae that subtly alter every part of a digital work. This will not interfere with the legitimate use of the work but the fingerprint will be distributed throughout every part of the work as subliminal noise which can never be fully eliminated from the work. These fingerprint systems will mark an image as the property of the copyright holder and they enable the distribution of the work to be tracked. Systems in use today can survive any data compressions, format conversions and even conversion to print form. Ultimately, it is intended that these systems will allow the automatic charging of fees for using digital works by sending signals over the Internet.[70]

[70.] Chudy, 'Handcuff Digital Thieves', BYTE, April 1996.

Chapter 9

Trade Secrets and Confidential Information

[9.01] It is well established that facts and ideas cannot be protected by copyright. Although protection is available under the Patents Act for inventions, computer programs as such cannot be the subject of a patent.[1] If a person has a new idea which might be included into a program or another part of a computer system, then he may fear that his idea will not be protected by intellectual property law. In this situation, he may wish to treat his idea as a trade secret or confidential information.[2]

[9.02] In *The Gates Rubber Co v Brando Chemical Industries Ltd*,[3] the plaintiff developed a computer program which allowed a salesman who entered a number of values to calculate the size of rubber belts needed for a particular machine. The defendant hired a former employee of the plaintiff to write a similar program for it. The programmer used the plaintiff's program code and data to write this program. The US Tenth Circuit Court of Appeal found that the data used in the program could not be protected by copyright but could be protected as a trade secret.

EQUITABLE PROTECTION OF TRADE SECRETS & CONFIDENTIAL INFORMATION

[9.03] Equity will protect confidential information. In the words of Lord Denning:

> "The law on this subject ... depends on the broad principle of equity that he who has received information in confidence shall not take unfair advantage of it. He must not make use of it to the prejudice of him who gave it without obtaining his consent."[4]

[1.] PA 1992, s 9(2).

[2.] It is impossible to define a trade secret. "Secret processes of manufacture provide obvious examples, but innumerable other pieces of information are capable of being trade secrets, though the secrecy of some information may only be short lived": *Faccenda Chicken v Fowler* [1987] Ch 117.

[3.] 28 USPQ 2d 1503, 10th Circuit 1993.

[4.] *Seager v Copydex Ltd* [1967] 2 All ER 4153; [1969] 2 All ER 718 which was quoted with approval by Costello J in *House of Spring Gardens v Point Blank Ltd & Ors* [1984] IR 611, at 661.

This protection will be given independently of any rights arising under a contract or a statute such as the Copyright Act 1963. It will be given to all forms of confidential information and not just commercial information.[5] The Law Reform Commission has recommended that 'property' should be defined to include confidential information for the purposes of the criminal law on dishonesty. This would protect confidential information by making it a crime to steal it.[6]

[9.04] The leading case in Ireland is *The House of Spring Gardens v Point Blank Ltd and others*.[7] The plaintiff had given the defendants confidential information regarding the design of a bullet proof vest. The defendants used this information in the production of their own bullet proof vests without paying the plaintiff royalties. In his judgment (which was upheld by the Supreme Court) Costello J stated that where:

> "the court's equitable jurisdiction is invoked in relation to the law of confidence, the court ... is being asked to enforce what is essentially a moral obligation."[8]

The court must first decide whether there exists an obligation of confidence between the parties with regard to any information which has been imparted and the court must then decide whether this information is confidential. In considering both these points, the court may regard as relevant the degree of skill, time and labour involved in compiling the information. With regard to the relationship, if the informant has expended skill, time and labour in compiling the information, then he can reasonably regard it as being valuable and he can reasonably consider that he is conferring on his recipient a benefit. If this benefit is conferred for a specific purpose then an obligation may be imposed to use it for that purpose and for no other purpose. With regard to the nature of the information, if it has been compiled through skill time and labour, then the information may be regarded as confidential even if it has been obtained from public sources.[9] In the *House of Spring Gardens* case Costello J found that there was an obligation of confidence on the

---

5. For example, the courts will treat information which has been imparted in a marital relationship as confidential: *Argyll v Argyll* [1967] Ch 302.
6. Law Reform Commission Report on Dishonesty, LRC 43/1992, p 181.
7. [1984] IR 611. For facts, see para **[4.14]** *et seq.*
8. On this point, McCarthy J stated in the High Court that: "I would venture the view that an obligation of secrecy whilst enforced by equitable principles, depends more upon commercial necessity than moral duty".
9. The plaintiff had lodged an application with the Patents Office. This required that the plaintiff publish details of the designs. See also *Schering Chemicals Ltd v Falkman Ltd* (1982) QB 1 which took the view that a secret could remain a secret even if published to all the world.

defendants and that the information relating to the design of the bullet proof vests was confidential.[10]

[9.05] If a party wishes to protect confidential information, it should stipulate this at the earliest possible stage. The obligation to protect this information should be explicitly stated in any contract and before opening any negotiations. This has benefits in many situations.[11] In *Data General Corporation v Grumman Systems Support Corporation*,[12] the plaintiff had created a program to help diagnose problems with computers manufactured by it. The plaintiff leased these programs to its customers, placing restrictions on its use and prohibiting its disclosure. The plaintiff's employees had to sign non-disclosure agreements and those who left the company were reminded of their obligations to maintain the plaintiff's confidences. The defendants acquired copies of the program from customers of the plaintiff and ex-employees. They then used these copies to diagnose problems on Data General computers belonging to its customers. The plaintiffs successfully sued the defendants and recovered $78 million in damages for both infringement of copyright and trade secrets.

[9.06] Obviously, any contractual obligation will not be directly binding on any third party. However, equity may protect confidential information in this situation. In *Prince Albert v Strange*,[13] the plaintiff was given an injunction restraining the publication of a catalogue containing unpublished etchings which had been made by himself and Queen Victoria. There was no contract between the plaintiff and the defendant.[14]

THE RIGHTS OF THE PREVIOUS EMPLOYER

[9.07] Companies which employ programmers and engineers will obviously want to prevent those engineers and programmers from leaving their

---

[10.] In the judgment of the Supreme Court, O'Higgins CJ stated that he agreed entirely with Costello J's view of the law of confidence.

[11.] For a discussion on remedies for breach of confidence, see Capper, 'Damages for breach of the equitable duty of confidence', Legal Studies, Vol 14, No 3, November 1994, p 313. For a detailed treatment of this subject see Lavery, *Commercial Secrets - The Action for Breach of Confidence in Ireland*, (Round Hall Sweet & Maxwell, 1996).

[12.] D Mass 1993, 28 USPQ 2d 1481.

[13.] (1849) 1 H & Tw 1.

[14.] See also *Seager v Copydex Ltd* [1967] 2 All ER 4153; [1969] 2 All ER 718. It is even possible that the duty of confidence will extend to a passer-by who picks up a confidential document or a private diary, see the judgment of Geoff LJ in *Attorney General v Guardian Newspapers Ltd (No 2)* [1990] 1 AC 109 (the 'Spycatcher' case). See also Wei, 'Surreptitious takings of confidential information', Legal Studies, Vol 12, No 3, November 1992, p 302.

company with any of their confidential information. Restraint of trade clauses in employment contracts may allow the company to do this. However, the application of such clauses is limited. Costello J stated in *Orr Ltd v Orr*:[15]

> "All restraints of trade in the absence of special justifying circumstances are contrary to public policy and are therefore void. A restraint may be justified if it is reasonable in the interests of the contracting parties and in the interests of the public. The onus of showing that a restraint is reasonable as between the parties rests on the person alleging that it is so ... A covenant by an employee not to compete may ... be valid and enforceable if it is reasonably necessary to protect some proprietary interest of the covenantee such as may exist in a trade connection or trade secrets. The courts may in some circumstances enforce a covenant in restraint of trade even though taken as whole the covenant exceeds what is reasonable, by the severance of the void parts from the valid parts."[16]

A restraint of trade clause cannot be used to prevent an ex-employee from using his training which may have been supplied by the previous employer to compete with that employer. In *Faccenda Chicken Ltd v Fowler*,[17] the defendants, who had been employed by the plaintiff, could not be prevented from using the names, addresses and delivery routes of the plaintiff's customers to compete with the plaintiff. At trial, Goulden J divided information into three categories. First, there is information which because it is trivial or easily accessible cannot be confidential. Secondly, there is confidential information which becomes part of the employee's knowledge and skill. The employer may protect this type of information by inserting an express restraint of trade clause into the employee's contract of employment. However, the clause must be reasonable, particularly with regard to the geographical area which it covers and the length of time which it lasts.[18] Finally, there are specific trade secrets which are so confidential that they cannot be used by the employee upon termination of employment.

THE OBLIGATIONS OF THE NEW EMPLOYER

[9.08] The computer industry in part owes its current success to the ability of some employees to leave one company and to set up another.[19]

---

15. [1987] ILRM 702.
16. *Ibid*, at 704.
17. [1987] Ch 117.
18. *ECI v Bell* [1981] ILRM 345. *Skerry & Ors v Moles* (1907) 42 ILTR 46.
19. For example, Compaq computers, the first company to manufacture clones of the IBM PC was set up by three ex-employees of Texas Instruments. See Cringely, *Accidental Empires*, (Viking, 1992).

Programmers, engineers and other personnel frequently move between computer companies. When they move they carry with them their own expertise and often quite detailed information about their employer's products. Sometimes they bring more than this. In *Computer Associates International Inc v Altai Inc*,[20] the plaintiff had employed a programmer, Arney for five years before he left to join Altai, a rival firm. When he left, he took with him a copy of the source code for one of Computer Associate's programs. At Altai he worked on a project to develop a program to compete with that of Computer Associates and he used the stolen source codes to do so without Altai's knowledge. It was only when they were sued for breach of copyright that Altai discovered the copying. They were forced to remove Arney from the project and programmers unfamiliar with the Computer Associate's program were assigned to write a new version.

[9.09] Sometimes companies may deliberately set out to recruit personnel from other companies so that they may benefit from their expertise and knowledge of their old employer's products. In *Telex Corp v International Business Machines Corp*[21] Telex had recruited IBM employees so that they could help Telex to manufacture equipment based on secret IBM information. This was found to be an abuse of IBM's confidentiality. In general, companies should be very wary of recruiting personnel from their competitors. In *House of Spring Gardens v Point Blank Ltd*, Costello J adopted a test developed by Willmer LJ in *LB Plastic v Swish*[22] to aid the identification of copying which infringed the Copyright Act 1963. This test required that there must be objective similarity between the copy and the original and a causal connection between the two. If a company recruits programmers from a rival it will be establishing this causal connection. If the new program has any substantial similarities with the original then the company may expect its rival to make full use of this connection in court. This is what happened in *Computer Associates v Altai* and this forced Altai to go to the expense of rewriting its program.

[9.10] Merely waiting until the expiration of any restrictive covenants will not be enough to protect an employer from any claims of breach of copyright. In *Ibcos Computers Ltd v Barclays Mercantile Highland Finance Ltd*,[23] Mr Poole was employed as a computer programmer by the plaintiff to

---

[20.] 982 F 2d 693 (1992) and 775 F Supp 544 (1991).
[21.] 510 F 2d 894, 10th Circuit 1975 discussed by Tunick, 'Legal advice for a company hiring computer programmers from another company', Rutgers Computer & Technology Law Journal, Vol 19, 1993, p 405.
[22.] [1977] FSR 87.
[23.] [1994] FSR 275.

write a program for use by agricultural dealers. He signed a restrictive covenant which prevented him from being employed by a competitor of the plaintiff for two years after he ceased employment. After he ceased employment, he wrote a similar program in his spare time. When the two years had expired he offered this program to the defendant. The plaintiff sued alleging breach of his contract of employment and breach of copyright. It was held that the restrictive covenant would not have prevented him from writing this program. However, this fact and the fact that he had waited the two years before marketing the program did not prevent the court from finding that there had been breach of copyright.

THE POSITION OF THE EMPLOYEE

[9.11] The South African case of *Northern Office Microcomputer Ltd v Rosenstein*,[24] concerned a computer programmer who developed a program similar to a program which he had developed for his previous employer. It was held that programs could be protected by the law of confidence but that the protection would be limited. The programmer would not be required to wipe clean the slate of his memory as this would restrict the use of his skill, training and experience. However, he could not be permitted to simply plagiarise his previous work.

[9.12] The right of the ex-employer to enforce his contract with the employee will have to be balanced with the ex-employee's personal right to earn a livelihood under Article 40.3.1° of the Constitution.[25] This right however is qualified and has been unsuccessfully invoked to try to permit underage children to sing[26] and to let dockers past retiring age continue to work.[27] This right may also be a property right capable of being commercially used under Article 40.3.2°.[28]

---

24. [1982] FSR 124.
25. The right to earn a livelihood was recognised in *Murtagh Properties v Cleary* [1972] IR 330 and *Murphy v Stewart* [1973] IR 97. See Hogan & Whyte, *Kelly: The Irish Constitution*, (3rd ed, 1994) p 761.
26. *Landers v The Attorney General* (1975) 109 ILTR 1.
27. *Rodgers v ITGWU* [1978] ILRM 51.
28. *Caffolla v O'Malley* [1985] IR 48; [1986] ILRM 177.

Chapter 10

Protection of Semiconductor Chips

INTRODUCTION

[10.01] Semiconductor chips have replaced the transistors and valves that were once used in computers, radios and other electrical goods. These chips have allowed computers to become increasingly smaller even as their processing capabilities have increased dramatically. They are made of wafers cut from a crystal of pure silicon or another semiconducting material such as germanium or gallium arsenide. The wafer is treated by heating it and coating it with silicon dioxide an insulator. Then a minute electrical circuit is etched onto the wafer. This circuit or topography is crucial to the performance and efficiency of the chip.

[10.02] The market for semiconductor chips is huge. There are approximately 200 billion semiconductor chips in use in the world at present and they control everything from airplanes to musical greeting cards.[1] In view of this, it is not surprising that special protection for their designs has be introduced.

[10.03] The Semiconductor Regulations of 1988[2] implement the Council Directive on the Legal Protection of Topographies of Semiconductor Products.[3] The Directive recognised that the increasing role of semiconductors in a broad range of industries had caused semiconductors to become of fundamental importance for the Community's industrial development.[4] Different levels of protection between EU Member States threatened to have negative effects on the market for semiconductors.[5]

[1.] *The Economist*, 23 March 1996. The average house has 50 such chips in everything from the toaster to the washing machine. Chips now make up around 15% of the world's equipment market. They are also very profitable with profit margins for Taiwanese chip manufacturers estimated at 60% in 1995. The memory chip manufacturing industry made profits of nearly $30 billion on sales of $55 billion that year. However, the semiconductor chip industry can be very risky, a chip manufacturing plant could cost well over $1 billion. Chip manufacturers invested $30 billion on new capacity in 1995, $3 billion of this was invested by Intel alone.

[2.] European Communities (Protection of Topographies of Semiconductor Products) Regulation 1988 (SI 101/1988).

[3.] Council Directive 87/54 of 16 December 1986.

[4.] Recital 1 of the Directive.

[5.] Recital 4.

127

However, the main inspiration for the Directive was the US Semiconductor Chip Protection Act 1984. This created a *sui generis* property right which would last for ten years. Under reciprocity provisions, only those chip manufacturers whose countries offered equivalent protection to US chips could receive protection in the USA. Therefore failure to agree to the Semiconductor Directive would have left European manufacturers of semiconductors without protection in the USA.

DEFINITIONS

[10.04] The Regulations offer no definition of a semiconductor chip. They define a topography but only as a 'a topography of a semiconductor product'.[6] 'Semiconductor products' and 'the topography of a semiconductor product'' are defined by the Directive. These specifically apply to the Regulations under Regulation 2(2) which states that a word or expression which is used in the regulations and is also used in the Council Directive will have the same meaning that it has in the Directive unless the contrary appears.

[10.05] 'Semiconductor product' means the:

final or an intermediate form of any product consisting of a body of material which includes a layer of semiconducting material and having one or more other layers composed of conducting, insulating or semiconducting material, the layers being arranged in accordance with a predetermined three dimensional pattern; and intended to perform, exclusively or together with other functions, an electronic function.[7]

A 'topography' of a semiconductor product means:

a series of related images, however fixed or encoded:

(i) representing the three dimensional pattern of the layers of which a semiconductor product is composed; and

(ii) in which series, each image has the pattern or part of the pattern of a surface of the semiconductor product at any stage of its manufacture;[8]

THE BENEFITS OF THE TOPOGRAPHY RIGHT

[10.06] The owner of the topography has the right to authorise or prohibit:

(i) the reproduction of a topography; or

---

6. Regulation 2.
7. Article 1(1)(a) of the Directive.
8. Article 1(1)(b) of the Directive.

(ii) the commercial exploitation or the importation for that purpose of a topography or of a semiconductor product manufactured by using the topography.[9]

However, this latter right will not apply after the topography or the semiconductor product has been put on the market in a Member State by the person entitled to authorise its marketing or with his consent[10] (This is known as the Exhaustion Doctrine[11]).

[10.07] In spite of the existence of the above rights, any person may reproduce a topography privately for non-commercial purposes or reproduce a topography for the purpose of analysis or evaluation or teaching of the concepts, processes, systems or techniques embodied in a topography.[12]

[10.08] It is not an infringement to reproduce or market a topography which is created on the basis of an analysis and evaluation of another topography. This allows reverse engineering which makes it possible for semiconductor manufacturers to analyse one another's products with a view to creating their own chips. The new topography must however, satisfy the requirements of Regulation 3(1), ie, it must be original and not commonplace in the semiconductor industry.[13]

[10.09] To what extent this right to reverse engineer another's chip can be relied on in court is open to question. The Regulations and the Council Directive apply without prejudice to any other protection conferred by the Patents or Copyright Acts.[14] It would appear that reproducing circuitry may infringe against copyright as there is no similar exception in copyright law. Electronic circuits were found to be the subject of copyright protection as both literary and artistic works in *Anacon Corporation Ltd v Environmental Research Technology Ltd*.[15] The plaintiff claimed that the defendant had infringed copyright in three classes of work which related to an electronic dust meter. These were a computer program, engineering drawings and circuit diagrams. The Court was satisfied that the plaintiff's claim was good as regards the copyright in the software and the drawings. However, the court also had to decide whether the defendant had infringed the plaintiff's

---

9. Regulation 4(1).
10. Regulation 4(4).
11. Discussed at para **[12.34]**.
12. Regulation 4(2).
13. Regulation 4(3).
14. Regulation 8 as amended by European Communities (Protection of Topographies of Semiconductor Products) Regulation 1993 (SI 310/1993).
15. [1994] FSR 659.

copyright in its circuit diagrams by making a net list and circuit boards from the plaintiff's circuit boards. Jacob J was satisfied that the creation of the plaintiff's circuit diagram had involved sufficient original work to create a copyright work. He found as fact that the defendant had taken the plaintiff's circuit as laid out on a circuit board and had made at least a net list from it (a net list is a list of the electronic components of the circuit board with details of their interconnection). He was satisfied that the defendant's circuit board was made using information derived from the plaintiff's circuit diagrams. These circuit diagrams were artistic works. However, the alleged infringements had not reproduced a substantial part of the circuit diagram's artistic work. The essential nature of an artistic work was that it was something that was looked at. What matters is what is visually significant. The alleged infringements simply did not look like the artistic work. However, he found that the circuit diagrams were also literary works. So long as a work was written down and contained information which could be read as opposed to being appreciated with the eye, it was a literary work. In this case the diagram was held to be an original literary work because it was a compilation of written matter. When the defendant had made its net list, it had reproduced the information which was the literary work contained in the diagram. Thus it had infringed the plaintiff's copyright.

[10.10] The US Semiconductor Chip Act 1984 has a similar provision.[16] In *Brooktree Corporation v Advanced Micro Devices*[17] the plaintiffs alleged that the defendants had copied parts of their semiconductor chips. The defendants claimed that they had produced their own topographies through legitimate reverse engineering but the plaintiffs argued that the differences between the topographies "were very minor, trivial, insignificant". The defendants were found liable and damages of $25 million were awarded. The defendants appealed unsuccessfully. The American Federal Court applied the principles of copyright law and held that infringement under the US Semiconductor Chip Act 1984 does not require that every part of an

---

16. 17 USC s 11906(a) 1988 which provides: "it is not an infringement of the exclusive rights of the owner of a mask work for:
    (i) a person to reproduce the mask solely for the purposes of teaching analysing or evaluating the concepts or techniques embodied in the mask work or the circuitry, logic flow or organisation of components used in the mask work; or
    (ii) a person who performs the analysis or evaluation described in paragraph (i) to incorporate the results of such conduct in an original mask work which is made to be distributed."
17. *Brooktree Corporation v Advanced Micro Devices* 977 F 2d 1555. (Fed Cir 1992).

infringing chip be copied from another, the requirement was that of substantial similarity.[18]

[10.11] The infringement of a topography right is actionable at the suit of the owner of that topography right.[19] In an action for infringement, all reliefs such as damages, injunctions or accounts of profits are available to the owner as would be available in any other proceedings in respect of an infringement of other proprietary rights.[20] This regulation may prove problematic since in its published form, Regulation 6(2) states that the reliefs available to an applicant are subject to paragraph 4 of Regulation 6 but there is no paragraph 4 in Regulation 6.

[10.12] In an action for infringement of a topography right the owner will not be entitled to any relief other than damages if the infringement was committed by reproducing, importing, distributing or dealing in a topography or a semiconductor product, or incorporating an infringing topography and at the time of the acquisition of a topography or a semiconductor product incorporating an infringing topography, the defendant did not know and had no reasonable grounds to believe, that the topography or the semiconductor product was protected by law. If damages are awarded in these circumstances then they will be limited to an amount which, in the opinion of the court, would have been a reasonable royalty payment under a licence.[21] The right to protection conferred by the Regulations will apply to successors in title to the right.[22]

THE TOPOGRAPHY RIGHT

[10.13] Regulation 3(1) provides that a topography right will exist in favour of its creator where that topography is the result of the creator's own intellectual effort and it is not commonplace in the semiconductor industry. If such a topography consists of elements that are commonplace in the industry, then it may be protected by the Regulations. However, this protection will only apply to the extent that the combination of such elements taken as a whole are not commonplace in the industry.[23]

---

18. For a full discussion of this case see Sayadian, 'Substantial Similarity and Reverse Engineering Under the Semiconductor Chip Act', The Journal of Corporation Law, 1993, p 103.
19. Regulation 6(1).
20. Regulation 6(2).
21. Regulation 6(3).
22. Regulation 3(6).
23. Regulation 3(2).

[10.14] The Regulations restrict the application of protection to those who are EU nationals or employers. This restriction would appear to have been introduced for the purposes of bargaining with the USA since later Regulations have extended the protections to a host of countries including the USA.[24] This has now been extended to persons from a Member State of the World Trade Organisation.[25] Where a topography is created in the course of employment or pursuant to a contract other than a contract of employment, the topography right will apply in favour of the employer or the person who commissioned the topography unless the terms of the contract provide otherwise.[26] The right to protection will apply in favour of creators of topographies who are:

    (i) natural persons who are nationals of a Member State or who habitually reside in the territory of a Member State, or

    (ii) persons having a real and effective industrial or commercial establishment on the territory of a Member State.[27]

[10.15] The right to protection conferred by the Regulations also applies to those persons who:

    (a) first exploit commercially a topography in a Member State which has not yet been exploited anywhere in the world, and,

    (b) have been exclusively authorised to exploit commercially the topography throughout the territories of the Member States by the person entitled to dispose of the rights in that topography.[28]

The right to protection afforded by the Regulations has been extended by the European Communities (Protection of Topographies of Semiconductor Products) Regulation 1993.[29] Regulation 9 extends the protection to natural persons who are nationals of a country listed in the First Schedule[30] to the regulations or who have their habitual residence in the territory of one of

---

[24.] European Communities (Protection of Topographies and Semiconductor Products) Regulations 1993 (SI 310/1993).

[25.] Council Decision on extension of the legal protection of topographies of semiconductor products to persons from a member of the World Trade Organisation, 94/824 22 December 1994; OJ L 349/86. This decision has be implemented since 1 January 1996. The extension of the protection of the Regulation is now expressly subject to decisions of the Council, see para **[10.18]** below.

[26.] Regulation 3(4).

[27.] Regulation 3(3).

[28.] Regulation 3(5). For this to apply the person must also satisfy the criteria of Regulation 3(3).

[29.] SI 310/1993.

[30.] This lists countries such as Australia, Japan and Switzerland.

those countries. It also extends to companies and other legal persons in those countries.

[10.16] The right to protection will also extend to natural persons who are nationals of a country or territory listed in the Second Schedule[31] to the Regulations or who have their habitual residence in the territory of one of those countries or territories and companies and other legal persons of a country or territory listed in the Second Schedule which have a real and effective individual or commercial establishment in such a country or territory. This is subject to the condition that a country or other legal persons of a Member State which have a right to protection under the Council Directive benefit from the protection in the country or territory in question.[32]

[10.17] The protection of the Regulations also extends to individual persons who are nationals of the USA or who have habitual residence in the territory of the USA. This includes companies or other legal persons of the USA which have a real and effective industrial or commercial establishment in the USA subject to the condition that companies or other legal persons of a Member State which have a right to protection under the Council Directive benefit from protection in the USA.[33]

[10.18] The right to protection conferred by the Regulations will in future extend to natural persons, companies or other legal persons if future decisions of the Council of Europe provide for this.[34]

[10.19] The right to protection in a topography will commence either when the topography is first fixed or encoded or where the owner of the right owns it because he was the first to exploit the topography in the EU then the right will commence from the date of first commercial exploitation anywhere in the world.[35] The rights subsisting in a topography will come to an end 10 years from the end of the calendar year in which the topography is first commercially exploited anywhere in the world. If the right is not commercially exploited anywhere in the world then it will come to an end within a period of 15 years from its first fixation or encoding.[36]

[10.20] A semiconductor product manufactured using a protected topography may be marked with the letter T.[37]

[31.] This includes Hong Kong, Bermuda and the Channel Islands.
[32.] Regulation 9(a) and 9(b).
[33.] Regulation 9(c) and 9(d).
[34.] Regulations 12 and 13.
[35.] Regulation 5(1).
[36.] Regulation 5(2).
[37.] Regulation 7.

Chapter 11

Patents and Computer Programs

INTRODUCTION

[11.01] The patents systems can trace its roots directly back to medieval England.[1] In 1326 the English Crown began to award monopolies to individuals who imported new products or processes into England.[2] These monopolies were published by 'letters patent'. The passage of the Patent Law Amendment Act 1852 created the system which exists today. The Industrial and Commercial Property Act 1927 created the office of the Controller of Industrial and Commercial Property who is now known as the Controller of Patents, Designs and Trade Marks. His responsibilities include assessment of applications to register patents in Ireland.

[11.02] Once an invention is patented the owner will be able to prevent others from using this invention or can charge them for the privilege. Deciding whether or not to patent an invention is an important decision. Just because an invention is new does not mean that anyone will want to buy it. On the other hand failure to patent an invention which becomes popular can be very costly. In the 1980s, a researcher at IBM developed a new way of making computer chips but IBM failed to patent this new invention. It was subsequently adopted by Japanese manufacturers for whom it made considerable sums of money.[3]

THE PATENTS ACT 1992

[11.03] The Patents Act 1992 replaces the Patents Acts 1964 and Patents (Amendment) Act 1966. It also gives effect to the European Patents Convention. Chapter II of the Act sets out the requirements which must be met if an invention is to be patented. There is no definition of invention but it must be susceptible of industrial application, novel and involve an inventive step. Even if an invention overcomes these three hurdles it may still not receive a patent if it comes within the exceptions laid down by s 9.

---

1. One of the earliest patents dates back to the third century BC when a Greek city granted a patent for a recipe. See Stobbs, *Software Patents*, (Wylie, 1995).
2. The first application for a patent for something actually invented by the applicant was not made until 1559. See Stobbs, *ibid.*
3. Carroll, *Big Blues - the Unmaking of IBM*, (Weidenfeld & Nicolson, 1993).

Novelty

[11.04] An invention will not be considered new if it does not form part of the state of the art. The state of the art comprises everything made available to the public (whether in Ireland or abroad) by means of a written or oral description, by use or in any other way before the date of filing of the patent application. This means that an invention will not be new if it can be shown that it already existed elsewhere at the time of the application. If a separate patent application has already been filed and published prior to this application, then the invention will not be new.[4] A disclosure of the invention will not be taken into consideration if it occurred within six months of the application and was due to a breach of confidence or the unlawful obtaining of the invention or the display of the invention at an international exhibition.[5]

[11.05] A patent application must be published 18 months after it is applied for.[6] The date of filing of an application is the earliest date on which the applicant paid the filing fee and filed the necessary documentation.[7] A person who has duly filed an application within the State or within any other State which is party to the Paris Convention will enjoy a right of priority over later patent applications.[8]

Inventive Step

[11.06] An invention will be considered as involving an inventive step if having regard to the state of the art it is not obvious to a person skilled in the art. In *Valensi v British Radio Corporation Ltd*[9] this person was stated to be:

> "not a person of exceptional skill and knowledge ... he is not to be expected to exercise any invention nor any prolonged research, inquiry or experiment. He must, however, be prepared to display a reasonable degree of skill and common knowledge of the art in making trials and to correct obvious errors in the specification if a means of correcting them can readily be found."

If the state of the art includes documents which are part of another prior patent application, these documents will not be considered in deciding whether or not there has been an inventive step.[10]

---

4. PA 1992, s 11.
5. PA 1992, s 12.
6. PA 1992, s 28.
7. PA 1992, s 23.
8. PA 1992, s 25.
9. [1973] RPC 337.
10. PA 1992, s 13.

Industrial Application

[11.07] An invention will be considered as susceptible of industrial application if it can be made or used in any kind of industry including agriculture.[11] A method of surgery, therapy or diagnosis used on human or animals will not be regarded as an invention susceptible of industrial application. This exception does not apply to a product and in particular a substance or composition used in such methods.[12] The rationale is that the saving of human life is more important than rewarding the inventors of new medical techniques.

Exceptions

[11.08] Section 9 of the 1992 Act provides that an invention will not be patented if it falls within the following categories:

    (a) a discovery, a scientific theory or a mathematical method;

    (b) an aesthetic creation;

    (c) a scheme, rule or method for performing a mental act, playing a game or doing business or a program for a computer;

    (d) the presentation of information.[13]

The provisions of subs 9(2) "shall exclude patentability of subject-matter or activities referred to in that subsection only to the extent to which a patent application or patent relates to such subject matter or activities as such".[14] There are few areas of technology which do not make use of computers and a large number of inventions are associated with computer technology. Many items of computer hardware will certainly be the subject of patents. However, it may be possible to patent a computer program in certain circumstances.

PATENTING COMPUTER PROGRAMS IN THE EUROPEAN PATENT OFFICE

[11.09] There are obvious advantages to having a single patent system for the whole of Europe. The European Patent Convention led to the establishment of the European Patent Office (EPO) in Munich.[15] The signatories to the Convention include Austria, Belgium, Denmark, France, Greece, Ireland, Italy, Liechtenstein, Luxembourg, Monaco, the

---

11. PA 1992, s 14.
12. PA 1992, s 9(4).
13. PA 1992, s 9(2).
14. PA 1992, s 9(3).
15. The European Patent Convention, Munich, 5 October 1973.

Netherlands, Portugal, Spain, Switzerland and the United Kingdom. If an applicant wishes to patent an invention in three or more of these countries he can do so by making a single application to the EPO. This is cheaper and more efficient than making individual applications to each of the countries. However, if the EPO rejects an application it will automatically fail in all the Member States of the Convention. For this reason, applicants may prefer to make individual applications to each Member State.

[11.10] The Patents Act 1992 is intended to enable effect to be given to certain international conventions on patents.[16] One of these international conventions is the European Patent Convention. On several occasions the European Patent Office and its Boards of Appeal have examined the patentability of computer programs. The importance of these decisions should not be underestimated. In *Gale's Application* Nicholls LJ in the Court of Appeal stated that:

> "it is of the utmost importance that the interpretation given in section 1 of the Act by the courts in the UK and the interpretation given to Article 52 of the European Patent Convention by the European Patent Office should be the same. The intention of parliament was that there should be uniformity in this regard ... any substantial divergences would be disastrous."

Article 52(2) of the European Patent Convention states that discoveries, scientific theories and mathematical methods, aesthetic creations, schemes, rules and methods for performing mental acts, programs for computers and presentations of information cannot be regarded as inventions. This provision is replicated in s 9 of the Irish Patents Act 1992.[17]

[11.11] EPO guidelines have clarified the circumstances in which a computer program will be patentable. The guidelines state that the matter not to be regarded as an invention is either abstract (such as discoveries or scientific theories) or non-technical (such as aesthetic creations or presentations of information). For an invention to be patentable it must be of a concrete and technical character.[18] The guidelines recognise that a data processing operation can be implemented either by means of a computer program or by means of special circuits and that the choice may have nothing to do with the inventive concept but rather with factors of economy or practicality. This views computer programs as simply a means to an end. It is the technical end which is material in determining whether the subject

---

16. Preamble to the Act.
17. For a discussion of the procedure of the EPO see *European Patents Handbook*, (Longman, 1995). Also, see Paterson, *European Patents*, (Sweet and Maxwell, 1995).
18. Guideline C-IV, 2.1.

matter may be considered an invention under the European Patent Convention since the computer program may in any event be replaced with suitably arranged digital circuits. Therefore, if an invention makes a technical contribution to the known art it will not be refused a patent simply because it is implemented using a computer program.[19]

[11.12] In *Re VICOM*,[20] the application was for a method and apparatus for digitally processing data (which represented a stored image). The initial application was for a method of digitally filtering the data using mathematical operations. This application was refused by both the Examining Board and by the Board of Appeal. The refusal was based on the fact that the application was for a mathematical method. This did not have a technical result. However, the Board of Appeal did allow an amended claim for a method of digitally processing images in the form of data using the same mathematical operations. The Board of Appeal stated that the basic difference between a mathematical method and a technical process can be seen in the fact that a mathematical method is carried out on numbers and provides a result also in numerical form. No direct technical result is produced by the method as such. In contrast, if a mathematical method is used in a technical process, that process is carried out on a physical entity (which may be a material object but equally an image stored as an electric signal) by some technical means implementing the method and provides as its result a certain change in that entity. The technical means might include a computer comprising suitable hardware or an appropriately programmed general purpose computer. The Board concluded that even though the idea underlying such a technical process might reside in a mathematical method, a claim directed to a technical process in which the method was used did not claim a mathematical method as such. The claim in this form could be allowed.

[11.13] The Boards of Appeal of the EPO have refused applications for what were essentially word processing programs as in their view these processes could just as easily have been carried out by a person with a pencil and paper. The subject matter of the applications related to correcting errors, listing of semantically related linguistic expressions, spell checking, text processing and document retrieval.[21] The Boards held that these applications were essentially for methods of performing mental acts and were not

---

[19] Guideline C-IV, 2.3.
[20] Decision 208/84.
[21] *Correcting contextual errors re IBM,* T65/86, [1990] EPOR 181. *Listing of semantically related linguistic expressions re IBM* T52/85, [1989] EPOR 454. *Text processing re IBM* decision T38/86, OJ EPO 384. *Document Abstracting and Retrieving re IBM* T22/85.

inventions. In *Spell checking re IBM*,[22] the invention related to an 'automatic spelling checking and correction process for parsing the words of a text in a word processing system'. The Board of Appeal rejected the application on the basis that spell checking is basically of a linguistic and not technical character. A wrong spelling is detected by performing mental acts with no technical means involved. The Board distinguished this case from *VICOM* where a program controlled computer was used for processing data which represented physical entities in a technical process. In *Re IBM*, linguistic information was processed to obtain other linguistic information.

[11.14] In a recent case,[23] an application concerned the automatic generation of a computer program. The source code for this program would be generated once certain specifications were given. The Board of Appeal held that it was not patentable as it was not an invention. The rejection was based on the fact that computer programs are not patentable. The activity of a programmer writing a program is excluded because it is the performance of a mental act. In this case, the computer program generator merely imitated the activities of a human programmer and so was not patentable. Developing hardware devices to create programs will not necessarily make programming patentable.

[11.15] If a computer program is part of a technical process then an application for that process will not fail merely because a computer program is used. In *Kock & Sterzel GmbH*,[24] the application related to an x-ray apparatus which included a data processing unit, controlled by a computer program. Siemens and Philips filed oppositions to the claim on the basis that it involved a new program for a known computer. The Board of Appeal allowed the application, stating that the invention must be considered as a whole. If the subject matter of the application uses technical and non-technical means then the use of non-technical means will not detract from the technical character of the overall subject matter. The European Patent Convention does not require that a patentable invention be exclusively or largely of a technical nature.[25]

Patenting Computer Programs in the UK

[11.16] Section 1(2) of the UK Patents Act 1977 is identical to both Article 52(2) of the European Patents Convention and s 9 of the Irish Patents Act

---

22. T121/85.
23. T204/93.
24. T26/86.
25. See Hanneman 'Patentability of Computer Programs', *The Law of Information Technology in Europe 1992*, Kluwer, 1991 for a discussion of the patentabilty of software in Europe.

1992. The first case in which it was considered whether or not computer programs could be patented was *Merrill Lynch's Application*[26] which concerned a data processing system for trading markets. The application was rejected by the Court of Appeal which held that the words 'only to the extent that' and 'relates to that thing as such' (in the Irish Act this appears as 'relates to such subject matter or activities as such') should be read together as meaning that the matters listed in (a)-(d) in para **[11.08]** above shall not be an invention for the purpose of the Act. If that section did not apply they would have constituted inventions and they would only be disqualified to the extent that the patent application related to disqualified subject matter. In this case the Court of Appeal rejected the application for a patent not because it was a computer program but because the application was a claim to a method of doing business.

[11.17] This ruling was applied by the Court of Appeal in *Gale's Application*[27] which concerned an improved method of calculating the square root of a number with the aid of a computer. The applicant placed the necessary instructions into the circuitry of a read only memory (ROM) chip. Aldous J in the Patent Court stated:

> "that the fact that the inventive step is a program will not disqualify the invention from being patentable. It will be patentable, assuming it is novel and not obvious, provided that the invention as claimed is the practical application of the program in that it is claimed as applied in a technique or a process not itself disqualified or incorporated into a product."

He held that if the claim for a patent is drafted so that it relates to any of the disqualified subject matter then the invention will not be patentable. If, however, the claim is drafted to include a process or technique or product, the basis of which is disqualified, then the court must decide as fact whether the claimed invention is more than just a claim for a disqualified matter. If it is more, then the invention will be patentable. Aldous J held that the Patent Examiner was incorrect to equate a ROM chip with a floppy disk containing the same program. He stated that a ROM chip is more than just a carrier of a program. It is a manufactured article having circuit connections which enable the program to be operated.

[11.18] This approach was unanimously rejected by the Court of Appeal which applied the judgment of the European Patent Office, Board of Appeal in *Re IBM Text Processing Application*[28] which stated that:

[26.] [1988] RPC 1.
[27.] [1991] RPC 305.
[28.] T65/86 [1990] EPOR 181.

"since the only conceivable use for a computer program is the running of it on a computer, the exclusion from patentability of programs for computers would be effectively undermined if it could be circumvented by including in the claim a reference to conventional hardware features, such as a processor, memory, keyboard and display which in practice are indispensable if the program is to be used at all".

Nicholls LJ noted that the claim was for an algorithm which was not patentable as it was a mathematical method. However, the subject matter of the claim had a practical application which would allow instructions to be written for computers which would expedite calculations. In Nicholls LJ's view the application of the mathematical formulae for the purpose of writing computer instructions is sufficient to dispose of the contention that the applicant is claiming a mathematical method as such. However, he found that these instructions did not define a new way of operating the computer in any technical sense and were therefore not patentable. Browne-Wilkinson VC held that anything excluded from being an invention by s 1(2) of the 1977 Act could not qualify as being patentable by being incorporated in a product or process unless such product or process was either itself novel or produces a technical result which is novel. He further held that it was established that the incorporation of excluded matter in a product or process does not render it patentable if the only effect of such incorporation is to produce something which is itself an excluded matter.

[11.19] *Wang's Application*[29] concerned an expert system which allowed an expert to store his information in a computer system shell from which it could be accessed. The claim was for the computer system shell and the expert system. The applicant's claim failed in the Patents Office and was appealed to the Patents Court where the appeal was dismissed. Aldous J held that the claim relating to the 'computer system shell' was a claim for a computer program and nothing more. The computer remained separate even when programmed and did not combine with the program to form a new machine. The claim for the expert system was a claim for a scheme or method for performing a mental act using a computer program. This also was disallowed.

[11.20] In *Raytheon's Application*,[30] the applicant had developed an invention which could identify ships and other objects. The silhouette of an unknown ship could be matched with those of known ships. The claim for a patent related to an apparatus for and a method of digitally measuring and comparing images by a series of steps set out in the claim. The application

---

29. [1991] RPC 463.
30. [1993] RPC 427.

failed in the Patents Office as it was held to be a mental process and this decision was appealed to the Patents Court. The applicant suggested that performing a mental act was a conscious process, something deliberate that was done in the mind and that identifying or recognising a shape with the eye was not a mental process. Jeffs QC[31] rejected this submission holding that where the eye was the judge, the eye was the instrument which fed the mind. He also found that the words 'mental act' must be construed as they would be understood in ordinary language. This invention was no more than a scheme for performing a mental act. The process did no more than provide a briefing for a computer programmer to write a program that would enable conventional pieces of apparatus to perform a particular mental act. The invention was effectively a program for a computer and was not patentable.

[11.21] The law relating to the patentability of computer software was cogently analysed by Laddie J in *Fujitsu's Application.*[32] The applicant had developed software which would help a chemist to design new compounds. It allowed the user to depict images of the chemical structure of known chemical compounds on a computer screen. The images could then be rotated at will and their scale altered relative to each other, enabling the face of one crystal structure to be aligned with a complimentary face of another thereby creating on the screen the structure of a hybrid 'designer' chemical. The applicant did not claim to have created any new computer hardware, only to have produced software which might be used as a tool. Laddie J examined the case-law on this area, paying particular attention to the *VICOM* and *IBM* decisions of the European Patent Office's Technical Board of Appeal and the decisions of the English Court of Appeal in *Merrill Lynch's Application* and *Fujitsu's Application*. He came to the following conclusions:

1. The types of subject matter referred to in s 1(2) of the UK 1977 Act (s 9 of the Irish Patent Act 1992) and Article 52 of the European Patent Convention are excluded from patentability as a matter of policy. This is so whether the matter is technical or not.

2. The exclusion from patentability is a matter of substance not form. Therefore the exclusion under s 1(2) extends to any form of passive carrier or recording of excluded subject matter. Although a piece of paper is in principle patentable (but for the fact that it lacks novelty) it is not permissible to record a literary work or a computer program (which are both excluded from patentability under s 9) and then seek a patent for the paper bearing the

---

[31.] Sitting as a deputy judge.
[32.] [1996] RPC 511.

recorded work. Similarly, it will not be permissible, without more, to seek protection for a computer program when it is stored on a magnetic medium or when it is merely loaded onto a computer.

3. *Prima facie*, a computer running under the control of one program is a different piece of apparatus from the same computer when running under the control of another program. Therefore, a claim to a computer when controlled by a program or to a method of controlling a computer by a program or to a method of carrying out a process by use of a computer so controlled can be the subject of patent protection. However, because the court is concerned with substance not form, it is not enough for the designer of a new program to seek protection for his creation merely by framing it in one of these terms. The court must direct its attention not to the fact that the program is controlling the computer but to what the computer so controlled is doing.

4. It follows from the above that a data processing system operating to produce a novel result would not be deprived of protection on the ground that it was a program as such. On the other hand, even if the effect of the program is to make the computer perform in a novel way, it is still necessary to look at precisely what the computer is doing. This means looking at the nature of the process being carried out. If all that is being done is one of the activities defined as being unprotectable then it will not be protected by patent.

[11.22] Laddie J suggested that if it is possible to obtain a patent for a faster chip or a more effective storage medium or for a computer containing such a chip or storage medium there is no reason in principle or logic why a modification of the computer to achieve the same speed or storage capacity by means of software should be excluded from protection. He took the view that the fact that the advance is achieved by software rather than hardware should not affect patentability. To do so would be to "exalt form over substance". It would not matter whether a patent claim was drafted in terms of a process controlled by a computer, a computer when programmed in a particular way or a method of controlling a computer, in each case the substance of the invention would be the same.

[11.23] Laddie J rejected the application as it was a method for performing a mental act. The user of the Fujitsu program would have to select the data to work on, how to work on it, how to assess the results and what results to use. This is an abstract process with an undefined result. The result will not be the inevitable result of taking a number of defined steps but is determined by the personal skill and assessment of the operator.

MAKING AN APPLICATION FOR A PATENT IN IRELAND

[11.24] Any person may apply for a patent either alone or jointly with another.[33] The right to a patent belongs to the inventor or his successor in title. If two or more persons have made an invention independently of each other, the right to the patent for the invention will belong to the person whose patent application was filed first. However, this provision will only apply if the first application has been published.[34] The inventor has the right to be mentioned in the patent specifications and in any published patent application. The applicant must supply the Controller of Patents with the identity of the inventor. If the applicant is not the inventor then he must explain how he is entitled to file this application. If the applicant fails to do this, his application will be deemed to be withdrawn. Where a person has been mentioned as an inventor, any person who objects to this may complain to the Controller.[35]

[11.25] An Irish patent application must include a request for the grant of a patent, the specifications of the invention and abstract, the appropriate fee and must be filed in the Patents Office.[36] A patent application must disclose the invention sufficiently clearly and completely for the invention to be carried out by a person skilled in the art.[37] The applicant may request the Controller to conduct a search in relation to the invention which will disclose any patents granted to similar inventions.[38] If the applicant wishes to receive a short term patent,[39] then he need not have the search conducted.[40] The Controller may refuse or grant the patent.[41] Once a patent is granted, notice of the grant must be published in the Patents Office Journal.[42]

THE EFFECT OF A PATENT

[11.26] Patents are treated as personal property.[43] A patent will take effect on the date on which its grant is published in the Patents Office Journal and (subject ot the payment of fees) will continue in force for 20 years from the

---

33. PA 1992, s 15.
34. PA 1992, s 16. Alexander Graham Bell was fortunate to file his patent application for the telephone before Elisha Gray who lodged his application later on the same day.
35. PA 1992, s 17.
36. PA 1992, s 18.
37. PA 1992, s 19(1).
38. PA 1992, s 29.
39. This will only last ten years as opposed to 20 years for a full patent: PA 1992, s 63.
40. PA 1992, s 65.
41. PA 1992, s 31.
42. PA 1992, s 34.
43. PA 1992, s 79.

date of filing the application. If the appropriate fees are not paid then the patent will lapse.[44] A patent confers on its owner the right to prevent third parties from doing the following without his consent:

(1) making, offering, putting on the market or using a product which is the subject matter of the patent, or importing or stocking the product for those purposes;

(2) using a process which is the subject matter of the patent or when the third party knows or it is obvious to a reasonable person in the circumstances that the use of the process is prohibited without the consent of the proprietor of the patent, or offering the process for use in the State;

(3) offering, putting on the market, using or importing or stocking for those purposes the product obtained directly by a process which is the subject matter of the patent.[45]

A patent will also give its owner the right to prevent the supply of means for putting into effect an essential element of the invention which is the subject of the patent.[46] The rights conferred by the patent will not extend to acts done privately for non-commercial purposes or acts done for experimental purposes relating to the subject matter of the relevant patented invention. Neither will they extend to the preparation of medicines in emergencies or the use of items on foreign ships, planes and vehicles temporarily or accidentally within the territory of the State.[47]

[11.27] An action for infringement of a patent may be brought in the High Court by the owner where the Court may grant one of the following remedies:

(1) an injunction restraining the defendant from any apprehended act of such infringement;

(2) an order requiring the defendant to deliver up or destroy any product covered by the patent;

(3) an award of damages;

(4) an account of profits derived by the defendant from the alleged infringement;

(5) a declaration that the patent is valid and has been infringed by the defendant.

[44.] PA 1992, s 36.
[45.] PA 1992, s 40.
[46.] PA 1992, s 41.
[47.] PA 1992, s 42.

The Court cannot award an account of profits together with damages for the same infringement.[48] No award of damages or account of profits can be made where the defendant proves that at the date of infringement he was not aware and had no reasonable grounds for supposing that the patent existed. The defendant cannot be said to be aware of the existence of a patent merely because the words 'patent' or 'patented' appear on an article, unless the article also displays the number of the relevant patent.[49]

[11.28] Where any person is threatened with proceedings for infringement whether by circulars, advertisement or otherwise, they may apply to the High Court for relief. If the plaintiff is not infringing the patent, then he may get a declaration to the effect that the threats complained of are unjustifiable, an injunction against the continuance of threats, and damages. Notification of the existence of a patent does not constitute a threat of proceedings.[50] The Court also has the power to make a declaration that a person is not infringing a patent.[51]

[11.29] The Register of Patents is kept at the Patents Office. It contains particulars of published patent applications, patents in force, assignments, transmissions and licences for patents, and applications.[52]

[11.30] In order to prevent the proprietor of a patent from depriving society of useful inventions, any person may apply for a compulsory licence to the Controller. This may be done only after the expiration of three years since the publication of the grant of the patent or such other time as may be specified.[53] Patents may also be assigned to the State[54] and patents have the same effect against the State as they have against individuals.[55]

REVOCATION OF PATENTS

[11.31] Any person may apply to the High Court or the Controller of Patents for the revocation of a patent.[56] An application for revocation of a patent may only be made on the following grounds:

(1) the subject-matter of the patent is not patentable under the Act;

---

48. PA 1992, s 47.
49. PA 1992, s 49.
50. PA 1992, s 53.
51. PA 1992, s 54.
52. PA 1992, s 84.
53. PA 1992, s 70.
54. PA 1992, s 76.
55. PA 1992, s 77.
56. PA 1992, s 57.

(2) the specification of the patent does not disclose the invention in a manner sufficiently clear and complete for it to be carried out by a person skilled in the art;

(3) the matter disclosed in the specification of the patent extends beyond that disclosed in the application for the patent;

(4) the protection conferred by the patent has been extended by an amendment of the application or the specification of the patent;

(5) the proprietor of the patent is not entitled to the patent.[57]

The Controller also has the power to revoke patents on his own initiative if he feels that a patent has been granted for something which formed part of the state of the art. He must, however, give the proprietor of the patent an opportunity to make observations and of amending the patent specifications.[58] The Controller may also revoke patents on his own initiative where an applicant for a patent has duplicated his application.[59]

THE EUROPEAN PATENT CONVENTION AND THE PATENTS ACT 1992

[11.32] Applications for a European patent may be made through the Irish Patents Office provided the applications are in English.[60] Applications for a European patent which designates Ireland may be made in other countries which have implemented the Convention. These applications will be administered by the European Patents Office in Munich. A European patent which designates Ireland will be treated as if it were a patent under the Patents Act 1992 from the date of publication of the mention of its grant in the European Patent Bulletin. The proprietor of a European patent will have the same rights and remedies and will be subject to the same conditions as the proprietor of an Irish patent.[61] An application for a European patent which designates Ireland will have the same effect in most aspects as though the application was made under the Patents Act 1992.[62] The Minister for Enterprise and Employment may make regulations to implement the European Patent Convention and any other international treaty.[63]

[57.] PA 1992, s 58.
[58.] PA 1992, s 60(1).
[59.] PA 1992, s 60(2).
[60.] PA 1992, s 127.
[61.] PA 1992, s 119.
[62.] PA 1992, s 120.
[63.] PA 1992, s 128. See also European Patent Organisation (Designation and Immunities) Order (SI 392/1996).

Chapter 12

Competition Law

INTRODUCTION

[12.01] The computer industry has always been prone to control by one large corporation. Until recently, the entire computer industry was dominated by IBM. However, the PC software industry is now dominated by Microsoft, which has a 90% share of the operating systems market for desktop PCs and a 90% share of the market for software 'suites' of word processor spreadsheets and databases. Microsoft holds 42% of the total world market for PC software.[1] It enjoys gross margins of approximately 85% on its products with an annual turnover of approximately $8 billion.[2] Other examples of dominant computer companies are Intuit which provides personal finance software, Intel and Cisco, which dominates the market for Internet routers.[3] The reason why the computer industry is prone to such dominance is because the standards in the industry are usually set by the dominant company, for example employers will want to use the word processing program which is most familiar to their employees. Furthermore, the developing economic theory of 'increased returns' suggests that such control may be inevitable in markets for high technology goods.[4]

[12.02] In view of such dominance it is not surprising that governments and competitors have believed that the computer industry is being controlled by the dominant company for its own, anti-competitive, ends. IBM was the defendant in a host of anti-trust actions in the USA in the 1970s.[5] Abuse of a

---

[1.] *The Economist*, 21 October 1995. Although, IBM remains the world's largest hardware company: *The Economist*, 13 December 1996.

[2.] *The Economist*, May 25 1996.

[3.] *The Economist*, 21 December 1996.

[4.] Arthur, 'Increasing Returns and the New World of Business', Harvard Business Review, July-August 1996, p 100. The traditional doctrine of 'diminishing returns' suggests that as a business expands it will eventually reach a point where its costs rise and so it loses its competitive advantage. Arthur suggests that in 'knowledge based' industries such as software this point is not reached by successful companies. This view has been questioned, see *The Economist*, 28 September 1996.

[5.] *Telex Corp v IBM Corp* 510 F 2d 894 (10th Cir 1975); *ILC Peripherals Leasing Corp v IBM Corp* 458 F Supp 423 (ND Cal 1978); *In re IBM EDP Devices Antitrust Litigation* 481 F Supp 965 (ND Cal 1979); *Greyhound Computer Corporation v IBM Corporation* 559 F 2d 488 (9th Cir 1978). Antitrust issues in the USA are discussed by Iannaccone and Volonino, 'Marginal Cost and Relevant Market Determination in Information Technology Antitrust Cases', Rutgers Computer and Technology Law Journal, Vol 18, 1992, p 681.

dominant position is prohibited by Article 86 of the Treaty of Rome which provides that:

> Any abuse by one or more undertakings of a dominant position within the common market or in a substantial part of it shall be prohibited as incompatible with the common market in so far as it may affect trade between Member States. Such abuse may, in particular, consist in:
>
> (a) directly or indirectly imposing unfair purchase or selling prices or other unfair trading conditions;
>
> (b) limiting production, markets or technical development to the prejudice of consumers;
>
> (c) applying dissimilar conditions to equivalent transactions with other trading parties, thereby placing them at a competitive disadvantage;
>
> (d) making the conclusion of contracts subject to acceptance by the other parties of supplementary obligations which, by their nature or according to commercial usage, have no connection with the subject of such contracts.

[12.03] The European Commission also instituted proceedings against IBM for anti-competitive practices.[6] They concerned the allegation that IBM held a dominant position in the EEC for the supply of the central processing unit (CPU) and the operating system of the System/370. It was alleged that IBM was using this position to control the markets for the supply of all products compatible with their system.[7] IBM was alleged to have abused its position in the following ways:

(i) by failing to supply other manufacturers in sufficient time with the technical information needed to permit competitive products to be used with System/370, (known as interface information);

(ii) by not offering System/370 CPUs without a main memory installed;

(iii) by not offering System/370 CPUs without the basic software included in the price; and

(iv) by discriminating between users of IBM software by refusing to supply certain software installation services to users of non-IBM CPUs.

---

6. Competition in the European Union is regulated by Article 85 of the Treaty of Rome.
7. It was the failure of IBM to retain this control over the CPU (which is now controlled by Intel) and the operating system (which is controlled by Microsoft) in the PC which allowed the current industry to develop and ultimately led to the decline of IBM.

[12.04] IBM did not admit the existence of a dominant position nor did it admit that it was abusing its position. However, it did undertake to offer its System/370 CPUs for sale without memory and to disclose sufficient interface information to allow other manufacturers to produce products which would work with the System/370.[8] The Commission monitored the activities of IBM to ensure that it complied with its undertaking. In total, there were 212 requests for disclosure of technical information from 23 competitors containing 1565 questions. Seven of these companies received information under technical information disclosure agreements. Three companies signed a subcontractor confidential disclosure agreement. The Commission was satisfied that IBM was complying with its undertaking. In July 1994, IBM exercised its right to terminate the undertaking. Since 6 July 1995 IBM has no longer been bound by it.[9]

[12.05] IBM was also the subject of a complaint by Phoenix International Computers Ltd in 1992. According to the complaint, IBM had unlawfully refused to cover, under the standard maintenance contracts concluded with its customers, a reworked memory card marketed by Phoenix on the pretence that they infringed the IBM trade mark.[10] The memory cards which were sold by Phoenix as original IBM products had been modified by third parties so as to increase their memory capacity with IBM's prior agreement. IBM had no control over this practice but it was alleged that IBM had for years turned a blind eye to it. The Commission rejected the request due to a lack of *prima facie* evidence.[11]

[12.06] On 30 June 1993 the Commission received a complaint from Novell, one of the world's largest PC software companies. This complaint concerned the licensing practices of Microsoft which was alleged to be using anti-competitive practices to block competitors out of the market for PC operating systems software. The structure of Microsoft's standard agreements for licensing software to PC manufacturers was said to exclude competition contrary to Article 86 of the Treaty of Rome. The Commission was particularly concerned with the following issues:

    (1) The use of 'per processor' and 'per system' licences which are licences requiring the payment of a royalty on every computer produced by a PC manufacturer either containing a particular processor or belonging to a particular model series designated by

---

8. The Fourteenth Commission Report on Competition Policy 1985.
9. The Twenty Fourth Commission Report on Competition Policy 1994.
10. IBM sued Phoenix in the English Courts for infringement of its trade marks: *IBM v Phoenix* [1994] RPC 251.
11. The Twenty Second Commission Report on Competition Policy 1992.

that manufacturer regardless of whether a particular computer is shipped with reinstalled Microsoft software.

(2) The use of 'minimum commitments' in these contracts which forced the licensees to pay a minimum royalty regardless of their actual use of Microsoft products.

(3) The duration of Microsoft's licence agreements.

[12.07] The Commission felt that as a result of these activities, the European market for PC operating systems software was being foreclosed. Just before the Commission was about to issue a statement of objection, Microsoft indicated its willingness to reach a settlement. As a result, an undertaking was given by Microsoft to the Commission which provided firstly, that Microsoft would not enter into licence contracts with a duration of more than one year. Secondly, Microsoft agreed not to use per processor type licences in future. Thirdly, per system licences would be allowed only if licensees were clearly given the freedom to purchase non-Microsoft products and to avoid payment of royalties in such cases. Finally, Microsoft agreed that it would not enforce existing licence contracts which breach these provisions and licensees have an option to end any existing contracts of these types. The undertaking will last for six and a half years. The Commission hoped that the undertaking would open up the market for operating systems software but there is no evidence that this has occurred as yet.[12]

[12.08] These negotiations with Microsoft were conducted in parallel with the US Department of Justice. The Federal Trade Commission began investigating Microsoft in 1990. Four years later on 15 July 1994 the Federal Justice Department filed a complaint against Microsoft which alleged that:

(1) Microsoft had a monopoly on the market for PC operating systems.

(2) Rather than licence directly to computer users, Microsoft licensed its operating systems to original equipment manufacturers for inclusion in the PCs that they make.

(3) Microsoft's use of per processor licences and its use of long term licensing agreements amounted to "exclusionary and anti-competitive contract terms to maintain its monopoly".

(4) Microsoft's non-disclosure agreements with independent software developers for information concerning the development of Microsoft's new Windows operating system, Windows 95,

---

[12.] The Twenty Fourth Commission Report on Competition Policy 1994.

were overly restrictive and anti-competitive as they discouraged independent software developers from developing competing operating systems.

Microsoft entered a consent to a decree which was agreed with the Department of Justice and which was identical to the undertaking given to the Commission. However, the judge hearing the case refused to approve the decree on the basis that it was not in the public interest and it did not include an admission that Microsoft had engaged in anti-competitive practices.[13] Microsoft and the Department of Justice appealed this decision and it was reversed.[14] Although Microsoft undoubtedly dominates the software industry, nobody has been able to prove that this is due to anti-competitive practices.

[12.09] More recently, the European Commission has opened an inquiry under Article 85 of the Treaty of Rome into the planned alliance between the US company America Online, a German publisher Bertelsmann and Deutsche Telecom. The intention of this alliance is to provide European computer users with e-mail and other material.[15] The Commission has also investigated another provider of on-line services, Europe Online. The Commission's concern is that these alliances will prevent others from accessing the libraries and material of some of the participants. The Europe On-line venture involved four of Europe's largest publishing groups including Germany's Axel Springer and the Pearson Group. The Commission sought two assurances: firstly that the publishing companies would make their material available to other on-line services at reasonable rates; and secondly, that they would treat competing content providers fairly if they should seek to use the network. As a result of these requirements several of the participants pulled out of the venture.[16]

COMPUTERISED RESERVATION SYSTEMS

[12.10] Computerised reservation systems are essential for the efficient working of airlines. These are extremely complex and expensive, only the largest airlines are able to afford to develop such systems. If these airlines can abuse their control of the system, they may distort the market to benefit themselves and to discriminate against smaller airlines. The abuse of such control over a computerised reservation system was the subject of a complaint to the European Commission in *London European Airways v*

---

13. Costa, '*US v Microsoft*', Computer Law and Security Report 1995, Vol 11, p 212.
14. *Op cit*, p 336.
15. [1996] 5 EIPR, D-154.
16. Gringras, 'Competition in Cyberspace' (1996) 2 ECLR 71.

Sabena.[17] London European was a low cost airline which ran a commercial service from London to Brussels. As the national airline of Belgium, Sabena controlled the major Belgian reservations system known as 'Saphir'. London European sought to be included in the Saphir system. Sabena refused this request and evidence uncovered by the Commission revealed that Sabena intended to recoup any losses which it might suffer as a result of London Europeans low fares by forcing London European to pay for access to the system and by insisting that London European contract the handling of its aircraft to Sabena. Ultimately, London European was refused access to the system by Sabena and complained to the Commission. Sabena was held to have abused its dominant position and a fine of 100,000 ECUs was imposed.

[12.11] The EU has regulated the provision of computerised reservation systems which are run by airlines.[18] System vendors[19] must allow any airline to participate on an equal basis in its distribution facilities. System vendors may not attach unreasonable conditions to any contract with an airline or make it a condition of participating in its system that airlines do not participate in other systems. Airlines must be able to terminate their contracts within six months.[20] All airlines who use the system must get equal access to any improvements to the system.[21] System vendors must not manipulate data on the system and must load and process all airlines' information with equal efficiency.[22] The displays used by the system must be clear and non-discriminatory.[23] Information relating to individual bookings is restricted and marketing, booking and sales data may only be made available on the basis that it includes no identification of a passenger or corporate user.[24]

[12.12] The Council has also specifically applied the provisions of Article 85(3) to computer reservation systems. This regulation essentially requires that system vendors and other users of the systems abide by conditions similar to those continued in the code of conduct.[25]

---

17. [1989] CMLR 662.
18. Commission Regulation No 2299/89 of 24 July 1990 on a Code Of Conduct For Computerised Reservation Systems For Air Transport Services, OJ L220 29/7/89 p 1 as amended by Regulation no 3089/93 of 29 October 1993, OJ L278 11/11/93 p 1.
19. This is defined in Article 2(h) as any entity which is responsible for the marketing of a computerised reservation system.
20. Article 3(3).
21. Article 3(4).
22. Article 4.
23. Article 5.
24. Article 6.

THE BLOCK EXEMPTION FOR PATENTS AND KNOW-HOW

[12.13] Where there are several companies competing in a market they may be tempted to agree amongst themselves to divide up the market for their own benefit. This is obviously not in the interests of the European Union and is prohibited by Article 85 of the Treaty of Rome.[26]. However, the European Union has no desire to let competition law become a further hindrance to the effective exploitation of modern technology by European companies. Therefore, it is willing to exempt from the provisions of competition law, certain agreements relating to the exploitation of patents and know-how. It is permitted to do so by Article 85(3). Until recently patent licensing[27] and

---

[25.] Commission Regulation No 83/91 of 5 December 1990 on the application of Article 85(3) of the Treaty to certain categories of agreements between undertakings relating to computer reservation systems for air transport services, OJ L 010, 15/1/91, p 9.

[26.] Article 85 provides that "The following shall be prohibited as incompatible with the common market:

1. all agreements between undertakings, decisions by associations of undertakings and concerted practices which may affect trade between Member States and which have as their object or effect the prevention, restriction or distortion of competition within the common market, and in particular those which:
   (a) directly or indirectly fix purchase or selling prices or any other trading conditions;
   (b) limit or control production, markets, technical development, or investment;
   (c) share markets or sources of supply;
   (d) apply dissimilar conditions to equivalent transactions with other trading parties, thereby placing them at a competitive disadvantage;
   (e) make the conclusion of contracts subject to acceptance by the other parties of supplementary obligations which, by their nature or according to commercial usage, have no connection with the subject of such contracts.
2. Any agreements or decisions prohibited pursuant to this Article shall be automatically void.
3. The provisions of paragraph 1 may, however, be declared inapplicable in the case of:
   - any agreement or category of agreement between undertakings;
   - any decision or category of decisions by associations of undertakings;
   - any concerted practice or category of concerted practices;

   which contributes to improving the production or distribution of goods or to promoting technical or economic progress while allowing consumers a fair share of the resulting benefit, and which does not:
   (a) impose on the undertakings concerned restrictions which are not indispensable to the attainment of these objectives;
   (b) afford such undertakings the possibility of eliminating competition in respect of a substantial part of the products in question."

[27.] Regulation No 2349/84 of 23 July 1984. OJ No 219, 16 August 1984, p 15.

certain categories of know-how licensing agreements[28] were regulated separately by the European Union. These two regulations have now been replaced by a single regulation: The Commission Regulation (EC) No 240/ 96 of 31 January 1996 on the Application of Article 85(3) of the Treaty to Certain Categories of Technology Transfer Agreements[29] which came into force on 1 April 1996. It applies until 31 March 2006. The regulation means that individual agreements do not have to be individually assessed for their compliance with competition law provided that the agreement is within the criteria of the regulations. The Regulation applies to agreements between undertakings and a complaint under Article 86 that a dominant position was being abused in a market would raise separate issues.[30]

The Exemption

[12.14] Article 1(1) of the Regulation exempts from the effects of Article 85(1) of the Treaty of Rome pure patent licensing or know-how[31] licensing agreements and mixed patent and know-how licensing agreements. This provision also applies to agreements which contain ancillary provisions[32] relating to intellectual property rights other than patents. Recital 6 to the Regulation suggests that the exemption may apply in particular to such ancillary provisions where they refer to trade marks, design rights and copyright, especially software protection rights. It is not clear what constitutes 'ancillary'. The specific inclusion of trade marks is a reflection of the fact that the marketing of a technology is often as important as the product itself. The inclusion of design rights and copyrights does not in all likelihood mean that this is a loophole which may allow agreements for the transfer of rights other than those to patents and know-how, to come within the provisions of the exemption. Rather it probably means that where the use of a design or a software program is necessary for the implementation of the patents or the know-how, then these rights may be transferred as part of the agreement.

---

28. Regulation No 556/89 of 30 November 1988. OJ No L61, 4 March 1989, p 1.
29. OJ L 31, 9 February 1996, p 2.
30. See generally Kerse, 'Block Exemptions under Article 85(3)', [1996] 6 ECLR 331. Also Antill and Burdon, 'The New Technology Transfer Block Exemption - a Whiter Shade of Grey?', Patent World, March 1996, p 14.
31. 'Know-how' is defined as a body of technical information that is secret, substantial and identified in any appropriate form: Article 10(1).
32. 'Ancillary provisions' are provisions relating to the exploitation of intellectual property rights other than patents which contain no obligations restrictive of competition other than those also attached to the licensed know-how or patents and exempted under the Regulation: Article 10.

[12.15] The Regulation is able to do this pursuant to Article 85(3) of the Treaty which states that agreements which contribute "to improving the production or distribution of gods or to promoting technical or economic progress while allowing consumers a fair share of the resulting benefit" may be permitted. The Regulation details the agreements to which this exemption applies.

The Scope of the Regulation

[12.16] The Regulation applies to the licensing of Member States' own patents, Community patents and European patents. It also applies to agreements for licensing know-how such as non-patented technical information including descriptions of manufacturing processes, recipes, formulae, designs or drawings. Finally, it applies to agreements which combine patent and know-how licensing. For the purpose of the Regulation 'patents' are deemed to include *inter alia* patent applications and topographies of semiconductor products.[33]

[12.17] Under Article 5 the Regulation has no application to:

(1) agreements between members of a patent or know-how pool which relate to the pooled technologies;[34]

(2) licensing agreements between competing undertakings which hold interests in a joint venture or between one of them and the joint venture, if the licensing agreements relate to the activities of the joint venture.[35] The Regulation will apply however, where a parent undertaking grants the joint venture a patent or know-how licence, provided that the licensed products[36] and the other goods and services of the participating undertakings which are considered by users to be interchangeable or substitutable in view of their characteristics, price and intended use represent:

- in the case of a licence limited to production, not more than 20%, and

- in the case of a licence covering production and distribution, not more than 10%

of the market for the licensed products and all interchangeable or substitutable goods and services.[37] However the Regulation will continue to apply where these market shares are not exceeded by

---

[33.] Article 8.

[34.] Article 5(1)(1).

[35.] Article 5(1)(2).

[36.] 'Licensed products' are goods or services the production or provision of which requires the use of the licensed technology: Article 10.

[37.] Article 5(2)(1).

more than one tenth, if that limit is exceeded the Regulation will continue to apply for a period of six months from the end of the year in which the limit was exceeded;[38]

(3) agreements under which one party grants the other a patent and/or know-how licence and in exchange the other party, albeit in separate agreements or through connected undertakings,[39] grants the first party a patent, trademark or know-how licence or exclusive sales rights, where the parties are competitors in relation to the products covered by those agreements;

(4) licensing agreements containing provisions relating to intellectual property rights other than patents which are not ancillary;

(5) agreements entered into solely for the purpose of sale.[40]

The Regulation will still apply to pool agreements and to reciprocal licences provided the parties are not subject to any territorial restriction within the common market with regard to the manufacture, use or putting on the market of the licensed products or to the use of the licensed or pooled technologies.[41]

[12.18] The similarity between a sale of a right and an exclusive licence for that right caused concern, as it was feared that the Regulation might be evaded by presenting exclusive licences as assignments. As a result, the Regulation applies to the following:

---

38. Article 5(3).
39. 'Connected Undertakings' are:
    (a) undertakings in which a party to the agreement directly or indirectly:
        - owns more than half the capital or business assets, or
        - has the power to exercise more than half the voting rights, or
        - has the power to appoint more than half the members of the supervisory board, board of directors or bodies legally representing the undertaking, or
        - has the right to manage the affairs of the undertaking;
    (b) undertakings which, directly or indirectly, have in or over a party to the agreement the rights or powers listed in (a);
    (c) undertakings in which an undertaking referred to in (b) directly or indirectly has the rights or powers listed in (a);
    (d) undertakings in which the parties to the agreement or undertakings connected with them jointly have the rights or powers listed in (a): such jointly controlled undertakings are considered to be connected with each of the parties to the agreement: Article 10.
40. Article 5(1).
41. Article 5(2)(2).

(1) agreements where the licensor is not the holder of the know-how or the patentee, but is authorised by the holder or the patentee to grant a licence;

(2) assignments of know-how, patents or both where the risk associated with exploitation[42] remains with the assignor, in particular where the sum payable in consideration of the assignment is dependent on the turnover obtained by the assignee in respect of products made using the know-how or the patents, the quantity of such products manufactured or the number of operations carried out employing the know-how or the patents;

(3) licensing agreements in which the rights or obligations of the licensor or the licensee are assumed by undertakings connected with them.[43]

Agreements to which the block exemption applies

[12.19] The block exemption will only apply to certain types of agreements. To avail of the exemption only two undertakings may be party to the agreement and the agreement must include one or more of the obligations referred to below.[44] The exemption for know-how agreements is temporally limited as it is difficult to determine the point at which know-how ceases to be secret.[45] The period for such agreement may be extended for individual decision. If the know-how transferred is improved, a new agreement may be made to licence the improvements and this may benefit from the exemption.[46] One or more of the following objectives must be contained in the agreement:

1. an obligation on the licensor not to licence other undertakings to exploit the licensed technology[47] in the licensed territory;[48]

[42.] 'Exploitation' refers to any use of the licensed technology in particular in the production, active or passive sales in a territory even if not coupled with manufacture in that territory, or leasing of the licensed products: Article 10.

[43.] Article 6.

[44.] 'Obligation' includes both contractual obligations and concerted practices. Article 10.

[45.] Recital 13 to the Directive.

[46.] Recital 14.

[47.] 'Licensed technology' is the initial manufacturing know-how or the necessary product and process patents or both, existing at the time the first licensing agreement is concluded and improvements subsequently made to the know-how or patents irrespective of whether and to what extent they are exploited by the parties or by other licensees: Article 10.

[48.] 'The licensed territory' is the territory covering all or at least part of the common market where the licensee is entitled to exploit the licensed technology: Article 10.

2. an obligation on the licensor not to exploit the licensed technology in the licensed territory himself;

3. an obligation on the licensee not to exploit the licensed technology in the territory of the licensor[49] within the common market;

4. an obligation on the licensee not to manufacture or use the licensed product or use the licensed process in territories within the common market which are licensed to other licensees;

5. an obligation on the licensee not to pursue an active policy of putting the licensed product on the market in the territories within the common market which are licensed to other licensees and in particular not to engage in advertising specifically aimed at those territories or to establish any branch or maintain a distribution depot there;

    If the agreement is a pure know-how licensing agreement, the period for which the exemption of the obligations referred to in points 1-5 above is granted may not exceed 10 years from the date when the licensed product is first put on the market within the common market by one of the licensees.[50] If the agreement is a mixed patent and know-how licensing agreement, the exemption of the obligations referred to in points 1-5 will apply in Member States in which the licensed technology is protected by necessary patents[51] for as long as the licensed product is protected in those Member States by such patents if the duration of such protection exceeds the periods specified for pure know-how agreements;[52]

6. an obligation on the licensee not to put the licensed product on the market in the territories licensed to other licensees within the common market in response to unsolicited orders;

    The exemption of this obligation from competition law is granted for a period not exceeding five years from the date when the licensed product is first put on the market within the common

---

49. 'Territory of the licensor' means territories in which the licensor has not granted any licences for patents and/or know-how covered by the licensing agreement: Article 10.
50. Article 1(3).
51. 'Necessary patents' are patents where a licence under the patent is necessary for the putting into effect of the licensed technology in so far as, in the absence of such a licence, the realisation of the licensed technology would not be possible or would be possible only to a lesser extent or in more difficult or costly conditions. Such patents must therefore be of technical, legal or economic interest to the licensee: Article 10.
52. Article 1(4).

market by one of the licensees to the extent that and for as long as, in these territories, this product is protected by parallel patents.[53] If the agreement is a pure know-how licensing agreement the period for which the exemption is granted may not exceed five years from the date when the licensed product is first put on the market within the common market by one of the licensees.[54] The duration of the exemption provided for mixed patent and know-how agreements may not exceed the five year period provided for pure patent and know-how agreements.

7.   an obligation on the licensee to use only the licensor's trade mark or get up to distinguish the licensed product during the term of the agreement provided that the licensee is not prevented from identifying himself as the manufacturer of the licensed products;[55]

8.   an obligation on the licensee to limit his production of the licensed product to the quantities he requires in manufacturing his own products and to sell the licensed product only as an integral part of or a replacement part for his own products or otherwise in connection with the sale of his own products provided that such quantities are freely determined by the licensee.[56]

If the agreement is a pure know-how agreement, then the exemption referred to in points 7 and 8 are exempted during the lifetime of the agreement for as long as the know-how remains secret[57] and substantial.[58]

[12.20] If the agreement is a pure patent licensing agreement, then the exemption is granted only to the extent that and for as long as the licensed product is protected by parallel patents in the territories of the licensee, the

---

[53.]   Article 1(2). 'Parallel patents' are patents which in spite of the divergences which remain in the absence of any unification of national rules concerning industrial property, protect the same invention in various Member States: Article 10.

[54.]   Article 1(3).

[55.]   Article 1(1)(7).

[56.]   Article 1(1)(8).

[57.]   'Secret' is defined as the know-how package as a body or in the precise configuration and assembly of its components is not generally known or easily accessible so that part of its value consists in the lead which the licensee gains when it is communicated to him. It is not limited to the narrow sense that each individual component of the know-how should be totally unknown or unobtainable outside the licensor's business: Article 10.

[58.]   'Substantial' is know-how including information which must be useful, ie, which can reasonably be expected at the date of conclusion of the agreement to be capable of improving the competitive position of the licensee, eg, by helping him to enter a new market or giving him an advantage in competition with other manufacturers or providers of services who do not have access to the licensed secret know-how or other comparable secret know-how: Article 10. See also Article 1(3).

licensor and other licensees respectively, save for the obligation referred to in point 6 above where a period not exceeding five years applies.[59] Where pure know-how agreements are concerned, the exemption will only apply where the parties have identified[60] in any appropriate form the initial know-how and any subsequent improvements to it which become available to one party and are communicated to the other party pursuant to the terms of the agreement and to the purpose thereof and only for as long as the know-how remains secret and substantial.[61] Agreements for mixtures of patent and know-how will qualify for the exemption only for as long as the patents remain in force or to the extent that the know-how is identified and for as long as it remains secret and substantial whichever period is the longer.[62] The exemption will also apply where in a particular agreement the parties undertake obligations of the types referred to above but with a more limited scope than is permitted above.[63]

[12.21] Article 2 provides that the exemption from competition law applies even though any of the following clauses are present in the agreement. The Regulation states that these clauses are generally not restrictive of competition. Therefore, even if one of these clauses falls within the scope of Article 85(1) of the Treaty it will be exempt from the effect of competition law even if it is not accompanied by any of the clauses referred to above or more limited forms of them.[64] The list is not exhaustive:[65]

(1) an obligation on the licensee not to divulge the know-how communicated by the licensor; the licensee may be held to this obligation after the agreement has expired;

(2) an obligation on the licensee not to grant sublicences or assign the licence;

---

59. Article 1(2).
60. 'Identified' means that the know-how is described as or recorded in such a manner as to make it possible to verify that it satisfies the criteria of secrecy and substantiality and to ensure that the licensee is not unduly restricted in his exploitation of his own technology, to be identified that know-how can either be set out in the licence agreement or in a separate document or recorded in any other appropriate form at the latest when the know-how is transferred or shortly thereafter, provided that the separate document or other record can be made available if the need arises: Article 10.
61. Article 1(3).
62. Article 1(4).
63. Article 1(5).
64. Article 2(2) and (3).
65. Recital 18.

(3) an obligation on the licensee not to exploit the licensed know-how or patents after termination of the agreement in so far and so long as the know-how is still secret or the patents are still in force;

(4) an obligation on the licensee to grant to the licensor a licence in respect of his own improvements to or his new applications of the licensed technology provided:

- that in the case of severable improvements such a licence is not exclusive, so that the licensee is free to use his own improvements or to licence them to third parties in so far as that does not involve disclosure of the know-how communicated by the licensor that is still secret;

- and that the licensor undertakes to grant an exclusive or non-exclusive licence of his own improvements to the licensee;

(5) an obligation on the licensee to observe minimum quality specifications, including technical specifications, for the licensed product or to procure goods or services from the licensor, in so far as these quality specifications, products or services are necessary for:

(a) a technically proper exploitation of the licensed technology;

(b) ensuring that the product of the licensee conforms to the minimum quality specifications that are applicable to the licensor and other licensees;

and to allow the licensor to carry out related checks;

(6) an obligation:

(a) to inform the licensor of misappropriation of the know-how or of infringements of the licensed patents; or

(b) to take or to assist the licensor in taking legal action against such misappropriation or infringements;

(7) an obligation on the licensee to continue paying the royalties:

(a) until the end of the agreement in the amounts, for the periods, and according to the methods freely determined by the parties in the event of the know-how becoming publicly known other than by action of the licensor without prejudice to the payment of any additional damages in the event of the know-how becoming publicly known by the action of the licensee in breach of the agreement;

      (b) over a period going beyond the duration of the licensed patents in order to facilitate payment;

(8) an obligation on the licensee to restrict his exploitation of the licensed technology to one or more technical fields of application covered by the licensed technology or to one or more product markets;

(9) an obligation on the licensee to pay a minimum royalty or to produce a minimum quantity of the licensed product or to carry out a minimum number of operations exploiting the licensed technology;

(10) an obligation on the licensor to grant the licensee any more favourable terms that the licensor may grant to another undertaking after the agreement is entered into;

(11) an obligation on the licensee to mark the licensed product with an indication of the licensor's name or of the licensed patent;

(12) an obligation on the licensee not to use the licensor's technology to construct facilities for third parties. This is without prejudice to the right of the licensee to increase the capacity of his facilities or to set up additional facilities for his own use on normal commercial terms, including the payment of additional royalties;

(13) an obligation on the licensee to supply only a limited quantity of the licensed product to a particular customer, where the licence was granted so that the customer might have a second source of supply inside the licensed territory; this provision will also apply where the customer is the licensee and the licence which was granted in order to provide a second source of supply provides that the customer is himself to manufacture the licensed products or to have them manufactured by a subcontractor;[66]

(14) a reservation by the licensor of the right to exercise the rights conferred by a patent to oppose the exploitation of the technology by the licensee outside the licensed territory;

(15) a reservation by the licensor of the right to terminate the agreement if the licensee contests the secret or substantial nature of the licensed know-how or challenges the validity of licensed patents within the common market belonging to the licensor or undertakings connected with him;

(16) a reservation by the licensor of the right to terminate the licence

---

[66.] Article 2(1)(13).

agreement of a patent if the licensee raises the claim that such a patent is not necessary;

(17) an obligation on the licensee to use his best endeavours to manufacture and market the licensed product;

(18) a reservation by the licensor of the right to terminate the exclusivity granted to the licensee and to stop licensing improvements to him when the licensee enters into competition within the common market with the licensor, with undertakings connected with the licensor or with other undertakings in respect of research and development, production, use or distribution of competing products and to require the licensee to prove that the licensed know-how is not being used for the production of products and the provision of services other than those licensed.

Application for exemption

[12.22] Article 4 states that the exemption provided for in Articles 1 and 2 also applies to agreements containing obligations restrictive of competition which are not covered by those Articles and do not fall within the scope of Article 3, on condition that the agreements in question are notified to the Commission[67] and that the Commission does not oppose such exemption within a period of four months.[68] It must oppose an exemption if it receives a request to do so from a Member State within two months of the transmission to the Member State of the notification.[69] This request must be justified on the basis of considerations relating to the competition rules of the Treaty.[70]

---

[67] This must be in accordance with the provisions of Articles 1, 2 and 3 of Regulation (EC) No 3385/94.

[68] This period of four months runs from the date on which the notification takes effect in accordance with Article 4 of Reg 3385/94.

[69] The Commission may withdraw the opposition to the exemption at any time. However, where the opposition was raised at the request of a Member State and this request is maintained, it may be withdrawn only after consultation of the Advisory Committee on Restrictive Practices and Dominant Positions: Article 4(6). If the opposition is withdrawn because the undertakings concerned have shown that the conditions of Article 85(3) are satisfied, the exemption will apply from the date of notification: Article 4(7). If the opposition is withdrawn because the undertakings concerned have amended the agreement so that the conditions of Article 85(3) are satisfied, the exemption will apply from the date on which the amendments take effect: Article 4(8). If the Commission opposes exemption and the opposition is not withdrawn, the effects of the notification is governed by the provision of Regulation No 17: Article 4(9).

[70] All information obtained must only be used for the purposes of the Regulation: Article 9.

[12.23] The notification procedure will apply in particular where:

(a) the licensee is obliged at the time the agreement is entered into to accept quality specifications or further licences or to procure goods or services which are not necessary for a technically satisfactory exploitation of the licensed technology or for ensuring that the production of the licensee conforms to the quality standards that are respected by the licensor and other licensees;

(b) the licensee is prohibited from contesting the secrecy or the substantiality of the licensed know-how or from challenging the validity of patents licensed within the common market belonging to the licensor or undertakings connected with him.[71]

Agreements to which the exemption does not apply

[12.24] Article 3 sets out several types of agreements to which the exemption will not apply, In particular, it will not apply in cases where parties refuse to meet demand from users or resellers who wish to purchase goods for export or otherwise try to restrict parallel imports. These agreements are excluded because Article 85(3) of the Treaty only allows exemptions if consumers receive a fair share of the benefit.[72] The agreements excluded from the Regulation are as follows:

(1) Where one party is restricted in the determination of prices, components of prices or discounts for the licensed products;

(2) Where one party is restricted from competing within the common market with the other party, with undertakings connected with the other party or with other undertakings in respect of research and development, production, use or distribution of competing products;[73]

(3) Where one or both of the parties are required without any objectively justified reason:

(a) to refuse to meet orders from users or resellers in their respective territories who would market products in other territories within the common market;

(b) to make it difficult for users or resellers to obtain the products from other resellers within the common market and in particular to exercise intellectual property rights or

---

[71] Article 4(2).
[72] Recital 17.
[73] This is without prejudice to Article 2(17) and (18).

take measures so as to prevent users or resellers from obtaining outside, or from putting on the market in the licensed territory, products which have been lawfully put on the market within the common market by the licensor or with his consent;

or do so as a result of a concerted practice between them;

(4) Where the parties were already competing manufacturers[74] before the grant of the licence and one of them is restricted within the same technical field of use or within the same product market, as to the customers he may serve, in particular, by being prohibited from supplying certain classes of user, employing certain forms of distribution or with the aim of sharing customers using certain types of packaging for the products, save as provided in Article 1(1)(7) and Article 2(1)(13);

(5) Where the quantity of the licensed products one party may manufacture or sell or the number of operations exploiting the licensed technology he may carry out are subject to limitations save as provided in Article 1(1)(8) and Article 2(1)(13);

(6) Where the licensee is obliged to assign in whole or in part to the licensor rights to improvements to or new applications of the licensed technology;

(7) Where the licensor is required, albeit in separate agreements or through automatic prolongation of the initial duration of the agreement by the inclusion of any new improvements, for a period exceeding that referred to in Article 1(2) and (3) not to licence other undertakings to exploit the licensed technology in the licensed territory or a party is required for a period exceeding that referred to in Article 1(2) and (3) or Article 1(4) not to exploit the licensed technology in the territory of the other party or of other licensees.

Withdrawal of the exemption

[12.25] Article 7 provides that the Commission may withdraw the benefit of the Regulation where it finds in a particular case that an agreement exempted by the Regulation is nevertheless anti-competitive. The Regulation specifies four situations where this may occur. Firstly, where the

---

[74.] 'Competing manufacturers' or manufacturers of 'competing products' are those manufacturers who sell products which in view of their characteristics, price and intended use are considered by users to be interchangeable or substitutable for the licensed products: Article 10.

effect of the agreement is to prevent the licensed products from exposure to effective competition in the licensed territory from identical goods or services or from goods or services considered by users as interchangeable or substitutable in view of their characteristics, price and intended use, which may in particular occur where the licensee's market share[75] exceeds 40%. Secondly, where the licensee refuses, without justification, to meet unsolicited orders from users or resellers in the territory of other licensees. Thirdly, where the parties without justification refuse to meet orders from users or resellers in their respective territories who would market the products in other territories within the common market or they make it difficult for users or resellers to obtain the products from other resellers within the common market. In particular, this will apply where they exercise intellectual property rights or take measures so as to prevent resellers or users from obtaining outside or from putting on the market in the licensed territory products which have been lawfully put on the common market by the licensor or with his consent. Finally, where the parties were competing manufacturers at the date of the grant of the licence and obligations on the licensee to produce a minimum quantity or to use his best endeavours as referred to in Article 2(1)(9) and (17) respectively have the effect of preventing the licensee from using competing technologies.

THE COMPETITION ACT 1991

[12.26] The Competition Act 1991 is stated to be an Act to prohibit, by analogy with Articles 85 and 86 of the Treaty of Rome and in the interests of the common good, the prevention, restriction or distortion of competition and the abuse of dominant positions in trade in the State.[76] The Act also establishes a Competition Authority to regulate the application of the Act.

The Rules of Competition

[12.27] All agreements between undertakings, associations and concerted practices which have as their object or effect the prevention, restriction or distortion of competition are prohibited and void. These in particular include those agreements which:

---

75. 'The licensee's market share' refers to the proportion which the licensed products and other goods or services provided by the licensee which are considered by users to be interchangeable or substitutable for the licensed products in view of their characteristics, price and intended use, represent the entire market for the licensed products and all other interchangeable or substitutable goods and services in the common market or a substantial part of it: Article 10.
76. The preamble to the Act.

(i)   directly or indirectly fix purchase or selling prices or any other trading conditions;

(ii)   limit or control production, markets, technical development or investment;

(iii)   share markets or sources of supply;

(iv)   apply dissimilar conditions to equivalent transactions with other trading parties thereby placing them at a competitive disadvantage;

(v)   make the conclusion of contracts subject to acceptance by the other parties of supplementary obligations which by their nature or according to commercial usage have no connection with the subject of such contract.[77]

The Competition Authority may, however, licence agreements, decisions or concerted practices which, in the opinion of the Authority, contribute to improving the production or distribution of goods or services or which promote technical or economic progress. This must allow consumers a fair share of the resulting benefits. The licence must not impose terms which are dispensable or allow the undertakings to eliminate competition in respect of a substantial part of the products or services in question.[78] The Authority may alternatively certify that the agreement, decision or practice does not distort competition.[79] It may invite any Minister to offer observations on the proposed licence.[80] The Authority must publish the licence or certificate in *Iris Oifigiúil* and a daily newspaper.[81]

Abuse of Dominant Position

[12.28] Any abuse by one or more undertakings of a dominant position in trade for any goods or services in the State or in a substantial part of the State is prohibited. Such abuse may consist of:

(i)   directly or indirectly imposing unfair purchase or selling prices or other unfair trading conditions;

(ii)   limiting production, markets or technical development to the prejudice of consumers;

(iii)   applying dissimilar conditions to equivalent transactions with other trading parties, thereby placing them at a competitive advantage;

[77.] CA 1991, s 4(1).
[78.] CA 1991, s 4(2).
[79.] CA 1991, s 4(4).
[80.] CA 1991, s 4(5).
[81.] CA 1991, s 4(6).

(iv)   making the conclusion of contracts subject to the acceptance by other parties of supplementary obligations which by their nature or according to commercial usage have no connection with the subject of such contracts.[82]

Any person who has suffered as a result of such an agreement, decision, concerted practice or abuse may complain to the High Court,[83] which may grant an injunction, declaration or award damages, including exemplary damages.[84]

Every agreement decision or concerted practice which may restrict competition must be reported to the Authority which may grant a licence permitting the activity.[85]

[12.29] In *RTE and ITP v Magill TV Guide*[86] the European Court of Justice held that RTE and ITV had abused their dominant position as broadcasters. These television stations had enjoyed a *de facto* monopoly over information relating their programmes. They used the control which this gave them to ensure that the market was reserved for their own publications such as *The RTE Guide*. The European Court of Justice upheld the Court of First Instance orders requiring the broadcasters to end their abuse by supplying third parties with the advance weekly listings for their programs and by permitting reproduction of those listings.

THE COMPETITION AMENDMENT ACT 1996

[12.30] This Act amends the Competition Act 1991 by making it an offence to enter into or implement an agreement or make or implement a decision or engage in a concerted practice.[87] It also makes it an offence not to comply with the terms and conditions of a licence issued by the Competition Authority.[88] The 1996 Act is somewhat unusual in that the penalty on conviction on indictment is not fixed by the Act. It may be a fine not exceeding the greater of either £3 million or 10% of the turnover of the undertaking or individual in the financial year ending in the twelve months

---

82. CA 1991, s 5.
83. CA 1991, s 4(1) & 4(2). An action may be brought in the Circuit Court but any relief is limited to the Circuit Court jurisdiction.
84. CA 1991, s 6(3).
85. CA 1991, s 7. The Competition Authority has considered agreements relating to trade marks in *Irish Distillers* Decision No 284, 7 February 1994. It considered agreements relating to the licensing of copyright in *The Performing Rights Society* Decision 326, 18 May 1994.
86. [1995] Irish Competition Law Reports 294.
87. CA 1996, s 2.
88. CA 1996, s 2(5).

prior to the conviction. An individual may also receive a prison term not exceeding two years. On summary conviction, a fine not exceeding £1,500 may be imposed and an individual may also be imprisoned for a term not exceeding six months.[89] It is difficult to see how the District Court could be used to uphold competition law. Any concerted practice which would only merit a fine of £1,500 would probably not be worth prosecuting or even engaging in. The inclusion of these offences in the Act has been criticised by the chairman of the competition authority.[90] It will be extremely difficult to produce evidence of the 'beyond reasonable doubt' standard of criminal trials.[91]

THE FREE MOVEMENT OF GOODS

[12.31] Article 30 of the Treaty of Rome provides that "quantitative restrictions on imports and all measures having equivalent effect shall ... be prohibited between Member States". This in essence means that the European Union is a free trade area.

[12.32] This is qualified by Article 36 which provides that the provisions of the Treaty relating to free movement of goods:

> shall not preclude prohibitions or restrictions upon imports, exports or goods in transit justified on the grounds of ... the protection of industrial or commercial property. Such prohibitions or restrictions shall not however, constitute a means of arbitrary discrimination or disguised restriction on trade between Member States.

[12.33] However, the effectiveness of Article 36 was limited in *Deutsche Grammophon*[92] where the European Court of Justice stated that it "only admits derogations from the freedom of trade to the extent to which they are justified for the purpose of safeguarding rights which constitute the specific subject matter of such property".[93] Over the years a considerable jurisprudence has been built up in Europe concerning the free movement of intellectual property. These cases have related to recordings of live

---

[89]. CA 1996, s 3(1).
[90]. "They might just as well have produced the death penalty for all likelihood there will be of a successful conviction": Paddy Lyons, 6 June 1996 quoted by Whittaker 'New competition law does not deal with malpractice', *Sunday Business Post*, 9 June 1996.
[91]. "It will be extremely difficult to take and win criminal cases. Its primary role will be as deterrent", Richard Bruton, 30 November 1995, *ibid.*
[92]. *Deutsche Grammophon GmbH v Metro-SB-Grossmärkte GmbH & Co KG* [1971] ECR 487; [1971] CMLR 631.
[93]. Article 222 of the Treaty has caused problems. It states that "this Treaty shall in no way prejudice the rules in member states governing the system of property ownership".

performances,[94] copyright in the design of spare car parts,[95] and films.[96] In any event, controls over the free movement of computer programs and other intellectual property in Europe will be weakened by the Internet.

[12.34] One provision of European law relating to the free movement of goods is specifically relating to the doctrine of exhaustion. This means that once a computer program has been sold within the territory of the European Union the copyright owner can no longer control its distribution. In other words the right of the copyright owner to control the distribution of the program will have been exhausted. The doctrine of exhaustion is applied to computers by Article 4(c) of the Council Directive on the legal protection of computer programs[97] and by Regulation 5(c) of the Regulations.[98] This also applies to semiconductor chips under the Regulations of 1988[99] which implement the Council Directive on the Legal Protection of Topographies of Semiconductor Products.[100]

[12.35] The Council of Europe has adopted a programme for the establishment of an internal information services market[101] acknowledging that there are numerous, legal, administrative, fiscal and technical barriers to the development of an internal information market which is causing distortions of competition.[102]

CONCLUSION

[12.36] It is unclear how the development of the Internet and other similar services will affect competition. Some see it as a new beginning where Microsoft and other similar large companies will be made redundant just as they previously marginalised IBM.[103] Others see the Internet as spelling the end of competition as it forces companies to co-operate with each other. Microsoft, Sun Microsystems and other companies are seen to be moving together rather than competing.[104] It is not clear how the computer industry

---

[94.] *Phil Collins v IMTRAT* [1993] 3 CMLR 773.

[95.] *Consorzio Italiano v Renault* [1990] 4 CLMR 265.

[96.] *Coditel SA v Cine Vog Films* [1981] 2 CMLR 362.

[97.] Council Directive 91/250, OJ L 122 p 42.

[98.] SI 26/1993.

[99.] European Communities (Protection of Topographies of Semiconductor Products) Regulation 1988, SI 101/1988.

[100.] Council Directive No 87/54/EEC, 16/12/1986.

[101.] Council decision of 12 December 1991, OJ L 377, 31/12/91, p 41.

[102.] Recital 4.

[103.] *The Economist*, 'A World Gone Soft', 25 May 1996.

[104.] Hyslop, 'Does the Internet Spell the End of Competition?', NLJ 7 June 1996.

will develop in the coming years. However, Microsoft has proven surprisingly agile in responding to this challenge.[105]

[12.37] The Internet is already having an effect on competition in other markets. German exporters have blamed the Internet for a decline in their international markets. They have found that they are losing lucrative niche markets because the Internet has made it easier to compare prices and thus increasing competition. Previously, German companies could be fairly sure that their initial offer would be accepted, now they are finding that the customer will quote more competitive prices from several other suppliers.[106]

---

105. *The Economist*, 28 June 1996.
106. *The Financial Times*, 27 March 1996.

Chapter 13

Computer Misuse

INTRODUCTION

[13.01] The feature of computers which has made them ubiquitous in modern life is their ability to rapidly access and process large amounts of information. This feature also makes computer misuse a unique problem, since users can also access and use that information without permission. As a result, most technologically modern countries have enacted computer crime legislation and Ireland is no exception in this regard. However, criminalising computer misuse is a difficult challenge for legislators as it does not easily fit into previously developed categories of crime. The creation of a computer crime law will not necessarily solve the problem as evidence of such crimes is usually difficult, if not impossible, to acquire and law enforcement agencies are often ill-equipped to acquire such evidence.

[13.02] Computer crimes, particularly those of professionals, are committed in secret and may not be discovered until long after the crime is committed. There is no need even to leave the house to commit a computer crime and the criminal may not even be in the same hemisphere as his victim. He may never interact with a human in the course of his crime and may not directly interact with the computer of his victim. He may instead write a program to do so which will destroy itself and any other evidence once the crime is committed. He will not leave fingerprints or DNA samples to be analysed and he will almost certainly cover his tracks by disguising the location of his computer.

HACKING

[13.03] The term 'hacker' is ambiguous and it may be divided into two categories. Hacker originally meant a technologically adept individual who could write computer games or other programs.[1] However, hacker has also come to mean an individual who applies his skills to breaking into other

---

[1.] BYTE cites Steve Wozniak who helped found the Apple computer company as an example of this: BYTE September 1995. Many in the computer industry remain attached to the original meaning of the term hacker and have tried to prevent its use to describe those engaging in criminal activities. BYTE suggests 'cracker' as an appropriate term for those who carry out computer crimes. See also Sterling, *The Hacker Crackdown*, (Bantam Books, 1992) p 56.

people's computer systems and generally creating chaos. Kevin Mitnick is the seminal hacker. He was arrested in 1981 for stealing manuals from the Pacific Telephone company in the US and received a six month prison sentence. In 1983, he was found to be hacking into computers at the University of Southern California. In 1986 he acquired an account with a computer run by the US National Security Agency through 'social engineering'. He found out the name of someone with an account on the computer and rang them up claiming to be the system administrator who needed to know the user's password, telephone number and name. At one stage, he gained control of the New York and Californian telephone systems. He used this control to create chaos, one individual who fell out with Mitnick was surprised to receive a $30,000 telephone bill. In 1989, Mitnick was convicted of stealing software from Digital and he received a two year jail sentence. The authorities were so concerned about Mitnick's skills that he was banned from using the phone in jail. When released, Mitnick went on the run. On his arrest in February 1995, he was found to have 20,000 credit card numbers in his possession.[2]

[13.04] This latter use of the term 'hacker' has become the more popular of the two and is the one adopted here. Hackers often never meet face to face but communicate through the Internet and by leaving messages on bulletin boards.[3] They are numerous, for example in 1995, 250,000 attacks were made against the Pentagon's computer system in the USA. Two thirds of these attacks resulted in unauthorised access.[4]

COMPUTER VIRUSES

What is a virus?

[13.05] A computer virus is frequently defined as a program which copies or replicates itself. The Texas Computer Crime Code defines a virus as:

[2.] See Hofner & Markoff, *Cyberpunk*, (Fourth Estate, 1991) for an account of Mitnick's early career. The events leading up to his capture in 1995 are dealt with in Shimomura & Markoff, *Takedown*, (Hyperion, 1996) and also in Littman, *The Fugitive Game: Online with Kevin Mitnik*, (Little, Brown, 1996).

[3.] See generally: Branscomb, 'Common Law for the Electronic Frontier', Scientific American, September 1991, p 112; Stefanac, 'Dangerous Games', California Lawyer, October 1994, p 56; Garner 'The Growing Professional Menace', Open Computing, July 1995, p 33; Arthur, 'Hackers Code', New Scientist, 22 October 1994, p 26; Black, 'The Computer Hacker-Electronic Vandal or Scout of the Networks?', Journal of Law and Information Science, 1993, Vol 4 No 1, p 65; Wallich, 'Wire Pirates', Scientific American, March 1994, p 72.

[4.] *The Times*, 24 May 1996.

an unwanted computer program or other set of instructions inserted into a computer's memory, operating system, or program that is specifically constructed with the ability to replicate itself and to affect the other programs or files in the computer by attaching a copy of the unwanted program or other set of instructions to one or more computer programs or files.[5]

Some viruses are mere practical jokes, they can be benign and simply play tunes such as 'Yankee Doodle'. Other viruses are designed with the sole intention of causing as much chaos as possible. However, all viruses are potentially destructive.[6] They may attack any type of computer but they are most frequently written for the PC because of its popularity and the vast amounts of information available about PCs and their operating systems. In 1995, an estimated 1,400 new viruses were detected and there are over 7,400 known viruses in existence.[7]

[13.06] Computer viruses are an increasing problem in Ireland. The 1995 Price-Waterhouse Survey[8] found that 53% of organisations surveyed had suffered a virus attack, the incidence of such attacks had more than doubled since 1991. Financial institutions were the organisations worst affected (72%). The lowest rates of attack were experienced by smaller companies and companies in Northern Ireland, of which 35% were attacked. The incidence of virus attacks was higher in those organisations that had a large number of PCs. The survey found that 21% of respondents did not know the source of the infection. Of the identified sources of infections, disks from outside the organisation affected accounted for 18% of cases and employees' disks accounted for 17%. Other sources were widely varied and included banks, consultants and auditors, customers, educational institutions, laptops, other group companies, suppliers and software vendors. The survey found that 50% of respondents believed that the danger posed by viruses would increase in the future, 38% believed that the danger would remain the same and 12% thought that it would decrease. The Audit Commission Report on computer abuse in the United Kingdom in 1994

---

5. Texas Penal Code, Title 7 para [33.01].
6. Even the most benign virus can have devastating consequences if users panic or take inappropriate actions when they realise that their PC is infected. *Dr Soloman's Anti-Virus Book*, (Newtech, 1994), p 82, gives the example of a company whose virus scanner encountered a virus called "12 tricks". This virus was not actually creating any problems, however, when the company decided to upgrade their DOS to avoid the virus, the virus became considerably more malevolent.
7. *The Irish Times*, 5 February 1996.
8. The Price-Waterhouse - Priority Data Systems Computer Virus and Security Survey, February 1995, p 7.

found that virus attacks accounted for a very high percentage of incidents of computer abuse (48%).[9] The 261 cases of virus attacks reported cost a total of £255,000 or an average of £977 per attack. One single attack forced an organisation to check over 450 computers and 4,000 disks at a cost of £50,000. Although there is a bewildering array of virus types, four important types of viruses or 'malevolent programs' are outlined below.[10]

(1) Virus

[13.07] The most well-known type of malevolent program is commonly referred to as a *virus*. This is a program which attaches itself to a copy of a program file. When the program is run, the virus will cause the computer to make further copies of the virus. Its main objective is to replicate itself and to spread itself as far and wide as possible. However, viruses frequently carry out more destructive tasks by damaging data or causing computers to shut down.

[13.08] Viruses have become increasingly sophisticated. In order to make them harder to detect, virus authors have developed several variations. *Polymorphic* viruses change their code every time they are copied. This means that if a computer is infected with hundreds of copies of a particular virus, every one of them will be different. 'Pathogen' and 'Queeg' were polymorphic viruses which were created by Christopher Pile who was eventually convicted under the UK Computer Misuse Act 1990 and sentenced to eighteen months in prison. One victim of the virus estimated that it cost almost £500,000 and 480 staff hours to undo the damage caused by the virus. Pile also distributed his *Smeg* encryption program which could be used to write similar viruses. This was distributed to various bulletin boards including one based in Belfast. However, Pile had infected the *Smeg* program with the *Pathogen* virus. This is alleged to have led to his downfall as other virus authors became so annoyed at being infected themselves that they informed on Pile.[11]

[13.09] Another variant is the *Stealth* virus which derives its name from the stealth bombers used in the Gulf War. The objective of a stealth virus is to remain hidden within programs and to be undetectable by anti-virus scanning programs while they look for valuable information such as passwords or credit card numbers.[12]

---

9. The Audit Commission, *Opportunity Makes a Thief: An Analysis of Computer Abuse*, 1994.
10. See Jones 'Computer Terrorist or Mad Boffin', 1996 NLJ 46.
11. *The Daily Telegraph*, 16 November 1995.
12. Dehaven, 'Stealth Virus Attacks', BYTE, May 1993, p 137.

(2) Trojan Horse

[13.10] The second category of malevolent program is the *Trojan Horse*. This is a program which may cause destruction but has been disguised as an innocent program. When the unsuspecting user runs the program, it will damage the data or other programs on the user's computer. An example of a Trojan was the 'AIDS Information disk' which was received by a large number of people (around 20,000) in late 1989. It stated that it was a guide to AIDS however when the programs on the disk were installed, a message would appear on the screen stating that if a fee was not sent to an address in Panama then all the files on the user's computer would be encrypted and so rendered unusable. Eventually an American scientist was arrested in New Jersey and extradited to the UK. Due to his mental condition he was found unfit to plead and all charges were ultimately dropped.[13]

(3) Worm

[13.11] The third category is the *Worm*. This program hides within the computer and waits until a certain event such as a specific date or a keystroke occurs which will cause it to operate. Unlike a virus, worms are complete in themselves and do not need to attach themselves to other programs. The most infamous worm was that created by Robert Morris, which was known as the 'Internet Worm'. In 1988, Morris, a student at Cornell University in the US, wrote a program which would roam the Internet taking advantage of flaws which Morris had found in the UNIX operating system. To ensure that the program would spread, Morris designed it so that it would copy itself every seventh time it entered a computer. Unfortunately, Morris failed to include a command in the program which would stop the replication once it had accomplished its task. Like the magician's apprentice, Morris found that his program rapidly replicated itself and soon swamped the Internet causing it to shut down. He tried to send out an 'antidote', however by then it was too late and he could not communicate with anyone else. The damage caused was estimated at between $5 million and $186 million.[14] Morris has the dubious distinction of being the first person to be convicted of a felony under the US Federal Computer Fraud and Abuse Act 1986. He was sentenced to three years probation, 400 hours of community service and fined $10,050, a penalty which has been criticised as too lenient.[15]

---

13. Davis, 'It's Virus Season Again', Washington University Law Quarterly, Vol 72:411, 1994.
14. Mello, 'Administering the Antidote to Computer Viruses: A Comment on *US v Morris*', Rutgers Computer Law and Technology Journal, Vol 19, No 1, 1993, p 259.
15. Mello, 'Comment on *United States v Morris*', Rutgers Computer Law & Technology Journal, 1993, Vol 19 No 1.

(4) Logic bombs

[13.12] Finally, there are *Logic Bombs*. These are adaptations to an existing computer program which will cause destruction if a certain event should occur. The classic logic bomb is inserted into a corporation's computers and checks once a week if its author still on the payroll. If it finds that he is not then the program will close down the system or otherwise cause damage.[16] An example of this occurred in the US in the case of *Werner, Zaroff, Slotnick & Askenazy v Lewis*.[17] The plaintiffs had installed software for processing insurance claims. This had been modified by the defendant. The software ceased working when it reached the 56,789th claim. Another computer expert employed by the plaintiffs found alterations to the software which had been installed by the defendant. The plaintiff was awarded damages of $25,000.

Protection against Viruses

[13.13] Programs have been developed which search for viruses. If viruses are detected, these programs will try to disable or remove the virus and repair the damage caused.[18] Such programs will either try to detect alterations to programs and data caused by the virus or else they will look for specific characteristics of the virus which have already been noted. The disadvantage with these programs is that they only detect known viruses. As new viruses appear, the anti-virus programs must be updated to deal with them. Such anti-virus programs are only effective if they are continuously updated. The Price Waterhouse Survey[19] found that most Irish companies update their anti-virus software either monthly, or quarterly. However, 11 of the top 200 Irish companies surveyed either updated annually, did not know when they updated or did not update at all. The Price Waterhouse Survey found that only 66% of respondents had installed anti-virus software on all their PCs. Amongst the top 200 companies this rose to 74% which had increased from 40% in 1991. However, only 24% of home PCs had such software installed. This is a concern because employees may transfer data between home and work computers and so transfer viruses.[20]

[13.14] The Price Waterhouse Survey found that only 49% of respondents had a specific policy on viruses. Only 43% of respondents had a policy regarding the playing of computer games. These were more common in

---

16. See Hurka, *Computer Viruses and Anti-Virus Warfare,* 2nd edition, (Ellis-Horwood, 1992) p 23.
17. 588 NYS 2nd 960 (NY Civ Ct 1992).
18. Eg *Norton Anti-Virus* and *Dr Solomon's Anti-Virus.*
19. See para **[13.06]** above.
20. See generally, Nance, 'Keep Networks Safe from Viruses', BYTE, November 1996, p 167.

government departments (66%) and financial institutions (72%). Installing games on a computer greatly increases the risk of virus infection as games are more frequently transferred between users. Such policies must be enforced to be effective. The Audit Commission Report gives the example of an administrative officer who introduced a virus onto three computers when he loaded software from another organisation. This contravened the company's policy and as a result he was suspended and was called before a full disciplinary hearing. The incident caused the company £5,000 worth of damage.[21]

CATEGORIES OF COMPUTER MISUSE

[13.15] The European Committee on Crime Problems was set up under the auspices of the Council of Europe. This body identified twelve areas of computer misuse as being suitable for the attention of the criminal law which are outlined below.[22] It was recommended that for a minimum standard of protection, the first eight specific activities should be criminalised. In addition to these, a further four were identified as being optional.

(1) Computer-related fraud

[13.16] Computer related fraud is essentially entering, altering or erasing computer data or programs with a fraudulent intention.[23] Fraud is a major problem for Irish companies. The KPMG Fraud Survey[24] found that Irish firms reported losses of £9.4 million between 1993 and 1995 due to fraud. This figure was described as being "only the tip of the Irish fraud iceberg" by one of the authors of the survey.[25] The gardaí knew of 3610 frauds committed in Ireland in 1995, 3050 of which were detected by the gardaí.[26] Computer fraud accounted for 9% of reported incidents in 1995. This was unchanged from the 1993 survey.

[13.17] Computer related frauds on a company may be perpetrated by employees or third parties. An example of an internal fraud is given in the

---

[21.] The Audit Commission, *Opportunity Makes a Thief*, 1994 p 18.

[22.] Computer Related Crime, Council of Europe, Recommendation No R 89(9).

[23.] "The input, alteration, erasure or suppression of computer data or computer programs or other interference with the course of data processing, that influences the result of data processing thereby causing economic or possessory loss of property of another person with the intent of procuring an unlawful economic gain for himself or for another person (alternative draft: with the intent to unlawfully deprive that person of his property)".

[24.] 1995.

[25.] *The Irish Times*, 24 June 1995.

[26.] Garda Siochána, *Annual Report 1995*, p 62.

UK Audit Commission Survey. The perpetuator, a temporary employee in a bank, accessed both her own and her husband's personal debtors' accounts and amended the debts due to reduce the amounts owed. She used a colleague's workstation which had been left open so that the transaction appeared to have been processed by the colleague. The UK Audit Commission Survey reported 108 incidents of computer related fraud costing a total of £3,042,318.

[13.18] In *R v Lennon*[27] the appellant was involved in a conspiracy to steal SF70,000,000 from the bank which employed him. The conspiracy involved using a computer to credit a fraudulently set up account with the money. The appellant was convicted and was ultimately sentenced to four years imprisonment. A spectacular external fraud was allegedly perpetrated by a 28 year old Russian working from his laptop computer in St Petersburg. In June of 1995, he hacked into the Wall Street Branch of CitiBank and obtained $400,000 from the accounts of three banks, two Argentinean and one Indonesian. After the police were called, a further $11.6 million was transferred whilst the police tried to track the hacker. Six other people were eventually arrested but Citibank denies that any of their employees were involved in the fraud.[28] There have been suggestions that other similar thefts have not been reported for fear of commercial embarrassment and bad publicity. One estimate suggests that in just two months in 1995 about $300,000,000 disappeared by electronic means from US banks.[29]

(2) Computer forgery

[13.19] Computer forgery is the alteration or creation of computer documents or other electronic material in a manner which would have been forgery had the actions been committed with regard to paper documents or other materials.[30] The Irish Forgery Act 1913 does not define the term 'document'. This may mean that it is already an offence to forge an electronic signature or other methods used to authenticate electronic messages.

---

27. English Court of Appeal, unrep, 14 November 1995, Curtis J.
28. *The Sunday Times*, 3 September 1995
29. See Flohr, 'Bank Robbers Go Electronic', BYTE, November 1995, p 48. See also Dunne, 'Fiddling by Computer', Business & Finance, 18 August 1994, 17. See also para **[15.13]** below.
30. "The input, alteration, erasure or suppression of computer data or computer programs or other interference with the course of data processing, in a manner or under such conditions as prescribed by national law, that it would constitute the offence of forgery if it had been committed with respect to a traditional object of such an offence".

(3) Damage to computer data or programs

[13.20] This is the erasing, damaging or otherwise interfering with computer data or programs.[31] Section 2 of the Criminal Damage Act 1991 specifically criminalises this type of computer misuse.[32]

(4) Computer sabotage

[13.21] Computer sabotage is the alteration or erasure of computer data or programs so as to hinder the working of a computer or a telecommunications system.[33] Computer sabotage is a particular worry for governments. The nightmare scenario of air traffic control computers being reset so that planes fly into each other has been a major motivation in legislating against computer crime in Ireland. So called 'denial of service' attacks are increasingly common on the Internet. This occurs when large numbers of spurious messages are sent to a computer with the object of overloading its communications channels and preventing legitimate users from accessing it.

(5) Unauthorised access

[13.22] This is accessing a computer system and overcoming security measures without permission.[34] This has already been made an offence in Ireland by s 5 of the Criminal Damage Act 1991. However, the offence does not require the offender to overcome any security measures and as a result, the offence is open to abuse. Accessing a computer in this way sounds dramatic but it need not be. In the 1980s VAX Computers made by Digital were found to have a simple but potentially devastating security flaw. When a false password and identification number were entered into the computer, it was meant to display an 'error' message and deny access. Unfortunately, the computers did not do this. If a user simply ignored the error messages, access would be allowed.[35]

(6) Unauthorised interception

[13.23] This involves intercepting messages between computers and networks.[36] Credit card numbers and other valuable information may be intercepted on the Internet and elsewhere. Due to this perceived lack of

---

31. "The erasure, damaging, deterioration or suppression of computer data or computer programs without right."
32. See para **[14.17]** *et seq.*
33. "The input, alteration, erasure or suppression of computer data or computer programs or interference with computer systems with the intent to hinder the functioning of a computer or a telecommunications system."
34. "Access without right to a computer system or network by infringing security measures".
35. Clough & Mungo, *Approaching Zero*, (Faber & Faber, 1992) p 170.
36. "The interception, made without right and by technical means, of communications to, from and within a computer system or network".

security, such networks have as yet to develop their anticipated commercial benefits. However, there is a problem with criminalising all interceptions, as monitoring the use of computers and communications to them may be essential for some security measures which protect computer systems themselves. The interception of telecommunications is already illegal under s 98 of the Postal and Telecommunications Services Act 1983.[37]

(7) Unauthorised reproduction of a protected computer program

[13.24] This is the copying of computer programs without permission.[38] It is an offence under the Copyright Act 1963 and the European Communities (Legal Protection of Computer Programs) Regulations 1993. Many software manufacturers are extremely vigorous in the protection of their copyright but it remains a serious problem in Ireland.[39] This is examined in detail in Chapters 2-5.

(8) Unauthorised reproduction of a topography

[13.25] This is the copying of the topography of a semi conductor chip without permission.[40] Protection is conferred on such chip topographies by the European Communities (Protection of Topographies of Semiconductor Products) Regulation 1988.[41]

OPTIONAL OFFENCES

[13.26] The Council of Europe also identified four additional areas where abuses occur but there was not the same consensus on the creation of offences to deal with these abuses. As a result they were only included on an optional list of possible offences.

(1) Alteration of computer data or computer program

[13.27] It is difficult to see how the alteration of data is different from the destruction or damaging of data.[42] If anything alteration is a more insidious offence as the user or owner of the data may not realise that the alteration has occurred. In any event, the alteration of data is an offence under s 2 of the Criminal Damage Act 1991.[43]

[37.] See Ch 26.

[38.] "The reproduction, distribution or communication to the public without right of a computer program which is protected by law".

[39.] *The Irish Times*, 12 March 1996.

[40.] "The reproduction without right of a topography, protected by law, of a semiconductor product, or the commercial exploitation or the importation for that purpose done without right of a topography or of a semiconductor product manufactured by using the topography." See Ch 10.

[41.] SI 101/1988; Council Directive No 87/54/EEC, 16/12/1986.

[42.] "The alteration of computer data or computer programs without right." p 61.

[43.] See para **[14.17]** *et seq.*

(2) Computer espionage

[13.28] This is the acquisition and disclosure of commercial information.[44] The Council of Europe seems to have only considered commercial espionage. This is similar to the offence of theft of information advocated by the Law Reform Commission.[45] Espionage for foreign governments or other similar activities would presumably be dealt with by existing laws. The US government has enacted an offence of accessing a computer to obtain classified information which carries a potential penalty of twenty years in prison.[46]

[13.29] In the 1980s West German hackers attempted to access various US government computers in order to access information on secret projects such as 'Star Wars'. They hoped to sell this information to the KGB, but they were caught after they were detected by an administrator at the University of California who traced their calls over the Internet.[47]

(3) Unauthorised use of a computer

[13.30] This is using a computer without permission.[48] The Council envisage that this will be an offence only if loss is caused to the person entitled to use the computer. It is difficult to use a computer without causing loss to the owner even if the loss is only the loss of electricity. In practice, it might be better to allow the civil law to deal with these cases unless there is some malicious intent.

(4) Unauthorised use of a protected computer program

[13.31] This is using a computer program without permission.[49] Its intent is to protect intellectual property by creating a further offence of using a pirated computer program. It is difficult to see how this law could be

---

44. "The acquisition by improper means or the disclosure, transfer or use of a trade or commercial secret without right or any other legal justification, with intent either to cause economic loss to the person entitled to the secret or to obtain an unlawful economic advantage for oneself or a third person."
45. Law Reform Commission Report on Dishonesty 1992, p 174.
46. Computer Fraud and Abuse Act 18 USCS S 1030 (1991).
47. Stoll, *The Cuckoo's Egg*, (Doubleday, 1989).
48. "The use of a computer system or network without right, that either: (i) is made with the acceptance of a significant risk of loss being caused to the person entitled to use the system or of harm to the system or its functioning; or (ii) is made with the intent to cause loss to the person entitled to use the system or harm to the system or its functioning; or (iii) causes loss to the person entitled to use the system or harm to the system or its functioning."
49. "The use without right of a computer program which is protected by law and which has been reproduced without right, with the intent, whether to procure an unlawful economic gain for himself or for another person or to cause harm to the holder of the right."

enforced even if a pirated copy of a program is found, it may be difficult to prove its use.

CONCLUSION

[13.32] The Council of Europe gives a comprehensive list of forms of computer misuse. There are other types of criminal or undesirable activity which they did not mention. The theft of computer parts and computers themselves is a particular problem in Ireland.[50]

[13.33] Networks such as the Internet have given rise to other activities which are not illegal but may be considered undesirable such as using the Internet to inflate the price of certain stocks and shares. The stock of one Canadian company, Interlock Consolidated Enterprises, rose from 42 cents to $1.30 before falling back to 60 cents because of messages on the Internet falsely claiming that the company had won a contract in the Russia. Some unfortunates lost as much as $20,000 as a result.[51]

The following chapters examine the issues and difficulties which arise and the measures that have been adopted to tackle computer misuse.

---

50. The small size of computer components means that they can be easily stolen. See *The Irish Independent*, 2 September 1995.
51. Kiernan, 'Internet Tricksters Make a Killing', New Scientist, 16 July 1994. See also *The Irish Independent*, 5 February 1996.

Chapter 14

Offences under the Criminal Damage Act 1991

INTRODUCTION

[14.01] The Criminal Damage Act 1991 ('the 1991 Act') was primarily intended to implement the recommendations of the Law Reform Commission Report on Malicious Damage 1988. However, sections were added to make computer abuse a crime which was not suggested in the Commission's Report. These sections were primarily intended to deal with a perceived danger of computer hackers and the Minister for Justice at the time identified three types of danger: (1) hackers might enter computers to steal or damage data; (2) hackers might cause problems for operational systems such as those used by air traffic control with potentially disastrous consequences; (3) hackers might perpetrate financial frauds.[1]

[14.02] The 1991 Act creates four basic offences:

(1) The offence of causing damage to property;

(2) The offence of threatening to damage property;

(3) The offence of unauthorised access to a computer; and

(4) The offence of possession of anything with intent to cause damage to data.

There has never been a prosecution for computer misuse in Ireland under this legislation. It is not yet known therefore, how the courts would interpret the main provisions.[2]

DEFINITIONS

'Computer'

[14.03] The 1991 Act does not contain any definitions of terms as basic as 'computer'. It avoids such definitions because they may become obsolete as a result of changing technology, a legislative approach which was

---

[1.] Parliamentary Debates, Dáil Éireann, 29 November 1990, p 575.

[2.] See generally: Murray, 'The Criminal Damage Act, 1991', ILT May 1995; Murray, 'Computer Crime in Ireland', ILT October 1995 and Osborne, *The Irish Criminal Legal Response to Computer Misuse,* in Wasik (ed) *International Yearbook of Law Computers & Technology,* (Carfax, 1995) Vol 9, p 65.

fashionable at the time of its enactment. The Data Protection Act 1988 does not provide any definition of the term computer either. Neither does the UK's Computer Misuse Act 1990 or Data Protection Act 1984. The Law Reform Commission has recommended that a definition of computer should be included in any legislation dealing with computer crime. It preferred the definition given in the US Federal legislation which defines a computer as:[3]

> an electronic, magnetic, optical, electrochemical or other high speed data processing device performing logical, arithmetic or storage functions, and includes any data storage facility or communications facility directly related to, or operating in conjunction with, such device but such term does not include an automated typewriter or typesetter, a portable hand held calculator or other similar device.[4]

The last part of this definition which states that it does not include a typewriter and other such devices should avoid the problem of computer crime legislation being potentially applicable to all sorts of machines which just happen to contain computer chips. The disadvantage with trying to define terms such as computer with such precision is that doing so can sometimes lead to ludicrous results. In Florida, a computer is defined as "an internally programmed, automatic device that performs data processing".[5] This covers a computer but it also covers a digital watch. The difficulty with broad definitions is that they may be too broad to be practical.[6] It is unclear what is and what is not illegal under the 1991 Act. The Oireachtas has left it to the courts to decide what exactly a computer, data, a storage medium or access actually is. This may render those sections of the Act which deal with computer crime unconstitutional as the terms are ambiguous and vague.

[14.04] The absence of definitions of terms such as 'computer' has not prevented the use of the UK Computer Misuse Act 1990[7] and Data Protection Act 1984[8] to successfully prosecute crime. However the pace of technological change is extraordinarily rapid in the computer industry and it is undoubted that new types of computer will be developed which would have seemed inconceivable to the drafters of the 1991 Act. Computers based on neural networks which attempt to mimic the functioning of the human

---

3.   Law Reform Commission Report on Dishonesty (LRC 43/1992), p 246.
4.   The Computer Fraud and Abuse Act 18 US CS s 1030 (1991).
5.   Fla Stat, s 815.0(3).
6.   This difficulty was explicitly accepted by Ian Taylor, the UK Technology Minister who stated "It's not going to be easy for us to frame legislation to limit uses of the Internet", in the New Scientist, 'Internet anarchy in the UK', 25 February 1995, p 4.
7.   For example the conviction of Christopher Pile at Exeter Crown Court, on 15 November 1995.
8.   *R v Brown* [1996] 1 All ER 545.

brain are already being built,[9] very fast computers based on quantum mechanics are at least a theoretical possibility[10] and even computers which use light to carry out processing instead of electrical charges are being used.[11] Although the 1991 Act does not define computer it cannot avoid including a definition of data which it defines as "information in a form which can be accessed by means of a computer and includes data." How these terms may be interpreted by the courts in the future is unknown, but the Supreme Court judgment in *Keane and Naughton v Clare County Council*[12] suggests that the courts will have some difficulty in doing so. That case concerned an application by the Commissioners of Irish Lights to build a mast for the Loran-C radio navigation system in County Clare. The Commissioners were a statutory corporation and their powers were limited by the legislation which regulated their activities, in this case the Merchant Shipping Act 1894. Their powers as set out by s 638 of the 1894 Act included *inter alia* the power to "erect or place any buoy or beacon". Buoy or beacon was defined as including all marks or signs of the sea other than lighthouses.[13] Obviously, radio navigation was not contemplated by the drafters of this legislation so the Supreme Court had to decide whether buoy or beacon could be extended to include this modern technology. The Court refused to extend the definition of buoy to include a mast for the Loran-C navigation system. Hamilton CJ agreed with the judgment of Murphy J in the High Court that he had:

> "... no difficulty in accepting the desirability and in general the necessity for giving to legislation an 'up-dating construction'. Where terminology used in legislation is wide enough to capture a subsequent invention there is no reason to exclude from the ambit ... of the legislation. But a distinction must be made between giving an updated construction to the general scheme of legislation and altering the meaning of particular words used therein."[14]

[14.05] Hamilton CJ stated that in interpreting a statute the text of a statute is to be regarded as the pre-eminent indication of the legislator's intention and its meaning is to be taken to be that which corresponds to the literal meaning. It was submitted by the Commissioners that the true intention of the Act was to provide navigational aids to mariners and that the language

---

9. For an account of neural networks, see Laddie, Prescott and Vitoria, *The Modern Law of Copyright and Design* (Butterworths, 1995) p 849.
10. *The Economist*, 28 September 1996, p 105.
11. *The Economist*, 4 May 1996, p 83.
12. Supreme Court, unrep, 18 July 1996.
13. The Merchant Shipping Act 1894, s 742.
14. *Ibid* p 30 of transcript.

used by the Act allowed for a very wide range of such aids. Hamilton CJ rejected this submission as not reflecting the true original intention of the legislature. He stated that:

> "Buoys and beacons are stated in the Act to include all ... marks and signs of the sea. At the time of the enactment of the Act 'Buoys' and 'Beacons' were regarded as visual aids to navigation. As a result of the development of technology and the current use of language the mast proposed to be erected by the Commissioners can be described as a beacon but the mere fact that it can be so described in the current use of the term does not entitle it to be so described for the purposes so of the Act if it is something which is altogether beyond the scope of the Act..."[15]

[14.06] Four of the judges[16] explicitly indicated that they were in favour of allowing old statutes "to operate in the light of new discoveries in science or elsewhere which can be taken to be within the ambit of what the particular act seeks to achieve".[17] However, they differed on whether the interpretation of this Act could be extended as far as was desired by the Commissioners. Barrington J suggested that had the 1894 Act simply entrusted the Commissioners with the management of 'aids to navigation' then he would have been happy to include the erection of radio masts as being within their remit.[18] Denham J dissenting, quoted *Bennion* who states:

> "It is presumed that Parliament intends the court to apply to an ongoing Act a construction that continuously updates its wording to allow for changes since the Act was initially framed ... While it remains law it is to be treated as always speaking. This means that in its application on any date, the language of the Act, though necessarily embedded in its own time, is nevertheless to be construed in accordance with the need to treat it as current law."[19]

[14.07] Denham J took the view that as the 1894 Act defined buoys and beacons as being all signs of the sea other than lighthouses they included all devices which give information to seafarers. She argued that as the definition of beacons was not limited to aids which may be seen or heard, it could be extended to radio masts. Denham J cited in support of her decision

---

15. *Ibid* p 35.
16. Hamilton CJ, O'Flaherty J, Denham J and Barrington J, Blayney J did not express any view on this point.
17. *Per* O'Flaherty J, p 5.
18. *Per* Barrington J, p 10.
19. Bennion, *Statutory Interpretation, A Code*, 2nd ed, s 288, quoted by Denham J at p 15. Hamilton J quotes *Bennion* to the same effect, however he notes that it also states that if "changed technology produces something which is altogether beyond the scope of the original enactment the Court will not treat it as covered."

a judgment of the Supreme Court in *McCarthy v O'Flynn*.[20] That case concerned the question of whether X-ray photographs were documents for the purposes of Order 31 rule 12 of the Rules of the Superior Courts. Like the 1991 Act, the RSC do not contain definitions of many terms used therein. However the Supreme Court was able to extend the definition of document to include an X-ray.[21] The very broad interpretation taken unanimously by the Supreme Court in that case strongly contrasts with its much more limited approach in *Keane and Naughton v Clare County Council*. This difference may result from the fact that in *McCarthy v O'Flynn* the Court was interpreting rules which are written by the Superior Courts Rules Committee as opposed to the Oireachtas. It may also be due to the fact that as the term 'document' was not defined by the Rules of the Superior Courts the court found it easier to give a broad definition of the term. If this latter proposition is correct, then there may be no substantial difficulty as a result of the lack of definitions in the 1991 Act. The judgment of the Supreme Court in *Keane and Naughton v Clare County Council* does make it clear that the courts will not automatically interpret statutes to take account of all changes in technology but it is difficult to generalise further from the judgments in that case. Although the court declared itself willing to apply updated definitions to terms in old legislation it declined to do so in the instant case. It is impossible to judge how the court would interpret a different statute dealing with different technology and different changes in that technology. On balance, inserting definitions into the 1991 Act would be a welcome reform. The Minister for Justice has announced that she wishes to create a system whereby annual amendments could be made to the criminal law where it has become outdated or outmoded. This would involve the introduction of an annual Criminal Justice (Miscellaneous Provisions) Bill.[22] If this is done then any statutory definitions of terms such as data or computer could be adapted to take account of technological change.

[14.08] If the 1991 Act is not amended then there is a danger that it may be unconstitutional because of the vagueness of its terms. In *King v AG*,[23] the appellant was convicted of loitering with intent under s 4 of the Vagrancy Act 1824. This section provided that "every suspected person or reputed thief" found loitering with intent to commit a felony could be committed to prison for up to three months. The Act contained no definition of suspected person or reputed thief. On appeal, the Supreme Court found that this

---

20. [1979] IR 127.
21. Para **[18.09]** *et seq.*
22. Speaking at the Committee stage of the Criminal Justice (Miscellaneous Provisions) Bill 1996, *The Irish Times*, 3 October 1996.
23. [1981] IR 233.

provision was unconstitutional on the grounds (*inter alia*) that it was inconsistent with the defendant's right to be tried on a criminal charge only in due course of law[24] and only to be deprived of his liberty in accordance with law.[25] Kenny J stated:

> "It is a fundamental feature of our system of government by law that citizens may be convicted only of offences which have been specified with precision by the judges who made the common law, or of offences which, created by statute, are expressed without ambiguity. But what does 'suspected person' mean? Suspected of what? What does 'reputed thief' mean? Reputed by whom? It does not mean a person who has been convicted of theft, for then 'convicted thief' would have been the appropriate words. So one is driven back to the conclusion that it is impossible to ascertain the meaning of the expressions. In my opinion, both governing phrases 'suspected person' and 'reputed thief' are so uncertain that they cannot form the foundation for a criminal offence."[26]

He cited the judgment of O'Byrne J in *Attorney General v Cunningham* as authority for the proposition "that a person may be convicted of a criminal offence only if the ingredients of, and the acts constituting, the offence are specified with precision and clarity". As many essential terms are not defined in the 1991 Act it lacks this element of precision and clarity.

'Property' and 'data'

[14.09] The 1991 Act extends the definition of property to include data.[27] Data is defined as "information in a form in which it can be accessed by means of a computer and includes a program". Programs are normally seen as being separate to data. Data is the information which computers, using programs, manipulate.[28] However, the meaning of the 1991 Act would appear to be that anything stored on a computer is to count as data. This will undoubtedly lead to confusion should any case be tried under the Act. It is almost certain, unless there is a guilty plea, that the court will have to hear evidence from computer experts and other professionals who use the terms 'program' and 'data' to refer to separate and distinct concepts.

[14.10] The definition of data as "information in a form in which it can be accessed by means of a computer ..." would include information held on a

---

24. Article 38.1.
25. Article 40.4.1°.
26. *Ibid*, at 263.
27. CDA 1991, s 1
28. *The Concise Oxford Dictionary*, (8th ed, 1990), defines data as "known facts or things used as a basis for inference or reckoning" and "quantities or characters operated on by a computer etc".

floppy disk. Stealing or damaging a floppy disk, or altering the data on a floppy disk would entail the same penalties as damaging the data on the hard disk of a computer. Property of a tangible nature[29] is also protected by the 1991 Act. If a hacker were to cause damage to property other than data by, for example, altering the commands used by the computers which control a factory's machinery, then he would be liable to be prosecuted for any damage caused by the machinery as well as the damage caused to the data. It has been suggested that this may lead a gap in the law in relation to non-tangible property. If a computer is used to obtain a benefit or service or to cause loss where the thing obtained in the misuse cannot be stolen in the ordinary sense, then there may not be an offence.[30]

[14.11] The question of whether a computer program or other materials stored in a computer can be property was examined in the English decision of *Cox v Riley*.[31] In that case the accused was employed by a company to operate a computerised saw. The saw was controlled by a printed circuit card which contained programs and the saw was of no use to the accused's employers unless the card contained those programs. For reasons which were not dealt with by the court, the accused operated a "program cancellation facility" which erased the programs from the circuit card. Section 1(1) of the UK Criminal Damage Act 1971 states that:

> A person who without lawful excuse destroys or damages any property belonging to another intending to destroy or damage any such property ... shall be guilty of an offence.

Property is defined in s 10(1) of that Act as meaning "property of a tangible nature, whether real or personal ...". The accused was convicted at first instance and appealed by way of a case stated. The accused argued that as the programs could not be seen or touched in the ordinary physical sense, the erasure of the programs could not amount to damage within the meaning of the Act. The Court relied on the judgments in *Henderson & Battley*[32] where the defendants caused building waste to be dumped on development land. Although no lasting damage was caused to the land it cost £2,000 to remove the waste. The Court also relied on *Fisher*[33] a case from 1865 where an employee had put a steam engine out of action and which required two hours labour to restart although no materials were required. The common thread in

---

[29.] CDA 1991, s 1(1) provides that property means "property of a tangible nature, whether real or personal including money and animals that are capable of being stolen and data".
[30.] The Report of the Government Advisory Committee on Fraud 1993, p 27.
[31.] (1986) 83 Cr App Rep 54.
[32.] English High Court, unrep, 29 November 1984, Cantley J.
[33.] [1865] LR 1; 1 CCR 7.

both these cases would appear to be that although no lasting physical damage was caused, the actions of the accused required time, labour and money to be expended. In *Cox v Riley* Stephen Browne LJ held that it was untenable to argue that the accused had not damaged property. He accepted that the court was living in the age of computers and computerised machines were part of the industrial and social scene and emphatically rejected the arguments of the accused.

[14.12] In *R v Whiteley*,[34] the accused was similarly charged with causing criminal damage contrary to s 1(1) of the UK Criminal Damage Act 1971. The defendant was a hacker who gained unauthorised access to the Joint Academic Network system (JANET) in the UK. Once he had access, Whiteley deleted and added files, sent messages, created user names for his own purposes, changed the passwords of authorised users, and regularly deleted files which contained records of his own and others' activity on the system. The computers on the system failed, were unable to operate properly or had to be shut down for periods of time. Whiteley was prosecuted on two grounds: first, that he caused criminal damage to the computers by bringing about temporary impairment of their use by causing them to be shut down for periods of time or preventing them from operating properly; secondly, that he caused criminal damage to the disks by altering the state of magnetic particles on them so as to delete and add files. This viewed the disks and the magnetic particles on them as being one entity and so capable of being damaged. Whiteley was acquitted by the jury of the former charge of causing criminal damage to the computers however he was convicted on the latter charge of damaging the computer disks and appealed to the Court of Appeal. At the trial the jury heard evidence that the disks were constructed to contain upon them millions of magnetic particles. Commands issued to the computer will produce impulses which will magnetise or demagnetise these particles in a particular way. This allows data or information to be written on the disks. The same method would allow the deletion or alteration of data, information or instructions which have been previously written on the disk. Whiteley's appeal rested on the argument that since the state of the magnetic particles on the disk was not perceptible by the unaided human senses such as touch or sight therefore the hacking carried out by him, which he admitted, only affected the "intangible information contained" on the disk itself. The argument of the defence was in essence that interference with these magnetic particles could not amount to criminal damage in law.

[34.] (1991) 93 Cr App Rep 25.

[14.13] This argument was rejected as fallacious by the Court of Appeal. The court referred to several other cases in which damage had been found to occur although no lasting physical damage had been caused to property including *Tacey*[35] in which it was found that removing a part of a machine and so making the whole of the machine useless could amount to damage. The Court agreed with the judgment of Stephen Brown LJ in *Cox v Riley*[36] and referred to the judgment of Auld J in *Morphitis v Salmon*[37] in which he stated that:

> "the authorities show that the term damage for the purpose of this provision, should be widely interpreted so as to include not only permanent or temporary physical harm, but also permanent or temporary impairment of value or usefulness."

The Court of Appeal held that the effect of these decisions was that any alteration to the physical nature of the property concerned may amount to criminal damage. Whether this alteration would amount to damage would depend on the effect that it had on the owner of the computer. If the hacker's actions did not go beyond mere "tinkering with an otherwise 'empty' disk, no damage would be established". However, if the interference impaired the value or usefulness of the disk to the owner then damage would be established. Since it is not the disk which is of any real value but rather the information contained upon it, this means that the Court of Appeal would appear to have effectively created an offence of damaging information.

[14.14] It has been suggested that as a result of the *Whiteley* case the introduction of specific legislation to deal with computer crime may have been unnecessary.[38] However, this case exposed a significant difficulty in prosecuting computer crime using legislation which does not specifically deal with computers. Firstly, Whiteley was only convicted of causing damage to a computer disk, although in reality his activities went far beyond this. In particular, Whiteley was not convicted of unauthorised access to a computer. At his trial both the judge and the prosecution agreed that there was a fundamental difference between "mere snooping" and "leaving annoying messages" which were not crimes and deleting files and impairing the usefulness of a computer system which were. Although Whiteley admitted damaging extensive and expensive computer networks, he was only actually convicted of damaging the computer disks which are just one

---

35. [1821] Rus and Ry 452.
36. [1986] 83 Cr App Rep 54.
37. [1990] Crim LR 48.
38. Lloyd, *Information Technology Law*, (Butterworths, 1993), p 151.

part of those networks. Secondly, the Irish courts may not be willing to include computer crimes within the ambit of other legislation.

'Damage'

[14.15] In relation to data, 'damage' is defined as:

> to add to, alter, corrupt, erase or move to another storage medium or to a different location in the storage medium in which they are kept (whether or not property other than data is damaged thereby), or to do any act that contributes towards causing such addition, alteration, corruption, erasure or movement.

and "to make an omission causing damage".

[14.16] The inclusion of omissions in the definition of 'to damage' means that the 1991 Act will cover a situation where a part of a program or data is deliberately omitted, however it would also apply in the situation, where for example, an employee neglects to turn off his or her computer at night and while they are gone a fault in the system damages or erases data. The definition of 'damage' probably does not include taking a copy of data while leaving the original in place. Copying of data or other computer materials may have been excluded from this definition because the authors felt that this was already prohibited under intellectual property law. This is certainly true of programs and copyright works. Factual data such as bank records may be protected as confidential information.[39] Copying data is probably not included because of difficulties which have arisen in prosecutions concerning the copying of films and examination papers and the difficulties of proving that there was an intention to permanently deprive the owner of the information.[40] In general, it is not a criminal offence to copy or 'steal' information.[41] If copying data were to be made an offence then records held on computer would have protection which is not available to other forms of data.

OFFENCES AND PENALTIES

(1) Damage to Data

[14.17] The first offence under the 1991 Act is damage to property as contained in s 2(1) which states:

---

39. See Ch **9**.
40. See *R v Lloyd* [1985] 2 All ER 661 and *Oxford v Moss* 68 Cr App Rep 183. See para **[18.02]** *et seq*.
41. Although the Law Reform Commission has recommended the creation of such an offence.

A person who without lawful excuse damages any property belonging to another intending to damage any such property or being reckless as to whether any such property would be damaged shall be guilty of an offence.

Even if it can be proved that an accused damaged a particular piece of 'data', assessing the amount of damage done may be difficult. Most computer users will back-up their data as a matter of course. If data can be easily and quickly replaced then it is difficult to attach much value to the data. In *United States v Riggs*,[42] the accused was charged with stealing a document relating to E911 or emergency calls using his computer. At the trial, the value of the document was accessed at $79,449 in total. Unfortunately for the prosecution, the phone company actually sold the document for $13.[43]

[14.18] Section 2 could be used to deal with the problem of viruses, but it does not make placing a virus on a computer an offence, only where it damages the data. This would create a problem since even if it can be shown that data on a computer was damaged, a virus was present on the computer and a known individual had introduced that specific virus to the computer, it may be impossible to show that the damage was caused by the operation of the virus. Accidental damage can occur to data in many ways, loss of electricity supply, jostling the computer and switching off a computer without closing files can all accidentally damage or erase data.[44]

[14.19] Section 2(1) states that the accused must have intended to damage the property, which would include malicious actions. Hackers frequently claim that they only access computers with the intention of 'looking around' and for the thrill of breaching the computer's defences. In this situation the hacker might not be liable for the damage although he could be prosecuted for unauthorised access. However, if it could be shown that the hacker had acted recklessly then he could be convicted. A person is defined as being reckless "if he has foreseen that the particular kind of damage that in fact was done might be done and has gone on to take the risk of it".

[14.20] It is arguable that any person who breaks into a computer without the owner's consent is acting recklessly. Owners of computer systems should

---

42. 739 F Supp 414 (ND III 1990) and 743 F Supp 556 (ND III 1990), also Smedinghoff ed, *Online Law,* (Addison Wesley, 1996) p 480.
43. The telephone company included the costs of buying the computer at $31,000 on which the document was written, $4,500 for the software, $6,000 for the printer and $17,099 for bureaucratic overheads. The document was 12 pages long and had taken 5 weeks to write and 1 week to type: Sterling, *The Hacker Crackdown,* (Bantam Books, 1992) p 258.
44. Breakdown was seen as being the most serious threat to computers, closely followed by viruses and hacking in the Price Waterhouse, *Priority Data Systems Computer Virus and Security Survey 1995,* p 12.

ensure that whenever a person attempts to access a system, a message is displayed on the monitor stating that only authorised users may access the system, anyone who is in doubt about their authorisation should contact an official within the company and that anyone who accesses the system without authorisation will be liable to prosecution under the 1991 Act.[45]

[14.21] The inclusion of recklessness as a requirement for an offence may have unexpected consequences. It is easy to damage data on a computer unintentionally. An authorised user may unintentionally but recklessly alter data in the course of his work but under this section will commit a criminal offence.

[14.22] A particular problem may occur when employees unwittingly use floppy disks which contain viruses. Any sensible organisation will warn employees against the use of floppy disks of unknown origin or which have been used elsewhere. If this is so and the computer is infected with a virus as a result, then it could be held that the employee who used the disks was acting recklessly and so had committed an offence.

[14.23] The 1991 Act also criminalises several other activities. Section 2(2) states that:

> A person who without lawful excuse damages any property, whether belonging to himself or another - intending to damage any property or being reckless as to whether any property would be damaged, and intending by the damage to endanger the life of another or being reckless as to whether the life of another would be thereby endangered, shall be guilty of an offence."

This is covers the scenario where as a result of computer misuse, lives are put at risk. An example was cited in the UK Audit Commission Report[46] where a nurse hacked into a hospital's computer system and prescribed potentially lethal drugs for a patient. He altered treatment records for others. The nurse used a doctor's personal identification code which he had memorised some months earlier. Fortunately, the prescription changes were noticed by a colleague before the drugs were administered. The nurse was

---

45. This method has also been used by hackers in the UK. Police Chiefs have complained that messages have been placed at the access points to Bulletin Boards stating that "law enforcement officials are not permitted to enter the system". Such a warning has been considered to be effective in restricting the police from accessing Bulletin Boards since the police would commit an offence of 'unauthorised access' under s 1 of the Computer Misuse Act 1990. This difficulty has been dealt with in the UK by the enactment of s 162 of the Criminal Justice and Public Order Act 1994.

46. The Audit Commission, *Opportunity Makes a Thief* (1994).

successfully prosecuted under the UK Computer Misuse Act 1990 for unauthorised modification of computer data.

[14.24] Section 2(3) of the 1991 Act states that:

> a person who damages any property whether belonging to himself or another, with intent to defraud shall be guilty of an offence.

This section deals with traditional forms of insurance fraud where a person deliberately crashes their car or burns down a building to claim the insurance on it. Altering computer data is a common means of committing financial fraud by altering entries on a payroll or creating false invoices. Altering data in this way would amount to damaging the data and would therefore amount to an offence.

[14.25] Where data kept within Ireland has been damaged by someone outside the State, presumably by use of a computer network, that person may still be prosecuted and the offence will be treated as though it had been committed within Ireland.[47] This provision also applies where property other than data is damaged.

Penalties

[14.26] The penalties for committing an offence under s 2 is on summary conviction a fine not exceeding £1,000 or imprisonment for a term not exceeding 12 months or both. If a person is convicted of causing damage with intent to endanger life then they may be fined or sentenced to life imprisonment or both. Where a person is found guilty of any other offence on indictment under this section he will be liable to a fine not exceeding £10,000 or imprisonment for a term not exceeding 10 years or both.[48]
The court may also make an alternative order requiring that compensation be paid to the injured party.[49]

(2) Threatening to damage property

[14.27] Hackers often will spend considerable amounts of time and energy trying to enter a computer system. If the administrator of the system detects these attempts then he will be forced to spend time and ultimately his employer's money countering these threats. Often a hacker who successfully

---

[47] CDA 1991, s 7(1).

[48] Where damage is caused to property by fire, it will be charged as arson. A conviction on indictment for arson under sub-s 1 or 3 is punishable by a fine or imprisonment for life or both: CDA 1991, s 2(4).

[49] See para **[15.21]** *et seq.* The penalties under the 1991 Act are mild by some international standards. The Chinese authorities are reported to have executed a computer hacker: The Audit Commission, *Opportunity Makes a Thief*, 1994, p 12.

enters a system undetected will tire of the anonymity and will boast of his accomplishment by leaving messages in files where they will be read by the administrators of the system. Nick Whiteley[50] was to acquire fame by hacking into mainframe computers throughout Britain during 1988. Whiteley's notoriety partially stemmed from rumours that he had successfully hacked into computers belonging to the Ministry of Defence and M15. Whiteley left numerous messages, particularly to the administrator of the computer at Queen Mary College in London. Ultimately, he was convicted of criminal damage and sentenced to one year's imprisonment. While hackers may not intend to cause damage, the administrator has no way of knowing this for certain and he must treat any such attack with the utmost seriousness. Although attempting to enter a system and leaving messages in a system once it is entered may not cause any actual damage in themselves, there is a clear threat in these actions that damage may or will be caused. The 1991 Act makes it an offence to threaten to cause damage to property which includes data.

[14.28] Section 3 of the 1991 Act states that:

> a person who without lawful excuse makes to another a threat intending that that other would fear it would be carried out -
>
> (a) to damage any property belonging to that other or a third person, or
>
> (b) to damage his own property in a way which he knows is likely to endanger the life of that other or a third person
>
> shall be guilty of an offence.

The person who makes the threat need not be actually capable of carrying out his threat. All he must do is intend that another will fear that it would be carried out. So if a hacker were to be charged under this section as a result of threatening to cause damage he could not defend himself by saying that he was not in fact able to cause any damage. This is important as often a hacker will try to access a system over long periods of time. The administrator may not note all these attempts and in particular if the hacker is successful in entering the system, the administrator may not know about it.

Penalties

[14.29] Any person convicted of an offence under this section is liable to a fine not exceeding £1,000 and/or to imprisonment for a term not exceeding 12 months on summary conviction. On conviction on indictment, he will be

---

50. *R v Whiteley* (1991) 93 Cr App Rep 25. See para **[14.12]**.

liable to a fine not exceeding £10,000 and/or imprisonment for a term not exceeding 10 years.[51]

(3) Possession of anything with intent to damage property

[14.30] In practical terms, s 4 is potentially the most useful section of the 1991 Act. It provides that possessing anything with the intent of using it to damage property is an offence. This is important as it may be difficult to prove that a hacker has actually caused criminal damage or accessed a system without authorisation. If it can be shown that the hacker had things in his possession which would be used for hacking then he could be convicted of an offence.

[14.31] Section 4 states:

> a person (in this section referred to as the possessor) who has any thing in his custody or under his control intending without lawful excuse to use it or cause or permit another to use it -
>
> (a) to damage any property belonging to some other person, or
>
> (b) to damage his own or the intended user's property -
>
> > (i)   in a way which he knows is likely to endanger the life of a person other than the possessor, or
> >
> > (ii) with intent to defraud,
>
> shall be guilty of an offence.

'Anything' implies that this section is intended to have an extremely broad effect. It would include having a virus program present on the computer, having a program to write viruses on the computer, but it could also include a modem and other hardware and also books, such as hacking guides.[52] The obvious difficulty for prosecutors would be that they would have to show that the possessor was intending to use the 'thing' to cause damage. Having a virus on a computer is probably evidence of misfortune rather than criminal intent. Similarly, the authors of viruses may never intend them to cause damage and may merely wish to satisfy themselves of their own expertise. For example, the *Tequila* virus was written by an amateur programmer to show off his sophisticated programming techniques and to prove to himself that he could do it. Unfortunately, he showed it to a friend who had fallen out with his father. The friend stole a copy of the virus and infected his father's computer from where the virus spread out to infect computers all over the world.[53]

---

[51] CDA 1991, s 3(i) and (ii).

[52] For example the German Chaos Computer Club promotes *Die Hackerbibel* (the hacker bible), a two volume reference of hacker techniques.

[53] *Dr Solomon's Anti-Virus Book*, (Newtech, 1994) p 183.

[14.32] Prosecutors might have to show that the possessor had something more incriminating. If the possessor held large numbers of passwords to which he would not normally be entitled or credit card numbers, then it could be very strongly argued that the possessor must have held these things with the intent to cause damage. The standard of intent is higher than that in s 2. There is no requirement that the possessor be reckless as to whether property is damaged. The possessor must be shown to have intended the damage to occur.

[14.33] The fact that the 'thing' may be held with the intention of causing or permitting another to use it to damage property, would mean that holding virus-infected disks could be an offence if it could be shown that these were to be used in another's computer. The difficulty with using this offence to prosecute computer crime is that it must be shown that the 'thing' is to be used in the future to damage property. Although this might be inferred from previous uses of the 'thing', it may be difficult to prove that the accused intended to use it to cause damage in the future.

Penalties

[14.34] Any person convicted of this offence is liable to a fine not exceeding £1,000 and/or not more than 12 months in prison on summary conviction. On conviction on indictment, they are liable to a fine not exceeding £10,000 and/or imprisonment not exceeding 10 years.[54]

(4) Unauthorised access

[14.35] This offence is different from the three discussed above. It is specifically intended to apply only to computer crime and has no other application. Although the section is entitled 'the unauthorised accessing of data' it is in fact the offence of accessing data without a lawful excuse. The offence of unauthorised access as found in the UK Computer Misuse Act 1990, amongst others, makes it an offence to access a computer without authorisation. Authorisation has a specific meaning, in computer terms it means that the accused has accessed a computer system with a password to which they are not entitled or by otherwise overcoming security measures. It may not be necessary to prove intent for this offence, all that has to be proved is that the accused used a password to which they were not entitled. The 1991 Act will force prosecutors to show that the accused did not have a lawful excuse. Although this might be inferred from the fact that the accused used a password to which they were not entitled, this may force the prosecution to deal with the question of the accused's intention. The offence

---

54. CDA 1991, s 4(a) and (b).

is very general and was probably included to catch hackers who entered a system where it was impossible to link them directly with any damage caused.

[14.36] Section 5(1) of the 1991 Act states that:

> a person who without lawful excuse operates a computer within the State with intent to access any data kept either within or outside the State, or outside the State with intent to access any data kept within the State, shall whether or not he accesses any data, be guilty of an offence.

This section potentially criminalises computer activities of every description, as it is for the operator of the computer to show that he has a lawful excuse. The meaning of operate is unclear, as is access. At its broadest 'operate' could mean just typing in a password or connecting to a computer over the Internet. A narrow interpretation would restrict 'operate' to interfering with programs on a computer or with the running of the computer itself. Similarly, a broad interpretation of 'access' might take it to mean simply plugging the computer in. The fact that the offence occurs regardless of whether any data is actually accessed or not, suggests that a very broad interpretation was intended. Data is defined as including programs. It is impossible to interact with a computer without interacting with the programs on the computer. Just about the only thing which can be done with a computer, without interacting with the programs is to turn it on or off. In fact even this involves accessing the programs as when a computer is turned on it automatically runs certain programs. In the event of a prosecution under the 1991 Act all the above terms would have to be defined in court.

[14.37] The one criteria which is made any way clear is that of intent. The accused must have "intent to access any data" however sub-s (2) states that the above:

> applies whether or not the person intended to access any particular data or any particular category of data or data kept by any particular person.

In other words, any type of data. Data is defined as "information in a form in which it can be accessed by means of a computer",[55] ie, any information held on any computer or computer disk. It would appear that if the accused intended to access data held by one person but in fact accessed data held by another, then he would still have the necessary intent. The definition of intent is as broad as it possibly could be and unlike the UK legislation, there is no requirement that the access be unauthorised. However, users may show

---

[55.] CDA 1991, s 1.

that they have a lawful excuse. The jurisdiction of this section is also very broad. It applies to a hacker within the State accessing a computer either in Ireland or elsewhere. It also applies to a hacker who accesses data within Ireland from abroad. Where data kept within Ireland has been accessed by someone outside the State, presumably by use of a computer network, that person may still be prosecuted and the offence will be treated as if it had been committed at any place within Ireland.[56] The Act is made more flexible by s 7(3) which provides that where a person is charged with damage to data under s 2, but the evidence is insufficient to convict, then the court may convict that person of the offence of unauthorised access under s 5 if the evidence so warrants.

[14.38] The definition of what constitutes access has been considered in the UK in the *Attorney General's Reference (No 1, 1991)*.[57] This case was referred to the Court of Appeal by the Attorney General. The defendant had been employed by a locksmith and he had full knowledge of his employer's computer system. After leaving the employment, he returned to the locksmith's premises to purchase an item valued at £710.96. While on the premises, he used an unattended computer terminal to enter a code which instructed the computer to give him a 70% discount. As a result he was only charged £204.76. The defendant was arrested pursuant to the UK Computer Misuse Act 1990, however, the trial judge dismissed the charges on the grounds that the Act required access to be obtained by using one computer to access another. He based this decision on s 1(1)(a) of the Act which states:

> a person is guilty of an offence if he causes a computer to perform any function with intent to secure access to any program or data held in any computer.

The decision of the trial judge was overturned by the Court of Appeal which stated that there was no reason to assume that access had to be from one computer to another. It would be possible to make this argument in Ireland, but it is probable that it would be unsuccessful.

[14.39] It may not be necessary for the accused actually to use the computer himself to commit an offence. In *R v Farquharson*,[58] the accused was found guilty of unauthorised access and given a six month term of imprisonment. Farquharson persuaded an unwitting accomplice who was employed by his victim to access the data and did not actually use the computer himself. His

---

[56.] CDA 1991, s 7(1). See para **[15.13]** *et seq.*

[57.] [1992] 3 WLR 432.

[58.] Croydon Magistrates, 9 December 1993. See Walden 'Update on the Computer Misuse Act 1990', Journal of Business Law, September 1994, p 522.

accomplice was given a £300 fine. This case would carry little weight in Ireland as it was only decided at the level of the Magistrates Court. In any event, the Irish Act refers specifically to a person who "operates a computer" which would seem to suggest that a similar case would not succeed here. The UK Act states that an offence is committed by any person who "causes a computer to perform any function". It might be possible to secure a conviction for causing damage to data or by proving a criminal conspiracy.

Penalties

[14.40] A person convicted of unauthorised access is liable on summary conviction to a fine not exceeding £500 and/or imprisonment for a term not exceeding three months. There is no provision for a conviction on indictment and the penalties are considerably lighter than those provided for criminal damage.[59] As this offence can only be prosecuted summarily, this may lead to problems as under s 10(4) of the Petty Sessions Ireland Act 1851 complaints must be brought within six months of the occurrence of the offence. This may be a short time within which to bring a prosecution in computer cases where the evidence of the crime may be difficult to prepare and the charges may be complex.

Conclusion

[14.41] The 1991 Act creates a comprehensive range of offences and most types of computer misuse are criminalised by the Act. Much of this comprehensiveness stems from ss 3 and 4 which make threatening and preparing to commit a computer crime an offence in itself. Later sections dealing with court procedures seem to take the view that prosecutions will only be taken for computer crimes under ss 2 and 5.[60] Unfortunately, it would appear that many legitimate activities are also criminalised and this will place a heavy burden on prosecutors and judges in deciding whether or not a prosecution is merited in a particular case. The main defence of a legitimate user is that they can claim to have a 'lawful excuse' and this will be examined in a later chapter.[61]

[14.42] One activity that is not specifically criminalised by the Act is the writing of viruses or other malicious programs. Instead the Act makes every

---

[59.] CDA 1991, s 5(1).

[60.] CDA 1991, s 7(3) provides that where an offence under s 2 is prosecuted, but there is not enough evidence for a conviction, then the accused may be convicted under s 5 if there is enough evidence for that offence. If the drafters had anticipated that prosecutions might be taken for computer crimes under ss 3 and 4 they would presumably have extended s 7(3) to deal with prosecutions under these sections.

[61.] See para **[16.04]** *et seq.*

innocent possessor of a virus a potential criminal. The reason for this is probably the difficulty in proving that an accused wrote a particular virus program. Furthermore it would be difficult to create an offence of virus writing which did not potentially criminalise the writing of any program. It is possible that the author of a virus could be prosecuted under s 2 for damaging property. Such a prosecution could only succeed if it could be shown that the specific virus written by the defendant had damaged property, which would probably be very difficult. The defendant's *mens rea* would be that of recklessness. Anyone capable of writing a virus will be very well aware of the damage it can cause and this would bring him within the definition of recklessness contained in s 2 which is that the defendant should have foreseen the damage which might be done and still gone ahead with his action.

Chapter 15

The Investigation and Prosecution of Offences under the Criminal Damage Act 1991

INTRODUCTION

[15.01] The investigation of computer crimes requires a knowledge of computers and information technology systems. *R v Vatsal Patel*[1] highlights the difficulties of prosecuting such offences. The accused was employed on a software development project. He seems to have been successful at his job, his contract was twice extended and only terminated with the completion of the particular project and he was immediately re-employed elsewhere. Unfortunately, his employer's project began to suffer difficulties. The product of all their software development was held as a set of database tables and these began to disappear. Sabotage was suspected and a pair of wrecking programs were identified on the network computer, normally used by the accused. One of these programs was called VAT, which was the accused's nickname. On the last day of his contract the accused was observed by police officers, but this was inconclusive. The accused was arrested and charged under the UK Computer Misuse Act 1990. During his trial it became clear that damage had occurred before the wrecking programs were allegedly first used. The project was plagued with both software and hardware difficulties and was already late when the accused first commenced work. More importantly, other employees used the accused's PC, which was on a network so the wrecking programs could have been only stored there and accessed from any other network PC. The accused was acquitted.

[15.02] The decision to prosecute the accused at all may seem surprising. The prosecution had no documentary evidence linking the wrecking programs with the alleged losses, for which there were many other potential causes. The accused was undoubtedly an intelligent man, indeed the prosecution depended on this fact and it is therefore hard to believe that he would have made such simple mistakes as using his own nickname to name the wrecking program or to store them in such an obvious position.

---

[1] M Turner, 'Case Report: The Computer Misuse Act 1990, s 3(1)' Computers and Law, Vol 5, Issue 1 [1994].

[15.03] The Law Reform Commission Report on Dishonesty[2] and the Report of the Government Advisory Committee on Fraud[3] both express serious concerns about how prosecutions for serious frauds are handled in Ireland. Many of these concerns will also probably be raised about potential future prosecutions for computer crimes. The Law Reform Commission has recommended that seminars for judges be held in areas such as information technology,[4] provision was made for the training of judges as recommended by the Commission in the Courts and Courts Officers Act 1995.[5] The Commission has recommended that the prosecution should be entitled to call an accountant as a witness to give evidence concerning accounting procedures,[6] the Advisory Committee on Fraud has recommended that an assessor sit with the judge and assist the jury in assessing complex technical evidence.[7] Finally the recommendation of the Advisory Committee that a National Bureau of Fraud Investigation[8] should be established has been implemented and the bureau has a computer crime section.[9]

POWERS OF ARREST

[15.04] The 1991 Act gives every person a very extensive power of arrest. This power of arrest does not however apply to the offence of unauthorised access under s 5, it only applies to the offences of causing damage to property, threatening to cause damage or possessing anything with the intent of causing damage. This omission downgrades s 5 and is consistent with the much lower penalties which may be imposed on anyone convicted under that section.[10]

[15.05] Anyone may arrest a person who is or whom they suspect with reasonable cause, to be in the act of committing an offence.[11] Where an offence has been committed then any person may arrest anyone who they suspect with reasonable cause to be guilty of committing the offence without a warrant.[12] A member of the gardaí may arrest anyone who is or who the

---

2. Part III of the Report p 323-361.
3. Section 5 of the Report p 37-58.
4. Page 351, para 39.32.
5. Section 48.
6. Page 351, para 39.30
7. Page 57, para 8.10.
8. Para 4.5.
9. See Collier and Spaul, *A Forensic Methodology for Countering Computer Crime,* in Carr & Williams Eds, *Computers and Law,* (Intellect, 1994) p 145.
10. CDA 1991, s 12(1).
11. CDA 1991, s 12(2).
12. CDA 1991, s 12(3).

garda believes is about to commit an offence without a warrant.[13] A garda may also arrest any person without a warrant, whom he suspects has committed an offence or who has obstructed or impeded a garda, or refused to give his name when the gardaí are carrying out a search warrant.[14] The gardaí may enter and search without a warrant, if need be by force, any place where they suspect a person whom they wish to arrest under this section is located.[15] These powers of arrest apply to attempts to commit offences as well as the actual commission of them.[16] Section 12 does not prejudice any other power of arrest conferred by any other law.[17]

Search Warrants

[15.06] Search warrants may be issued in the District Court. The judge must be satisfied by an information on oath of a member of the gardaí that there is reasonable cause to believe that a person has in his custody or under his control or on his premises anything which has been used or is intended to be used to damage another's property, to damage any property in a way likely to endanger life or with an intent to defraud or to access data without a lawful excuse.[18]

[15.07] Such a search will authorise a named member of the gardaí accompanied by other members to enter, if necessary by force, the premises named in the warrant, at any time within one month from the date of issue. The warrant will empower the gardaí to search the premises and anyone found there. They may seize and detain anything which they suspect has been used or is intended for use in the commission of an offence. The Police Property Act 1897 applies to any property which comes into the possession of the gardaí, under this section or any other provision of the Act.[19] If the warrant has been issued because it is suspected that computer crimes are being committed, then the gardaí or someone brought with them for the purpose, may operate any equipment in the premises for processing data, inspect and extract any data found there by operating the equipment or otherwise.[20] The fact that the gardaí may have to bring a non-garda with them to access and inspect data and equipment is an acknowledgement that the force may not have sufficient expertise or knowledge in this area.

[13.] CDA 1991, s 12(5).
[14.] CDA 1991, s 12(4).
[15.] CDA 1991, s 12(6).
[16.] CDA 1991, s 12(7).
[17.] CDA 1991, s 12(8).
[18.] CDA 1991, s 13(1).
[19.] CDA 1991, s 13(3).
[20.] CDA 1991, s 13(2).

[15.08] On 1 March 1990 the US Secret Service raided the offices of Steve Jackson in Austin, Texas. Pursuant to a search warrant, they confiscated Jackson's hardware, software and an about to be published book and business records. They held these for several months. As a result, Jackson was forced to lay off half his employees and his business suffered badly. In fact, Jackson was never suspected of any criminal activities, but had the misfortune to unknowingly employ a suspected member of the notorious 'Legion of Doom' hacking ring. He sued the government and received $51,000 in compensation.[21] If the gardaí can confiscate the computers or other equipment held at a suspect's address pursuant to a search warrant, this would be a powerful weapon to harass and intimidate those suspected of computer crimes. It would effectively allow the gardaí to close down any suspected business which relied on its computers. At this stage, there are few businesses which would not be badly affected if they lost their computer equipment. It is unclear whether the Act purports to give this power to the gardaí. Certainly, in 'normal' criminal damage cases, they can remove any suspect material pursuant to the search warrant. However, where they obtain a warrant in a computer crime case the gardaí are permitted to:

> operate or cause to be operated by a person accompanying him for that purpose, any equipment in the premises for processing data, inspect any data found there and extract information therefrom, whether by the operation of such equipment or otherwise.[22]

[15.09] This means that the gardaí may copy any data found on the premises. Whether this operates to supplement or is exclusive of the normal power of seizing any suspect equipment contained in the same subsection is unclear. However, the best evidence rule which requires that original evidence be preferred by the court might mean that the gardaí would have to recover hard disks and other items containing evidence rather than relying on copies of the contents of those items. If the gardaí can copy the data found in the premises, it is hard to understand why they should also need to confiscate the equipment itself. The fact that a non-garda is permitted to accompany them on any search would mean that the gardaí could not claim that having found the suspect data or equipment they were unable to extract or analyse it and so had to remove the equipment. If the gardaí uncover suspect equipment, they should call in experts to analyse the equipment and data to ascertain whether it poses any threat.

[21.] Kapor, 'Civil Liberties in Cyberspace', Scientific American, September 1991, p 16.
[22.] CDA 1991, s 13(2).

[15.10] The section allows for two offences. The first is committed by any person who obstructs or impedes the gardaí in the execution of the search warrant. This is punishable by a fine not exceeding £1,000 and/or 12 months in prison. The second offence is committed by any person found on the premises who fails or refuses to give his name and address or gives a false name and address to a member of the gardaí. This is punishable by a fine not exceeding £500.[23]

[15.11] The Government Advisory Committee on Fraud[24] has suggested that any search warrant should, where necessary, require any relevant person to surrender to the investigating officers any relevant computer passwords and to produce a copy of specified documents in legible form. Designers of computer programs or persons who operate computers should also be under a duty to provide the gardaí upon a request being made with all information concerning relevant programs and with all information necessary to enable the gardaí to gain access to computer records (including passwords or information about systems designed to erase records automatically). This latter request would presumably also have to be made on foot of a warrant or court order. In carrying out a search warrant the gardaí would have to be aware of the need to copy everything on a hard disk and not just to receive print-outs or other data.

[15.12] Hackers have shown that it is not necessary to enter the building containing a computer in order to access its contents. The gardaí or other authorities may be tempted to take a leaf out of the hacker's book and access computers held by individuals from outside. However, the courts may well look askance at efforts such as these if it is felt that they are carried out to avoid the necessity of getting a search warrant but it may be difficult to argue that a citizen's dwelling has been violated by sending electronic commands down the phone line.[25] If the authorities suspect that illegally copied programs, forged electronic documents or passwords are being held by individuals then it is at least theoretically possible to create a program which would search the memories of all computers connected to the Internet for an exact copy of the program, document or password.[26] If the program found such a copy it would report this fact back to its operator. The program

---

[23] CDA 1991, s 13(4).

[24] 1993 Report.

[25] Article 40.5 of the Constitution provides that "The dwelling of every citizen is inviolable and shall not be forcibly entered save in accordance with law". See generally: *The People (AG) v O'Brien* [1965] IR 142; *The People (DPP) v Lawless* (1985) 3 Frewen 30;

[26] Adler, 'Cyberspace, General Searches and Digital Contraband', Yale LJ, 1996, Vol 105: 1093.

would not examine or note any information other than the existence or non-existence of the relevant copy and so may not be intruding on the privacy of the individual.[27]

JURISDICTION

[15.13] One of the main characteristics of the computer crime is its international nature. Hackers may break into computers anywhere in the world, often huge physical distances from where they are operating.[28] The 1991 Act allows for proceedings to be brought under s 5 against anyone who operates a computer abroad in order to access data kept within Ireland. A prosecution could also be brought under s 2 against someone based abroad who damages data kept in Ireland. Where a prosecution is brought against somebody located outside the State then the offence may be treated as having been committed in any place in the State.[29] Section 5 also allows people who operate computers based in Ireland to be prosecuted where they access data kept outside the State.

[15.14] A miscreant working at a computer in Ireland may use his machine to dishonestly obtain money from computers located abroad or to commit other crimes in the belief that as the computer or data is not held within the State then he cannot be prosecuted in the Irish courts for his crimes. This belief may be mistaken, the English authorities suggest that the courts will take a flexible approach in deciding whether or not they have jurisdiction to try such offences. In *R v Tomsett*[30] the appellant was a telex operator employed by a Swiss bank in London. He was convicted of conspiracy to steal from the bank by diverting $7,000,000 from an account in New York to an account in Geneva. He appealed to the Court of Appeal where his counsel argued that the contemplated crime would have taken place in either New York or Geneva and so the English courts did not have jurisdiction.[31] The judges in the Court of Appeal suggested that the prosecution might use the argument that the appellant had appropriated the chose in action in New

---

27. For comparison see the argument concerning the legality of searching for marijuana plants by trying to spot the heat lamps used to grow them with infrared cameras. See Huskins 'Marijuana Hotspots: Infrared Imaging and the Fourth Amendment', The University of Chicago Law Review, Vol 63, No 2, Spring 1996, p 655.

28. For example, one hacker accessed the computers in a laboratory in New York from London: *The Times*, 24 May 1996.

29. CDA 1991, s 7(1).

30. (1985) Crim App R 369.

31. See also *R v Thompson* [1984] 3 All ER 565, where the applicant had entered computer instructions in Kuwait which transferred money to accounts in England. He was held to have committed the crime of larceny when he withdrew the money from the English banks.

York when he sent the telex from London and so the appropriation had occurred in England. This suggestion was not taken up by the prosecution which used the sole argument, which they did not support with any authorities, that the appellant had stolen his employer's money and so the courts had jurisdiction. This was rejected by the courts as *"prima facie* a theft takes place where the property is appropriated; *prima facie* appropriation takes place where the property is situated."[32]

[15.15] The question was also raised in *R v Governor of Pentonville Prison (ex parte Osman)*[33] where the applicant was appealing against a decision by a magistrate to extradite him to Hong Kong. It was alleged that he had been involved in a conspiracy which had netted hundreds of millions of dollars. As a result of the applicant's activities a telex would be sent from Hong Kong to a bank in New York instructing the bank to pay out a set amount to an account which was held in the name of a company. The applicant submitted that he should not be extradited to Hong Kong as he had not committed any offence there, if there had been a theft then it had occurred in the United States. The Court of Appeal examined the authorities and held that the question of whether the sending of the telex was an appropriation was fully open on the authorities.[34] The applicant submitted that even if the sending of a telex was appropriation than the appropriation takes place where the telex is received not where it is sent. He argued this by analogy to the acceptance of a contractual offer by telex. This analogy was not seen by the Court:

> "If we are right that the act of sending the telex was the act of appropriation, then the place where that act was performed, namely the place where the telex was dispatched, is the place where the (property) was appropriated. We do not rule out the possibility that the place where the telex is received may also be regarded as the place of appropriation, if our courts were ever to adopt the view that a crime may have a dual location.

[32.] Quoted by Lloyd LJ in *R v Governor of Pentonville Prison (ex parte Osman)* [1989] 3 All ER 701 at 714.

[33.] [1989] 3 All ER 701. See also *R v Smith (Wallace Duncan)*, *The Times*, 13 November 1995 where the Court of Appeal held that the English Courts did have jurisdiction to try a case where funds were transferred from one bank account based abroad to another bank account also based abroad by the defendant operating from England.

[34.] *Ibid* p 716. The Court of Appeal (Lloyd LJ and French LJ) referred to *R v Kohn* (1979) Cr App R 395; *R v Navvabi* [1986] 3 All ER 102; [1986] 1 WLR 1311; *Chan Man-sin v AG of Hong Kong* [1988] 1 All ER 1; [1988] 1 WLR 196; *R v Doole* High Court, unrep, 21 March 1985; *R v Wille* (1987) 86 Cr App R 296; See also Smith, *Law of Evidence* 5th ed, 1984 p 106. The court distinguished *R v Tomsett* (1985) Crim App R 369 on the basis that it did not examine the question of whether or not the sending of a telex could be appropriation.

But in the meantime, we would hold that Hong Kong was the place of appropriation ..."[35]

[15.16] The flexibility of the English courts on this question is illustrated by *R v Levin (orse R v* Governor *of Brixton Prison and Another, ex parte Levin)*[36] which was an extradition case. The applicant was a Russian computer hacker who had gained access to the computers of Citibank in New Jersey. It would appear that he transferred over $10,700,000 out of the accounts of customers of Citibank and into accounts controlled by accomplices. He argued that the act of appropriation had occurred when he typed in the appropriate instructions into his computer situated in St Petersburg in Russia. If this were so then the US courts would not have jurisdiction under English law and the applicant could not be extradited to the USA.[37] However, the English court was able to distinguish the *Osman* case. Beldam J argued that *Osman* had assumed:

"... the right of a right holder to give instructions and to have them met. Those instructions could be given by telex without more ado. Osman was simply sending an instruction to the correspondent bank in the United States. But in the present case no instructions could be given without first gaining entry into the Citibank computer in (New Jersey) ... We see no reason why the appropriation of the client's right to give instructions should not be regarded as having taken place in the computer ... the operation of the keyboard by a computer operator produces a virtually instantaneous result on the magnetic disk of the computer even though it may be 10,000 miles away. It seems to us artificial to regard the act as having been done in one rather than the other place. But in the position of having to choose on the facts of this case whether, after entering the computer in [New Jersey], the act of appropriation by inserting instructions on the disk occurred there or in St Petersburg, we would opt for [New Jersey]. The fact that the applicant was physically in St Petersburg is of far less significance than the fact that he was looking at and operating on magnetic disks located in [New Jersey]. The essence of what he was doing was done there."

[15.17] The flexibility of the courts in these cases is understandable. If the courts do not display this flexibility then serious crimes will go unpunished as occurred in *R v Tomsett*. However there is a danger that this may lead to international forum shopping. In an American case *United States v Thomas*[38]

---

35. *Ibid* at 717 *per* Lloyd LJ.
36. *The Times* 11 March 1996, (LEXIS transcript).
37. For the extradition to succeed it had to be shown that the offences which the applicant was accused of would be crimes under English if the acts he had carried out in the USA had occurred in England.
38. No 94-CR 20019 (WD Tenn 28 July 1994).

the accused were a couple who ran a San Francisco based internet service called Amateur Action which allowed paid subscribers to view and download pornographic images. The material was downloaded by a postal inspector in Tennessee and the couple were convicted in the Tennessee courts of interstate transportation of obscene materials. The Tennessee courts may be taken to be more conservative than those in San Francisco. This case has given rise to fears in the USA that the more conservative communities in America may be able to control the content of computer services in the more liberal parts of the country.[39]

OWNERSHIP OF PROPERTY AND DATA

[15.18] While data is specifically defined as property, deciding to whom data belongs may be difficult. This problem is dealt with by s 1(2) of the 1991 Act which states:

> Property shall be treated for the purposes of this Act as belonging to any person having lawful custody or control of it, having in it any proprietary right or interest (not being an equitable interest arising only from an agreement to transfer or grant an interest), or having a charge over it.

This definition of ownership is very broad. This is necessary for computers as often data will be held by companies or individuals who do not own the data. For example, auditors will often keep considerable amounts of data about the firms they audit even though this data ultimately belongs to the audited company. Section 8 provides that no rule of law which ousts the jurisdiction of the District Court to try offences where a dispute of title to property is involved shall prevent the District Court from trying offences under the 1991 Act.

[15.19] Two subsections of s 1 endeavour to simplify the process of proving ownership of property in court. Section 1(4) provides that where the property is subject to a trust, any person who can enforce the trust may be treated as the owner. Section 1(5) states that the property of a corporation sole may be treated as belonging to the corporation regardless of any vacancy in the corporation.

[15.20] The Law Reform Commission identified a problem where the owner of property would be required to attend court to identify the property as his in a situation where it patently did not belong to the accused.[40] To deal with this problem s 7(2)(a) was enacted which states that it is not necessary to name the owner of property in court and unless the defendant can show to

---

[39.] See Smedinghoff (ed) *Online Law*, (Addison-Wesley, 1996) p 323.
[40.] Law Reform Commission Report on Malicious Damage, 1988.

the contrary, it is presumed that property belongs to somebody other than the defendant. This provision greatly simplifies prosecutions as it is not necessary to bring the owner of the property into court to prove his ownership. This is particularly important with computers as many companies are owned and registered outside the State. This would make it impractical to prosecute offences if the owners of computers had to travel from the US to give evidence of ownership or appoint agents here to give evidence on their behalf.[41]

COMPENSATION ORDERS

[15.21] Where a person has been convicted of criminal damage under s 2, the court may order him to compensate the injured party. This order may be made in addition or in alternative to any other penalty imposed by the court.[42] The injured party is defined as any person who has suffered loss other than consequential loss[43] as a result of the actions of the accused.

[15.22] The compensation payable is the amount which the court finds appropriate having regard to the evidence and to the representations made to the court by the prosecutor and the offender. It would appear that the injured party cannot address the court in this matter. The compensation cannot exceed the amount that the injured party would have received in a civil action against the accused person. The court cannot award more than its jurisdiction in tort which at present stands at £5,000 for the District Court.[44]

[15.23] A compensation order may not be made unless the damage and the identity of the injured person can be readily ascertained at the time of conviction or within a reasonable period afterwards.[45] In determining the amount of compensation to be paid, the court will have regard to the means of the offender.[46] The court may order the compensation to be paid in instalments.[47] If the court feels that it would be appropriate to impose both a fine and a compensation order, but the offender does not have the means to pay both, the court may order the offender to pay compensation and then decide whether it is appropriate to impose a fine having regard to the means

---

41. This point was raised in *Roche v DJ Mary Martin and the DPP* [1993] ILRM 651 where on appeal by judicial review, the appellant tried unsuccessfully to claim that the failure of executives from 20th Century Fox to travel from the US to Ireland to prove their ownership of the copyright in a video, made the appellant's conviction unsafe.
42. CDA 1991, s 9(1).
43. Consequential loss may be defined as indirect loss.
44. CDA 1991, s 9(2).
45. CDA 1991, s 9(3).
46. CDA 1991, s 9(4).
47. CDA 1991, s 9(5).

which are left.[48] Proving the amount of damage in a computer case may not be easy. Although imposing a compensation order may punish the culprit, it may not fully compensate the victim. It is possible to cause huge amounts of damage by misusing computers which the culprit will never be able to repay.

[15.24] For the purposes of enforcement, a compensation order is treated as if it were a court order made in civil proceedings.[49] A compensation order or an order increasing the amount of compensation to be paid under s 9(7)(b) will be treated as if it were an instalment order within the meaning of Part I of the Enforcement of Court Orders Act 1940 without prejudice to the provisions of s 9(7) which allows for compensation orders to be varied.[50] If any other Act provides for the payment of compensation then the 1991 Act is expressed to operate without prejudice to it.[51] For the purposes of making compensation orders, conviction is defined as including the making of an order under the Probation Act 1907.

[15.25] The court can also make an order requiring the parent or guardian of a child to pay compensation under s 99 of the Children Act 1908.[52] The making of a compensation order against a parent or guardian does not give rise to any other liability on the part of the parent or guardian.[53]

Suspension of compensation orders

[15.26] The compensation order must be suspended in every case for one month from the date of conviction. It will also be suspended where notice of appeal or a notice of leave to appeal has been given until the appeal has been determined.[54] Where an appeal is made against conviction or sentence, then the appellant court may annul or vary the compensation order.[55] The accused may also appeal against the compensation order on its own.[56] When a compensation order has ceased to be suspended for any of the reasons outlined above, then the offender and the injured party may apply to the court to vary the compensation order before the order has been complied with. The offender may apply to the court to reduce the amount to be paid, to vary the instalments or to order that no further payments be made. The court may do so if it is satisfied that the means of the offender are insufficient to

---

48. CDA 1991, s 9(6).
49. CDA 1991, s 9(8).
50. CDA 1991, s 9(8).
51. CDA 1991, s 9(10).
52. CDA 1991, s 9(4).
53. CDA 1991, s 9(11).
54. CDA 1991, s 10(1).
55. CDA 1991, s 10(3).
56. CDA 1991, s 10(4).

satisfy the order in full. Alternatively, the court may vary the order if it is satisfied that the amount of damage caused by the offender was less than that imposed by the compensation order, having given the injured party an opportunity to be heard and having regard to the representations of that party. If the compensation order has been complied with by the offender and it appears to the court that the order exceeds a reasonable sum, then the court may order the injured party to repay that excess to the offender. If the court makes such an order then the compensation order ceases to have effect.[57] The injured party may apply to the court to have the amount of compensation or the amount of any instalment or the number of instalments varied. The court may do so if it is satisfied that the means of the offender are sufficient. Alternatively, it may increase the amount of compensation to the paid if it is satisfied that the amount of damage is greater than that imposed by the compensation order. It may only do so if the offender has been given an opportunity to make representations to the court and if the court takes those representations into account.[58]

[15.27] Even if a compensation order has been made, the injured party or a party who has suffered consequential loss may still sue in the civil courts. If damages are awarded and the sum assessed exceeds the amount awarded in the compensation order, then the civil court may only award damages which do not exceed the amount of the excess. If the amount of damages are less than the amount awarded by the compensation order, then the court may order that the appropriate sum be repaid by the injured party to the offender. Once the civil court makes an award of damages or another order, then the compensation order ceases to have effect.[59] This could have interesting consequences if at that time the offender has not paid the compensation required by the compensation order. If that is the case, then presumably the court would have to award the full sum of damages, that is the compensation order plus any excess. If the court does not do so, then the offender would be able to avoid fulfilling the compensation order.[60]

[57.] CDA 1991, s 7(a).
[58.] CDA 1991, s 7(b).
[59.] CDA 1991, s 11.
[60.] Normally, an individual could not claim against an insurance policy for the cost of an order such as a compensation order which was imposed as a criminal penalty. If civil proceedings were be taken, then it would be in the convicted person's interests to avoid paying the compensation order and waiting until the civil court makes an award of damages since he might be able to claim this against his insurance. In particular, the convicted person might be able to claim against public liability insurance for his home if this is the place from which he had been carrying out his computer crimes.

[15.28] The 1991 Act gives the court the power to impose compensation orders in addition to or as an alternative to any other penalty where a person is convicted of damaging property under s 2. Although damage may be caused by unauthorised access or by threatening to cause damage, a compensation order cannot be made in these cases and the injured party will have to pursue a claim in the civil courts. Compensation orders were clearly intended to force those who cause damage to pay for it. The difficulty with computer crimes is that the amount of damage caused may be beyond the ability of any defendant to pay. Morris, who created the Internet Worm which closed down the Internet in 1988, was estimated to have caused anything up to $186 million in damage, although the more extravagant figures have been questioned by some commentators. The actual restitutional cost was assessed at only $150,000. In any event, Morris had to pay a fine of $10,000 and was sentenced to 400 hours of community service plus three years probation.[61]

THE COUNCIL OF EUROPE'S RECOMMENDATIONS ON CRIMINAL PROCEDURE

[15.29] Following the recommendations of the Council of Europe on Computer Related Crime, the Council examined criminal procedure.[62] The Recommendations were adopted by the Committee of Ministers on 11 September 1995. The Recommendations do not just apply to computer crimes as described in Recommendation No R (89)9,[63] they apply to "offences connected with information technology". These are offences which may be committed by means of a computer but the system may also be the object or environment of the crime. The Recommendation sees such 'IT offences' as embracing any criminal offence where the investigating authorities must obtain access to information being processed or transmitted in computer systems.[64]

Search and Seizure

[15.30] The first recommendation is that the legal distinction between seizing data stored in a computer system and intercepting data in the course of transmission should be clearly delineated. The need for this stems from the fact that the distinctions between search and seizure and interception of communications may become blurred in relation to information technology

---

[61.] Susan M Mello, 'Administering the antidote to computer viruses: A comment on *US v Morris*', Rudgers Computer and Technology Law Journal, Vol 19, No 1, 1993, p 259.

[62.] Recommendation No R (95) 13 1995.

[63.] See para **[13.15]** *et seq.*

[64.] *Ibid* p 21.

as the form and location of computer data may be quickly changed. The second recommendation is that the police should be able to search computer systems and seize data in similar fashion as where search warrant is granted. There should also be a duty to inform the person in control of the system that the search has been carried out. The object of this is to allow the authorities to gather data from a computer without seizing the whole system. Third parties who have a legitimate interest in data seized during a search should also be informed as soon as possible. The third recommendation is that investigating authorities should have the power to extend the search to other computer systems within the jurisdiction which are connected by means of a network and to seize the data therein provided immediate action is required. The data stored on computer networks will be controlled by the network software which will administer the logical addresses, defined by the user and the physical addresses where the data is located. The user will not be aware of the physical location of the data within the system, he only knows its file name. In a complex computer network, the network software can place the data into connected systems and autonomously move them from time to time to other systems. From a technical point of view, it becomes increasingly difficult, if not impossible, to establish the location of data at any one time. "The relation between data and its character becomes nebulous".[65] The Internet may also be used to move data to other locations. If the data is stored on several systems, the authorities may have to get several different search warrants while the suspect may be able to destroy or move the data by means of a single phone call. Limitations are also suggested such as restricting search warrants to the parts of a computer system to which the suspect has access. The fourth recommendation is that where electronic documents exist they should be treated by the criminal law the same as traditional documents for the purpose of search warrants.

Technical Surveillance

[15.31] The distinction between forms of electronic communication such as radio, television, telephone and computer networks is disappearing. The Council has recommended that the laws relating to technical surveillance such as the interception of telecommunications should be amended to ensure their applicability. The sixth recommendation is that the criminal law should allow the authorities to use all necessary technical measures in order to gather traffic data in the investigation of crimes. This means that the authorities should be able to identify the source and destination of communications. Any information collected during the course of investigation should be secured appropriately. The criminal law should also

---

[65.] *Ibid* p 33.

be reviewed to make possible the interception of telecommunications in the investigation of telecommunication or computer crimes.

Obligations to co-operate with the investigating authorities

[15.32] The Council recommends that the authorities should have the power to order persons to submit specified data in their possession in the form required by the investigating authorities. The authorities should also have the power to order persons who have data in a computer system under their control to provide all necessary information to enable access to a computer system and the data on it. This latter provision should be extended to other people who have knowledge about the functioning of the system and the security measures used to protect it. This power is necessary because data may be encrypted or otherwise protected in a manner which make it extremely difficult or impossible to recover the data. All these powers would be subject to the normal legal privileges or protections extended to individuals. Network operators should be obliged to facilitate the interception of telecommunications by the authorities. They should also be obliged to identify users when ordered by the authorities. The Council has also suggested the creation of a Central Register to keep details of all service providers. For this register to be effective, registration would have to be mandatory.

Electronic Evidence

[15.33] The procedures and technical procedures for handling electronic evidence should be developed to ensure their integrity and also compatibility of evidence rules between Member States. Measures should also be adopted to minimise the negative effects of cryptography whilst allowing for its legitimate use.

Research, Statistics and Training

[15.34] To allow the authorities to keep abreast of new computer crimes and to develop counter measures, the collection and analysis of data on these crimes should be furthered. Specialised units should be established and criminal justice personnel should also be specially trained.

International co-operation

[15.35] The Council recommends that international agreements should be negotiated to allow searches of computer systems located in different jurisdictions to be carried out. A system of liaison should also be established to allow the authorities in one State to request foreign authorities to promptly collect evidence. Authorities should have the power to search and seize data with a view to its subsequent transfer abroad.

Chapter 16

Defences under the Criminal Damage Act 1991

[16.01] As outlined in Chapter 14, the Criminal Damage Act 1991 creates an extremely broad set of offences which may be applied to computer misuse. It is not going too far to suggest that the Act potentially criminalises every action involving a computer, beginning with turning it on. To avoid having to convict every computer user of criminal damage, the Act creates the defence of lawful excuse. If a person who damages or accesses data has such an excuse, then he can escape conviction. The Act explicitly allows any other defences, such as those available under the common law, to remain intact.

THE BURDEN OF PROOF

[16.02] In a criminal trial, the prosecution must always prove its case beyond reasonable doubt. There is no onus on the accused to raise any such doubt in the mind of the judge or jury. If the accused pleads that he has a defence, whether that of a lawful excuse or otherwise, then it is for the State to prove that the accused does not have this defence.[1] The accused is never under an obligation to establish a defence. If a person is accused of unauthorised access of a computer, under s 5, and he claims that he has a lawful excuse, then the judge need only decide whether or not he is satisfied beyond reasonable doubt that the accused accessed that computer and whether he is satisfied beyond reasonable doubt that the prosecution has negatived the issue of lawful excuse. If the judge is not satisfied beyond reasonable doubt on both of these matters the accused must be acquitted.[2]

[16.03] Where a person is charged with an offence of damaging data or other property, under s 2, it is presumed until the contrary is shown, that the damage has not been authorised. The only exception is where an employee or agent of the person keeping the data has been charged with causing damage to data.[3] The situation is similar where someone is charged with unauthorised access to data under s 5.[4] The reason for this exception is that

---

[1] The exception to this is insanity, where the onus is on the accused to establish that he is insane.

[2] *People (AG) v Quinn* [1965] IR 366.

[3] CDA 1991, s 7(2)(b).

[4] CDA 1991, s 7(2)(c).

often there may be misunderstandings about the extent of an employee's authorisation to modify data.[5]

'WITHOUT LAWFUL EXCUSE'

[16.04] The main defence allowed under the 1991 Act is that of a lawful excuse. The Act is designed to criminalise virtually every activity which may be carried out with a computer. Those who are legitimately using a computer may avoid prosecution and conviction by showing that they have a lawful excuse to carry out their actions. The definition of 'without lawful excuse' is contained in s 6. This section applies to every offence of causing damage to property or data under s 2(1). Where property is damaged with the intent of endangering life or with intent to defraud under s 2 then there is no lawful excuse. The defence may also be used against a charge of unauthorised access under s 5. It applies to any offence of threatening to damage property under s 3 other than a threat to damage property which the offender knows is likely to endanger life. It also applies to the possession of any article with the intent to use it to damage property except where the offender knows it is likely to endanger life.

If a person is charged with one of the offences above, he will have a lawful excuse in any of the circumstances outlined below.

(1) Ownership

[16.05] In the case of access to data, under s 5, the accused will have a lawful excuse if he is himself the person entitled to consent to or authorise the damage to data. The Act makes accessing all data, including your own, an offence. This section allows the owners of data to claim as a lawful excuse the fact that they own the data which is accessed by themselves.

(2) Consent

[16.06] The accused can avail of the defence if at the time he committed the offence, he believed that he had the consent of the person, who actually had, or who he believed had, the authority to consent to or authorise the damage or access to data. Alternatively, he will have a lawful excuse if he believed that the person who actually had, or who he believed had, the authority to authorise the damage, or the access to data, would have consented to it, had they known of it and its circumstances. This gives employees a defence where they damage or access data. Even if they damage or access data which they should not have, they will have a defence if they believed that they were allowed to do so.

---

5. See the Dáil Debates on the Bill, 29 November, 1990, p 582.

[16.07] Most computer systems will have various levels of access for different users. Some users such as the administrators of the system may have unlimited access to all data and programs on the system. Other users usually have only the limited access that is appropriate to their needs. Users may exceed the limitations placed on their access. If they do this, they will commit an offence as their access will be no longer authorised unless they can show that they made a legitimate mistake. However, they must realise that they have exceeded their authority. If they honestly believe that they are entitled to carry out certain actions then they will still have a lawful excuse.

[16.08] Deciding where the limits of an employee's access rights lie has caused difficulty in the UK. The *Independent* newspaper published a story illustrating how easy it was to access confidential information held on British Telecom's computers. BT claimed that the story was false, but an employee of theirs rang the *Independent* to offer a demonstration to prove the original report. A reporter attended at BT's offices where the employee accessed confidential information and printed some of it out. BT conducted an internal investigation and reported the matter to the police. The employee and the reporter were charged with the offence of gaining unauthorised access to a computer under s 1(1) of the UK Computer Misuse Act 1990. What made this case unusual was that the employee was given his password by BT so that he could access this information, doing so was part of his job. BT claimed that he was not authorised to access the computer for the purpose of showing reporters how easy it was to do so. His defence turned on s 17(5) which provides that access is unauthorised if the employee is:

> not himself entitled to control access of the kind in question to the program or data and he does not have consent ... from the person so entitled.

The court found that the employee had no case to answer and the case against the reporter was withdrawn as a result.[6] A similar case under the Irish legislation would have to result in the same conclusion. While the UK legislation required the court to examine the employee's access rights objectively, Irish law would only require the court to subjectively examine what authorisation an employee believed he actually had.

[16.09] The design of computer programs is still an inexact science. Even the simplest program can have many errors in its code, known as bugs. As programs become more complex the number of bugs is also increasing. A programming error can cause as much, if not more, damage than a malicious hacker.[7] The offences under the 1991 Act are easily broad enough to allow

---

6. Davis, 'Computer Misuse', NLJ 1 December 1995. See *The Independent*, 15 November 1995.

for the prosecution of an incompetent programmer in such a case. The question is whether the fact that they were acting pursuant to a contract or as an employee would be sufficient to amount to a lawful excuse. Obviously, they would not be contracted or employed to provide incorrect computer programs. At the same time, anyone who commissions or buys a new computer program will have to anticipate that it will contain numerous bugs which will have to be remedied in later versions. The programmer might cease to have a lawful excuse if the errors in the program were caused by more than normal human error and resulted from real negligence. Where errors or bugs in a program are fixed, this will necessitate altering the program, which involves damaging it. As programs are included in the definition of data, this would amount to an offence and anyone who wishes to carry out such work would need to have the program owner's permission. Both access and the rights to modify a program will have to be carefully defined by contract prior to any work being done. A particular problem is where a dispute arises between parties to a contract over payment or over the ownership of the intellectual property rights in the program.[8]

(3) Protection

[16.10] The defence of lawful excuse may be claimed if the accused person damaged or threatened to damage property or possessed something that would damage property in order to protect himself or somebody else or property belonging to himself or someone else. This will only apply if the accused person believed that the property was in immediate need of protection and that the means of protection adopted were reasonable in the circumstances. This could have interesting effects in computer law. If the administrator of a system discovers that a hacker has stolen passwords which would enable the hacker to enter his system, the administrator might be tempted to dispatch a virus to the hacker's computer which would destroy the passwords held on that system. This would appear to be legal under this section. However, it would be very difficult to write a virus which would only eliminate the passwords and to be certain, the administrator would probably want to destroy all the data on the hacker's system. If the administrator could show that his system was in imminent danger and the

---

7. In 1989, a computer in Paris read files on traffic violations and mistakenly sent out letters charging 41,000 traffic offenders with crimes including murder, drug trafficking, extortion and prostitution. Also in the same year, an anonymous British bank transferred an extra £2 billion to customers in one hour, when a bug permitted payment orders to be issued twice. Since there was no way to distinguish real from duplicate transactions, the bank had to rely on the honesty of its customers to ensure the repayment of the money: BYTE September 1995.

8. See para **[28.22]**.

only way he could reasonably protect it would be to damage all the data on the hacker's computer, then even this drastic course would seem to be legal. Obviously, the actions of the administrator would have to be reasonable. If the administrator could just as well protect his system by changing the stolen passwords, then action such as that suggested above would not be reasonable and the administrator could find himself convicted under s 2.

(4) Honest mistake

[16.11] For the purposes of deciding whether or not an accused has a lawful excuse, it is immaterial whether a belief is justified or not provided that it is honestly held. Therefore someone who damages data as a result of a honest mistake will have a defence. This was probably included because the level of authority of employees who control data may not always be clear and they may damage data without realising that it was not permitted. Another situation is where a person believes that under a contract or other legal right they are entitled to damage or access data. Even if they are mistaken in this belief they will have a defence so long as they are honestly mistaken. Many hackers are very young, naive and immature. Some may genuinely believe that their activities are condoned by the operators of the systems into which they gain access and that they are just involved in a game. If this is untrue, they argue, why do the operators not simply increase security to exclude them. If this belief is honestly held then there is no reason why they should not also be entitled to this defence. Particularly if the operators of the system engage in banter and other discussions with the hackers.[9]

Finally, the section may not be construed as casting doubt on any other defence recognised by the criminal law. This leaves any other defences to criminal damage intact.

UNCONSTITUTIONALITY

[16.12] The possibility that sections of the 1991 Act may be unconstitutional due to the vagueness of their terms has been referred to above.[10] The Constitution protects the private property of citizens.[11] Therefore, the State would obviously be entitled to protect private property against criminal damage. However, citizens also have a right to communicate.[12] Damage to data is defined as including the moving to another storage medium or to a different location in the storage medium in which the data is kept. If charges were to be brought relating to the moving

---

9. Hofner & Marksoff, *Cyberpunk*, (Fourth Estate, 1991).
10. See para **[14.08]**.
11. Article 43.1.
12. *Attorney General v Paperlink* [1984] ILRM 343.

of data in this way, then it is possible that constitutional rights of the accused such as the right to communicate would be infringed.

ENTRAPMENT

[16.13] One of the most controversial methods of police work is that of entrapment. This occurs when a member of a police force induces a member of the public to commit an offence which they might not have commited without the involvement of the police. Entrapment is recognised as a defence to criminal charges by the US courts[13] but not by those in England.[14] The Irish authority on this question is *The Dental Board v O'Callaghan*.[15] The Dental Board employed an inspector to investigate allegations that O'Callaghan, a dental mechanic, was practising illegally as a dentist. The inspector approached O'Callaghan and asked him to provide a replacement for his dentures. O'Callaghan duly took an impression of the inspector's mouth and sold him a set of dentures. In the District Court the District Justice stated that the law on this matter was that the evidence of accomplices could not be accepted without corroboration. He refused to hear the evidence of the inspector since he had induced and assisted in the commission of an offence and that as such he was an accomplice. This decision was appealed by way of case stated to the High Court where it came before Butler J. He referred to the English case of *Sneddon v Stevenson*[16] and quoted with approval the following passage from the judgment of Parker CJ:

> "... a police officer acting as a spy may be said in a general sense to be an accomplice in the offence, yet if he is merely partaking in the offence for the purposes of getting evidence, he is not an accomplice who requires to be corroborated".[17]

Butler J felt that this decision was correct and that this exception should be extended to:

> "... witnesses employed by an official body to secure evidence of the commission of an offence which it is the duty of that body to investigate with a view to prosecution ..."[18]

[16.14] Although these methods are not greatly used in Ireland, the difficulty of gathering evidence in computer crime cases may force authorities to adopt them. The authorities are certainly entitled to monitor vulnerable

---

13. *Sherman v US* (1958) 356 US 369.
14. *R v Sang* (1980) AC 402.
15. [1969] IR 181.
16. [1967] 1 WLR 1051.
17. *Ibid* at 1058.
18. [1969] IR 181, at 185.

systems or systems which are the object of computer crimes (if necessary by getting the appropriate permission to institute a wire tap). It would probably also be permissible to set up a computer system and wait to see if anyone attempts to hack into it. A difficulty would arise where the gardaí publicise the existence of their system in the hope of enticing a hacker to access it. Hackers are notorious for using bulletin board systems and other such systems to communicate information about their activities. If the gardaí, posing as hackers, merely posted a notice suggesting that their system was vulnerable and could be accessed, then it could be argued that they were are acting in a fashion analogous to that of the investigator in the Dental Board case. However, if they were to post detailed information on how to access the system or if they were to bombard suspected hackers with detailed information and suggestions as to how to access the system, this might be construed as entrapment.

ADDICTION

[16.15] Addiction may be defined as an habitual or compulsive dependence on something such as a drug.[19] It is not usually available as a defence to criminal charges.[20] However, in *R v Bedworth*[21] the accused successfully claimed that he was addicted to hacking and avoided conviction on charges of unauthorised modification of data under s 3 of the UK Computer Misuse Act 1990. The accused and two others were arrested in a co-ordinated operation by four separate police forces. They were members of a hacking group called Eight Legged Groove Machine (8 LGM) and were charged with offences relating to eight institutions in all and with causing damage of £25,000 to the Financial Times, and leaving the European Organisation for the Research and Treatment of Cancer with a £10,000 phone bill. Although the three never met, they communicated through a bulletin board system. Bedworth's two accomplices pleaded guilty and were sentenced to 6 months imprisonment.[22] Bedworth pleaded not guilty. At his trial, Bedworth's defence called an expert on addiction, Professor Griffith Edwards of the Maudsley Hospital, who had conducted psychological assessment interviews with Bedworth. During these interviews Bedworth made statements such as "I believe I am addicted to hacking ... I can't stop myself from doing it because it goes on and on and on and I can't stop".[23] There was also evidence that Bedworth would spend long hours on his computer and

---

[19.] *The Concise Oxford English Dictionary*, 8th ed.
[20.] *R v Lawrence* (1989) Crim LR 309.
[21.] *The Financial Times*, 18 March 1993.
[22.] *The Financial Times*, 22 May 1993.
[23.] *Computing*, 4 March 1993.

when possible he would continue to hack right throughout the night. The trial judge clearly told the jury that addiction, obsession and dependence could not be used as a defence to criminal charges. In spite of this the jury acquitted the accused. How successful the defence of addiction really was is unknown since the nature of the jury's deliberations are secret. It may well be that the jury took pity on the accused, a student, who was clearly extremely lonely and withdrawn from society.

[16.16] Spending long hours 'surfing' the Internet is not uncommon. A survey carried out in the University of Buffalo found that participating users spent an average of 21 hours a week on-line with 17% spending more than 40 hours. Almost all the participants exhibited addiction-like behaviour.[24] This has led to the identification of Internet Addiction Syndrome (IAD) whose existence has been confirmed by a professor of psychology at Pittsburgh University, who has founded the Centre for On-Line Addiction.[25]

[16.17] It is doubtful that this defence would succeed in a different trial or rather it is doubtful that categorising an accused's mental state as being one of addiction would be the best way of proceeding in the Irish courts. A better method might be to claim that the accused was unaware of the effect of his actions and that he believed that his actions were not harmful or illegal.

AUTOMATISM

[16.18] For the purposes of deciding whether or not an accused has a lawful excuse it is immaterial whether a belief is justified or not, provided that it is honestly held.[26] Bedworth, in the case discussed above, may well have felt that he was not in control of his activities when he was hacking into computer systems. Certainly his obsession with hacking and the very long hours spent on computers went far beyond a healthy interest in the subject. If a hacker such as Bedworth was deluded as to the nature of his activities, if he honestly believed that they were condoned by the operators of the systems, then he might be entitled to a defence of lawful excuse. 'Cyberspace' or the world of computer networks does not operate according to the normal rules of society. It is possible to speak to somebody in Durban with the same ease as someone in Dublin. Users are not bound by their physical limitations and frailties rather by the limitations of their technology. In such an environment it is possible to lose touch with reality and to believe that criminal activities are in fact normal.

[24.] *The Sunday Times*, 14 April 1996.
[25.] *The Sunday Times*, 9 June 1996.
[26.] CDA 1991, s 6(3).

[16.19] Hackers frequently spend extremely long periods of time working on their computers trying to access other systems. These sessions may spread over periods of days during which the hacker may go without food and rest and have no outside stimuli save that of the computer. An accused hacker might argue that they had ceased to control their actions and that they were acting in a state of automatism as a result of these unusual and arduous physical conditions. The problem for the accused is of course that these conditions are apparently self induced. Still the effect on body and mind of working with a computer over a long period of time is unknown. The courts already have accepted that where offences are committed while sleep walking, the accused may have a defence of non-insane automatism.[27] It may be possible for the courts to develop another category of non-insane automatism to deal with individuals who commit computer crimes while in a similar state of mind.

[16.20] Some commentators have suggested that dissociative states may amount to automatism. These states are hysterical neuroses, the most extreme of which will cause a 'split personality'.[28] Nick Whiteley, whose conviction for hacking offences led to the enactment of the UK Computer Misuse Act 1990, became a totally different person whenever he was hacking on his computer:

> "The contrast between Nick - generally polite, easy going and articulate - and his *alter ego,* the Mad Hacker, impressed everyone who met him. Nick Whiteley would never leave messages redolent with sexual aggression for Marilyn (a computer systems administrator): that was the Mad Hacker ... Like so many hackers Nick played out his fantasies on the computer keyboard ... With a computer he could become anyone he wanted. Without a computer he was just Nick Whiteley".[29]

MINORS

[16.21] Although there has been no survey of the characteristics of computer hackers, there is good reason to believe that they tend to be young males.[30] The prosecution of young offenders has become problematic in Ireland. The law has remained unchanged since the foundation of the State and there is an acute shortage of suitable accommodation for convicted offenders. Children

---

[27.] *Bratty v AG for Northern Ireland* [1963] AC 386.

[28.] See Glanville Williams, *Textbook of Criminal Law,* 2nd ed (Stevens and Son, 1983) p 672.

[29.] Clough & Mungo, *Approaching Zero,* (Faber & Faber, 1992) p 56.

[30.] For example, a 16 year old English boy accessed a US Air Force research laboratory in New York, "realising (that the police) had come to arrest him, he curled up on the floor and cried": *The Times,* 24 May 1996.

under the age of seven years are not punishable by criminal prosecution as they are *doli incapax*.[31] Children between seven and fourteen may be convicted of offences but only if it can be shown that they knew what they were doing was wrong.[32] Evidence of their state of mind may be gathered from the nature of the act, the intelligence and understanding of the child and the child's behaviour immediately subsequent to the offence. It is not necessary to show that the child knew that what he was doing was morally wrong but he must know that what he did was seriously wrong and not merely naughty or mischievous.[33] Where a child is over fourteen years of age, they are assumed to have the capacity to commit offences. That is, it is presumed that they can distinguish between good and evil. A person under the age of twenty one who is convicted of an offence may not necessarily be sent to prison. If they are under seventeen they may only be sent to prison if they are so unruly and depraved that they may not be held elsewhere. They can only be kept in prison for a maximum of three months. If they are over seventeen years, they may be sent to prison as a matter of course. There are a number of alternatives if it is decided that the convicted person should endure a period of detention but not go to prison. These include St Patrick's Institution and St Lawrence's School.[34]

NECESSITY

[16.22] Data may be damaged in many ways, turning off a computer or otherwise interfering with its use may damage or destroy the data held on it. In the 'Internet Worm' incident,[35] some computers were forced to shut down, others broke their communications link with the Internet in order to avoid suffering damage as a result of Morris's virus. In a situation such as this it is inevitable that some damage will be caused to data. However the administrators may be able to rely on the defence of necessity.[36] This defence will only apply where the person who commits a crime did so in a situation where he was forced to chose between the lesser of two evils and in the process committed an offence. The defence of necessity has never been raised in Ireland but it seems likely that it would be accepted. *Charleton* suggests that there are limitations on the defence. Firstly, there must be a real

---

31. It has been argued that mental age and not chronological age is what is important. See: Lloyd-Morris & Mahendra 'Doli Incapax and Mental Age' 1996 NLJ 8 November p 1622.
32. See the decision of the House of Lords in *C v DPP* [1995] 2 All ER 43.
33. *JM v Runeckles* (1984) 79 Cr App R 255.
34. Charleton, *Criminal Law, Cases and Materials*, (Butterworths, 1992) p 274.
35. See para **[13.11]**.
36. All system administrators should ensure that all users of their systems have consented to their data being damaged in this way prior to using the system.

danger to the accused or someone else. Secondly, there must be an inescapable necessity to commit the offence charged. Thirdly, there must be proportionality between the harm avoided and that done by breaching the law. Finally, the accused should not have brought about the situation giving rise to the defence by his own criminal or negligent conduct.[37]

DURESS

[16.23] If a person commits a criminal offence as a result of a threat by a third party, they may be entitled to the defence of duress. In general, threats perceived as duress have been threats of physical violence.[38] Although threats of serious commercial damage might also be sufficient in certain circumstances.

[16.24] In *R v Horne*[39] the accused had entered false information into the English DSS computer system and had fraudulently claimed over £17,000 as a result. His defence that he did so under duress failed as did his appeal. This defence would presumably be part of the defence of 'lawful excuse', in the 1991 Act, as the accused would have honestly believed that he owned the data.

IGNORANCE OF THE LAW

[16.25] Ignorance of the criminal law is not a defence to criminal charges *(ignorantia juris non excusat)*. This rule is justified on two grounds. First, the difficulty of proving that the defendant knew the law and secondly, the risk that the use of the defence would make it advantageous for people to avoid ascertaining their legal obligations. As the law becomes more complex, excluding this defence becomes less fair, particularly where the legislation is as difficult to interpret as the 1991 Act. However, this rule only applies to the criminal law, it has no application to civil law.[40] Where property or data belonging to one person is damaged by another who, due to ignorance of the civil law of property believed that the property or data belongs to him, he will have the defence of ignorance of the civil law. This defence would presumably be part of the defence of 'lawful excuse', in the Criminal Damage Act, as the accused would have honestly believed that he

---

37. Charleton, *Criminal Law, Cases and Materials*, (Butterworths, 1992) p 214.
38. *The People (AG) v Whelan* [1934] IR 518. Murnaghan J stated that "threats of immediate death or serious personal violence so great as to overbear the ordinary power of human resistance should be accepted as a justification for acts which would otherwise be criminal."
39. [1988] Crim LR 584.
40. See Glanville Williams *Textbook of Criminal Law,* 2nd Ed, (Stevens, 1983) Ch 20 at p 456, para 20.4. and *R v Gould* (1968) 2 QB 65.

owned the data. In a situation where the vendor of computer software has got into a dispute he may erroneously believe that he is entitled to repossess or disable the computer software. This may be an offence, possibly of unauthorised access or damaging data. If the contract of sale does not allow the repossession of the software or access for that purpose, the vendor may be prosecuted as has occurred in the UK in *R v Goulden* and *R v Whitaker*.[41]

[41.] See para **[28.22]** *et seq.*

Chapter 17

Reform of the Criminal Damage Act 1991

THE CRIMINAL DAMAGE ACT 1991

[17.01] The Criminal Damage Act 1991 has been described as:

> "... a fine example of law reform. Its provisions are clear and self-explanatory. It proceeds on a coherent basis which recognises and defines, in simple terms, both the mental and external elements of the offences created".[1]

This is undoubtedly correct with regard to 'normal' offences against property such as arson and vandalism. Unfortunately it would appear that the Act's application to computer crime will not be as easy. Potential problems may stem from the fact that the computer crime offences were shoehorned into the form of criminal damage offences. It is unclear why computer crime offences were included in the 1991 Act. The Law Reform Commission Report on Malicious Damage did not recommend the inclusion of any such offence in a reform of the law of criminal damage.[2] It would appear that the computer crime offences were included as an afterthought to meet a perceived threat that frauds could be committed and damage caused using computers.[3] The English Court of Appeal decision in *R v Whiteley*[4] that computer misuse could amount to criminal damage may also have been a factor.[5] Burning down a bank and altering its records by use of a computer are radically different crimes, yet they are treated as being the same by the Act. Arson and vandalism are by their nature very public crimes. The criminal has to be close to the property that he damages and physically present when the damage is caused. These crimes are by their nature unsophisticated and only the most professional criminal will be able to avoid leaving a trail of evidence behind. Computer crimes are totally different. Computer criminals may be remarkably sophisticated. Since all the evidence will often be contained in electronic code or data it is easy to destroy all of it

---

1. Charleton, *Criminal Law Cases and Materials*, (Butterworths, 1992) p 475.
2. LRC 26 1988.
3. Dáil Debates, 29 November 1990, pp 575-637.
4. (1991) 93 Cr App Rep 25.
5. However that decision suggests that only very limited types of computer misuse may be criminal damage see para **[14.12]** *et seq*.

and even the most junior of criminals may be adept at destroying evidence in this way.

[17.02] The computer crime offence is extremely broad and as a result the definition of lawful excuse is equally broad. This has the dubious effect of making every use of a computer a potential crime while giving every computer criminal a potential excuse for that crime. It is unknown how this will work in practice. This is not because there is any shortage of computer crimes. The Act is so broad that computer crimes are committed every day by the most unlikely perpetrators. The breadth of the Act is illustrated by Intel, the manufacturer of the 'Pentium' computer chip, who admitted that there was a fault in their chip. When the faulty chip carried out calculations with very large numbers an error could occur in the final digits, thus the chip would have altered and corrupted data within the meaning of the Act. Intel stated that the problem was not serious and affected only a small number of calculations. Pentium chips are manufactured in Ireland and if it could have be shown that one of these chips had altered the data in a computer anywhere in the world Intel could be charged with criminal damage. While Intel undoubtedly did not intend to damage property, they must have been aware that by selling faulty chips there was a danger that this sort of damage would be done but they proceeded to take the risk. It goes without saying that Intel has never been charged with an offence under the 1991 Act and most people would find it bizarre if they were to be prosecuted.[6] However the failure to prosecute 'offenders' such as Intel may give rise to the claim of unequal treatment which is in breach of the Constitution.[7] The first person to be prosecuted under the 1991 Act may point to the millions of 'offences' which have been committed since the legislation's enactment and argue that he is entitled to the same treatment as all of those 'offenders'.

[17.03] It is difficult to obtain reliable information about computer misuse. Prosecutions of computer misuse offences are problematic and as a result, reports of court cases give only a patchy impression of the problem. The victims of such offences may be unwilling to report them as they fear the embarrassment and bad publicity which may result. In view of these difficulties, the Law Reform Commission[8] examined the suggestion that

---

6. *The Irish Times*, 16 December 1994. A class action has been commenced in the Californian courts concerning this matter. It seems likely that a settlement will be reached with the purchasers of an estimated 4 million defective Pentium chips. See July-Aug, 11 CLSR, p 226, (1995). One beneficial effect of this controversy was that Microsoft admitted that there was a fault with the calculator applet in Windows. As a result of this fault the calculator would not give correct answers: BYTE, September 1995.
7. Article 40.1.
8. Law Reform Commission Report on Dishonesty p 528 at para 37.17.

there should be a compulsory obligation on companies and other major users of computers, to report incidents of computer misuse. This suggestion was rejected by the Commission as it would be unenforceable as well as unjust to force companies to reveal cases of misfortune or weakness to a central agency. There is no general duty upon anyone to report other crimes such as larceny or other frauds.

[17.04] This position will be altered by the Criminal Law Bill 1996 if enacted. Section 8(1) provides that:

> where a person has committed an arrestable offence, any other person who, knowing or believing that the offence or some other arrestable offence has been committed and that he or she has information which might be of material assistance in securing the prosecution or conviction of an offender for it, accepts or agrees to accept for not disclosing that information any consideration other than the making good of loss or injury caused by the offence, or the making of reasonable compensation for that loss or injury, shall be guilty of an offence and shall be liable on conviction on indictment to a term of imprisonment not exceeding three years.

[17.05] Assessing the effect of this section is difficult. What exactly "reasonable compensation" amounts to is not explained by the Bill. The obvious starting place is the amount of compensation which might be awarded by a court in a claim for damages. As already outlined above,[9] assessing the cost of damage done in a computer misuse case is extremely difficult. Many victims of crime may feel that compensation far in excess of what they would receive for a tort claim is reasonable and just.

Preventative Measures

[17.06] Preventing computer misuse is obviously easier and cheaper than dealing with the consequences. The first step for any organisation which wishes to deal with this problem is to appoint a computer security officer within the organisation. The Price Waterhouse Survey found that over 55% of financial institutions and over 40% of government institutions had appointed such an officer. Overall, the figure was about 28%, with smaller companies and companies in Northern Ireland being less likely to appoint such an officer.[10]

[17.07] Once such an appointment has been made the next step is to establish a clear policy on computer security. The Price Waterhouse Survey

---

[9] See para **[14.17]**.

[10] Cost appears to be one reason why some companies are unwilling to take on the services of a security officer. It is more important that someone within a firm should have responsibility for this even on a part time basis than to have a permanent appointment.

found that these policies were common amongst government departments (70%), the top 200 companies (58%) and financial institutions (48%) but were far less common in Northern Ireland (33%) and smaller companies (24%). Obviously, it is pointless to establish such a policy if computer users are not made aware of it and educated or trained to the necessary standard.

[17.08] In preventing computer crime there are several methods which have proven successful. First, there are authentication measures such as passwords. These are meant to ensure that only authorised users are able to access computers, however, in the past they have proven to be unreliable. This unreliability usually stems from the frailties of the user's memories. To prevent themselves forgetting passwords, users often select their name, phone number, children's names and other words which are easy to remember but also easy for hackers to guess. To overcome this, variants of passwords have developed. As well as the more traditional remembered passwords, there are also passwords which rely on smart cards or other forms of identifications. As these can be stolen, other methods have been developed such as checking a user's fingerprint or retina.[11]

[17.09] Secondly, controlling the access rights of users may prevent misuse. Some users may only need to use computers as word processors. Others, such as a computer security officer may need access to every file on the system. The operator of a computer system should ensure that only those who need access, receive it. A common method of screening out unwanted intruders from networks such as the Internet is to create a 'firewall'. This is an electronic barrier which will sort out those trying to access the system and only allow those in who satisfy the system's requirements. These systems are not without their disadvantages. They are not completely secure and the impression of security that they give may lull administrators into a false sense of security.[12]

[17.10] Thirdly, encrypting data will ensure that only those who are entitled to access the data can do so. Some encryption systems are remarkably sophisticated, but no such system can ever be totally secure.

[17.11] Finally, monitoring the use of a computer system will enable administrators to identify cases of computer misuse. It is important to realise

---

[11.] See Denning, 'Passwords' Scientific American, 1992, March-April, p 117; 'Token Authentication', Data Communications, May 1995, p 62; Clark and Hoffman, 'BITS: A Smartcard Protected Operating System', 1994 Communications of the ACM, November, Vol 37, No. 11, p 66.

[12.] See Bryan, 'Barricading the Net', BYTE, April 1995, 89 and 'Firewalls under Fire', Network Security, May 1995, p 3.

that while computers and computer systems give criminals unprecedented opportunities to commit crimes, they also allow employers and others to monitor the work of their employees to a remarkable degree. Issues such as this have given rise to privacy concerns and the concept of data protection.[13]

[17.12] No one method will be sufficient to protect a computer system and the data held on it. A combination of these methods must be used to ensure adequate protection.[14] It has been suggested that preventative measures such as these should be encouraged rather than forcing the State to legislate for, and police, computer crime. This approach is obviously not practical and the Law Reform Commission rejected it.[15] However, the experience of the UK Computer Misuse Act 1990 would suggest that computer crime laws may be abused in situations where normally only the civil law would apply. Both the *Independent* case[16] and *R v Goulden*[17] were cases which should have been decided by the civil courts if they had gone to court at all. As the drafting of computer crime legislation is so broad there is a danger that it will be abused.

[17.13] Where an employee has been found to be abusing his rights of access to his employer's computer system or otherwise misusing it, his employer may feel it necessary to dismiss him. The decision to dismiss must conform to the standards set out in the Unfair Dismissals Act 1977. In *Mullins v Digital Equipment International BV*[18] the claimant was dismissed after it came to the attention of the company that he attempted to access the

---

13. See Quest, 'Computer Fraud - The Auditor's Approach', Computer Law and Security Report, 1990, September, Vol 6 Issue 3, also, Hallinan, 'Human Factors in Computer Security: A Review', Journal of Law and Information Science, 1993, Vol 4 No 1, p 94.
14. See: Layland, 'A Plan of Attack for Network Security', Data Communications, 21 May 1995, p 19; Lampard, 'Making IT Secure', Byte, 1992, February, p 661 s-41; Onwusah, 'Have You Taken Precautions?' NLJ 19 April 1996 p 548; Worthy, 'Be Prepared - Protecting Computer Systems Against Disaster', 1993, Business Law Review, October, p 235; Gamesan and Sandhu, 'Securing Cyberspace', Communications of the ACM, November 1994, Vol. 37, No. 11, p 29. Kay, 'Distributed and Secure', 1994, BYTE, June p 165. Johnson, 'Enterprise Security, Better Safe Than Sorry', 1995 Data Communications , March, p 110.
15. Report on Dishonesty, 1992, p 242 at para 29.12.
16. Davis, 'Computer Misuse', NLJ, 1 December 1995. This case involved an employee of BT who allowed a journalist from the Independent to view files on his computer. Criminal charges were subsequently brought against both but dismissed. See para **[16.08]** above.
17. Southwark Crown Court, unrep, 1992. Goulden was a programmer who was contracted to write a program. After a dispute over payment, he set up the program so that no-one but himself could use it. His client claimed to have lost £36,000 as a result. Goulden was convicted under s 3 of the CMA 1990.
18. UD 329/1989.

accounts of various people in the company. There had also been an attempt to access a master directory which contained confidential data. The claimant was called to a meeting with management on 22 February 1989 and he admitted attempting to access the accounts of four individuals and explained his attempts as experiments with the system and as a search for games. He was told that he was dismissed on 24 February 1989, however the company agreed to defer this decision until 27 February 1989 to allow the claimant to make submissions. However by then the company had discovered further evidence of attempts by the claimant to access accounts. The claimant was asked to demonstrate how he tried to access the accounts and he did so, following this management held a meeting at which it was decided to uphold the decision and the claimant was duly informed. The Employment Appeals Tribunal (EAT) was told that the company's main concern was that the claimant had attempted to access the accounts of supervisors who hold confidential information about people who worked under the control of the supervisors. The claimant told the EAT that he had no interest in any confidential information and that he was simply experimenting with the system. He said that it had never occurred to him that he could be dismissed for such experimentation and that he had never tried to hide anything and that those present at the meetings were not competent to understand his explanation. He told the EAT that he did not think that what he had done was a dismissable offence. The EAT found that there were substantial grounds justifying the dismissal. It accepted the evidence of how seriously the company viewed the attempts by the claimant to gain access to the accounts and it found that the claimant was aware at all times of the effect of his actions. Accordingly the EAT found that the respondent was entitled to view the unauthorised access attempts as serious misconduct on the part of the claimant. It was the unanimous view of the EAT that the decision by the company to terminate the claimant's employment was reasonable and that the claimant had failed. In *Minihan v Dell Computer Corporation*[19], the claimant was employed as a supervisor in a warehouse. The location of goods in the warehouse was recorded on a computer system. There had been a problem with pilferage in the warehouse which had been investigated by the gardaí. The company did not believe that the claimant was associated with these thefts but it alleged that the claimant had instructed another employee to falsify the returns. It would appear that this was done to improve the appearance of efficiency at the warehouse. It was alleged that if stock appeared on the computer system which was not actually in the warehouse then the claimant would tamper with the records to make them appear correct. Minihan claimed that he was only correcting for human error which occurred when entering details of stock into the system. He appealed

---

[19.] IR Databank, Employment Appeals Tribunal. Vol 14, No 335, p 11 June 1996.

to the Employment Appeals Tribunal which held that the decision to dismiss him was not unreasonable in the circumstances. In *Denco Ltd v Joinson*[20] the UK Employment Appeals Tribunal dealt with a case in which a Trade Union official was dismissed for gross misconduct after he accessed his employer's computer system without authorisation. Joinson used the password of another employee to gain access to and print out a list of all his employer's customers, information which he was not entitled to. He was dismissed and appealed. Initially Joinson's appeal succeeded, however this decision was appealed by the company to the Employment Appeals Tribunal which overturned that decision and remitted the case to a different industrial tribunal for rehearing. The industrial members of the Employment Appeals Tribunal were of the view that:

> "... [I]n this modern industrial world, if an employee deliberately uses an unauthorised password in order to enter or to attempt to enter a computer known to contain information to which he is not entitled, then that of itself is gross misconduct which prima facie will attract summary dismissal, although there may be some exceptional circumstances in which a response might be held unreasonable. Basically, this is a question of 'absolutes' and can be compared with dishonesty."[21]

[17.14] The Tribunal was critical of the company's failure to clearly warn employees of the serious consequences of interfering with the integrity of their computer systems. It was accepted by the Tribunal that:

> "unauthorised use of or tampering with computers is an extremely serious industrial offence. However, it is clearly desirable to reduce into writing rules concerning the access to and use of computers and not only to post them but to leave them near the computers for reference".[22]

However decisions such as these do not give employers a *carte blanche* to dismiss any employee found interfering with a computer. In another UK case *British Telecommunications plc v Rodrigues*[23] the employee, Rodrigues, was a credit control manager for BT. He had requested access to BT's databases of indebted customers to aid him in his work, but he was refused so instead he altered and stole the passwords of others who had access. Once caught he was placed on suspension and then dismissed. The Employment Appeals Tribunal found that he had been unfairly dismissed, however when the question of compensation was determined Rodrigues was found to have been 50% responsible for his dismissal.

---

20. [1992] 1 All ER 463.
21. *Ibid*, at 467.
22. *Ibid*, at 468.
23. [1995] Masons Computer Law Reports 11.

[17.15] Although Ireland has yet to prosecute for computer offences under the 1991 Act, it has become an increasing problem in other jurisdictions. The UK legislation was enacted around the same time as the Irish, however, it has considerable differences. The US legislation is of particular interest because it has the greatest problem with computer crime and has been legislating for this type of crime for a lot longer. The following sections examine and compare the UK and US approaches to this problem.

UK COMPUTER MISUSE ACT 1990[24]

[17.16] Unlike Ireland, the UK rejected the criminal damage approach to computer crime.[25] Although the UK legislation contains offences broadly similar to the Irish, it makes no reference to property and so avoids the potential difficulties of defining property as data. The UK courts had previously convicted persons of criminal damage to data in the cases of *Cox v Riley* and *R v Whiteley*.[26]

[17.17] The UK Act contains three offences. A person is guilty of an offence if:

(1) he causes a computer to perform any function with intent to secure access[27] to any program or data held in any computer. The access he secures must be unauthorised and he must know at the time that that is the case. He need not have intended to access any particular program or data or type of program or data or a

---

24. See generally: Lloyd, *Information Technology Law*, (Butterworths, 1993), pp 169-193; Charlesworth, *Between Flesh and Sand: Rethinking the Computer Misuse Act 1990*, in Wasik (ed*), International Yearbook of Law Computers & Technology*, (Carfax, 1995) Vol 9, p 31; Charlesworth, 'Legislating against Computer Misuse: The Trials and Tribulations of the UK Computer Misuse Act 1990', Journal of Law and Information Science, 1993, Vol 4 No 1, p 81; Dumbill, 'Computer Misuse Act 1990', Computer Law & Practice, 1992, Vol 8 No. 4 p 105: and Wuermeiling, 'German and English Law against Computer Crime - a Comparative Survey', Computer Law and Security Report, 1990, Vol 6 No 3, p 15.
25. Under s 3(6) of the UK CMA 1990 a modification to the contents of a computer shall not be regarded as causing criminal damage unless it impairs the computers physical condition.
26. See para **[28.22]** for discussion of these cases.
27. A person is defined as securing access to any program or data held in a computer if by causing a computer to perform any function he:
    (a) alters or erases the program or data;
    (b) copies or moves it to any storage medium other than that in which it is held or to a different location in the storage medium in which it is held;
    (c) uses it; or
    (d) has it output from the computer in which it is held (whether by having it displayed or in any other manner): CMA 1990, s 17(2).

program or data held in any particular computer. This is known as unauthorised access.[28]

(2) he gains unauthorised access with intent to commit a further offence or to facilitate the commission of such an offence whether by himself or somebody else. It is immaterial whether the further offence is to be committed at the time of the unauthorised access or at a later date. The person may be guilty of this offence even though the commission of the further offence would in fact be impossible.[29]

(3) he does any act which causes an unauthorised modification of the contents of any computer and at the time when he does the act he has the requisite intent and the requisite knowledge. Intent is defined as the intention to impair the operation of any computer; to prevent or hinder access to any program or data held in any computer or to impair the operation of any such program or the reliability of any such data. The intention does not have to be directed at any particular computer or any particular program or data or any particular modification. The requisite knowledge is the knowledge that any modification which he intends to cause is unauthorised. It is immaterial whether the unauthorised modification is or is intended to be permanent or merely temporary.[30]

[17.18] The first offence is similar to the offence of unauthorised access as contained in s 5 of the Criminal Damage Act 1991. The second offence is not to be found in the 1991 Act. It is the offence of accessing a computer with intent to commit further offences. This type of offence is useful as it may not be possible to show that the accused caused any damage and in this situation he can only be convicted of unauthorised access under the 1991 Act, no matter how malicious his intent in doing so. The third offence is that of unauthorised modification of computer contents. This is similar to the offence of data damage under s 2 of the 1991 Act. It prohibits the use of viruses as they will obviously cause modifications.

[17.19] The offence of unauthorised access under s 1 has caused unexpected problems. UK police chiefs have complained that messages have been placed at the access points to bulletin board systems stating that "law enforcement officials are not permitted to enter the system". Such a warning has been considered to be effective in restricting the police from accessing

---

[28.] CMA 1990, s 1.
[29.] CMA 1990, s 2.
[30.] CMA 1990, s 3.

bulletin boards since the police would commit an offence of 'unauthorised access' under s 1 of the 1990 Act.[31] To deal with this problem, s 162 of the Criminal Justice and Public Order Act 1994 provides that notices of this type cannot make access by law enforcement officials unauthorised. If such notices were to be posted on Irish bulletin boards they might not be effective since the gardaí should be able to claim a lawful excuse unless the controllers of the board could argue that for the gardaí to access their board without authorisation would amount to a breach of their right to privacy.

[17.20] The UK Act has more complex definitions than its Irish equivalent. Whether this complexity makes the Act any clearer is open to question. The term *computer* is not defined and although the terms *program* and *data* are used separately they are also not defined. *Access* is defined as being unauthorised if the user is not entitled to control access and he does not have consent from the person entitled to do so.[32] A *modification* of the contents of any computer is said to occur when any program or data held on the computer are altered or erased or new programs or data are added to the contents.[33] The Computer Misuse Act only protects computers themselves. Devices such as floppy disks are only protected when they are inserted into the computer. If such devices were to be stolen or damaged these offences would have to be dealt with under other legislation.[34]

UNITED STATES LEGISLATION

[17.21] As the country which invented the modern computer and computer networks, it is inevitable that the USA should have the greatest experience of computer misuse. As a result they have developed extensive legislation to deal with this problem.

The Computer Fraud and Abuse Act[35]

[17.22] At federal level, there are several statutes which may be used in the prosecution of computer offences particularly the Computer Fraud and Abuse Act 1991. The Act creates six offences:

[31.] See: Reed and Walden, 'Legal Problems of Electronic Bulletin Board Operators', International Journal of Law and Information, Vol 2, No 1, p 286.

[32.] CMA 1990, s 17(5).

[33.] CMA 1990, s 17(7).

[34.] CMA 1990, s 17(6).

[35.] 18 USCS s1030 1991. See generally, Cavazos and Morin, 'Cyberspace and the Law', MIT Press, p 107-109; Rose, *Netlaw,* (McGraw-Hill, 1995); Smedinghoff (ed), *Online Law,* (Addison Wesley, 1996) pp 479-480; Charney, 'Computer Crime', Federal Bar News and Journal, 1994, Vol 41 No 7, p 489; Young, *United States Computer Crime Laws, Criminals and Deterrence,* in Wasik (ed), *International Yearbook of Law Computers & Technology,* (Carfax, 1995) Vol 9, p 1.

(1) Knowingly accessing a computer without authorisation and obtaining information which is to be used to injure the USA;

(2) Intentionally accessing a computer without authorisation or in excess of authorisation to steal financial information;

(3) Intentionally accessing a computer without authorisation, used by the US government and adversely affecting the use of that computer by the US government;

(4) Knowingly and with intent to defraud, accessing a 'Federal Interest' computer without authorisation to further a fraud;

(5) Knowingly causing the interstate transmission of "a program, information, code or command to a computer system" with intent to cause damage or cause the system to withhold service;

(6) Knowingly causing the interstate transmission of "a program, information, code or command to a computer system" with reckless disregard for the damage that may be caused or the fact that the system may withhold service;

(7) Trafficking in passwords or similar information.

[17.23] The Federal Act is far more specific in the offences it creates and it has a clarity which is missing from the Irish legislation. There is no provision for recklessness apart from the sixth offence which relates to the reckless transmission of viruses. To be convicted the defendant must have carried out his actions intentionally or knowingly for all other offences. There is no unauthorised access offence as contained in the Criminal Damage Act 1991. Unauthorised access only becomes an offence if it is done to obtain financial or government information, with a fraudulent purpose or if it adversely affects the government's use of the computer. The Act also avoids the problems which have occurred in the UK where the police have been prevented from accessing bulletin boards and other areas used by hackers.[36] The Act also deals with the theft of particular types of information. The suggestion by the Irish Law Reform Commission that an offence of theft of information should be created here has been criticised by the authors.[37] The only way that such an offence could work would be to make it specific to certain categories of information as done in the US legislation. Otherwise such an offence is open to abuse.

[17.24] The US Act lacks the generality of the Irish law. There is no general offence of data damage or anything similar. Instead, the US legislation

---

[36.] See para **[18.03]** below. Section 1030(f) provides that the section does not prohibit lawful investigations by law enforcement agencies.

[37.] See paras **[17.39]** & **[18.03]** below.

prohibits certain specific activities which lead to data damage. In particular, it prohibits the transmission, whether recklessly or intentionally of any program, information, code or command to a computer system which results in damage or causes the computer to withhold service. This provision prohibits the transmission of viruses and also the transmission of a direct command to the computer which causes damage. Trafficking in passwords is also made illegal which is a useful offence and has no parallel in Irish law.

[17.25] The federal legislation is limited in its effect. It only applies to crimes which involve interstate commerce or communications or where crimes directly impinge on the activities of the US government or financial institutions. The Act is very specific but this is partially due to the fact that the federal government does not have to legislate for every type of computer crime. This job is left to the individual States whose legislation operates in parallel with the federal laws.

The New York Computer Crime Statute[38]

[17.26] The New York Computer Crime Statute was revised in 1992. In essence, the New York Statute provides for four types of offences. First, using a computer without authorisation is an offence. The unusual feature of this section is that for an offence to be committed the computer must be equipped with security devices to prevent such unauthorised use. Secondly, computer trespass, which will be committed when a person gains unauthorised access to a computer with intent to commit a felony or gains unauthorised access to a computer and knowingly gains access to computer material. Thirdly, four offences of computer tampering, the penalties for which become more severe as the offence becomes more serious:

(a) Computer tampering in the fourth degree occurs where a person uses or causes to be used a computer and having no right to do so, alters or destroys computer data or programs belonging to another.

(b) Computer tampering in the third degree is committed where computer tampering in the fourth degree is done with intent to commit another offence, the offender has previous convictions for similar offences, he intentionally alters or destroys computer material or he intentionally alters or destroys material valued at over $1,000.

---

38. See also Bierce, 'The Crime of Technological Duress in New York', Computer Law & Practice, Vol 10, No 1, 1994 p 5.

(c) Where the damage exceeds $3,000 then the offence of computer tampering in the second degree will be committed and

(d) where the damage exceeds $50,000 then computer tampering in the first degree is committed.

Finally, the offence of duplication or possession of computer related material such as programs or data. The duplication must cause the owner a loss of at least $2,500 for the offence to be committed. This would make copying computer programs in breach of copyright an offence but it would also cover copying or possessing computer passwords or other material to enable further offences to be committed.

[17.27] These clearly drafted offences cover most, if not all, possible abuses of a computer. However, they do not penalise legitimate users. It is a defence to any charge under the Statute to be able to show that the defendant had reasonable grounds to believe that he could carry out the acts complained of. The New York Statute contains three offences which are not in the Irish Act. First, the Statute does not criminalise access to a computer, rather it makes unauthorised use of a computer an offence. The difference from the Irish Act is subtle but important. A user may be entitled to access a computer but not to use it in certain ways. The criminalisation of *use* rather than *access* is sensible and should avoid problems such as those which occurred in the *Independent* case.[39] Secondly, there is the offence of unlawful duplication of computer related material. Copying is not offence under the Criminal Damage Act 1991, although copying a program may be an offence under the Copyright Act 1963. Finally, the offence of criminal possession of computer related material. Arguably, there is a similar provision in s 4 of the Criminal Damage Act 1991 which makes it an offence to possess anything with intent to use it to cause damage. However, the offence contained in the New York Statute is much broader and covers computer criminals who hold onto illegally copied materials after the commission of their crimes and not just before as in the Criminal Damage Act. This provision is similar to the offence of theft of information recommended by the Law Reform Commission. American legislatures find it easier to enact such laws since any abuse of them will be prevented by the First Amendment protection of free speech, which has no equivalent in Ireland.[40]

[39.] See para **[16.08]** above.

[40.] The First Amendment to the American Constitution reads "Congress shall make no law ... abridging the freedom of speech, or of the press; or the rights of the people peaceably to assemble, and to petition the Government for a redress of grievances."

[17.28] The scope of the New York Statute is much broader then its Irish counterpart. The offence of unauthorised use of a computer, computer trespass and tampering in the fourth degree in the New York Statute apply to offences against computer services as well as offences against computers themselves. This extends the protection of the criminal law to:

> any and all services provided by or through the facilities of any computer communication system allowing the input, output, examination or transfer of computer data or computer programs from one computer to another.

This extends the protection to networks such as the Internet and is not available under the Criminal Damage Act 1991.

[17.29] In particular, the use of a computer without authorisation is clearly defined. This means the use of a computer without the permission of, or in excess of the permission of the owner after notice has been given to the user. This notice may be given either in writing or orally or prominently posted adjacent to the computer which is being utilised by the user, or displayed, printed out or announced by the computer being utilised by the user. Proof that the computer is programmed to automatically display, print or announce such notice or a notice prohibiting copying, reproduction or duplication will be presumptive evidence that such notice was displayed, printed or announced. Like the Irish Act, the New York Statute defines *computer program* and *computer data* as being property. Unlike the Irish Act, it defines both terms separately in keeping with common practice.

Computer program is defined as:

> property and means an ordered set of data representing coded instructions or statements that when executed by computer, cause the computer to process data or direct the computer to perform one or more computer operations, or both and may be in any form, including magnetic storage media, punched cards or stored internally in the memory of the computer.[41]

Computer data:

> is property and means a representation of information, knowledge, facts, concepts or instructions which are being processed or have been processed in a computer and may be in any form, including magnetic storage media, punched cards or stored internally in the memory of the computer.[42]

---

[41] NY CLS Penal, s 156, 1992.
[42] NY CLS Penal, s 156, 1992.

Texas Computer Crime Statute

[17.30] The Texas Computer Crime Statute[43] provides for nine offences in total. It includes the offences of data damage and unauthorised access, however it also includes several specific offences to deal with particular problems. Using a password or other code is made an offence if it is done without the consent of the person who controls the computer system. Causing a computer to disrupt communications, utilities or government business is an offence, as is tampering with government, medical or educational records. An offence will be committed where a person obtains information from or introduces false information into a computer system to damage or enhance the data or credit records of a person. Offences will also be committed by using a computer to remove, alter, erase or copy a negotiable instrument or knowingly and intentionally introducing a computer virus into a computer program, computer network or computer system. The only specific defence contained in the code is that if the accused was the employee of a phone company or electric utility and committed the act in the course of employment while engaged in any activity which is necessary for the rendition of a service or to protect the interests and property of his employer, then he will have a defence to criminal charges.

[17.31] The drafting of this Statute is not as impressive as that of the New York Statute. However, it contains several interesting features. Like the other US Statutes, the authors have tried to produce a large number of specific offences to deal with specific crimes. The Texas Statute provides for an offence for the unauthorised use of a computer. This will only apply if there are security measures to prevent such use. There is no requirement of recklessness. For an offence to be committed, the accused's actions must have been intentional. *Computer program* and *data* are clearly defined as separate concepts.

SUGGESTED REFORMS

[17.32] All the computer crime legislation outlined above have one crucial difference to the Irish legislation, they are all specifically designed to deal with computer misuse. It might be better therefore for the Irish legislature to create a number of specific offences rather than the three or four general offences which exist at present and which may prove difficult to apply to specific instances of computer misuse.

[17.33] First, s 5 of the Criminal Damage Act 1991 makes it an offence to operate a computer with intent to access data. It may simply be better to

---

[43.] Texas Penal Code s 33.

criminalise the unlawful use of a computer. Access is a difficult concept to define as is seen by s 17 of the UK Computer Misuse Act 1990. It also suggests that the authors of these Acts still saw computers as being large mainframe type machines, access to which was restricted and easy to control. The Law Reform Commission has suggested[44] the creation of an offence of dishonest use of a computer. They suggest creating an offence based on s 115 of the Australian Capital Territory Ordinance, which provides:

> (1) A person who, by any means, dishonestly uses, or causes to be used, a computer or other machine, or part of a computer or other machine, with intent to obtain by the use a gain for himself or herself or another person, or to cause by that use a loss to another person, is guilty of an offence punishable, on conviction, by imprisonment for 10 years.

[17.34] Secondly, not all computers contain valuable information. It is reasonable to assume that if a computer contains no security devices, it contains no valuable information. It might be beneficial to require the owners of computer systems to install such protection before receiving the protection of the criminal law. This would have obvious benefits as a crime prevention measure and would also ensure that only cases which definitely involved criminal intent would be prosecuted. A provision that accessing or using a computer would only be criminalised if it involved the breach of security measures would also prevent confusion arising about the access limits of users. Any abuse of information or other material acquired through authorised access or use could be dealt with as a civil matter. It would be clear when the access or use had become unauthorised since it would be necessary to breach the system's security measures.

[17.35] Thirdly, it is obviously beneficial for employers and other authorities to ensure that computer users are aware of the limitations placed on their access. A provision that where the limitations on access are given in writing, displayed beside the computer or appear on the monitor when accessing the computer, it will be assumed that the user was notified of his access limitations, will encourage this practice. This would also simplify court proceedings.

[17.36] Fourthly, the sale or other distribution of passwords and other information which may be used for computer misuse should be made an offence. It is unwise to make it an offence to access a computer but not to make it an offence to facilitate such access.

---

44. Law Reform Commission Report on the Law relating to Dishonesty 1992, Ch 29, p 244.

[17.37] Fifthly, the misuse of computer systems will often have implications for networks such as the Internet. While computers which are a part of such networks are protected, there is more to a network than just the computers connected to it. Networks or computer services should be protected and it should be an offence to interfere with the working of a network as it is an offence to damage the contents of a computer.

[17.38] Sixthly, the Criminal Damage Act 1991 lacks any clear definitions. Although such definitions may eventually become obsolete, it may be difficult to effectively prosecute computer crime without them.

[17.39] Finally, the Law Reform Commission has proposed that an offence of theft of information be created.[45] This is a difficult area in which to legislate. The example used by the Law Reform Commission to justify the creation of a new offence is that of the theft of an exam paper. The Law Reform Commission argue that it is wrong to prosecute someone for stealing an exam paper when what they have really done is to gain information to which they are not entitled. The problem with creating an offence of this nature is that it is open to abuse. What may be confidential information to one person may be an exposé of corruption to another. The creation of this offence could make the use of 'gagging writs' seem mild. A modern society needs information to function correctly. Computers can supply this information cheaply and effectively, creating an offence of this nature would impede the flow of that information. In particular, if information embarrassing to the government were to 'leak' out, this type of offence could be used to intimidate journalists and others. Valuable information is already adequately protected by intellectual property law and the law on confidential information.

[17.40] Fraud,[46] forgery[47] and similar crimes will all be prosecuted in Ireland under Statutes which pre-date the foundation of the State. If accounts are falsified, a prosecution may be taken under an enactment from the last century.[48] In this context, it may seem unreasonably optimistic to suggest the reform of an Act which is only six years old. However, the computer industry and the technology which it generates change with remarkable speed and it may be that the Criminal Damage Act 1991 will prove ineffective.

---

45. *Op cit* para 20.29. See para **[18.03]** below.
46. The Larceny Act 1916.
47. The Forgery Act 1913.
48. Falsification of Accounts Act 1895.

Chapter 18

Other Relevant Offences

INTRODUCTION

[18.01] As discussed in the previous chapters, the Criminal Damage Act 1991 has created several computer offences, but these may not be sufficient on their own and prosecutors may find it necessary to rely on other legislation to secure convictions. Laws which are not specifically written to prohibit criminal acts using computers are rarely satisfactory. However, these other offences may prove useful in the future. Often criminals who commit computer offences will commit other offences as a result. For example, someone who alters bank records on a computer may commit a separate offence when they actually withdraw the money to which they are not entitled. If a computer has been used to commit a fraud or another such crime it may be more practical to prosecute an offender for one of the more traditional offences such as larceny or obtaining by false pretences. Including charges other than those of criminal damage may be advisable if a prosecutor is worried that the defendant may successfully raise defences such as having a lawful excuse to charges of criminal damage. It should be borne in mind however that the courts are not always receptive to such prosecutions, one attempt was described as a "procrustean attempt to force these facts into the language of an Act not designed to fit them (which) produced grave difficulties for both judge and jury which we would not wish to see repeated".[1]

LARCENY

[18.02] Stealing something is an offence under s 1 of the Larceny Act 1916 which states:

> For the purposes of this Act:
>
> (1) a person steals who, without the consent of the owner, fraudulently and without a claim of right made in good faith, takes and carries away anything capable of being stolen with intent, at the time of such taking, permanently to deprive the owner thereof:

[1.] *Per* Lane CJ, in the English Court of Appeal in *R v Gold* [1987] 3 WLR 803 at 809 whose sentiments which were approved of by Brandon LJ giving judgment in the House of Lords [1988] 1 AC 1063, at 1073.

253

> Provided that a person may be guilty of stealing any such thing
> notwithstanding that he has lawful possession thereof, if, being a
> bailee or part owner thereof, he fraudulently converts the same to
> his own use or the use of any person other than the owner.

This makes it an offence to take and carry away anything capable of being
stolen with intent to permanently deprive the owner of it. It is difficult to see
how this could apply to computer data or programs as they can easily be
copied without permanently depriving the owner of possession. In the
English case of *R v Lloyd*,[2] the defendant was involved in a conspiracy to
take copies of films from cinemas and copy them onto video tape. He was
prosecuted under s 6 of the UK Theft Act 1968 which prohibits the
temporary appropriation of property and which has no equivalent in Ireland.
The case is important as the Court of Appeal held that notwithstanding this
section, there could only be a theft where the taker's intention was to return
the item when all of its value had been extracted. As the films could still be
projected in front of paying audiences, this had not occurred.

[18.03] It is also doubtful that data or other information could be a 'thing'
within the meaning of the Larceny Act. In *Oxford v Moss*[3] the defendant was
a student at Liverpool University. He stole a copy of an examination paper,
but intended to replace the paper once he had copied it. Because Moss
intended to return the paper, it was felt that he could not have stolen it.
Instead, he was prosecuted for stealing confidential information which was
the contents of the paper. He was acquitted as it was held that information
was not property and therefore could not be stolen. In a Scottish case, *Grant
v Allan*,[4] it was alleged that the appellant copied computer printouts of his
employer's confidential information and he offered to sell this information
to their rivals. The court held that this was "a matter for the civil and not the
criminal law"[5] and allowed the appeal.[6] The Law Reform Commission has
recommended creating a crime of theft of information.[7] They recommend
that this be done by defining property in the context of dishonesty as
including intellectual property protected by the equitable doctrine of
confidentiality, the personal data defined in and protected by the Data
Protection Act 1988, or other valuable, confidential information. The
Commission also recommends that the requirement of proving an intention

---

2. [1985] 2 All ER 661.
3. (1978) 68 Cr App Rep 183.
4. (1988) SLT 11.
5. *Ibid* per McDonald at 15.
6. The Court referred to two cases, *Dewar,* Burnett, Treatise on Criminal Law, 115 and *HM
   Advocate v Mackenzies* (1913) 7 Adam 189; 1913 SC(J) 107.
7. Report on Dishonesty p 181, para 20.49.

to permanently deprive the owner of the information be abolished.[8] Confidential information is already protected by the civil law,[9] but as computer networks expand, these protections may cease to be sufficient. If so it is probably better to reform the provisions of the civil law rather than introduce criminal penalties.

[18.04] Where someone is able to command a computer to part with money or other goods, it may be argued that the operator of the computer has consented to that transaction even though all other criteria for the offence of larceny have been satisfied. In the Australian case of *Kennison v Daire*[10] the defendant closed his bank account and withdrew all his funds. Later he was able to withdraw $200 from an automatic teller machine due to a flaw in the machine's programming. It was accepted that he had fulfilled all the other criteria for larceny and the court found that the bank could not have consented to the withdrawal of the money as his account was closed and he held no funds.

Stealing electricity

[18.05] Stealing electricity is an offence under s 10 of the Larceny Act 1916. This provides:

> Every person who maliciously or fraudulently abstracts, causes to be wasted or diverted, consumes or uses any electricity shall be guilty of felony and on conviction thereof liable to be punished as in the case of simple larceny.[11]

Prosecuting a computer misuse offence under this section is likely to be difficult. In a Hong Kong case of *R v Siu Tak-Chee*,[12] the defendant was charged with stealing electricity worth considerably less than one Irish penny. He was alleged to have done so when he gained unauthorised access to confidential information held on a computer. Due to the trivial amount of electricity stolen, the defendant was discharged unconditionally. In *Low v Blease*[13] the defendant had trespassed upon premises and made a phone call from there. He was charged with burglary as a result, the prosecution claiming that making a phone call had resulted in the theft of electricity. The

---

8. *Ibid* p 164, para 19.24.
9. See Ch 9.
10. (1986) 64 ALR 17.
11. Under s 6(1) of the Electricity (Supply) (Amendment) Act 1942 an offence may be tried summarily and will attract a maximum penalty of a £50 fine or six months imprisonment. Such proceedings may be brought by the ESB or any other person.
12. August 1984, Law Reform Commission of Tasmania, Report No 47, *Computer Misuse*, p 23.
13. [1975] Crim LR 513.

English High Court held that electricity could not be appropriated by switching on current and could not be described as property for the purposes of the UK Theft Act 1968. The Court took the view that Parliament had recognised that electricity cannot be 'appropriated' and had enacted s 13 of the UK Theft Act 1968 to deal with dishonest use of electricity as a result. It has been suggested that the 'dishonest borrower' of a vehicle such as a car which consumes electricity does commit the offence of dishonestly using electricity under the UK Act as may a person who uses electricity as a result of some fraud.[14] If this is so then unauthorised use of a computer, which also consumes electricity, would be an offence under s 10 of the Larceny Act 1916.

Stealing telephone calls

[18.06] Making telephone calls without payment is made an offence under s 99 of the Postal and Telecommunications Services Act 1983 which provides:

> (1) A person who wilfully causes the company to suffer loss in respect of any rental, fee or charge properly payable for the use of the telecommunications system or any part of the system or who by any false statement or misrepresentation or otherwise with intent to defraud avoids or attempts to avoid payment of any such rental, fee or charge shall be guilty of an offence.
>
> (2) A person who connects or causes to be connected any apparatus or device to, or places or causes to be placed an apparatus or device in associations or conjunction with, the telecommunications system operated by the company or any part of the system the effect of which might result in the provision by the company of a service to any persons without payment of the appropriate rental, fee or charge shall be guilty of an offence.

There are two separate offences. Firstly, causing Telecom Éireann a loss and secondly, attaching an apparatus or device to the telecommunications system. This offence might include connecting a computer to the telecommunications system, if that computer could be used to defraud Telecom by hacking into its computers and altering the billing records or other data within. This would be useful in a situation where a computer was found to be connected to the telecommunications system and where there was other evidence of such hacking such as programs or stolen passwords, but it was not possible to prove that such fraud had actually been perpetrated.

[14.] See Smith, *The Law of Theft*, 6th Ed, (Butterworths, 1989), para 306, p 157.

[18.07] The theft of telephone calls does not usually involve breaking into someone's home or office and using their phone. Rather it is usually accomplished by fooling a telephone company's computers into billing someone other than the caller for the call. At the most extreme level, this may be accomplished by hacking into the phone company's computers and transferring billing records.[15] Obviously, this is not usually feasible and there are easier methods. One is to acquire someone else's credit card number and use this to make calls, usually to international destinations. Another is used with cellular phones which involves 'cloning' or copying the phone of a legitimate user. When a mobile phone is used it will send out a radio signal which gives its electronic serial number and phone number. The cloner will intercept this signal and copy it. He will then transfer the numbers to another phone and all calls made on that phone will be charged to the legitimate user's account. This is a particular problem in the UK and has affected the Ministry of Defence and the Royal Family.[16] It has now become a problem in Ireland. In *DPP v Abdul Umarjee*,[17] the defendant was convicted of causing losses to Telecom Éireann. The gardaí were alerted to Umarjee's activities when Eircell subscribers complained about unexplained increases in their bills. Umarjee had cloned these users' phones and used the clones to sell international phone calls to places such as Pakistan, Kuwait, India, Surinam and America. By doing this, Umarjee ran up bills of £30,000 which ultimately had to be paid by Telecom Éireann. Umarjee received a three year sentence, however, O'Connor J ordered that he be released after one month provided that he returned to the UK.

[18.08] This crime is also a major problem in the US where it is known as 'phone phreaking'. Although other forms of stealing phone calls are common in the USA, a particular problem is so-called 'PBX' fraud. PBX stands for Public Branch Exchange which are computerised phone systems operated by companies to control their internal and external phone calls. Many of these systems are set up so that salesmen and other employees can ring into the company on a 1800 number and re-dial out to get international or long distance phone calls. All a hacker would have to do is dial 1800 and 7 random digits until he finds a PBX. To dial out he would usually need to give a password but these are frequently quite simple.[18]

[15.] See para **[13.03]**.
[16.] *The Sunday Times*, 23 July 1995.
[17.] *The Irish Times*, 26 April 1996.
[18.] Wallich, 'Wire Pirates', Scientific American, March 1994. Voice mail systems or answer phones are also easily interfered with.

FORGERY

[18.09] Section 1 of the Forgery Act 1913 makes it an offence to make a false document in order that it may be used as genuine. This might have an application in a situation where a password is entered into a computer by someone who is not entitled to use it in order to gain access. This overlaps with the offence of unauthorised access under s 5 of the 1991 Act. One attraction to charging somebody with an offence under the Forgery Act 1913, further or in the alternative to an offence under s 5 of the 1991 Act, is that the forgery offence may be punishable as a misdemeanour where it is done with intent to deceive.[19] Commerce and banking are increasingly reliant on EDI and other telecommunication technologies which allow documents, invoices and contracts to be created, transmitted and acted upon without ever using paper. If these documents are created electronically, the Forgery Act will apply to any attempts to falsify them.

[18.10] Section 1(2) of the Forgery Act 1913 provides that a document will be false:

> if the whole or any material part thereof purports to be made by or on behalf or on account of a person who did not make it or authorise its making; or if though made by or on behalf or on account of the person by whom or by whose authority it purports to have been made, the time or place of making where either is material or in the case of a document identified by number or mark, the number or any distinguishing mark identifying the document is falsely stated therein; and in particular a document is false:
>
> (a) if any material alteration, whether by addition, insertion obliteration, erasure, removal or otherwise has been made therein;
>
> (b) if the whole of some material part of it purports to be made by or on behalf of a fictitious or deceased person;
>
> (c) if, though made in the name of an existing person, it is made by him or by his authority with the intention that it should pass as having been made by some person, real or fictitious, other than the person who made or authorised it.

One difficulty with using the Forgery Act is that a forged electronic document may only be used to fool a computer which might fall outside the scope of the Act. The Forgery Act states that a forged document must purport to have been made 'by or on behalf of a person', this might exclude documents which purport to have been made by a particular computer. It is likely that communications between persons such as letters, which are transmitted by electronic means as opposed to being printed out and posted,

---

19. Section 4(1).

will be covered by this legislation. However, communications between computers or between humans and computers such as a command to print something, may not be covered.

[18.11] The term 'document' is not defined by the Act. It is not clear that an electronic document will be a document for the purposes of the Act. A clear definition of 'document' is difficult to come by. In the Supreme Court judgment of *McCarthy v O'Flynn*[20] Kenny J stated "I have looked at many attempted generic definitions of (document) but all of them are unsatisfactory".[21] That case concerned an application to have a X-ray discovered as a document for the purposes of discovery.[22] Kenny J suggested that the best course would be to consider what the origin of the words was and to try to ascertain from that what the main characteristic of a document was. He held that as the term document is originally derived from the Latin verb "docere" (to teach). Therefore, he found that "the main characteristic of a document is that it is something which gives information".[23] In support of his decision, Kenny J referred to a number of English cases[24] and quoted the judgment of Humphreys J in *Hill v The King*[25] where he stated that:

> "Whether I regard the derivation of the word 'document' from Latin or the decisions of the courts on the meaning of the word, I find that a document must be something which teaches you and from which you can learn something ie, it must be something which affords information. In the dictionaries the word is repeatedly defined as something admissible in a court of law, but as being something which makes evident that which otherwise would not be evident. To constitute a document, the form which it takes seems to me to be immaterial; it may be anything on which the information is written or inscribed- paper, parchment, stone or metal."[26]

Henchy J took the view that where 'document' occurs in the rules relating to discovery then it should be construed in terms of the scheme and purpose of those rules. He found that the term includes "any thing which if adduced in evidence at the hearing of the proceedings, would be put in, or become

---

[20.] [1979] IR 127.

[21.] *Ibid*, at 131.

[22.] See para **[14.07]**.

[23.] *Ibid*, at 131.

[24.] See *Lyell v Kennedy* (1884) 27 Ch D 1, where a photograph was held to be a document for the purposes of discovery and *Grant v South-Western Properties* [1974] 3 WLR 221, where a tape recording was held to be a document. There have also been a number of UK cases in which computer files have been found to be documents for the purposes of discovery: see para **[24.40]**.

[25.] [1945] KB 329.

[26.] *Ibid*, at 332.

adduced to, the court file of the proceedings".[27] Although the Law Reform Commission concluded that "One can survive as well with or without the definition"[28] it recommended that the word 'instrument' should be used instead of document and the most appropriate definition was that of s 8 of the UK Forgery and Counterfeiting Act 1981.[29]

Passwords

[18.12] The Irish definition of the term 'document' clearly encompasses documents in the form of a page with writing on it or a photograph. However it is unclear whether a computer password will count as a document for the purposes of the Forgery Act 1913. A password tells a computer that the person who has entered it is entitled to use that system. As such, a password would appear to be "something which gives information".[30] The question of whether a password can be an 'instrument' for the purposes of the UK Forgery and Counterfeiting Act 1981 was examined in the English case of *R v Gold*.[31] The appellant was involved in defrauding the Prestel system run by British Telecom. This is system which links users to a computer database using the British Telecom phone system. To access this system a user must first register with the company and pay a rental charge. The user is then given a Customer Identity Number (CIN) and also a password. To access the system the user must first enter his CIN and then his password, if the computer can verify that these are correct then the user would be allowed access to the system. These passwords were deleted once the system had verified that they were correct. The defendant used a password which belonged to a British Telecom engineer. This gave him unlimited access to all Prestel services and had the added advantage of not creating a billing record.[32] Eventually the appellant was caught and charged on four sample counts that he:

---

27. *Ibid*, at 129.
28. Report on Dishonesty, 1992 p 265, para 32.30.
29. This defines instrument as "(a) any document whether of a formal or informal character; (b) any stamp issued or sold by the Post Office; (c) any Inland Revenue stamp; and (d) any disc, tape, sound track or other device on or in which information is recorded or stored by mechanical, electronic or other means." The Commission also recommended that cash and credit cards be specifically included. *Ibid* p 266, para 32.31.
30. *Per* Kenny J in *McCarthy v O'Flynn* [1979] IR 127.
31. (1988) 1 AC 1063 and [1987] 3 WLR 803 (CA).
32. The acquisition of the password and user identification number was not a dramatic event. One night Gold dialled up Prestel from his home computer. Prestel asked him for his user ID. By chance, Gold entered ten twos. This was correct. Gold was then asked for a password and he tried 1234. As a result he received unlimited and free access to the Prestel System. Unfortunately for Gold, he decided to use his access to enter the mailbox of Prince Philip. See Clough and Mungo, *Approaching Zero*, (Faber & Faber, 1992), p 37.

"made a false instrument ... with the intention of using it to induce the Prestel Computer to accept it as genuine and by reason of so accepting it to do an act to the prejudice of British Telecommunications Plc."[33]

[18.13] Under the UK Forgery and Counterfeiting Act 1981 'instrument' is defined as *inter alia*: "any disc, tape, sound track or other mechanical device on or in which information is recorded or stored by mechanical, electronic or other means ..."[34] The appellant was convicted and ultimately his appeal came before the House of Lords. It had been accepted in the Court of Appeal that the electronic impulses which made up the passwords could not be an instrument for the purposes of the Act. Instead the deliberations in that Court and in the House of Lords focused on the question of whether or not the portion of the Prestel computer's memory[35] which recorded the passwords could be an instrument. The House of Lords decided unanimously that an instrument was not created in these circumstances as the Prestel computer would only record the passwords for a very short time. The Court was of the opinion that the Act required the recording and storage of information to be of a "lasting and continuous nature" whereas the passwords would only be "held momentarily ... while the checking of was carried out, and then being totally and irretrievably expunged".[36]

[18.14] The logical question to ask about *R v Gold* is if the Prestel computer had permanently recorded the passwords would the Court have then found that they were within the Act's definition of 'instrument'? The judgment of the English High Court in *R v Levin (orse R v Governor of Brixton Prison and another, ex parte Levin)*[37] suggests that they would. In that case the applicant was a Russian accused of accessing the computers of an American bank and transferring over $10,700,000 from customer accounts into accounts controlled by his associates. The court examined the question of whether passwords and other commands entered by the applicant into the bank's computer could be an 'instrument' for the purposes of s 8(1)(d) of the UK Forgery and Counterfeiting Act 1981. These commands were recorded on a magnetic disk. The court was willing to extend the definition of the term 'disk' to any information contained on such a disk in the same way as a document consists both of the paper and the printing upon it. The court quoted the judgment of Brandon LJ of the House of Lords in *R v Gold*:

---

33. [1987] 3 WLR 803, at 805 (CA).
34. Section 8(1)(d).
35. The information would appear to have been recorded on the computer's temporary electronic memory (the equivalent of the RAM on a PC) as opposed to its permanent memory such as its hard drive.
36. *Ibid, per* Brandon LJ, at 1072.
37. *The Times*, 11 March 1996, LEXIS transcript.

"The words 'recorded' and 'stored' are words in common use which should be given their ordinary and natural meaning. In my opinion both words in their ordinary and natural meaning connote the preservation of the thing which is as subject matter of them for an appreciable time with the object of subsequent retrieval and recovery. Further in relation to information recorded or stored on or in a disk, tape or soundtrack, that is the meaning of the two expressions which appears to me to be clearly intended."[38]

The court held that as the commands were stored permanently, then a false instrument was created. Unfortunately, this court did not refer to the judgment of the Court of Appeal in *R v Gold*. There Lane CJ referred to the UK Law Commission Criminal Law Report on Forgery and Counterfeit Currency[39] which pointed out that in 'normal' forgery cases a document will contain two distinct messages: firstly, a message about the document itself (eg, that it is a cheque) and; secondly, a message to be found in the words of the document that is to be accepted and acted upon (eg, that a banker has to pay £x). Lane CJ stated that "it is only documents which contain both types of message that require protection by the law of forgery".[40] The Court of Appeal held that the recording of the passwords did not carry these two types of message and as such was not an instrument. This may suggest that the conclusion reached in *Re Levin* is incorrect. Since the House of Lords held that due to the brevity of the password's existence an instrument was not created, they never proceeded to examine this question.

Forging valuable securities

[18.15] The judgment in *R v Gold* and the creation of an unauthorised access defence in the 1991 Act makes it unlikely that a case will be taken to prosecute somebody for forgery as a result of using an unauthorised password. This does not mean that the forgery offence has no application to information technology law. It might be applicable in a situation where a stolen credit card number has been entered into a computer to pay for services on the Internet.[41] Although credit card numbers are no more than streams of digits they are recorded for considerable periods of time and as such would overcome the hurdle set by the House of Lords judgment in *R v*

[38.] *Ibid* at 1072.

[39.] Law Com No 55 1973. In *Levin* Beldam LJ did refer to this report in his judgement however he does not appear to have drawn any conclusions from its findings or examined whether the passwords used in *Levin* satisfied its requirements for an document needing protection by the law of forgery.

[40.] [1987] 3 WLR 803, at 809 (CA).

[41.] If the credit card number was to be used to pay for goods then the offence could be prosecuted as larceny.

Gold. However the judgment of the Court of Appeal that a document must contain two messages, one about the document itself and the other requiring certain actions to be taken, may create problems. The forgery offence may also become relevant if digital cash becomes commonplace since it is inevitable that people will try to counterfeit it.[42]

[18.16] In *R v King & others*[43] the appellants had been convicted of procuring the execution of a valuable security by deception. The appellants were part of a conspiracy which involved a solicitor and a bank manager amongst others. They secured the execution of electronic money orders called CHAPS orders which instantaneously transferred money from the bank into accounts controlled by the appellants. The order was made out on an A4 sheet of paper, one side signed by one of the appellant, the other containing details of the electronic transaction. On appeal they argued that the CHAPS order was not a valuable security. The Court of Appeal held that it was and the court looked at the effect of the order as well as its form. The order required the bank officials to pay over considerable sums of money, £81,000 in one case. Lane LCJ stated that to argue that the transfer was the result simply of the actions of the bank officials was analogous to arguing that a cheque, incontestably a valuable security, was not efficacious to transfer property because there had to be bank activity before a credit appeared in the payee's account. The Court suggested that in future cases attention should focus firstly on what a document did and only afterward should it examine whether a document fell within the relevant statutory definition. Although this case did not examine the characteristics of electronic documents directly, by focusing attention on what a document does as opposed to what form it takes, the judgment suggests a way out of the conundrum of trying to manufacture a suitable definition of terms such as 'document'.

FALSE PRETENCES

[18.17] Obtaining money or other property by false pretences is made an offence under s 32 of the Larceny Act 1916. This provides that a person is guilty of an offence, where by any false pretence:

> (1) with intent to defraud, (he) obtains from any other person any chattel, money, or valuable security, or causes or procures any money to be paid, or any chattel or valuable security to be

---

[42.] Computer technology also makes it easier to counterfeit conventional legal tender. See, 'Making Money', Scientific American, March 1994.

[43.] *The Times*, 26 June 1991. See also *R v Bolton* (1992) 94 Cr App R 74.

delivered to himself or to any other person for the use or benefit or on account of himself or any other person; or

(2) with intent to defraud or injure any other person, (he) fraudulently causes or induces any other person:

   (a) to execute, make, accept, endorse, or destroy the whole or any part of any valuable security; or

   (b) to write, impress, or affix his name or the name of any other person, or the seal of any body corporate or society, upon any paper or parchment in order that the same may be afterwards made or converted into, or used or dealt with as, a valuable security ...

[18.18] On conviction for obtaining by false pretences, the maximum punishment is five years imprisonment.[44] This offence would be relevant in a situation where computer networks are used to perpetrate some scam or hoax. It has been claimed that the Internet has been used to perpetrate various frauds.[45] There would be no difference between this and the normal offence save that a computer was used to commit it. Whether the offence would have any other relevance to computer law is unclear. It has been suggested that in a case where a computer is fraudulently commanded to transfer money or other property then this may be the crime of obtaining by false pretences. This might be useful in cases where stolen or forged cashcards and passwords are used to remove cash from Automated Teller Machines (ATMs). In November 1996 seven men pleaded guilty in the UK to charges arising from a conspiracy to steal hundreds of millions of pounds from banks. The telephone lines which link the ATMs to the banks were to be tapped with the help of corrupt British Telecom employees. The gang would then have deciphered the information gathered and used it to create false cash cards which could then be used to withdraw cash from machines around the UK. However, the equipment held by the conspirators would not have actually been capable of de-ciphering the acquired information and the cards which they had been able to create did not have the correct Personal Identification Number (PIN) to gain access to the individual accounts.[46] In September 1996 the leader of criminal gang pleaded guilty to charges arising from a 'scam' which successfully removed £130,000 from bank accounts in the UK using fake cash cards. The gang filmed customers taking cash from ATMs and used the details gathered to make the fake cash cards.[47]

---

44. Larceny Act 1916, s 32.
45. For example one Texan lost $10,000 when he sent it to an individual based in Minnesota who falsely advertised on a computer network, that he was a money manager. See Kiernan, 'Internet tricksters make a killing', New Scientist, 16 July 1994.
46. *The Times*, 5 November 1996.
47. *The Daily Telegraph*, 13 September 1996.

[18.19] Where bank accounts are emptied in this fashion it is inevitable that disputes will arise between banks and their customers. In *Banks v AIB*,[48] the plaintiff had lodged over £1,000 in the bank, when two years later he went to withdraw some of it he found that there was nothing there except a few pence. Apparently, the money had been withdrawn from an ATM machine. The plaintiff claimed that he had never used the card, he left it in his bedroom after memorising the PIN number. Experts from the bank gave evidence of near invisible marks on the card which indicated that it has been used and the procedures under which the card was made. Carroll J held that the bank was free to pay out money unless it was aware of fraud, and he was satisfied that the bank was not aware of any unauthorised use of the PIN number. "The probability of a duplicate card and PIN number having been carelessly and negligently issued is so remote that it must be discounted". Judgment was given in favour of the bank together with costs. However not every court will make a similar finding, in *Judd v Citibank*[49] the court found in favour of the customer stating that "In this case we are met with a credible witness on the one hand and a computer printout on the other".[50]

[18.20] One case cited by the Law Reform Commission suggests that in this situation it may be possible to prosecute for obtaining by false pretences. In the case of *The State v Hamm*,[51] the defendant used another's bank card and PIN to obtain money from an ATM. He was held to have made false representations to the effect that he had the authority to use the card and PIN to get money from the machine. The problem with using this offence to prosecute computer crimes is that it is difficult to show how a machine such as a computer can be deceived.

[18.21] Analysis of this offence tends to turn on the question of whether or not a computer can be said to have consented to a transaction or to have been deceived. A computer will be programmed to carry out the commands of its owner and those authorised by its owner to give such commands. Anyone who enters false commands or passwords into a computer is arguably deceiving the owner of computer, although at one remove. It may be argued that if a computer is programmed by a bank to give out money to anyone who has a smartcard and an appropriate PIN then the computer cannot be deceived if someone enters a stolen smartcard and PIN, rather it is the bank which owns and programs the computer which is deceived. The Law Reform

---

48. Circuit Court, unrep, Carroll J: see *Irish Independent* 10 March 1995.
49. 435 NYS 2d 210 (1980).
50. *Ibid* at 211. Quoted in Ellinger, *Modern Banking Law* (Clarendon Press, 1987) p 400.
51. 569 SW 2d 289 (Mo App, 1978); referred to in the Law Reform Commission Report on Dishonesty, 1992, p 103, para 9.4.

Commission appears to have been of the view that a computer can not be said to have been deceived:

> "A machine or a computer can only respond to a physical shape or electronic impulse fed into it. There can be no question of a machine giving a meaningful consent. No mind is deceived. The machine or computer does what it is told or programmed to do. On that approach, if someone achievers unauthorised access to a machine or computer or having authority to use a machine or computer feeds in false information and obtains cash or a chattel, we have a straightforward case of theft or unlawful appropriation. Thus, if someone stole a person's Banklink card, found out his PIN (password) and withdrew cash from his account from a money dispensing machine, one could be charged with larceny."[52]

The Government Advisory Committee on Fraud has recommended the creation of a new offence of unauthorised use of an ATM card.[53] The question of whether or not a machine can be deceived did arise in the case of *Davies v Flackett*.[54] The defendant was driving his car out of a car park. When he approached the exit barrier, the occupants of the car ahead of him got out and manually lifted the barrier and avoided payment. When they left the defendant followed them and so also avoided payment. This was observed by the police who charged him with dishonestly obtaining a pecuniary advantage by deception. The charges against the defendant were dismissed on the basis that a machine could not be the victim of deception. This was appealed by the prosecution to the Divisional Court. However, this case does not bring the argument any further as this court did not consider the question of whether a machine could be deceived[55] and the *obiter* views of the judges differ on this question.

[18.22] The obtaining of property by deception as a result of computer misuse was considered in *R v Thompson*.[56] The defendant was employed in Kuwait as a computer programmer by a Kuwaiti bank. He opened five bank accounts in his own name with different Kuwaiti branches of that bank. He identified other bank accounts held at those branches which all had the same features. Firstly, they held substantial balances and secondly they were infrequently used. The defendant programmed the bank's computer to debit

---

52. The Law Reform Commission Report on the Law Relating to Dishonesty, 1992, p 243.
53. 1993 Report.
54. (1973) RTR 8.
55. Instead, their deliberations focused on whether the defendant had intended to evade payment.
56. [1984] 3 All ER 565. The Law Reform Commission has recommended changing the crime of obtaining by false pretences to one of obtaining by deception similar to the UK Theft Act 1968: Report on Dishonesty 1992, p 195, para 23.5.

each of these bank accounts and to credit his own accounts for an identical amount. The program was set to operate when the defendant was on a plane home to England and to erase itself afterwards. This it duly did. When the defendant arrived in England he telexed the Kuwaiti branches to forward the balance which he had created to accounts which he controlled in the UK. As a result the defendant received approximately £45,000. The defendant was caught, charged and convicted. On appeal he argued that as the fraud had taken place in Kuwait where the computer program had operated, then he could not be tried in an English Court. This view was rejected by the Court of Appeal which held that all the computer program had done in Kuwait was create a chose in action. That is he created a liability for a sum which the bank was obliged to pay him. He did not obtain any money until he withdrew it from his bank in England. The Court was therefore satisfied that the defendant's conviction was safe and it dismissed his appeal.[57]

[18.23] The view that altering bank accounts or other material to make it appear that an individual has a credit balance only creates a chose in action and so cannot result in the actual obtaining of any property is supported by the decision of the House of Lords in *R v Preddy*.[58] In that case the appellants had been convicted under s 15 of the UK Theft Act 1968 of obtaining property by deception. They had been engaged in mortgage fraud, by making false statements on their application forms for a mortgage they induced lending institutions to advance money to them. They appealed to the House of Lords which had to answer the question:

> "whether the debiting of a bank account and the corresponding crediting of another's bank account brought about by dishonest misrepresentation, amount to the obtaining of property within s 15 of the (Theft Act) 1968."

The House of Lords found that it did not. When a balance was transferred from the lender's bank to the appellants' own bank account the defendant acquired a "new chose in action constituted by the debt now owed to him by his bank, and represented by the credit entry in his own bank account".[59] It did not come into existence until the debt created by it was owed to the appellants by the bank, this meant that the property was not owned by anyone else. Goff LJ accepted that the credit in the appellants' bank account corresponded to the debit entered in the bank's account but it did not follow that the property which the defendant acquired can be identified with the property which the bank lost when its account was debited. Charging the defendants with obtaining property by deception was condemned as the

---

57. See also *R v Gent* [1990] 1 All ER 364.
58. [1996] 3 All ER 481. See also *R v Hawkins*, *The Times*, 6 August 1996.
59. *Ibid* at 490.

"adoption of a simplistic approach ignoring the nature of the precise transactions involved"[60] and as invoking the Theft Act for a purpose for which it was never designed, and for which it did not legislate.[61] It should be noted that the Law Reform Commission has recommended that property be defined so as to include choses in action.[62]

[18.24] This does not mean that if an offence similar to *R v Preddy* occurred in Ireland that it would not result in a prosecution. A prosecution could occur under s 13(1) of the Debtors (Ireland) Act 1872 which provides that it is an offence for a person, in incurring any debt or liability, to obtain credit under false pretences or by means of any other fraud. The offence carries a maximum sentence of one year's imprisonment.[63] It might also be taken under ss 2 and 5 of the Criminal Damage Act 1991. Like the fraud offences, the offence of false pretences will become more relevant to information technology law as electronic documents become more common.

EMBEZZLEMENT

[18.25] Embezzlement occurs when property is stolen before it comes into the possession of the thief's employer. This would occur when goods or other property are received by an employee who instead of giving them to his employer retains them for his own use. Obviously, the alteration of computer records would greatly facilitate the commission of this type of offence. Embezzlement is made an offence by s 17 of the Larceny Act 1916 which provides:

> Every person who:
>
> (1) being a clerk or servant or person employed in the capacity of a clerk or servant:
>
> > ... (b) fraudulently embezzles the whole or any part of any chattel, money or valuable security delivered to or received or taken into possession by him for or in the name of or on the account of his master or employer ...
>
> shall be guilty of felony ....

---

60. *Ibid* per Jauncey LJ, at 496.
61. *Ibid* per Goff LJ, at 490. Jauncey LJ was particularly critical of the reforms contained in s 15 of the UK Theft Act 1968: "My Lords it is singularly unfortunate that parliament has achieved ... the result of legalising fraudulent conduct of the type involved in these appeals - conduct which was almost certainly criminal prior to the 1968 Act." *Ibid* at 496.
62. Report on Dishonesty, 1992, p 175, para 20.35.
63. The Law Reform Commission has recommended that the theft of Choses in Action be made an offence. See Report on Dishonesty p 175, 20.35.

Clerks or servants may be very widely defined. In *Faulkes*,[64] a son was convicted of embezzling from his father.

FALSIFICATION OF ACCOUNTS

[18.26] Employees who falsify the accounts of their employer will be guilty of the offence of falsification of accounts as provided by s 1 of the Falsification of Accounts Act 1895:

> ... if any clerk, officer or servant, or any person employed or acting in the capacity of a clerk, officer, or servant, shall wilfully and with intent to defraud destroy, alter, mutilate or falsify any book, paper, writing, valuable security or account which belongs to or is in the possession of his employer, or has been received by him for or on behalf of his employer, or shall wilfully and with intent to defraud make or concur in making any false entry in, or omit or alter, or concur in omitting or altering, any material particular from or in any such book, or any document, or account, then and in every such case the person so offending shall be guilty of a misdemeanour, and be liable to imprisonment for a term not exceeding seven years.[65]

Although this offence dates back to 1895, it may be applicable to computer offences as it only applies to the falsification of "any book, paper, writing, valuable security or account". Presumably, the courts could extend "writing ... or account" to include computer records.

THE DATA PROTECTION ACT 1988

[18.27] Section 22 of the Data Protection Act 1988 creates an offence of gaining unauthorised access to personal data.[66] Any person who obtains access to personal data or information constituting such data, without the prior authority of the data controller or processor and who discloses the data or information to another is guilty of an offence. This provision does not apply to an employee or agent of the data controller or data processor and would appear to be aimed at hackers and others who gain access to such data without authorisation. The offence is punishable by a fine not exceeding £1,000 on summary conviction and a fine not exceeding £50,000 on conviction on indictment.[67]

---

64. 13 Cox CC 66 (CCA 1875).
65. Directors, officers or managers of a company who falsify accounts will be guilty of a misdemeanour under s 82 and s 83 of the Larceny Act 1861.
66. See para **[21.09]** *et seq.*
67. See also *R v Brown* [1996] 1 All ER 545; *McGregor v McGlennan* (1993) SCCR 852.

Proposed Fraud Bill

[18.28] The Minister for Justice has announced that a review of the law of fraud is being undertaken with a view to enacting a new law on fraud to take account of the recommendations of the Law Reform Commission and the Government Advisory Committee on Fraud. This will create a consolidated fraud statute to reduce confusion. The proposed statute will move away from the existing offences of larceny which are based on the physical taking of property and replace them with new offences based on the broader concept of appropriation. The proposed Act will also create new offences to deal with the misuse of information technology which will deal with developments such as home banking, payment via the Internet, electronic cash and other innovations.[68]

[68.] Address given by Nora Owen, Minister for Justice at a conference on combating corporate fraud on 25 March 1996.

Chapter 19

The Origins and Scope of Data Protection

INTRODUCTION

[19.01] Governments have always held extensive information about their citizens. The Roman census which caused Christ to be born in Bethlehem and the Doomsday book are examples of this. However, such records were always limited in their content. It was difficult to cross reference the information and the information had to be held centrally, which made dissemination difficult. In recent years, computers have allowed the size and use of these records to be greatly expanded. The dangers posed by modern information technology and data processing systems has been acknowledged by Hoffman LJ in the House of Lords who stated that:

> "one of the less welcome consequences of the information technology revolution has been the ease with which it has become possible to invade the privacy of the individual ... No longer is it necessary to open letters, pry into files or conduct elaborate inquiries to discover the intimate details of a person's business or financial affairs, his health, family, leisure interests or dealings with central or local government. Vast amounts of information about everyone are stored on computers, capable of instant transmission anywhere in the world and accessible at the touch of a keyboard. The right to keep oneself to oneself, to tell other people that certain things are none of their business, is under technological threat."[1]

Traditional paper files were limited in the amount of information which they could contain by their physical size. Computers allow huge amounts of personal information to be held in any one place and on any one individual. At one stage, Lotus proposed the creation of a database on the habits and spending of over 120 million consumers.[2] The use of identification numbers facilitates the processing and storage of personal data. Although there is no national identification card scheme in Ireland, it has been advocated in the UK.[3] Credit cards and so called 'loyalty cards' allow information to be gathered about a person's spending and leisure habits. The introduction of smart cards will make collecting information from individuals even easier.

---

[1] *R v Brown* [1996] 1 All ER 545 at 555.

[2] After public protests this idea was dropped. See Bibas, 'A Contractual Approach to Data Privacy', Harvard Journal of Law and Policy, Vol 17, p 594.

[3] Cullen, 'Nationwide ID Scheme on the Card', Patrol, 1996.

Smart cards with microprocessors can store considerable amounts of information. So called 'contactless cards' have an antenna which will pick up an electro-magnetic signal as the holder passes a device which can read the card. This device will transmit a signal which will power the card and cause it to transmit data held on it.[4] This means that information such as a person's location may be gathered without that person being aware of it.

[19.02] A computer can rapidly search through hundreds of thousands of licence plate numbers to find all the owners of blue cars bought in 1990. These searches can be as extensive or as limited as the user desires. Such a search can be accomplished in minutes using a computer but might take days using paper files. Databases can be powerful tools when they are combined with other technology. Number-plate recognition systems are now being developed which can automatically identify a number plate and compare it with a list of thousands of suspect numbers. When it matches a number it will send out an alert.[5] Data matching is the comparison of one file with another. In a US case, *Jaffess v Secretary, Department of Health, Education and Welfare*[6] the plaintiff was receiving benefits from both the US Veterans' Administration and Social Security. A computer program matched the files of both these departments and found that the plaintiff was receiving both benefits, although he had not disclosed this to the Veterans' Administration. As a result, his benefits were reduced. The plaintiff sued, claiming his right to privacy had been violated, but failed.[7]

[19.03] Profiles can be generated by a computer to predict which members of society or of a sub-group of that society are likely to exhibit certain behaviours.[8] If this processing is to be successful then large amounts of personal data about individuals must be collected and processed. Individuals may object to being arbitrarily assigned to particular groups by marketing firms or credit reference agencies and it may not be beneficial for society to be sub-divided using arcane criteria which is obscure to all but a few

---

4. Tomkowiak & Hofland, 'A Computer in your Wallet', BYTE, June 1996.
5. Collins, 'Database Detection Methods in Criminal Investigation', Computer Law and Security Report, Vol 11, 1995, p 2.
6. 393 F Supp 626, (SDNY 1975).
7. In 1982, the US Department of Education compared a file of defaulted student loans with a file of all federal employees. As a result, $3.4 million was recovered. see Cruse, 'Invasions of Privacy and Computer Matching Programs', Computer Law Journal, Vol XI 1992.
8. "Profiling is a technique whereby a set of characteristics of a particular class of person is inferred from past experience and data holdings are then searched for individuals with a close fit to that set of characteristics": Clarke, 'Profiling: a hidden challenge to the regulation of data surveillance', Journal of Law and Information Science, Vol 4, 1993.

experts.[9] In recent years, so called data mining techniques have become popular which use advanced software methods such as intelligence agents to analyse data more effectively. Such advanced statistical techniques may also be used to produce information about individuals which they may not be aware of and do not appreciate.[10]

[19.04] Computer networks also allow for records to be shared between computers which means that databases can be more geographically extensive and also more readily accessible, in the UK, the National Health Service network allows doctors throughout the UK to access any patient's medical records, regardless of location.[11] Computers also allow information from diverse sources to be combined to create a picture of a person's habits and activities. Facts which might be insignificant on their own may become important when combined with others.

Insurance

[19.05] Insurance companies in Ireland maintain significant databases to enable themselves to monitor the risks posed by their customers. One example is life assurance where the Republic of Ireland Register contains the names and dates of birth of people who have either been refused life assurance or offered cover on special terms. This database is maintained by the Irish Insurance Federation and holds the names of 'many thousands of people'. The database will normally contain anyone with a history of cancer, heart disease or another serious illness.[12]

[19.06] This type of database may seem unobjectionable but advances in medical science may allow more extensive databases to be created. 'Molecular epidemiology' will allow scientists to look for 'biomarkers' which show that a patient is likely to develop cancer. It is not yet feasible to examine a person and then give a meaningful assessment of the likelihood that they will suffer cancer but it may be possible in the future.[13] This will be very significant for medicine since it will allow cancer to be treated earlier.

[9.] The Office of Technology Assessment of the US Congress has noted that most federal US agencies use data processing techniques to develop various profiles including those of drug dealers, violent offenders, arsonists, rapists and child molesters. 'Federal Government Information Technology: Electronic Record Systems and Individual Privacy'. OTA-CIT-296 US Government Printing Office, Washington DC, June 1986.

[10.] One such system was used to analyse the death penalty related votes and opinions of US Supreme Court Justice Byron White. It was found that his voting patterns were linked to the race of the accused: BYTE October 1995, p 86.

[11.] *The Times*, 3 September 1995.

[12.] *The Irish Times*, 8 September 1995 and 29 September 1995.

[13.] Perera, 'Uncovering New Clues to Cancer Risk', Scientific American, May 1996.

However, it will also be very significant for insurance companies since they will be better able to predict their own risk. These and other methods of predicting the likelihood that an individual will become ill will have to be carefully controlled if they are not to be abused.

[19.07] Another important database maintained by the insurance industry is the Insurance Link Database maintained by the Irish Insurance Federation. This is specifically designed to target fraud. The database is used for 'data matching'. When an individual makes a claim, his details will be entered into the system and will inform the insurer if the claimant has made previous claims or whether there are any similarities between claims. Various State bodies also maintain similar databases and cross-checking takes place between these systems. The system is used by 19 insurance companies in Ireland and has saved almost £1 million on 166 claims in its first five years of operation.[14]

THE ORIGINS OF THE DATA PROTECTION ACT 1988

[19.08] In view of the dangers outlined above, most European countries have enacted legislation to ensure that personal data is protected. Ireland is no exception in this regard. The Data Protection Act 1988 ensures that Irish people have a considerable control over their personal data. The Minister for Justice stated that the purposes justified the need for the Bill when introducing it to the Dáil for the second time:

> "The Bill is designed to provide adequate safeguards to individuals against any abuse of their privacy arising from the automatic processing of personal data concerning them. It does this without imposing any undue burdens on industry or the taxpayer and without unnecessarily restricting transborder flows of data, including flows of data to this country for processing from countries which have ratified the Convention. There are other positive benefits. The Bill will encourage Government Departments and agencies and private sector companies to adopt better practices in the handling of personal data such as keeping data up to date and not keeping data for longer than necessary. That should lead to greater efficiency in the use of information technology in both the public and private sectors."[15].

However, this legislation was enacted with a minimum of debate within Ireland itself. The motivation for the legislation came from two international bodies, the OECD (Organisation for Economic Co-operation and Development) and the Council of Europe. The OECD guidelines governing

---

[14.] *The Irish Independent*, 19 March 1996.
[15.] *Dáil Debates*, 17 November 1987, Vol 375, Col 847 to 848.

the Protection of Privacy and Transborder Flows of Personal Data[16] and the Council of Europe Convention for the Protection of Individuals with Regard to Automatic Processing of Data[17] (the Strasbourg Convention) clearly influenced the Data Protection Act 1988 more than any internal Irish debate.

The Strasbourg Convention

[19.09] The Strasbourg Convention for the Protection of Individuals with regard to the Automatic Processing of Personal Data[18] is broadly similar to the OECD guidelines. The Convention contains eight basic principles for data protection which must be observed by the signatories to the Convention, of which Ireland is one:

1. Data must be obtained and processed fairly and lawfully;

2. It must be stored for specified and legitimate purposes and not used in a way incompatible with those purposes;

3. The data must be adequate, relevant and not excessive;

4. It must be accurate and up to date;

5. Data must be preserved in a form which permits identification for no longer than is necessary for the purpose for which it is stored;[19]

6. Sensitive data such as political opinions, racial origin, or religious beliefs may not be processed without appropriate safeguards;[20]

7. Appropriate security measures must be taken to protect personal data;[21]

8. Any person may establish the existence of personal data, rectify or erase such data and be able to appeal a refusal to rectify or erase data.[22]

The main difference between the Strasbourg Convention and the OECD guidelines is that the Convention contains clearer obligations to ensure transborder data flows and mutual assistance. The Council of Europe has

---

16. Recommendation of the Council of the OECD, 23 September 1980. The guidelines were mainly inspired by the United States delegation to the OECD. Members of the OECD should take all reasonable appropriate steps to ensure uninterrupted and secure transborder data flows. The OECD guidelines contain eight principles to ensure data protection.
17. Signed by Ireland on 28 January 1981.
18. 1981.
19. Article 5.
20. Article 6.
21. Article 7.
22. Article 8.

also produced a number of recommendations and resolutions on data protection.[23]

THE DATA PROTECTION ACT 1988

[19.10] The objective of data protection legislation is to give individuals some control over their personal data or information. It also attempts to regulate the data processing industry. The 1988 Act only applies to computerised data and not to personal information kept in paper files or otherwise, which obviously places serious limitations on the Act. The Act's application is limited, furthermore, one of the main requirements of the Act, that of registration for data controllers and processors, will only apply in certain circumstances.

Definitions

[19.11] The 'data subject' is the person who is the subject of the personal data. 'Personal data' is defined as data relating to a living individual who can be identified either from the data or from the data together with other information in the possession of the data controller. This means that databases containing information about corporations and companies will not be covered save where they refer to people alive and working in those companies. If the data on a computer is identified by a number which can be cross referenced to a name held by the controller elsewhere, then this will be covered by the Act. A data controller is any person who controls the contents and use of personal data.

[19.12] 'Processing' is defined as being the performance of an automatically logical or arithmetical operation on data and it includes the extraction of any information constituting the data. In relation to a data processor, the use by a data controller of data equipment[24] in the possession of the data processor[25] and any other services provided by him for a data controller is also processing. Processing does not include an operation performed solely for the purpose of preparing the text of documents. This means that word processing to prepare a document containing data will not be covered by the

---

23. See Resolution (73)22 on data protection in the private sector and Resolution (74)29 on data protection in the public sector. There are also various recommendations on, *inter alia*, medical data, scientific research and police data.
24. 'Data equipment' is equipment for processing data. Any document or other material used in connection with or produced by the data equipment is referred as data material.
25. A 'data processor' is a person who processes personal data on behalf of the data controller. He is not an employee of a data controller who processes such data in the course of his employment.

Act but so long as the data is retained and can be processed automatically it will be covered.

[19.13] 'Data' is any information in a form which can be processed.[26] Information held on the hard disk of a computer or on a floppy disk or CD-ROM will fall within the definition as will information which may be accessed on a network, such as the Internet. Information stored on a microfiche or a microfilm will not count as data, unless it is capable of being processed through an automated retrieval system. Print-outs of data will not come within the definition of data nor will information displayed on a visual display unit. However, information contained within print-outs or on VDUs cannot be disclosed save in compliance with the Act.

Scope

[19.14] The Act has no application to personal data that in the opinion of the Minister for Justice or Defence is or was kept for the purposes of safeguarding the security of the State. It does not apply to personal data which must be made available to the public by law nor does it apply to personal data kept by an individual for the purposes of managing his personal family or household affairs or for recreational purposes.[27] The Act does not apply to data controllers or data processors who hold or process data outside the State,[28] which has the potential for abuse, but the Data Protection Commission may issue a prohibition notice to prevent the transfer of data abroad.[29] Data is deemed to be kept by a data controller in the place where he controls its contents and use and processed by a data processor in the place where the relevant data equipment is located.[30] If a person is not resident in the State but controls or processes personal data through an employee or agent within the State, the Act will apply as if the employee or agent were acting on their own account.[31] The Act has no application to data processed wholly outside the State unless the data is used or intended for use in the State[32] and any restrictions on the transfer of registered data does not apply to data that is kept outside the State.[33] The provisions of the Act may be avoided if personal data is held and processed outside the State. Although the Act contains provisions to control the transfer of data to other countries,

---

26. DPA 1988, s 2.
27. DPA 1988, s 1(4).
28. DPA 1988, s 23(1).
29. DPA 1988, s 11(5).
30. DPA 1988, s 23(2).
31. DPA 1988, s 23(3).
32. DPA 1988, s 23(4).
33. DPA 1988, s 23(5).

in reality controlling such transfers is difficult. The EU aims to combat this problem with the Data Protection Directive which will control data protection throughout the Community.

THE DATA PROTECTION DIRECTIVE

[19.15] The Data Protection Act 1988 will now be supplemented by an EU Directive[34] on data protection which must be implemented by 24 October 1998. This Directive reflects the realisation that in the 1990s it is not the 'big brother' State which poses the greatest threat to data privacy but rather the hordes of 'little brothers' which gather scraps of mundane information. The collection of these individual bits of information poses no threat to anyone. It is only when thousands of such bits of information are combined together to produce a profile or picture of a person's life that there is a real threat to privacy.[35] In the following chapters, both the Act and the Directive are discussed in detail. Since both pieces of legislation deal with identical issues, we will first examine the provisions of the Data Protection Act 1988 and then the provisions of the Directive which affect that area.

[19.16] In 1990, the Commission of the European Communities published a "proposal for a Council Directive concerning the protection of individuals in relation to the processing of personal data". This was the subject of much controversy, notably in the European Parliament. The amended proposal or draft Directive was introduced on 15 October 1992 but proved to be equally controversial. It was originally intended that all EU Member States would have implemented legislation in line with the Directive by the end of 1994. The "Directive on the Protection of Individuals with Regard to the Processing of Personal Data and on the Free Movement of such Data" was finally adopted on 24 October 1995.

[19.17] The Directive attempts to balance the objectives of the EU to ensure economic and social progress by establishing an internal market with the need to preserve the privacy of the individual. The Directive states that data processing systems are designed to serve man,[36] however, more frequent use of data processing is being made in the EU and progress in information technology is making this ever easier.[37] The creation of a single market will greatly increase data processing and cross-border data flows within Europe. This will require the Member States to co-ordinate their data protection measures.[38] These cross-border flows of personal information will, in

---

[34.] OJ L 281, 23 November 1995, p 31.
[35.] *The Economist*, 10 February 1996, p 14.
[36.] Recital 2.
[37.] Recital 4.
[38.] Recital 5.

particular, be increased by the scientific, technical and telecommunications co-operation encouraged amongst Member States by the EU.[39]

[19.18] The levels of data protection differs between Member States, in particular, some States have different rights to privacy than others and this may prevent the transmission of personal data between States. This could constitute an obstacle to the pursuit of economic activities at Community level, distort competition and impede authorities in the discharge of their responsibilities under Community law.[40] The Directive therefore seeks to provide a high degree of uniform data protection throughout the EU.[41]

Scope of the Directive

[19.19] The objective of the Directive is that Member States shall protect the fundamental rights and freedoms of individuals and in particular their right to privacy with regard to the processing of personal data.[42] Member States must not restrict or prohibit the free flow of personal data between Member States to protect this right of privacy.[43]

Manual and computer files

[19.20] In comparison with the 1988 Act, the Directive extends the scope of data protection. The Directive applies to the processing of personal data wholly or partly by automatic means. 'Processing of personal data' means any operation or set of operations which is performed upon personal data, whether or not by automatic means such as collection, recording, organisation, storage, adaptation or alteration, retrieval, consultation, use, disclosure by transmission, dissemination or otherwise making available, alignment or combination, blocking, erasure or destruction.[44] 'Personal data' is defined as meaning any information relating to an identified or identifiable natural person (data subject). An identifiable person is one who can be identified directly or indirectly, in particular by reference to an identification number or to one or more factors specific to his physical, physiological, mental, economic, cultural or social identity.[45]

[19.21] This means that the Directive will apply to data which is wholly processed on a computer, however, it will also apply to a situation where extracts of data held elsewhere are processed on a computer. The Directive

---

39. Recital 6.
40. Recital 7.
41. Recital 10.
42. Article 1(1).
43. Article 1(2).
44. Article 2(b).
45. Article 2(a).

will also apply to the processing otherwise than by automatic means of personal data which form part of a filing system or are intended to form part of a filing system. A 'personal data filing system' ('filing system') is any structured set of personal data which is accessible according to specific criteria, whether centralised, decentralised or dispersed on a functional or geographical basis.[46] This means that the Directive will apply to paper (manual) files where they form part of a filing system. It will no longer be possible to avoid the obligations of data protection by dispersing files or holding some in paper files while processing extracts of data on computer. This is one of the most controversial parts of the Directive as the cost in implementation is expected to be very high. The UK has a derogation from this provision,[47] Ireland does not. However, the protection of manual files as well as computer files has become common in Europe and elsewhere. The Netherlands and Switzerland have data protection laws which apply to both computer and manual files, as has Australia.[48] It is unclear how much the application of data protection to manual files will cost. In any event, this provision does not have to be implemented until 2007 when the use of paper files may well be obsolete.

[19.22] The Directive states that the protection of individuals must apply as much to computer processing of data as to manual processing. It states that protection cannot depend on the techniques used, otherwise this would create a serious risk of circumvention. The Directive only covers filing systems of manual files not unstructured files. To come within the Directive, the content of a filing system must be structured according to specific criteria relating to individuals, allowing easy access to personal data. Member States may lay down the constituents of a structured set of personal data and the different criteria governing access to such a set.[49] Files, or sets of files including their cover pages which are not structured according to specific criteria will under no circumstances fall within the scope of the Directive.[50]

Sound and Image Data

[19.23] In recent years, the use of closed circuit television systems has become more common in Ireland where gardaí video cameras are a familiar

---

[46.] Article 2(c).

[47.] *The Economist.* A survey carried out for the Home Office in the UK indicated that this provision would cost at least £2 billion for the 625 organisations surveyed. Home Office: Costs of implementing the Data Protection Directive 1994.

[48.] OECD Privacy and Data Protection 1994.

[49.] See the definition of a 'filing system' at Article 2(c).

[50.] Recital 27.

sight in Dublin. Dublin Corporation operates approximately 20 such cameras.[51] Under the Prevention of Terrorism (Temporary Provisions) Act 1984, the UK police forces maintain records of photographs of suspected terrorists. They are able to do this under s 15 which provides that where is a person is detained under suspicion of terrorism:[52]

> any constable or prison officer or any other person authorised by the secretary of State may take all such steps as may be reasonably necessary for photographing, measuring or otherwise identifying him.

Once the photograph is taken it is held centrally by the special branch of the Metropolitan Police. This was the subject of a complaint to the European Commission on Human Rights in *McVeigh, O'Neill and Evans v UK*[53] where the Commission took the view that while taking these photographs was an interference with the individual's right to privacy, it was justified in this situation by the need to combat terrorism.[54]

[19.24] It is clear from European Court of Human Rights cases such as *Murray v The United Kingdom*[55] that the taking of a photograph of an individual may be an interference with her private life and so contravene Article 8 of the European Convention on Human Rights. However, that interference may be justified by the need to combat crimes such as terrorism. The Law Reform Commission has suggested that much more stringent measures should be introduced to monitor the gathering of video and photographic data about individuals. They suggest it should be made an offence to carry out video surveillance of an individual without their permission.[56]

[19.25] The scope of the Directive is extended to videos or tape recordings of individuals as "the techniques used to capture, transmit, manipulate, record, store or communicate sound and image data relating to natural persons, [mean that] this Directive should be applicable to the processing involving such data."[57] The processing of this type of data will be covered by

---

51. Closed circuit television cameras installed in the Temple Bar area of Dublin are monitored in Pearse Street Garda Station: Garda Síochána Annual Report 1995 p 34.
52. See Criminal Justice (Miscellaneous Provisions) Bill 1996, s 11(2) and 12 and Criminal Justice Act 1984 s 28.
53. (1982) 25 ECHR 15.
54. See also Beddard, 'Photographs and Rights of the Individual', [1995] MLR 771.
55. [1995] 19 EHRR 193. See also *McVeigh, O'Neill and others v UK* (1982) 25 ECHR 15 and *Friedl v Austria* [1995] 21 EHRR 83.
56. Law Reform Commission, Consultation Paper on Privacy, paras 10.41-10.45, p 234-235. They also suggest that the gardaí should get Ministerial permission before carrying out video surveillance: paras 10.56-10.66, p 238-242.
57. Recital 14.

the Directive only if the data is automated or if the data processed is contained or intended to be contained in a filing system structured according to specific criteria relating to individuals, so as to permit easy access to the personal data in question.[58] The processing of sound and image data such as in cases of video surveillance will not come within the scope of the Directive if it is carried out for the purposes of public security, defence, national security or in relation to criminal law or of other activities which do not come within the scope of Community law.[59] Similarly, the processing of such data for journalism or for artistic or literary purposes will only be covered in the restricted manner laid down by Article 9 of the Directive.[60]

Non-application of the Directive

[19.26] The Directive has no application to any activity which falls outside the scope of Community law,[61] and in any case does not apply to processing operations concerning public security, defence, State security (including the economic well-being of the State when the processing operation relates to State security matters) and the activities of the State in areas of criminal law.[62]

[19.27] Like the 1988 Act, the Directive will not apply to criminal investigations. However, the exceptions for the activities of the State are less extensive than in the 1988 Act. There is only a specific exception for criminal investigations while the Act allows an exception for personal data held for "accessing or collecting any tax or other moneys owed or payable to the State, a local authority, or a health board".[63] There is an exception in the Directive for processing relating to the economic well-being of the State but only when it also relates to State security. The legislatures of individual Member States may create exceptions to a variety of rights and duties under the Directive such as the subject's rights of access to data and rectification or erasure of data, the controller's duty to ensure the quality of his data and to supply the subject with information at the time of collection.[64] This may be done where it is necessary to ensure security, defence, the investigation of crimes, the economic interests of the State or Union, monitoring or regulatory functions, and the protection of the data subject or the rights or

---

[58.] Recital 15.
[59.] Recital 16.
[60.] Recital 17.
[61.] Such as those provided for by Titles V and VI of the Treaty on European Union.
[62.] Article 2.
[63.] DPA 1988, s 5(1)(a).
[64.] Article 13(1).

freedoms of others.[65] The Directive also has no application to processing by a natural person in the course of a purely personal or household activity.[66]

Exceptions for journalism, artistic and literary expression

[19.28] Member States must provide for exemptions from the rules relating to the processing of data, transferred data flows, and the supervisory authority in relation to processing of personal data carried out solely for journalistic purposes or artistic or literary expression only if these exemptions are necessary to reconcile the right of privacy with the rules governing freedom of expression.[67] This also applies to the processing of sound and image data.[68] However, these exemptions should not extend to the measures to ensure security of processing. The Supervisory Authority responsible for this sector should also be provided with certain *ex-post* powers, such as the power to publish an annual report or refer matters to the judicial authorities.[69]

The Application of National Law

[19.29] Member States must apply their own data protection legislation to the processing of personal data where:

(a) the processing is carried out by a controller established within the territory of the Member State. If the controller is established in several Member States, he must ensure that each of his establishments complies with the local data protection law;[70]
    The 'controller' is defined as the natural or legal person, public authority, agency or any other body which alone or jointly with others determines the purposes and means of the processing of the personal data. For the purposes of data protection, the controller may be nominated by national or community law;[71]

(b) the controller is not established on the Member States territory but in a place where its national law applies by virtue of international public law;[72]

(c) the controller is established outside Community territory, but for the purposes of processing personal data makes use of equipment, automated or otherwise, situated on the territory of the said

---

65. See para **[20.27]** and para **[21.18]** below.
66. Article 2.
67. Article 9.
68. Recital 17.
69. Recital 37.
70. Article 4(1)(a).
71. Article 2(d).
72. Article 4(1)(b).

Member State, unless the equipment is used only for purposes of transit through the territory of the Community;[73]

In this case, the controller must designate a representative established in the territory of the relevant Member State. This will not prejudice any legal action which might be initiated against the controller.[74]

Implementation of the Directive

[19.30] Member States must bring into force the necessary laws to implement the Directive three years after the adoption of the Directive,[75] at the latest.[76] Member States must ensure that processing which is already in operation on the date of adoption of the national position must be brought into conformity with these provisions within three years.[77] It is not necessary for the data subject to give his consent again to allow the controller to continue to process any sensitive data necessary for the performance of a contract freely entered into before the provisions come into force.[78]

[19.31] Member States may provide that the processing of manual files will only have to comply with the principles of data quality,[79] the criteria for making data processing legitimate[80] and the provisions relating to special categories of data[81] within 12 years of the date on which the Directive was adopted. Importantly, data subjects will still have the right to obtain the rectification, erasure and blocking of data which was incomplete or inaccurate or stored in a way incompatible with the legitimate purposes of the controller, particularly at the time of exercising his right of access.[82] Member States may also provide that data kept for historical research need not comply with the principles of data quality,[83] the criteria for making data processing legitimate[84] and the provisions relating to special categories of data[85] subject to suitable safeguards.[86] Member States must communicate to the Commission the text of the laws which they adopt pursuant to the Directive.[87]

[73.] Article 4(1)(c).
[74.] Article 4(2).
[75.] The Directive was adopted on 24 October 1995.
[76.] Article 32(1).
[77.] Article 32(2).
[78.] Recital 70.
[79.] Article 6. See para **[20.16]**.
[80.] Article 7. See para **[20.18]**.
[81.] Article 8. See para **[20.25]**.
[82.] Article 32(2).
[83.] Article 6. See para **[20.16]**.
[84.] Article 7. See para **[20.18]**.
[85.] Article 8. See para **[20.25]**.
[86.] Article 32(3).
[87.] Article 32(4).

Chapter 20

Control of Data Processing

[20.01] Although very extensive databases may be held, these are worthless if the information in them is incorrect or unreliable. Once the data is collected there is no guarantee that data processing techniques will be accurate. Even allowing for the huge processing and storage capabilities available on computers, many techniques are quite crude. In the UK, credit reference agencies often use addresses of credit applicants to determine their creditworthiness. This is because there are huge numbers of people in the UK with the same name, however, addresses are usually unique. In one case, an applicant was unsuccessful in her applications for credit because her landlord, previous tenants and neighbours had defaulted on loans. The applicant was only successful when she used the address of her grandmother.[1] The defects of software have been documented elsewhere in this book.[2] Modern statistical techniques may suffer from similar defects particularly when they are used to analyse large amounts of data. There is a danger that data processing will lead to a form of electronic red lining where those who exhibit certain characteristics will not be able to obtain credit or other services.

[20.02] Furthermore, data collected for one purpose may be used for another unrelated purpose. At the most extreme level, when the Germans invaded Holland during the Second World War they used the extensive population registers maintained by the Dutch authorities to facilitate the deportations of thousands of people.[3] On a more mundane level in the UK case of *The Data Protection Registrar v Amnesty International*,[4] Amnesty and another charity exchanged their mailing lists in order to send requests for donations to each other's subscribers. There was no exchange of monies. One donor to Amnesty complained to the Data Protection Registrar (the equivalent of Ireland's Data Protection Commissioner) when she received a request for funds from the other charity.

---

[1] *The Times*, 22 September 1995.
[2] See para **[24.06]** *et seq*.
[3] Lloyd, *Information Technology Law*, (Butterworths, 1993).
[4] High Court, Queens Bench, 8 November 1994.

[20.03] Once data has been collected, computers allow for records to be held for longer than the subjects of the records may realise or wish. The data may also be shared, sold or bought by different data controllers. In the US, databases have developed to quite an extraordinary degree. For example, the Employers' Information Service compiles lists of employees who have filed workers' compensation claims and lawsuits. The Medical Information Bureau holds records on more than fifteen million Americans and releases confidential medical information to insurance companies. Another database alerts doctors to patients who are prone to initiate litigation.[5]

DUTIES OF THE DATA CONTROLLER

[20.04] In order to regulate the activities of the data processing industry, the 1988 Act requires the data controller to uphold certain standards with regard to the data held by him. A 'data controller' is a person who either alone or with others controls the contents and use of the personal data. The data controller may be an individual or a company. The amount of control which a person has over data will determine whether or not they are a controller. Several people who are in control of data will all be data controllers.[6] Section 2 of the 1988 Act sets out the data controller's duties:

(1) The data must have been obtained, and must be processed, fairly.[7] Interestingly, this does not apply to personal data obtained or processed for the purposes of preventing, detecting or investigating offences or for collecting any tax, duty or other moneys owed or payable to the State, a local authority or a health board[8] which exempts many of the State's functions from the Act. Information will not be regarded as being unfairly obtained if the unfairness only relates to the fact that the data subject was not informed that the data was to be used for any purpose, provided that the data is not used in such a way as to cause damage or distress to the data subject.[9]

(2) The data must be accurate[10] and kept up to date.[11] This will not

---

5. Bibas, 'A Contractual Approach to Data Privacy', Harvard Journal of Law and Policy, Vol 17.
6. Ministers and other appropriate authorities who are data controllers or processors may designate civil servants to be data controllers or processors for the purposes of the Act. This provision does not apply outside the civil service although the Minister for Defence may nominate a commissioned officer as a data controller or processor: s 1(3).
7. DPA 1988, s 2(1)(a).
8. DPA 1988, s 2(3).
9. DPA 1988, s 5(b).
10. 'Inaccurate data' is data which is incorrect or misleading as to any matter of fact: s 1(2).
11. DPA 1988, s 2(1)(b).

apply to back-up data[12] which is defined as data kept only for the purpose of replacing other data in the event of its being lost, destroyed or damaged.[13]

(3) The data must be kept for only one or more specified and lawful purpose.[14] It is unclear what the specified purpose means. This will probably be the purpose specified in the register but it is likely that entries in the register will be drafted as broadly as possible to prevent difficulties of this type. In any event, only certain data controllers and processors have to register. If a data controller is unregistered it may be difficult to discover what the specified purpose is.

(4) The data must not be used or disclosed in any manner incompatible with that specified purpose or purposes.[15] There is no definition of 'used' but 'disclosed' is defined[16] as including the disclosure of information from data and the transfer of the data. It does not include disclosures made to an employee of the data controller or processor where the disclosure in made in order to allow the employee to carry out his duties. If the identification of a data subject depends on both the data and other information held by the controller, the data will not be regarded as disclosed where only the data is disclosed. So if a data subject is identified by a number in the data, disclosure of this data will not amount to disclosure of the subject's personal data unless it is possible to correlate the number with the identity of the data subject.

(5) Data must be adequate, relevant and not excessive in relation to the purpose or purposes specified.[17]

(6) The data must only be kept for as long as is necessary for the specified purpose.[18] This will not apply to personal data kept for historical, statistical or research purposes provided that the data will not be used in such a way as to cause damage or distress to any data subject.[19]

---

12. DPA 1988, s 2(4).
13. DPA 1988, s 1.
14. DPA 1988, s 2(1)(c)(i).
15. DPA 1988, s 2(1)(c)(ii).
16. DPA 1988, s 1.
17. DPA 1988, s 2(1)(c)(iii).
18. DPA 1988, s 2(1)(c)(iv).
19. DPA 1988, s 2(5)(a).

(7) The data controller must preserve the data by using appropriate security measures against unauthorised access to the data and by taking steps to prevent any alteration, disclosure or destruction of the data and against their accidental loss or destruction.[20] This places a duty on the controller to prevent hackers or other computer criminals from accessing and damaging or disclosing the data. A data processor must also take these preventative measures.[21]

The Minister for Justice may also amend these duties by creating regulations to provide additional safeguards in relation to personal data as to racial origin, political opinions, religious or other beliefs, physical or mental health, sexual life or criminal convictions.[22]

Enforcement of the data controller's duties

[20.05] The data subject has two methods of forcing the data controller to uphold his duties. He may assert his right of rectification or he may sue the data controller for negligence. The problem is that a data subject may find it difficult to prove that the data controller has actually failed in his duty. Although the data controller has a duty to keep data secure, companies are notoriously slow to admit that they have suffered breaches of security.[23]

[20.06] Section 7 of the 1988 Act provides that for the purpose of the law of torts a data controller or data processor owes a duty of care to the data subject with regard to the collection of personal data or information intended for inclusion in such data or with regard to the dealing in the data. However, the data controller will be deemed to have kept the data up to date and accurate if the personal data he holds is an accurate record of data or other information received or obtained by him from the data subject or a third party. The controller also has to include in his data and in any disclosures of his data, firstly, an indication of how the information constituting the data was received or obtained. Secondly, if necessary, an indication that the data subject has informed the data controller that he regards the information as inaccurate or not kept up to date and finally, any statement supplementing the data pursuant to the subject's right of rectification.[24]

[20.07] The equivalent UK section was discussed in *Bamber v Dental Practice Board*,[25] where the plaintiff, who was a dentist, claimed that the

---

[20.] DPA 1988, s 2(1)(d).
[21.] DPA 1988, s 2(2).
[22.] DPA 1988, s 2(6).
[23.] See para **[17.03]**.
[24.] DPA 1988, s 7.
[25.] Court of Appeal, unrep, 9 February 1995.

defendants had wrongly sent money to his partner in his dental practice together with an indication of the patients in relation to whom the money had been earned. The plaintiff argued that this disclosure was detrimental to him because it contained the names of his patients. Section 23 of the UK Data Protection Act 1984 provides that any individual who is the subject of data held by a data user and who suffers damage by reason of the loss, destruction or disclosure of the data will be entitled to compensation. Kennedy LJ in the Court of Appeal accepted that there might be some right to compensation for unlawful disclosure of data but in this case the plaintiff was unable to establish that he had suffered any loss. This case illustrates the difficulty with suing for damages due to inappropriate use of personal data. It is extremely hard to prove damage, in this case the plaintiff claimed that as a result of this disclosure he had spent four days in the County Court suing his partner. Kennedy LJ rejected this as any damage which the plaintiff may have suffered as a result of taking this action would be compensated in the judgment of the County Court.

The disclosure of personal data

[20.08] Under s 2(1) the data controller may not disclose data in any manner incompatible with its stated and lawful purpose, however the Act provides that in certain situations disclosure of personal data cannot be restricted by the Act. Disclosure is permitted in the following situations:

(1) If a member of the gardaí[26] or an Army officer[27] is of the opinion that it is required to safeguard the security of the State.[28]

(2) If it is required for the purpose of preventing, detecting or investigating offences, apprehending or prosecuting offenders or assessing or collecting any tax, duty or other moneys owned or payable to the State, a local authority or a health board.[29]

(3) If it is required to protect the international relations of the State.[30]

(4) If it is required urgently to prevent injury or other damage to the health of a person or serious loss of or damage to property.[31]

(5) If it is required by or under any enactment or by a rule of law or court order.[32]

[26.] "Not below the rank of chief superintendent".
[27.] "Who holds an army rank not below that of colonel and is designated by the Minister for Defence".
[28.] DPA 1988, s 8(a).
[29.] DPA 1988, s 8(b).
[30.] DPA 1988, s 8(c).
[31.] DPA 1988, s 8(d).
[32.] DPA 1988, s 8(e).

(6) If it is required for the purposes of obtaining legal advice or for the purposes of, or in the course of legal proceedings in which the person making the disclosure is a party or a witness.[33]

(7) If it is made to the data subject concerned or to a person acting on his behalf.[34]

(8) If it is made at the request or with the consent of the data subject or a person acting on his behalf.[35]

Criminal offences

[20.09] Although the Data Protection Act 1988 creates certain criminal offences, they are very limited. A data processor, his employees or agents, must not disclose personal data which he is processing without the prior consent of the data controller.[36] Any person who knowingly contravenes this provision will be guilty of an offence.[37] Any person who obtains access to personal data or information constituting such data, without the prior authority of the data controller or processor and who discloses the data or information to another is guilty of an offence.[38] This provision does not apply to an employee or agent of the data controller or data processor.[39] This offence deals with the problem of unauthorised access to data as might occur if a hacker gained access to a system. It ignores the more likely situation of where employees and employers abuse their access rights to gain access to information which they then sell or use for their own purposes.

[20.10] There appears to be a market for the sale of confidential information about individuals in Ireland. It has been alleged that a full personal profile of a person including bank details, credit card transactions, PRSI number, passport details, salary and job prospects and outstanding debts may be bought for approximately £200. Much valuable information may be culled from ESB bills, tax returns and itemised phone bills.[40] Since nobody has ever been prosecuted for the above offences it is hard to say whether they could be successfully used to deal with this problem.

[20.11] The market for personal information about individuals has been well documented in the United Kingdom.[41] *R v Brown*[42] concerned a police

---

33. DPA 1988, s 8(f).
34. DPA 1988, s 8(g).
35. DPA 1988, s 8(h).
36. DPA 1988, s 21(1).
37. DPA 1988, s 21(2).
38. DPA 1988, s 22(1).
39. DPA 1988, s 22(2).
40. *The Sunday Tribune*, 22 August 1993.
41. Report of the Data Protection Registrar (UK) 1992, p 10.
42. [1996] 1 All ER 545.

constable in the Kent Constabulary who was friendly with the owner of a debt collection business. On two occasions the defendant used the UK Police National Computer to check the registration numbers of vehicles owned by debtors who were being pursued by the debt collection agency. The defendant was charged with 'using' personal data[43] contrary to the UK Data Protection Act 1984. There is no equivalent to this in the 1988 Act. Ultimately, the defendant's conviction was quashed by the House of Lords who found that accessing or retrieval of information on a computer so that it could be read either on screen or by means of a print-out was not 'using' the information but simply transferring the information into a different form prior to possible use being made of it. The House of Lords held that if the information was thereafter made use of, then it was used within the meaning of the Act but if no further action was taken there was no use made of it. In the Scottish case of *McGregor v McGlennan*,[44] McGregor, who was a police officer, was approached by a neighbour who was concerned that his adolescent daughter was living with a forty-four year old man. McGregor duly accessed the police computer and found that the man had previous convictions and that he was suffering from AIDS and infected with hepatitis. He then phoned the girl and suggested that she leave the man. McGregor was subsequently convicted of 'using' personal data contrary to the UK Data Protection Act 1984.

[20.12] To deal with such problems s 161 of the UK Criminal Justice and Public Order Act 1994 states that a person who procures the disclosure of personal data in contravention of the Data Protection Act 1984 knowing that his procurement is in contravention of that Act, commits an offence. A person who sells or offers to sell personal data is guilty of an offence if he has procured the disclosure of that data in contravention of the Data Protection Act. An advertisement indicating that personal data is for sale is to be deemed an offer to sell the data. Selling or offering to sell data includes information extracted from the data. Although this is similar to the Irish offence of obtaining access to personal data, the UK provision is much broader as it makes it an offence to actually sell the data. It may be easier to prove the sale of the data than to prove access alone. The Law Reform Commission has recommended that 'property' should be defined so as to include personal data protected by the Data Protection Act 1988 for the purposes of the criminal law on dishonesty. This would protect personal data by making it a crime to steal it.[45]

---

43. The UK Data Protection Act 1984, s 5(2)(b).
44. (1993) SCCR 852.
45. Law Reform Commission Report on Dishonesty. LRC 43/1992, p 181.

DATA PROCESSING AND THE DIRECTIVE

[20.13] The requirements of data quality are virtually identical in the 1988 Act and in the Directive. However, the Directive greatly increases the data controller's duties in other regards. The controller can only process data if:

- he has the consent of the data subject;
- he is required to do so by the law;
- it is in the interests of the subject; or
- it is in his own legitimate interests.

[20.14] The controller must supply the subject with information about his processing activities at the time of collecting the data or the time of disclosing it to third parties. The controller may only process sensitive data in specific circumstances, however there is an exemption created for journalists and for artistic and literary works.

[20.15] The Directive places limits on how data may be processed. However, Member States must determine more precisely the conditions under which the processing of personal data is lawful.[46]

Data quality

[20.16] The data controller must ensure that all the provisions relating to personal data are complied with.[47] Personal data must be:

(a) processed fairly and lawfully;[48]

(b) collected for specified, explicit and legitimate purposes and not further processed in a way incompatible with those purposes. Any processing of data for historical, statistical or scientific purposes will not be considered as incompatible provided that each Member State has provided appropriate safeguards.[49] These safeguards must rule out the use of such data in support of measures or decisions regarding any particular individual;[50]

(c) adequate, relevant and not excessive in relation to the purposes for which they are collected and/or further processed.[51] The purposes for which data is collected must be explicit, legitimate, and determined at the time of collection. The purpose of

---

[46.] Article 5.
[47.] Article 6(2).
[48.] Article 6(1)(a).
[49.] Article 6(1)(b).
[50.] Recital 29.
[51.] Article 6(1)(c).

processing cannot be incompatible with the purposes as they were originally specified;[52]

(d) accurate and where necessary, kept up to date. Every reasonable step must be taken to ensure that data which is inaccurate or incomplete, is erased or rectified;

(e) kept in a form which permits identification of data subjects for no longer than is necessary. Appropriate safeguards must be laid down by Member States for personal data stored for longer periods for historical, statistical or scientific use.[53]

Exceptions and restrictions

[20.17] Member States may allow exceptions to the principles of data quality and to the data controller's duty to supply information to the data subject[54] if it is necessary to ensure:

- national security, defence or public security;

- the prevention, investigation, detection and prosecution of criminal offences or breaches of ethics for regulated professions;

- an important economic or financial interest of a Member State or of the EU including monetary, budgetary and taxation matters;

- a monitoring, inspection or regulatory function connected, even occasionally with the exercise of official authority in the cases of public security, crime and the economic interests of the State and the EU;

- the protection of the data subject or of the rights and freedoms of others.[55]

Criteria for legitimate data processing

[20.18] The Directive limits the situations in which processing can be carried out. Personal data may only be processed if the data subject has unambiguously given his consent.[56] 'The data subject's consent' means any freely given specific and informed indication of his wishes by which the data subject signifies his agreement to personal data relating to him being processed.[57] This may mean that the current situation where the subject is asked to mark a box if he objects to his data being processed will have to be

---

52. Recital 28.
53. Article 6(1).
54. See para **[20.27]**.
55. Article 13(1).
56. Article 7(a).
57. Article 2(h).

replaced with a box which will be marked if the subject consents to his data being processed. If this is so, it will make it more difficult to gather information about individuals. Alternatively, data processing will be permitted where:

(1) the processing is necessary for the performance of a contract to which the data subject is a party or in order to take steps at the request of the data subject prior to entering into a contract;[58]

(2) processing is necessary for compliance with a legal obligation to which the controller is subject;[59]

(3) processing is necessary in order to protect the vital interests of the data subject;[60]

(4) processing is necessary for the performance of a task carried out in the public interest[61] or in the exercise of an official authority vested in the controller or in a third party to whom the data is disclosed.[62]

- A 'third party' is defined as any natural or legal person, public authority, agency or any other body other than the data subject, the controller, the processor and the persons who, under the direct authority of the controller or the processor, are authorised to process the data;[63]

- A 'processor' is a natural or legal person, public authority, agency or other body which processes personal data on behalf of the controller;[64]

(5) processing is necessary for the purposes of the legitimate interests pursued by the controller or by the third party or parties to whom the data is disclosed except where such interests are overridden by the interests for fundamental rights and freedoms of the data subject which require protection under Article 1(1).[65] It is unclear what the legitimate interests of the controller are but it may be

---

58. Article 7(b).
59. Article 7(c).
60. Article 7(d).
61. Recital 32 states that "it is for national legislation to determine whether the controller performing a task carried out in the public interest or in the exercise of an official authority should be a public administration or another natural or legal person governed by public law or by private law such as a professional association."
62. Article 7(e).
63. Article 2(f).
64. Article 2(e).
65. Article 7(f).

assumed that controllers will seek to have them defined as broadly as possible.

The data subject also has the right to object to the processing of his data. If his objection is justified then the controller must cease processing. Article 14 provides that Member States must ensure that the data subject has this right at least in (4) and (5) above. This gives the data subject considerable control over the processing of his data as this means that he will either be able to object or withhold his consent to processing unless it is done in his own vital interests or it is necessary for compliance with a legal obligation to which the controller is subject.

[20.19] In order to maintain a balance between the interests of the data subject and effective competition, Member States may determine the circumstances in which personal data may be used or disclosed to a third party in the context of the legitimate ordinary business activities of companies and other bodies. Member States may similarly specify the conditions under which personal data may be disclosed to a third party for the purposes of marketing, whether carried out commercially or by a charitable organisation or any other association or foundation, of a political nature for example, subject to the provisions allowing a data subject to object to the processing of data regarding him,[66] at no cost and without having to state his reasons.[67]

Information to be given to the data subject

[20.20] One of the main problems with the Data Protection Act 1988 is that data subjects may not realise that their data is being processed or that it is being processed inaccurately until it is too late. Most data subjects do not realise this is happening until they are refused a loan or suffer other adverse consequences. The Directive tries to prevent this by ensuring that data subjects are given as much information as possible and as early as possible.

Information to be supplied to the data subject at time of collection

[20.21] In situations where the data subject supplies information to the data controller about himself, then the subject must be supplied with accurate and full information bearing in mind the circumstances of the collection. This is to ensure that any processing is carried out fairly.[68] Member States must ensure that the data subject is supplied with information from the data controller, unless the subject already has it. This information must consist of the identity of the controller and the purposes of the processing for which the

---

66. Article 14.
67. Recital 30.
68. Recital 38.

data is intended. If necessary, further information may have to be supplied but this would depend on the specific circumstances in which the data is collected, and the guarantee of fair processing for the data subject. This further information may include the recipients[69] or categories of recipients of the data. Data can be legitimately disclosed even if the disclosure was not anticipated at the time the data was collected from the data subject. However, the subject should be informed at the latest, when the data is first disclosed to a third party.[70] It must also disclose whether replies to the questions are obligatory or voluntary, as well as the possible consequences of failure to reply and the existence of the right of access to and the right to rectify the data concerning him.[71]

Information to be supplied to the data subject when the data has not been collected from him

[20.22] Where the data has not been obtained directly from the data subject, the controller must provide the data subject with the identity of the controller and the purposes of the processing. It may be necessary to give the data subject further information depending on the circumstances of processing and the guarantee of fair processing. This may include the categories of data concerned, the recipients or categories of recipients and the existence of the right of access to and the right to rectify the data concerning him.[72] This information must be given to the data subject at the time of recording the personal data or if a disclosure to a third party is envisaged, no later than the time when the data is first disclosed.

[20.23] This requirement to supply information will not apply where the provision of such information proves impossible, would involve a disproportionate effort or if recording or disclosure is expressly laid down by law. In deciding this, the number of data subjects, the age of the data, and the availability of compensation must be taken into account.[73] The Directive anticipates that this will occur in particular where data is processed for statistical, scientific or historical purposes. However, suitable safeguards must be supplied.[74]

---

69. Article 2(g). The 'recipient' is a natural or legal person, public authority, agency or any the body to whom data is disclosed, whether to a third party or not. However, any authority which receives data in the framework of a particular inquiry shall not be regarded as recipients.
70. Recital 39.
71. Article 10.
72. Article 11(1).
73. Recital 40.
74. Article 11(2).

Processing sensitive data

[20.24] Some types of data may be so sensitive that it is arguable that it should not be processed by a computer at all, such as some types of medical information. One hospital in the USA has reported complaints about employees searching for their co-workers' medical records before asking them out socially. Other reported abuses in the USA include the sale of abortion patient names to anti-abortion organisations, extortion based on the knowledge that the patient was treated for venereal disease and an employer requesting a list of HIV infected employees with a view to firing them.[75] Australia has also been host to a significant market in confidential information illicitly obtained from government databases.[76]

[20.25] Member States must prohibit the processing of personal data which reveals racial, or ethnic origin, political opinions, religious or philosophical beliefs, trade union membership and the processing of data concerning health or sex life.[77] This will not apply in the following situations:

(a) Where the data subject has given his explicit consent to the processing of data unless the national laws invalidate this consent.[78]

(b) Where processing is necessary for the purposes of carrying out the obligations and specific rights of the controller in the field of employment law, provided this is authorised by national law which must contain adequate safeguards.[79]

(c) Where processing is necessary to protect the vital interests of the data subject or of another person where the data subject is physically or legally incapable of giving his consent.[80] This would apply in cases of wards of court, children or people in a coma. The processing of personal data will be regarded as lawful where it is carried out in order to protect an interest which is essential for the data subject's life.[81]

[75.] Arnold, 'Let Technology Counteract Technology', Hasting Communications and Entertainment Law Journal, Vol 15:455.

[76.] Mandeville, 'Marketing Public Sector Information', Computer Law and Security Report, Vol 10, 1994, p 234. See also, Hughes, 'An Overview of Data Protection in Australia', Melbourne University Law Review, Vol 18, June 1991, p 83.

[77.] Article 8(1).

[78.] Article 8(2)(a).

[79.] Article 8(2)(b).

[80.] Article 8(2)(c).

[81.] Recital 31.

(d) Where processing is carried out in the course of its legitimate activities with appropriate guarantees by a foundation, association or any other non-profit seeking body with a political, philosophical, religious or trade union aim and on condition that the processing relates solely to the members of the body or to persons who have regular contact with it in connection with its purposes and that the data is not disclosed to a third party without the consent of the data subjects.[82]

(e) Where the processing relates to data which is manifestly made public by the data subject or is necessary for the establishment, exercise or defence of legal claims.[83]

Member States may extend these exemptions for reasons of substantial public interest,[84] provided they include suitable safeguards. These extensions may be made by the legislature or supervisory authority.[85]

Medical data

[20.26] The processing of sensitive data is allowed where it is required for preventative medicine, medical diagnosis, the provision of care or treatment or the management of health care services and where the data is processed by a health professional under national law or rules established by national bodies relating to the obligation of professional secrecy or by another person subject to similar obligations.[86] This processing will especially be allowed to ensure the quality and cost effectiveness of health insurance and also for scientific research and government statistics.[87]

Criminal and civil records

[20.27] The processing of data relating to offences, criminal convictions or security measures may only be carried out under the control of an official authority. Alternatively, if appropriate, specific safeguards are provided under national law, subject to derogations which may be granted by the

---

[82.] Article 8(2)(d).

[83.] Article 8(2)(e).

[84.] These reasons of substantial public interest include religious and political reasons. The processing of personal data by official authorities for achieving aims, laid down in constitutional law or international public law, of officially recognised religious associations is carried out on important grounds of public interest: Recital 35.

Also, in the course of electoral activities, the operation of the democratic system requires in certain Member States that political parties compile data on peoples political opinion, the processing of such data may be permitted for reasons of important public interest, provided that appropriate safeguards are established: Recital 36.

[85.] Article 8(4).

[86.] Article 8(3).

[87.] Recital 34.

Member State, then processing may also occur. However, a complete register of criminal convictions may only be kept by an official authority. Member States may also provide that data relating to administrative sanctions or judgments in civil cases must also be processed under the control of an official authority.[88] Any provisions creating derogations from the prohibition on the processing of sensitive data must be notified to the Commission.[89] Member States may determine the conditions under which a national identification number or any other such identifier may be processed.[90] This means that Ireland may determine its own rules for the processing of RSI numbers and other identification numbers. In the UK it is now common for employers to request that potential employees supply them with a copy of their criminal record. The employees do this by exercising their access rights and requesting a copy of their record from the police. In the draft Directive, a provision existed to allow data subjects the right "to refuse any demand by a third party that he should exercise his right of access in order to communicate the data in question to that third party or to another party, unless the third party's request is founded on national or Community law".[91] This provision did not appear in the Directive as adopted.[92]

Confidentiality and security of processing

[20.28] The Directive tries to ensure that personal data will not be abused in the fashion of the *R v Brown* case.[93] Like the 1988 Act, it tries to do this by ensuring that employees will not abuse their positions and securing data from outside access. Any person who is acting under the authority of the controller or the processor, including the processor himself, who has access to personal data must not process it except on instructions from the controller, unless he is required to do so by law.[94] This means that employees may not process data on their own behalf or otherwise abuse their positions.

---

88. Article 8(5).
89. Article 8(6).
90. Article 8(7).
91. Proposal for a Council Directive concerning the protection of individuals in relation to the processing of personal data (COM (92) 422 final - SYN 287, Article 13.
92. The UK Home Office has recently announced plans to make it even easier for employers to check out the criminal records of potential workers. Separate categories of employers would be entitled to different levels of information about the criminal careers of prospective employees. Employers in sensitive areas such as nurses, homes, banks and accountants would be able to get a full criminal record check including details of offences committed in the distant past. At present, statutory authorise in the UK such as social services and education departments can carry out checks on those who may work with children: *The Times*, 25 May 1996.
93. [1996] 1 All ER 545, see **[20.11]**.
94. Article 16.

Security

[20.29] In order to secure data, the controller must implement appropriate technical and organisational measures to protect personal data against accidental or unlawful destruction or accidental loss, alteration, unauthorised disclosure or access and against all other unlawful forms of processing. Appropriate technical and organisational measures must be taken, both at the time of the design of the processing system and the processing itself, in order to maintain security and prevent unauthorised processing.[95] In particular, where the processing involves the transmission of data over a network, appropriate security measures must be installed. These measures must ensure a proportionate level of security having regard to the risks represented by the processing, the nature of the data, the state of the art and the cost of implementation.[96]

[20.30] If the controller does not process the data himself, then he must choose a processor providing sufficient guarantees on the technical security and organisational measures governing the processing and must ensure compliance with those measures.[97] The processor must sign a contract binding him to the controller and ensuring that the processor will only act on the instructions of the controller and that he will fulfil the obligation to ensure the security and processing of the data.[98] The contract must be in writing or in another equivalent form.[99] Where a message containing personal data is transmitted by means of a telecommunications or electronic mail service, the sole purpose of which is the transmission of such messages, the controller in respect of the personal data contained in the message will normally be considered to be the person from whom the message originates, rather than the person offering the transmission services. Nevertheless, those offering such services will be considered controllers and respect of the processing of the additional personal data necessary for the operation of the service.[100]

Enforcement of the controller's duties

[20.31] Member States must provide for a judicial remedy for any breach of the data subject's rights under the Directive. This is without prejudice to any other remedies available from the supervisory authority which may be invoked prior to referral to a judicial authority.[101] Any person who has

---

[95.] Recitals 46.
[96.] Article 17(1).
[97.] Article 17(2).
[98.] Article 17(3).
[99.] Article 17(4).
[100.] Recital 47.
[101.] Article 22.

suffered damage as a result of unlawful processing is entitled to compensation from the controller.[102] If the controller is not responsible for the damage, then he will be exempt from liability.[103] The controller must prove that he is not responsible for the damage, in particular, in cases where he establishes fault on the part of the data subject or in the case of *force majeure.*[104] Member States must adopt suitable measures to ensure the full implementation of the Directive and must in particular lay down sanctions for infringements of the Directive.[105] These provisions would appear to replicate those of the Data Protection Act. As already stated, there is some doubt about how enforceable these provisions are and therefore a data subject may have to rely on his rights such as access and rectification to ensure that his data is protected.

REGISTRATION

[20.32] The purpose of registration is to ensure that there is a public record of data processing operations in Ireland. However, the groups who must register are limited and they are also very obvious, such as banks, insurance companies and government departments. It is the data processing operations which are not obvious which probably should be included in this register. Public use of the register is minimal although it does form a useful record which aids the Data Protection Commissioner in the execution of his duties. There are at present 2161 entries, but only 297 of these are data processors, the remainder being data controllers. There are essentially two groups who must register, financial and governmental institutions and these institutions and those who maintain databases of sensitive data. The Commissioner has stated that he is satisfied that most institutions have registered, however, he has difficulties with those who maintain registers of sensitive data. It is often unclear who must register on a practical level.[106]

REGISTRATION UNDER THE DATA PROTECTION ACT

The Effect of Registration

[20.33] A data controller who is required to register under the 1988 Act may not keep personal data unless he is registered. A registered data controller must not keep any personal data, other than that specified in his register entry. He may not keep or use personal data for a purpose other than that

---

[102.] Article 23(1).
[103.] Article 23(2).
[104.] Recital 55.
[105.] Article 24.
[106.] Sixth Annual Report of the Data Protection Commissioner 1994, p 16.

stated in the entry or obtain data or information from a source other than that registered. He may not disclose any of his data to a person who is not described in his entry or directly or indirectly transfer such data outside the State, unless it is mentioned in his entry.

[20.34] An employee of a data controller is subject to the same restrictions in relation to the use, source, disclosure or transfer of the data as the data controller. A data processor who is required to register may only process personal data if he is registered. If someone who is registered changes their address, they must notify the Commissioner of the change. Any data controller or processor who is required to register and who processes data without being registered is guilty of an offence as is any person who is registered and fails to notify a change of address to the Commissioner. If a person knowingly uses, obtains, discloses or transfers data in breach of the requirements of registration he will be guilty of an offence.[107] Any person who knowingly furnishes false or misleading information in an application for registration is guilty of an offence.[108]

[20.35] Unlike the UK legislation which requires all those who hold or provide services in respect of personal data to register,[109] the Irish legislation only requires certain groups to register. The most noticeable exception is the defence forces and the Gardaí Siochána. The UK Data Protection Act 1984 does not exempt the police from its provisions although an exemption is granted where it is required for the purposes of national security.[110] This is a much more limited form of exemption. Whether such a broad exemption as that provided for the Irish police is justified, is unclear. In *Friedl v Austria*[111] the applicant was photographed during a demonstration and arrested. The applicant's complaint against his treatment was ultimately brought before the European Commission of Human Rights which found that there had been a breach of Article 13 of the European Convention on Human Rights as the applicant did not have access to an effective remedy against his questioning and recording of personal data. When the applicant appealed against this gathering and use of his personal data to the Austrian Constitutional Court it found that these aspects of his complaint were inadmissible as they related to police activities. A similar Irish complainant might argue that the gathering and holding of his personal data was in breach of his human rights as the Data Protection Act exempts the gardaí from the

---

[107.] DPA 1988, s 19.
[108.] DPA 1988, s 20.
[109.] UK Data Protection Act 1984, s 4(1).
[110.] DPA 1988, s 27(1).
[111.] [1995] 21 EHRR 83.

requirement of registration and so makes it more difficult to control the use of his personal data.

[20.36] The following groups must register with the Data Protection Commissioner:

(1) Data controllers consisting of the government, Ministers of the government, the Attorney General, the Auditor General, the Ombudsman, local authorities, health boards and other bodies[112] established under any enactment[113] which are financed wholly or partly by means of moneys provided or loans made or guaranteed, by a Minister of the government or the issue of shares held by or on behalf of a Minister of the government. A subsidiary of any such body is included as are companies a majority of whose shares are held by or on behalf of government Ministers. Bodies appointed by the government, individuals appointed to statutory office by the government and any other public authority, body or person financed by the Oireachtas must also register with the Commissioner.[114]

(2) Data controllers who are financial institutions,[115] insurers or persons whose business involves direct marketing, providing credit references or collecting debts.[116]

(3) Data controllers who keep personal data relating to racial origin, political opinions, religious or other beliefs, physical or mental health,[117] sexual life or criminal convictions.[118] This would, for example, include doctors who hold medical records on computers.

(4) Data processors who process data on behalf of data controllers.[119]

[112.] Other than the Garda Síochána and the defence forces.

[113.] Other than the Companies Acts 1963-1990. However, bodies established under the Companies Acts in pursuance of powers conferred by or under another enactment are included in this category.

[114.] DPA 1988, s 16(1)(a), and the Third Schedule to the Act.

[115.] Financial institutions are:

(a) persons who hold or have held a licence under s 9 of the Central Bank Act 1971; or

(b) a person referred to in s 7(4) of that Act.

Therefore, associated banks are registerable as is the Trustee Savings Banks, buildings societies, credit unions, investment trust companies and the manager of a unit trust scheme.

[116.] DPA 1988, s 16(1)(b).

[117.] Other than data on the physical or mental health of employees kept in the ordinary course of business administration and not used or disclosed for any other purpose.

[118.] DPA 1988, s 16(1)(c).

(5) Categories of data controllers and processors who may be prescribed by law.[120]

The Register

[20.37] The Data Protection Register is established and maintained by the Data Protection Commissioner.[121] The following particulars must be included in an entry in a register in respect of a data controller:

  (i)   his name and address;

  (ii)   the purposes for which the data is kept;

  (iii)   a description of the data;

  (iv)   persons to whom the data may be disclosed;

  (v)   countries to which the data my be transferred;

  (vi)   if required by the Commissioner, the source of the data must be included;

  (vii)   persons to whom requests for access to data should be addressed if it is not the data controller himself;

  (viii) the date on which the entry was made; and

  (ix)   a reference to any other entry in the register relating to the data controller.[122]

[20.38] If an entry is made in respect of a data processor, then the entry must include his name and address.[123] Members of the public may inspect the register free of charge and may copy entries in the register. Those who wish to obtain certified copies of entries may do so for a fee.[124]

Applications for Registration

[20.39] An application for registration may be made in writing to the Commissioner. If a data controller intends to keep personal data for two or more purposes, he may make separate applications for each particular purpose. The Commissioner will accept the application unless he is of the opinion that the information provided in the application is insufficient or the applicant is likely to contravene the provisions of the Act. The Commissioner will not accept an application unless he is satisfied that the

---

[119.] DPA 1988, s 16(1)(d).

[120.] DPA 1988, s 16(1)(e). This categories may include those who have been served with enforcement or prohibition or information notices, if the notices are in force and have not been appealed.

[121.] DPA 1988, s 16(2).

[122.] Data Protection (Registration) Regulations 1988 (SI 351/1988), Reg 6.

[123.] *Ibid*, Reg 7.

[124.] DPA 1988, s 16(3). Certified copies are evidence of the entry or extract which they have copied in all proceedings.

privacy of the data subject is provided for. If he refuses an application then he must notify the applicant in writing stating the reasons for the refusal and inform the applicant that he may appeal to the Circuit Court within 21 days. If the Commissioner refuses to register an applicant and he believes that the refusal should take effect urgently, then he must notify the applicant with a statement to this effect. He must also inform the applicant that he has 7 days within which to appeal the refusal. An applicant for registration will be treated as if his application was successful until he is either notified that the application has been accepted or until the expiry of the period in which he may appeal, if he has been refused. These rules also apply to applications for continuance of registration or for alterations to the particulars of registration.[125]

[20.40] Registration can only last for one year and at the end of the year the entry must be removed from the register unless it is continued.[126] The Commissioner may continue a registration subject to the other provisions of the Act but he must remove any entry if the applicant requests it.[127]

REGISTRATION UNDER THE DIRECTIVE

[20.41] The Directive allows Member States to exempt certain categories from notification. This may allow the position in the Act where only the government, financial institutions, insurers, direct marketing and credit rating agencies and those processing sensitive data are required to register to continue. More importantly, the supervisory authority will have a new duty to check processing operations which are likely to present specific risks to data subjects before they actually begin. The procedures for notifying the supervisory authority[128] are designed to ensure disclosure of the purposes of any processing operation and to verify that the operation is in accordance with the Directive.[129]

Notification

[20.42] The data controller must notify the supervisory authority before carrying out any wholly or partly automatic processing operation intended to achieve either a single purpose or several related purposes.[130]

---

125. DPA 1988, s 17.
126. The Data Protection (Registration Period) Regulations 1988 prescribe a period of one year as the registration period: SI 350/1988, Reg 2.
127. DPA 1988, s 18. At present, the fee for registration is £250 for an application for registration made by a person with more than 25 employees or £50 for a person who employs more than six but less than 25 employees. For any person who employs less than six people the fee is £20. Data Protection (Fees) Regulations 1996, SI 105/1996.
128. The supervisory authority is the equivalent of the Data Protection Commissioner. See Article 28 at para **[22.22]**.
129. Recital 48.

[20.43] Notification may be simplified or eliminated where processing operations are unlikely to adversely affect the rights and freedoms of data subjects, taking account of the data to be processed. If the notification is simplified then it must still specify the purposes of the processing, the data categories undergoing processing, the category of data subject, the recipients to whom the data is to be disclosed and the length of time the data is to be stored. Alternatively, the data controller may appoint a personal data protection official, in compliance with a national law. This official will be responsible for independently ensuring the internal application of the national data protection law and for keeping a register of processing operations carried out by the controller.[131] This must be done to protect the rights and freedoms of the data subject. Member States may provide that the requirement of registration will not apply to processing whose purpose is to maintain a register which is intended to provide information to the public and which is open for consultation by the public or by anyone displaying a legitimate interest. This may also apply to processing carried out by a foundation, association or other non-profit seeking body with a political, religious or trade union aim and on the condition that the processing relates solely to the members of the body or persons in regular contact with it. This is to avoid unwieldy administrative formalities.[132] Member States may stipulate that certain or all non automatic processing operations involving personal data must notify the supervisory authority, although these procedures may be simplified.[133] However simplification or exemption from the obligation to notify will not release the controller from any of the other obligations of the Directive.[134] In this context, *ex post facto* verification by the competent authorities will in general be considered a sufficient measure.[135]

The Contents of Notification

[20.44] Member States must specify that the notification contains at least the name and address of the controller and the purpose of the data processing. It must also include a description of the categories of data subject and of the data relating to them together with a list of the persons to whom the data might be disclosed. Details of any proposed transfers of data to third countries must be included and also a general description allowing an

---

130. Article 18(1). See para **[21.23]** *et seq*.
131. This must contain the information specified in Article 21(2).
132. Recital 49.
133. Article 18.
134. Recital 51.
135. Recital 52.

assessment to be made of the appropriateness of the security measures taken to protect the data.[136] Member States must also specify how changes in the information contained in a notification may be notified to the supervisory authority.[137]

Prior Checking of Processing Operations

[20.45] It is likely that certain processing operations will pose specific risks to the rights and freedoms of data subjects by virtue of their nature, scope, purpose or the technology they use. The Member States must determine which processing operations are likely to present specific risks to the rights and freedoms of data subjects and must ensure that these operations are examined before they begin processing. These prior checks must be carried out by the supervisory authority upon receipt of a notification from the controller or any other data protection official who must consult the supervisory authority in cases of doubt. Member States may not legislate or otherwise specify the nature of processing or create safeguards for processing without carrying out such prior checks.[138]

Publicising Processing

[20.46] Member States must ensure that the existence of processing operations is publicised. A register of processing operations which have been notified must be kept by the supervisory authority. The register must contain at least the minimum information required by the Directive. It need not include the general description of the security measures taken by the controller. This did not appear in the draft Directive and it was suggested that forcing data controllers to disclose their security measures might negate the effectiveness of those measures.[139] This register may be inspected by anyone. Where processing operations do not have to be notified, controllers or another body appointed by the Member State must make information similar to that contained in the register available to any person on request. This need not apply to processing where the sole purpose is the keeping of public information.[140] The requirement that a register be kept need not apply where it is necessary to safeguard the following:

-   national security;
-   defence;
-   public security;

---

136. Article 19(1).
137. Article 19(2).
138. Article 20. See also Recital 53.
139. See Murray, 'The Future of Data Protection', ILT, August 1995.
140. Article 21.

- the prevention, investigation detection and prosecution of crime;
- the important economic or financial interests of a Member State or the EU;
- a monitoring, inspection or regulatory function; and
- the protection of the data subject or of the rights and freedoms of others.[141]

---

141. Article 13(1).

Chapter 21

Rights of the Data Subject

[21.01] If individuals are worried about their privacy, then the most effective way of allowing them to protect their privacy is to allow them to enforce their rights themselves. Individuals must check that data relating to them is properly handled and accurate, if they are dissatisfied with the conduct of a controller then a complaint may be made to the Data Protection Commissioner.

RIGHTS UNDER THE DATA PROTECTION ACT 1988

[21.02] The Data Protection Act 1988 provides three basic rights for data subjects.

1. Right to establish the existence of personal data

[21.03] Where a person suspects that another is keeping personal data relating to him, he may write to that person requesting that he be informed as to whether any data is being kept. If it is, then the data subject must be given a description of the data and the purposes for which it is kept. This must be done within 21 days of the request being sent.[1]

2. Right of Access

[21.04] If the data subject makes a written request, the data controller must inform the subject whether he holds personal data relating to the subject and supply him with a copy of the information. This must be done within 40 days of the data subject making any necessary payments to the controller or complying with any other relevant provisions of the Act. If the data cannot be understood by the average person, then the information must be accompanied by an explanation. A letter enquiring as to the existence of any information must be treated as being a request for a copy of the information in the absence of any indication to the contrary. The data controller is entitled to charge a reasonable fee for supplying the information.[2] If he does not comply with the request then the fee must be returned. If the data controller rectifies, supplements or erases part or all of the data as a result of the application of the data subject or in compliance with a court order, then

---

[1.] DPA 1988, s 3.
[2.] DPA 1988, s 4(1).

the fee must be returned. If the data controller uses the data for two or more registered purposes, then the subject must make separate requests for each purpose and pay a separate fee.[3]

[21.05] Anyone who requests information from a data controller must supply the controller with reasonable information to satisfy the controller of his identify and to help locate any relevant personal data.[4] A data controller is not obliged to disclose personal information relating to one data subject to another unless that data subject has consented or unless the data can be disclosed without identifying the other data subject.[5] This last provision will not apply if the other individual is a health professional involved in the health care of the data subject making the application[6] or if it is social work data[7] and the individual concerned is a social worker.[8]

[21.06] Where information is supplied in response to a request, then it must take account of any amendments of the data since the receipt of the request, provided that the amendments would have been made regardless of the making of the request.[9] If an individual requests the results of an examination sat by him, then the request is deemed to have been made on the date of the first publication of the results of the examination or on the date of the request, which ever is later. The data controller has 60 days within which to respond.[10] If the data controller refuses to reply to a request for personal data information, he must write to the subject stating the reasons for the refusal and informing the subject that he may complain to the Data Protection Commissioner about the refusal.[11]

[21.07] One of the most controversial aspects of data protection is that of access to medical records. Traditionally, doctors and other health and social

---

3. DPA 1988, s 4(2).
4. DPA 1988, s 4(3).
5. DPA 1988, s 4(4).
6. Data Protection (Access Modification) (Health) Regulations 1989 (SI 82/1989), Reg 6.
7. The Data Protection (Access Modification) (Social Work) Regulations 1989, Reg 3, (SI 83/1989) defines social work data as personal data kept for, or obtained in the course or, carrying out social work by a Minister of the government, a local authority, a health board, or a voluntary organisation or other body which carries out social work and is in receipt of monies provided by such a minister, authority or board but excludes any health data with the meaning of the Data Protection (Access Modification) (Health) Regulations 1989 (SI 82/1989). 'Social work' is construed accordingly.
8. Data Protection (Access Modification) (Social Work) Regulations 1989, Reg 5, (SI 83/1989).
9. DPA 1988, s 4(5).
10. DPA 1988, s 4(6).
11. DPA 1988, s 4(7).

workers have been reluctant to allow access to such records.[12] The Minister for Justice may modify the right of access in relation to personal data relating to physical or mental health, or kept for the purposes of social work. This modification may be carried out by means of a regulation after consultation with the Minister for Health and any other Minister.[13] The Data Protection (Access Modification) (Health) Regulations 1989,[14] provide that a data controller who is not a health professional must not supply or refuse to supply medical records or other 'health data' in response to a request for access unless he has consulted the person who appears to him to be the appropriate health care professional. The appropriate health professional is the doctor or dentist most recently responsible for the clinical care of the data subject.[15] Data collected by social workers may not be supplied to a data subject in response to a request for access if that data would be likely to cause serious harm to the physical or mental health or emotional condition of the data subject. However, all the information which can be supplied without causing such harm must be supplied. If social work data includes information supplied by an individual then the data controller must not give that information to the data subject.

[21.08] The European Court of Justice considered a patient's right of access to his own medical records in *Gaskin v The United Kingdom*.[16] The applicant had spent virtually all his life, until he attained the age of majority, in the care of Liverpool City Council where the Council was under a duty to keep certain confidential records on him. The applicant sought access to these records but the Council objected as it felt that disclosure would be contrary to the public interest. Various public officials had contributed to the records in the strictest confidence, if such officials feared that their comments might be read by the subject or his legal advisors they might not be so frank in the future. The applicant's motion to discover the records was ultimately rejected by the Court of Appeal and leave to appeal to the House of Lords was refused. The applicant's case went to the European Court of Justice, where it was alleged that his right to privacy under Article 8 of the Convention on Human Rights and his right to freedom of expression under

---

12. The Freedom of Information Bill 1996 provides that everyone has a right of access to public records: s 6. It will not be possible to access the medical records of others and where an individual wishes to access their own medical or social work records and the information might be prejudicial to that persons physical or mental health, well being or emotional condition, the request may be refused: s 28.
13. DPA 1988, s 4(8).
14. SI 82/1989.
15. *Ibid*, Reg 5.
16. 12 EHRR 36.

Article 10 had been violated. His claim under Article 10 was unanimously rejected by the Court but his claim under Article 8 succeeded. The Court found that individuals such as the applicant had:

> "a vital interest which is protected by the Convention in receiving the information necessary to know and to understand their childhood and early development. On the other hand it must be borne in mind that confidentiality of public records is of importance for receiving objective and reliable information, and that such confidentiality can also be necessary for the protection of third persons. Under the latter aspect, a system like the British one, which makes access to records dependent on the consent of the contributor, can in principle be considered to be compatible with the obligations under Article 8, taking into account the State's margin of appreciation. The Court considers, however, that under such a system the interests of the individual seeking access to records relating to his private and family life must be secured when a contributor to the records either is not available or improperly refuses consent. Such a system is only in conformity with the principle of proportionality if it provides that an independent authority finally decides whether access has to be granted in cases where a contributor fails to answer or withholds consent. No such procedure was available to the applicant in the present case."[17]

[21.09] The English Court of Appeal re-examined this question in *R v Mid-Glamorgan Family Health Services*[18] where the plaintiff had a history of psychological problems and had requested access to his medical records which were held by the defendants. The defendants refused to release them, the refusal was based on two grounds: the fear that the plaintiff might use the records in litigation and a suggestion that it might not be in the plaintiff's interests to see the records. The plaintiff brought a legal action, in the course of which he stated that he had no interest in becoming involved in further legal action or that he wished to see the records for medical reasons but rather because he wished to have a greater knowledge of his "childhood, development and history".[19] Although the court accepted that the defendants did not have:

> "... an absolute right to deal with medical records in any way that it chooses ... the doctor's general duty ... is to act at all times in the best interests of the patient. Those interests would usually require that a patient's medical records should not be disclosed to third parties; conversely, that there should usually, for example, be handed on by one

---

17. *Ibid* at 50.
18. [1995] 1 All ER 356 .
19. *Per* Evans J at 364.

doctor to the next or made available to the patient's legal advisers if they are reasonably required for the purposes of legal proceedings in which he is involved. The respondents' position seems to be that no practical difficulty could arise in such circumstances, but that they would act voluntarily and not because they were under a legal duty to do so. If it ever became necessary for the legal position to be tested, it is inconceivable that this extreme position would be vindicated."[20]

In the future the question of controlling access to medical records will become a major issue. Large networks are being built in the UK and the USA which allow for the electronic storage, retrieval and transfer of data.[21] Controlling access to these records will be difficult, particularly in view of their potentially huge size. At the same time, rising health care costs will greatly increase the value of such information to employers and health insurers.[22]

Restrictions on the Right of Access

[21.10] Data processing may be a powerful tool for the detection of criminals. At the most basic level, a fingerprint from a crime scene can be compared with those of known offenders and others on record. The use of computers to carry out this comparison has greatly improved the usefulness of fingerprint evidence.[23] At a more advanced level, in a murder case, a profile of suggested characteristics of the murderer may be created. This may be compared with the characteristics of suspects or the general population. This technique may be quite simple, it may just involve searching for those who have committed similar crimes. Alternatively, it might involve creating a psychological profile of the murderer which could then be compared with a list of suspects or even with the general population.

[21.11] The use of data processing in crime prevention represents the convergence of two trends. One is the traditional role of the police and the State in compiling intelligence about citizens and potential criminals. The

---

20. *Per* Nourse J at 363.
21. There have been allegations that medical data and records have been lost and misplaced in the UK see *Computing,* 12 September 1996.
22. Apparently 90% of health care insurance costs are caused by 10% of subscribers: *The Irish Times,* 9 January 1997, p 12. Anything which makes it easier to identify potentially unhealthy subscribers, such as medical records, will become valuable information provided it is legally possible to exclude those potential subscribers.
23. An automatic fingerprint identification & retrieval system was installed in the Garda Technical Bureau in 1995. It contains databases of fingerprints, palm prints and prints from unsolved scenes of crimes (latents). The computer allows prints taken from a crime scene or from a suspect to be compared with those in the database: *Garda Siochána Annual Report* 1995 p 20.

other is the belief that science and scientific techniques can be used to predict human behaviour.[24] Most crime is committed by a surprisingly small number of people. A study of 10,000 males born in Philadelphia in 1945 found that just 6% of them committed 71% of the murders, 73% of the rapes and 69% of the assaults attributed to the entire group.[25] If that small group of people could be identified and dealt with appropriately, then the crime rate would fall and society would benefit.[26] One initiative proposed in the UK is to use data processing to predict which 6-year-olds will grow up to commit crimes. Information such as the areas in which the children grow up, their records at school and their parents' criminal records will be used to build up profiles of potential offenders. This plan has been 'enthusiastically' received by the police.[27]

[21.12] In view of the sensitivity of this data, it is not surprising that the Data Protection Act 1988 exempts data held for criminal investigations, amongst other types, from the right of access. These exceptions are set out in s 5. The right of access will not apply to:

(1) Personal data kept for the purpose of preventing, detecting or investigating offences, apprehending or prosecuting offenders or assessing or collecting any tax, duty or other moneys owed or payable to the State, a local authority or a health board.[28] In 1992, the Data Protection Commissioner investigated a complaint on behalf of a taxpayer. It emerged that the Revenue Commissioners had adopted a policy of refusing access to personal data held by them on the grounds that this would prejudice the collection of taxes. The Revenue Commissioners refused to give this information to the Data Protection Commissioner so he served them with an information notice.[29] The Revenue Commissioners then appealed to the Circuit Court, but their application was refused on the grounds that replying to the information notice would not be contrary to the provisions of this section;[30]

[24.] See Gould, *The Mismeasure of Man* (Penguin, 1984) for an account of efforts to predict intelligence from scientific questionnaires.

[25.] *Scientific American*, March 1995, p 77.

[26.] The most notorious example of this is the, now discredited view that those men with an 'extra Y chromosome' or XYY chromosome was thought to be more likely to commit violent crime. This technique has been discredited but it has been suggested that the UK government may start searching for those males with this chromosome: *The Sunday Times*, 9 June 1996.

[27.] *The Sunday Times*, 15 October 1995.

[28.] DPA 1988, s 5(1)(a) and (b).

[29.] See para [22.05] *et seq*.

[30.] Fourth annual report of the Data Protection Commissioner 1992, p 14.

(2) Personal data which might prejudice the security of a prison, a place of detention, military prison or St Patrick's Institution;[31]

(3) Personal data which is kept to protect the public against financial loss caused by dishonesty, incompetence or malpractice on the part of persons concerned with the provision of banking, insurance, investments or other financial services or in the management of companies or by persons who have been declared bankrupt.[32] Under the Data Protection Act 1988 (Section 5(1)(d) (Specification) Regulations 1993, access to personal data will not be allowed when it is acquired by auditors, the Central Bank, the Director of Consumer Affairs, inspectors and examiners under the Companies Acts, the Stock Exchange, liquidators, receivers, accountancy bodies, the Minster for Industry and Commerce, Official Assignees in bankruptcy and the Registrar of Friendly Societies. These exemptions only apply when functions are being carried out pursuant to specified legislation;[33]

(4) Applications which might prejudice the international relations of the State;[34]

(5) Estimates kept for the purposes of assessing claims for damages or compensation where the data controller's interests would be prejudiced;[35]

(6) Communications between a client and a lawyer or communications between lawyers, which are privileged;[36]

(7) Information which is kept for the purposes of statistics or carrying out research if the data is not used or disclosed for any other purpose and the results of the research do not allow the data subjects to be identified;[37]

(8) Back-up data.

The Minister for Justice may make regulations providing that any other type of information may not be accessed, if it is in the interests of the data subject or any other individual.[38] The Data Protection Act 1988 (Restriction of Section 4) Regulations 1989 provide that the subject will not be able to

---

[31.] DPA 1988, s 5(1)(c).
[32.] DPA 1988, s 5(1)(d).
[33.] Regulation 4.
[34.] DPA 1988, s 5(1)(e).
[35.] DPA 1988, s 5(1)(f).
[36.] DPA 1988, s 5(1)(g).
[37.] DPA 1988, s 5(1)(h).
[38.] DPA 1988, s 5(3)(b).

exercise his right of access with respect to information held pursuant to s 22(5) of the Adoption Act 1952[39] and s 9 of the Ombudsman Act 1980.[40]

3. Right of rectification or erasure of data

[21.13] If the data controller fails to comply with his duties under the Act, then the data subject may request in writing that the data be rectified or erased. The data subject must make his complaint in writing and the controller must comply with the request within 40 days. If the data is inaccurate or not kept up to date, the controller may comply with the request by supplementing the data with a statement (on terms agreed with the subject) relating to the matters dealt with by the data.[41] Once a data controller complies with the request, he must inform the individual of the rectification, erasure or statement within 40 days of the request.[42] If compliance with the request materially modifies the data, the controller must inform any person to whom the data has been disclosed within the last 12 months.[43] Unfortunately, this last provision has never come into effect.[44]

Direct Marketing

[21.14] Identifying potential consumers is important as advertising is expensive.[45] If a business can identify its potential consumers more accurately then it will get more value from advertisements. Marketing firms must therefore develop extensive databases on consumers' habits.[46] The ability of credit cards to generate information about consumers has always been very attractive to marketing firms, hence the enthusiasm of supermarket chains for cards which are tied to their stores. These allow supermarkets to know exactly which customers are buying what. One credit card company in the UK sends advertising to each of its customers which is customised to correlate with the spending habits of the consumer, so a

---

39. This provides that with regard to the Adopted Children's Registers shall have an "index to make traceable the connection between each entry and the corresponding entry in the register of births. That index shall not be open to public inspection; and no information from it shall be given to any person except by order of a court or the Board".

40. This provides that information or a document or thing obtained by the Ombudsman or his officers in the course of their investigations must not be disclosed except where it is necessary for the Ombudsman in the exercise of duties or any proceedings arising under the Officials Secrets Act 1963.

41. DPA 1988, s 6(1)(a).

42. DPA 1988, s 6(2)(a).

43. DPA 1988, s 6(2).

44. Data Protection Act (Commencement Order) Regulations 1988, (SI 349/1988).

45. Irish estate agents have recently began holding computerised databases of potential buyers: *The Irish Times*, 18 January 1996.

46. The marketing firm, AC Nielsen, monitors all the purchases of 40,000 households in the USA: *The Economist*, 22 July 1995.

vegetarian will not receive an invitation to go to a steak restaurant. To create these customised bills, the company has hired 50 mathematicians who have spent 18 months building models to work out which offers will best suit the buying habits of each cardholder by techniques known as 'data mining'. The techniques allow the company to tailor the advertisements to the location of the customer's spending (the company's software assigns longitude and latitude co-ordinates to the location of each purchase for this). As a result, the company has found that people may carry out their major spending up to 40 miles from where they live. This may make the old methods of sending out direct mail according to postal district obsolete. The company is enthusiastic about this service, even suggesting that in time customers would be willing to pay more for it.[47] This may be naive. Many may feel that analysing every detail of their spending is an invasion of privacy.[48]

[21.15] Direct marketing is defined in the Act as including direct mailing. The Council of Europe has further defined direct marketing as:

> all activities which make it possible to offer goods or services or to transmit any other messages to a segment of the population by post, telephone or other direct means aimed at informing or soliciting a response from the data subject as well as any service ancillary thereto.[49]

[21.16] The data subject has the right to prevent his data being used for this purpose. Unfortunately the Irish Act only applies within Ireland, as some direct marketing operations will be based in the UK and other countries where these rights may not be enforceable. Where personal data is kept for the purpose of direct marketing, the data subject concerned may request in writing that the data controller cease to use the data for that purpose. The data controller must erase the data if it is kept for the purposes of direct marketing purposes. If the data is used for direct marketing and other purposes, then its use for direct marketing must cease. The data subject must be notified in writing of these actions before the expiry of 40 days after the written request being sent.[50]

---

47. *The Sunday Times*, 14 April 1996.
48. Direct mailing has also expanded to the Internet. An American company, Juno Online, is offering free e-mail access to any subscriber who is willing to part with their demographic details and view advertisements in the corner of their screens. This has several advantages over the normal post. As it is a voluntary scheme, only those who wish to view advertisements will receive them. The companies involved estimate that this method will be about eight times cheaper than traditional direct mail. *The Economist*, 27 April 1996
49. The Council of Europe Recommendation on the protection of personal data used for the purposes of direct marketing (1985).
50. DPA 1988, s 2(7).

RIGHTS UNDER THE DIRECTIVE

[21.17] The Directive has maintained the subject's right of access and rectification. It also provides new rights such as the right of objection to processing and the right not to be subject to an automated decision. As the controller must give the subject information when collecting data, this gives the data subject considerable control over any processing of his data.

1. Right of access

[21.18] The right of access under the Directive is similar to that provided for in the Act. The data subject has the right to obtain certain information from the Controller. He must receive confirmation as to whether or not data relating to him is being processed; also information as to the purposes of the processing, if any, the categories of data concerned and the recipients of the data. He must also receive the data undergoing processing in an intelligible form and information as to its source. However, Member States may restrict the right of access in the interests of the subject or to protect the rights and freedoms of others. Therefore, the State may specify that access to medical data may only be obtained through a health care professional.[51]

2. Right of rectification or erasure

[21.19] This right is similar to that provided for in the Act. The data subject has the right to ensure the rectification, erasure or blocking of data, whose processing does not comply with the directive, especially, where the data is incomplete or inaccurate.[52] Where this rectification, erasure or blocking of data has been carried out, then all third parties who have received the data must be notified, unless this proves impossible or involves a disproportionate effort.[53]

Exceptions

[21.20] Member States may allow exceptions to the rights of access and of rectification or erasure, if it is necessary to ensure:

    (a) national security;

    (b) defence;

    (c) public security;

    (d) the prevention, investigation, detection and prosecution of criminal offences or of breaches of ethics for regulated professions;

[51.] Recital 42.
[52.] Article 12(b).
[53.] Article 12(c).

(e) an important economic or financial interest of a Member State or of the EU including monetary, budgetary and taxation matters;

(f) a monitoring, inspection or regulatory function connected, even occasionally with the exercise of official authority in the cases of public security, crime and the economic interests of the State and the EU;

(g) the protection of the data subject or of the rights and freedoms of others.[54]

The State may restrict the right of access where data is processed for scientific research or where it is kept in a personal form only until statistics can be created. There must be adequate legal safeguards, the data cannot be used for taking measures or decisions regarding any particular individual and there can be no danger of breaching the privacy of the subject.[55]

3. Right to Object

[21.21] Member States must grant the data subject the right to object to the processing of data relating to him. This right of objection must at least allow the subject to object to the processing of data which is necessary for the performance of a task carried out in the public interest or in the exercise of official authority vested in the controller or in a third party to whom the data is disclosed.[56] The subject must also be able to object to processing which is necessary for the purposes of the legitimate interests pursued by the controller or by the third party or parties to whom the data is disclosed.[57] He must object on compelling legitimate grounds which relate to his particular situation save where otherwise provided by national legislation. Where the objection is justified, the processing may no longer include the data which is being objected to.[58] The right to object is very extensive. A subject must have the right to object to all processing unless he has previously given his consent, it is necessary for the performance of a contract to which he is party, it is in his vital interests or the controller is obliged to carry out the processing by law. Although this right was present in the Act, it was restricted to direct marketing activities. The Act and the rights of access and rectification merely give the subject the right to ensure that data processed relating to him is accurate. This right goes some way towards providing data subjects with real control over the processing of their data.

[54.] Article 13(1).
[55.] Article 13(2).
[56.] Article 7(e).
[57.] Article 7(f).
[58.] Article 14(a).

Direct Marketing

[21.22] The Directive will not prevent a Member State from regulating marketing activities aimed at consumers resident in the State provided such regulation does not infringe on data protection.[59] The data subject may object, free of charge, to the processing of personal data which relates to him and which the controller anticipates being used for direct marketing. Member States must ensure that subjects are aware of these rights, presumably by advertising. The subject also has the right to be informed before personal data is disclosed for the first time to third parties or used on their behalf for the purposes of direct marketing. The subject must be expressly offered the right to object free of charge to such disclosures or uses.[60] This last provision will make it more difficult to sell or swap mailing lists as occurred in *The Data Protection Registrar v Amnesty International*[61] as informing every member of any lengthy mailing list would be a huge undertaking.

4. Right not to be Subjected to Automated Individual Decisions

[21.23] Every person has the right not be subject to a decision which significantly or legally affects him and which is based solely on automated processing of data intended to evaluate certain personal aspects relating to him, such as his performance at work, creditworthiness, reliability, conduct, etc.[62] This means that companies cannot rely on processes such as data profiling or data mining alone. It is not clear how much must be done to ensure that a decision is not made 'solely' on the basis of computer processing. It may well be that a person reviewing the output of the computer would be sufficient, if the reviewer had the power to alter or reverse the conclusion of the machine. An interview with the person should be sufficient, provided the interview affected the outcome of the decision.

[21.24] However, a person may be subjected to a decision of this kind if that decision is taken in the course of entering into or performance of a contract, but only if the request for the entry into the contract or performance of it, which must have been lodged by the data subject, has been satisfied. Alternatively, there must be suitable measures to safeguard the subjects legitimate interests such as allowing him to put his point of view. These types of decisions may also be made where they are authorised by law which also lays down measures to protect the subjects legitimate interests.[63]

---

59. Recital 71.
60. Article 14(b).
61. High Court, Queen's Bench, 8 November 1994.
62. Article 15(1).
63. Article 15(2).

[21.25] Why decisions made solely by a computer are so bad is unclear. The intention of the Directive may be to prevent electronic red lining where those from certain deprived areas or with other characteristics may be deprived of benefits by computer processing which can identify these characteristics. Unfortunately, humans are quite capable of bias and prejudice without the aid of computers. An important ancillary right is that the subject must receive knowledge of the logic involved in any automatic processing of the data, at least, in the case of automated decisions.[64] Although, this right must not adversely effect trade secrets, or intellectual property and in particular the copyright protecting the software, this cannot lead to the data subject being refused all information.[65] This essentially means that a company which carries out automated processing will have to be able to explain these processes to data subjects who may have no knowledge of mathematics or computers. Such automated processes may be extremely complicated and only understood by a few technicians within a company.[66] Indeed, if the software to carry out such decisions is bought in from outside the company, nobody within the company may understand it. The main benefit of this provision is that it may prevent banks and other institutions from making arbitrary decisions or decisions based on the analysis of sensitive data such as sex or ethnic origin.

---

[64]. Article 12(a).
[65]. Recital 41.
[66]. For example, those engaging in data mining may use extremely complex tools such as intelligence agents, multi-dimensional analysis tools or query and reporting tools: BYTE October 1995, p 92.

Chapter 22

The Supervision of Data Protection

FUNCTIONS OF THE DATA PROTECTION COMMISSIONER UNDER THE 1988 ACT

[22.01] The Data Protection Commissioner is appointed by the Government but he performs his functions independently. The Commissioner's term of office is 5 years but he may be re-appointed. A member of the Oireachtas, the European Parliament or a local authority may not be appointed Commissioner. If he is elected to one of those bodies, he must cease to act as Commissioner. He may not hold any other paid office or employment. The Commissioner is paid by the Minister for Justice who determines his conditions of employment and who also has the power to appoint his staff.[1] The main duty of the Data Protection Commissioner is to ensure that the provisions of the 1988 Act are adhered to. He has eight functions which enable him to do this, these are listed below.

1. Enforcement Notices

[22.02] The Commissioner may investigate whether any of the provisions of the 1988 Act have been, are being, or are likely to be, contravened by a data controller or processor. He may do this either upon receipt of a complaint or if he of the opinion that there may be such a contravention.[2] If a complaint is made to the Commissioner, he must investigate the complaint unless he is of the opinion that it is vexatious or frivolous. He must then notify the individual who made the complaint of his decision. The complainant may then appeal the decision to the Circuit Court within 21 days.

[22.03] If the Commissioner decides that a data controller or processor is in contravention of a provision of the Act, the Commissioner may serve an 'enforcement notice' requiring the controller or processor to take specified steps within a specified time to ensure compliance with the Act. The enforcement notice may require the controller either to rectify or erase his

---

[1.] DPA 1988, s 9.

[2.] DPA 1988, s 10(1)(a). The Commissioner received 24 formal or serious complaints in 1994 and the same number in 1993. 12 of these related to the public sector, 5 to insurance, 5 to banking and 2 in other areas. He received 37 such complaints in 1995, 14 relating to banking and insurance and 9 relating to the public sector: *Seventh Annual Report of the Data Protection Commissioner*, 1995 p 9.

data or to supplement it with a statement which is approved of by the Commissioner.[3] The notice must specify the provisions which the Commissioner believes have been contravened and the reasons for his opinion together with a statement that it may be appealed to the Circuit Court within 21 days. In general, the time specified in an enforcement notice may not expire before the 21 days in which the controller or processor may appeal. If an appeal is brought, then the controller or processor need not comply with the notice pending the determination of the appeal. However, if the Commissioner is of the opinion that the enforcement notice must be complied with urgently, then he may require compliance within seven days. The Commissioner must insert a statement to this effect in the notice and inform the controller or processor of his right to appeal. If the enforcement notice is urgent, then it must be complied with regardless of whether the controller or processor wishes to appeal.

[22.04] Once the data controller complies with the notice, he must within 40 days inform the data subject concerned and if he materially modifies the data any person to whom the data was disclosed in the previous 12 months of the relevant rectification, erasure or statement. This last provision has never commenced.[4] Any person who fails to comply with an enforcement notice will be guilty of an offence unless they have a reasonable excuse. If the Commissioner cancels the enforcement notice, he must notify the data controller or processor in writing.[5]

2. Information Notices

[22.05] The Commissioner may request information from any person by sending him an 'information notice' which will require the person to give the information specified within a set time. The information notice must state that the person may appeal to the Circuit Court within 21 days. If the person appeals against the request, the notice need not be complied with pending the outcome of the appeal. If the Commissioner requires information urgently, then this must be stated in the notice which must include a statement that there is a right of appeal to the Circuit Court and must allow the person seven days in which to comply with the notice. An urgent notice must be compiled with regardless of whether or not the person appeals.

---

3. If the data is supplemented in this way then the controller will not be in breach of his duty to keep the data up to date and accurate.
4. Data Protection Act (Commencement Order) Regulations 1988: SI 349/1988.
5. DPA 1988, s 10.

[22.06] No law prohibiting disclosure of information will prevent any person from providing the Commissioner with any information. This does not apply in the case of information which in the opinion of the Ministers for Justice or Defence should not be disclosed in the interests of state security or to information which is privileged from disclosure in court proceedings. Any person who fails or refuses to comply with an information notice or furnishes the Commissioner with false information, will be guilty of an offence, unless they can show a reasonable excuse.[6]

3. Prohibition Notices

[22.07] A 'prohibition notice' may be issued to prevent the transfer of personal data abroad.[7] Such a notice may either prohibit the transfer absolutely or specify conditions which must be complied with before the transfer can take place. These are fully dealt with in the section below on transborder data flows.[8]

Service of notices

[22.08] Notices may be served on an individual by delivering the notice to him, sending it by post addressed to his usual or last known place of residence or business, or by leaving it at that place. Notices may be served on a body corporate or an unincorporated body by posting it or leaving it at its registered office or principal place of business.[9]

Court proceedings

[22.09] The Circuit Court may hear appeals against: the requirements of enforcement or information notices, a prohibition notice; a refusal by the Commissioner to register an entry in the Data Protection Register; or, a decision of the Commissioner in relation to a complaint made by an individual about the activities of a data controller or processor. Such appeals must be brought within 21 days from the service of the relevant notices or notifications of decisions of the Commissioner.

[22.10] The appeal will be heard by the Circuit Judge who is assigned to the Circuit where the appellant resides or carries on his profession, business or occupation. Alternatively, the appeal may be heard in Dublin Circuit Court at the option of the appellant. In general, the decision of the Circuit Court will be final although an appeal on a point of law may be brought to the High Court. If a person appeals against an enforcement, information or

---

6. DPA 1988, s 12.
7. DPA 1988, s 11(5).
8. See para **[22.30]** *et seq*.
9. DPA 1988, s 25.

prohibition notice or a refusal by the Commissioner to register an entry in the Register which the Commissioner has stated must be carried out urgently then the Court may allow the appellant to ignore the notice or refusal pending the determination of the appeal. If the Court allows this, the appellant will not be guilty of any offence as a result.[10] The whole or any part of proceedings under the 1988 Act may be heard otherwise than in public at the discretion of the Court.[11]

Evidence

[22.11] In any proceedings a certificate signed by the Minister for Justice or Defence stating that personal data was in his opinion kept for reasons of State security, will be evidence of that opinion. A certificate signed by a member of the gardaí[12] or an army officer[13] stating that in his opinion personal data is required for reasons of State security, will be evidence of that opinion. Any such document will be presumed to be a signed certificate unless the contrary is proven. Information supplied by a person in response to an individual exercising his right to establish the existence of personal data or his right of access, will not be admissible in proceedings for an offence under the Act against the supplier or his spouse.[14] This means that data controllers do not have to worry about incriminating themselves when they respond to access requests.

Authorised officers of the Data Protection Commissioner

[22.12] To assist the Commissioner in his duties, he may appoint authorised officers. These are persons who are authorised to exercise certain powers in writing. If it is necessary or expedient for the Commissioner to obtain any information for the performance of his functions, then an authorised officer has the following powers:

(1) He may enter onto the premises of any data controller or data processor, inspect those premises and any data kept there and inspect, examine, operate and test any equipment kept there at all reasonable times;

(2) He may require any data controller, processor or employee to disclose any data or data material that is within their control or power and give him information that he may reasonably require.

---

10. DPA 1988, s 26.
11. DPA 1988, s 28.
12. Not below the rank of chief superintendent.
13. Not below the rank of colonel.
14. DPA 1988, s 27.

(3) He may inspect, copy or extract information from the data or data material either on the premises or elsewhere.

(4) He may require any person on the premises to give him whatever information he may reasonably require with regard to the procedures employed on the premises to ensure compliance with the Act, the sources of data, the purposes for which data is kept, the persons to whom it is disclosed and the data equipment held on the premises.

In general, the authorised officer may not exercise these powers in relation to a financial institution. However, if the Data Commissioner decides that it is necessary or expedient for an authorised officer to exercise his powers with regard to a financial institution, he may apply to the High Court for an order to enable him to do so. The High Court may make such an order, if it is satisfied that it is necessary or expedient that an authorised officer should exercise his powers subject to whatever conditions the court specifies in the order. Any person who obstructs or impedes an authorised officer in the exercise of a power or without reasonable excuse does not comply with a requirement of the officer or the Act, or who gives information which he knows to be materially false or misleading, will be guilty of an offence.[15]

4. The Prosecution of Offences

[22.13] Where an offence has been committed by a body corporate and the offence is proven to have been committed with the consent or connivance or to be attributable to any neglect by an officer of that body corporate, then that person as well as the body corporate will be guilty of the offence. If the affairs of the body corporate are managed by its members, then if any offence has been committed as a result of the acts or defaults of a member, in connection with his managerial function, that member will also be guilty of an offence as if he were a director or manager of the body corporate.[16]

[22.14] Summary proceedings under the 1988 Act may be prosecuted by the Commissioner and must be instituted within one year from the date of the offence.[17]

Penalties

[22.15] A person found guilty of an offence under the 1988 Act, will be liable on summary conviction to a fine not exceeding £1,000 or on conviction on indictment to a fine not exceeding £50,000. The court may

---

[15.] DPA 1988, s 24.
[16.] DPA 1988, s 29.
[17.] DPA 1988, s 30.

order any data material connected to the offence to be forfeited or destroyed. The court may not order the destruction of such data unless it is satisfied that there is no person other than the offender who is the owner of the data unless reasonable steps have been taken to notify that person and to give him an opportunity to show why the order should not be made.[18]

5. Codes of Practice

[22.16] The Commissioner is required to encourage trade associations and other bodies to prepare codes of practice for dealing with personal data. The Commissioner may approve of any such code if he is satisfied that it provides a suitable level of protection for data subjects. If the code is approved by the Oireachtas, then the code will have the force of law and it will be treated as a statutory instrument. The provisions relating to codes of practice for data controllers may also apply to data processors, however codes for data processors will only relate to the security of the data.[19] Such codes of practice also exist in other countries such as Germany, Sweden and the UK. There are a wide variety of codes in use in Europe today, some apply to sectors of society such as the code for Catholic primary schools in the Netherlands others apply to specific companies such as IBM and American Express.[20] To date, there has only been one such code developed in Ireland, the Irish Direct Marketing Association Code of Practice. This is because there is a danger that such codes of practice could be used to dilute the provisions of the 1988 Act. To prevent this, any such code would result in being a restatement of the Act's provisions.

6. Annual Report

[22.17] The Commissioner must prepare an annual report and lay it before the Oireachtas.[21] Seven reports have been produced since the commencement of the Act.

7. Mutual Assistance

[22.18] The Commissioner is required to provide mutual assistance to each member of the Strasbourg Convention.[22] The Commissioner must furnish information on the provisions of the 1988 Act and other factual information to every other country's equivalent authority.[23] Each country must assist any data subjects resident abroad to exercise their rights. If those data subjects

---

18. DPA 1988, s 31.
19. DPA 1988, s 13.
20. OECD Privacy and Data Protection Report, 1994, p 40.
21. DPA 1988, s 14.
22. DPA 1988, s 15.
23. Article 13.

live in another country which is a party to the Convention, then they may exercise their rights through the designated authority of that country. This request for assistance must contain all the relevant particulars such as the identity of the subject, the relevant data and the purpose of the request.[24] Any such transfers of information may only be used for the purposes specified in the request. There must be appropriate safeguards for confidentiality and secrecy and no such request for information may be made by an authority without the consent of the data subject.[25] An authority may refuse a request for assistance if it is incompatible with the authority's data protection powers; if it is incompatible with the Convention; or if compliance would be incompatible with the sovereignty, security or public policy of the country.[26] Such mutual assistance cannot give rise to costs or fees, except for those incurred by experts or interpreters. These costs must be borne by the country whose authority has made the request for assistance. The data subject may not be charged costs or fees in respect of this mutual assistance other than those costs or fees which would be paid by residents of that country.[27] Although the commitment to mutual assistance is commendable, it may be difficult to enforce the provisions of the Data Protection Act on behalf of people resident abroad and vice versa. The Sixth Report of the Data Protection Commissioner cites the example of an Irish person who wished to have his name removed from a magazine circulation list. As the company concerned operated outside Ireland, the Irish Act did not apply.

The Consultative Committee of the Strasbourg Convention

[22.19] Chapter 5 of the Strasbourg Convention sets up a consultative committee to monitor the application of the Convention. The Committee consists of the representatives of the parties to the Convention.[28] The Committee may make proposals to improve or facilitate the application of the Convention; make proposals for the amendment of the Convention; formulate opinions on proposed amendments to the convention and express opinions on any question concerning the Convention.[29]

8. Maintenance of the Data Protection Register

[22.20] See para **[20.33]** *et seq.*

---

24. Article 14.
25. Article 15.
26. Article 16.
27. Article 17.
28. Article 18.
29. Article 19.

THE DATA PROTECTION DIRECTIVE: SUPERVISORY AUTHORITY AND REGISTRATION

[22.21] In the future all data protection laws in Europe will have to be compatible and to ensure this, the Directive creates a Supervisory Authority with a far wider role in the EU than that of the Data Commissioner. The Directive also creates a working party to monitor the standards of data protection within the EU and elsewhere. In particular, the working party must report to the Commission any divergences in data protection between Member States. The working party will be made up of representatives of each country's supervisory authorities. The Directive also creates a committee to consider data protection measures which the commission has decided to implement. As the Directive is implemented, it would appear that increasingly control of data protection will be exercised by the EU directly. In time, the Irish Data Protection Commissioner may become an adjunct of an EU data protection authority, in the same way as the Irish Controller of Patents is becoming a subsidiary of the European Patents Office.

Supervisory Authority

[22.22] The establishment of independent supervisory authorities is seen as being an essential component of the protection of individuals and their personal data.[30] Member States must provide one or more public authorities to monitor the application of the Directive within their territory. These authorities will have complete independence in the exercise of their functions[31] and must be consulted when drawing up administrative measures or regulations relating to data protection.[32] Each authority must have the following powers:

(1) Investigative powers, such as powers of access to data used in processing and the power to collect information necessary for the performance of its supervisory duties;

(2) Effective powers of intervention, for example that of delivering opinions before processing beings, ensuring publication of opinions, of ordering the blocking, erasure or destruction of data, of imposing a temporary or definitive ban on processing, or warning or admonishing the controller, referring the matter to the legislature or other political institution;

(3) The power to engage in legal proceedings where the national

---

[30.] Recital 62.
[31.] Article 28(1).
[32.] Article 28(2).

provisions adopted pursuant to the Directive are violated and to bring these violations to the attention of the judicial authorities.

Any decision made by the supervisory authority which gives rise to a complaint may be appealed through the courts.[33] The supervisory authority must hear claims lodged by any person concerning the protection of his rights and freedoms with regard to processing of personal data. That person must be informed of the result of any claim. The supervisory authority must in particular hear claims on the lawfulness of data processing lodged by a person where Article 13 of the Directive which limits, *inter alia*, the application of the right of information and access, has been invoked. He must at least be informed that a check has been carried out.[34]

[22.23] The authority must help to ensure the transparency of processing.[35] It must draw up a report on its activities at regular intervals which must be made public.[36] Each authority may be requested to exercise its powers by the authority of another Member State. They must co-operate with one another, in particular by exchanging all useful information.[37] Member States must provide that the members and staff of the supervisory authority will be subject to a duty of professional secrecy even after their employment has ceased.[38]

The Working Party

[22.24] The authorities of the different Member States will need to assist one another so as to ensure that the rules of data protection are properly respected throughout the EU.[39] The Directive creates a 'Working Party on the Protection of Individuals with regard to the Processing of Personal Data' ('the working party') which will contribute to the uniform application of national data protection laws.[40] It has an advisory status and acts independently. It is composed of a representative of each of the national supervisory authorities as well as a representative of the authority established for Community institutions and bodies and a representative of the Commission. If a country has more than one supervisory authority, then they must nominate a joint representative. The working party must make decisions by a simple majority of the representatives of the Supervisory

---

[33.] Article 28(3).
[34.] Article 28(4).
[35.] Recital 63.
[36.] Article 28(5).
[37.] Article 28(6).
[38.] Article 28(7).
[39.] Recital 64.
[40.] Recital 65.

Authorities and will adopt its own procedural rules. It must elect its chairman and his term of office will be two years, which may be renewed. It must consider items placed on its agenda by the chairman who may act on its own initiative or on the request of a representative of a supervisory authority or at the request of the Commission. The working party secretariat will be provided by the Commission.[41]

[22.25] Its functions include:

(1) examining any question regarding the application of the national measures adopted under the Directive in order to contribute to the uniform application of such measures;

(2) giving the Commission an opinion on the level of protection in the Community and in third countries;

(3) advising the Commission on any proposed amendment of the Directive, on any additional or specific measures to safeguard data protection and any other proposed Community measures affecting such rights and freedoms;

(4) giving an opinion on codes of conduct drawn up at Community level.[42]

If the working party finds that the data protection legislation of Member States is diverging in a manner likely to affect data protection, then it must inform the Commission. It may make recommendations on its own initiative on all matters relating to data protection. The opinions and recommendations of the working party must be forwarded to the Commission and to the Committee established under Article 31. The Commission must inform the working party of any action that is taken in response to these recommendations or opinions. This will be done in a report which will be sent to the European Parliament and the Council. This report will be made public. The working party must draw up an annual report on data protection in the EU and in third countries which will be sent to the European Parliament, the Commission, and the Council. It must also be made public.[43]

The Committee

[22.26] The Commission will be assisted by a committee made up of representatives of the Member States and chaired by a representative of the Commission. The representative of the Commission must submit to the Committee a draft of the measures to the taken on which the committee must

---

[41.] Article 29.
[42.] Article 30(1).
[43.] Article 30.

deliver its opinion on within a specified time limit, according to the urgency of the matter. The opinion must be delivered by a majority laid down in Article 148(2) of the Treaty. The chairman will not vote. The Commission will adopt measures which will apply immediately. If these measures are not in accordance with the opinion of the Committee, then they must be communicated by the Commission to the Council immediately. If this occurs the Commission will defer application of the measures for three months and the Council may take a different decision within that time acting by a qualified majority.[44]

[22.27] The Commission has particular powers in regard to transborder data flows. If the Commission, using the above procedures finds that a third country does not have a suitable level of data protection, then it may prevent such data flows, however it may negotiate with such third countries to improve their data protection.[45] The Directive gives only data protection authorities a voice in decision making at European level. There are no provisions for data controllers, processors or data subjects to be heard.

Codes of conduct

[22.28] Member States and the Commission must encourage the drawing up of codes of conduct which will aid the proper implementation of the Directive while taking account of the features of different sectors. Member States must make provisions for trade associations and other organisations representing controllers to submit to the Supervisory Authority any draft national codes which they have drawn up or which they intend to implement or extend so that they may be approved. The Authority must ascertain whether the drafts submitted are in accordance with the Directive amongst other things. The Authority may seek the opinions of data subjects if it sees fit. Draft Community codes and amendments or extensions to those codes may be submitted to the working party. They must decide whether the drafts comply with national provisions. If it sees fit, the working party may consult with data subjects. If they approve a code, then the Commission must ensure appropriate publicity for it.[46]

TRANSBORDER DATA FLOWS

[22.29] One of the most controversial aspects of data protection is transborder data flows which involves the transmission of data from one country to another. One of the objectives of the Directive is to allow free

---

[44.] Article 31
[45.] Article 25.
[46.] Article 27.

flows of personal data between Member States.[47] Once transfers of data out of Ireland have taken place, it is unclear how much real control Irish data subjects will have over their data. The object of controlling transborder data flows is to at least ensure that this data will remain within countries which are subject to the Directive. The trend in computer and telecommunications technology in recent years has been to make such transfers easier. Whether legislation will have much success in controlling such transfers is unclear.

Transborder Data Flows Pursuant to the Data Protection Act 1988

[22.30] The 1988 Act contains provisions which allow transfers of data outside Ireland to be controlled by the Commissioner who may, in certain circumstances, prohibit the transfer of data outside the State.[48] In deciding whether or not to prohibit the transfer, the Commissioner must have regard to the provisions of Article 12 of the Strasbourg Convention.[49] Article 12 provides that a party to the Convention must not prohibit or subject to special conditions the transfer of data between parties to the Convention, if the sole reason is to protect privacy. The objective of this is to ensure that States do not use protestations about their citizens' right to privacy as a disguise for the restriction of trade. However, the parties to the Convention may disregard this if their legislation regulates certain categories of personal data unless the recipient State has equivalent protection. The parties may also disregard this provision to prevent transfers of data to a State which is not a party to the Convention with the intention of circumventing the legislation of the contracting party. The Commissioner must not prohibit the transfer of data outside the State unless he believes that the transfer would lead to a contravention of the basic principles for data protection as set out in Chapter II of the Convention.[50] The Commissioner must also have regard for the possibility that damage or distress would be caused to any person as a result of any transfer and the desirability of facilitating international transfers of data.[51]

Prohibition Notice

[22.31] If the Commissioner decides to prohibit transborder data flows, then he may issue a 'prohibition notice' to the person who wishes to transfer the data.[52] Such a notice may either prohibit the transfer absolutely or specify conditions which must be complied with before the transfer can take place.

[47.] Article 1(2) of the Directive.
[48.] DPA 1988, s 11(1).
[49.] DPA 1988, s 11(2).
[50.] See para **[19.09]**.
[51.] DPA 1988, s 11(4).
[52.] DPA 1988, s 11(5). For procedure, see para **[22.07]** above.

If the Commissioner cancels a prohibition notice he must notify the person on whom it was served, in writing.[53] In any event, a person who fails or refuses to comply with a prohibition notice, without a reasonable excuse, will be guilty of an offence.[54] These restrictions on transborder data flows do not apply where the transfer is authorised under any enactment or by any Convention or other instrument which imposes an international obligation on the State.[55] The restrictions on transborder data flows apply to transfers of information which is to be converted into personal data in the same fashion as it applies to personal data itself. This means that the controls on transborder data flows cannot be circumvented by gathering information in Ireland, transferring it to another country and converting it there into computerised data.

[22.32] The blocking of transborder data flows has occurred in other countries. In a Swedish case, a company wished to set up and keep files of personal data for its own marketing purposes in Ireland. This would involve the delivery of personal data from Sweden to Ireland. The transfer was permitted as Ireland had a Data Protection Act and the data involved was not sensitive.[56] In *IG Metall v Adam Opel*[57] a German trade union complained that Opel which was a subsidiary of General Motors was transferring personnel data to another subsidiary, EDS, which was also based in Germany. The union was concerned that such data might be transferred to the headquarters of EDS in the United States. The court held that the transfer was legal and that the theoretical possibility of the data being transferred out of Germany was insufficient to restrict transfers of data. In another German case, the German supervisory authority forced an American multi-national to set up a subsidiary in Germany to process personnel data as there were no guarantees of data protection if the data was transferred to the USA. The German supervisory authority has also prevented the transfer of personal data to Eastern European Countries which do not have appropriate data protection safeguards.[58]

Transborder Data Flows Pursuant to the Directive

[22.33] There are two major differences between the 1988 Act and the Directive. First, the Directive allows for the free flow of personal data

---

53. DPA 1988, s 11(9).
54. DPA 1988, s 11(13).
55. DPA 1988, s 11(10)
56. Data Inspectorate Decision No, 747-89. OECD privacy and data protection, 1994.
57. Privacy, Laws and Business 1987.
58. Vassilaki, 'An Empirical Survey of Cases Concerning the Transborder Flow of Personal Data', Computer Law and Security Report, 9 1993 Jan-Feb, p 34.

between all Member States of the EU. Secondly, the European Commission is given the role of overseeing the transfer of data to States outside the EU. The Directive recognises that the transfer of personal data is necessary for the expansion of international trade and protections that are afforded to data subjects by the Directive will not stand in the way of any transfers of data to countries with adequate data protection.[59]

[22.34] Transfers of personal data to third countries (outside the EU) for processing will only be permitted if the third country has an adequate level of data protection. This is without prejudice to compliance with the other provisions of the Directive.[60] The adequacy of data protection in the third country must be assessed in the light of all the circumstances surrounding the data transfer. In particular, consideration must be given to the following:

- the nature of the data;

- the purpose and duration of the proposed processing;

- the country of origin and of destination;

- the rules of law both general and sectoral in force in the third country; and

- the professional rules and security measures which are in force in that country.[61]

Particular attention must be paid to the processing of sensitive data.[62] The Member States and the Commission must inform each other where they consider that a third country does not ensure an adequate level of protection.[63] Where the Commission is of the opinion that a third country does not provide adequate protection,[64] Member States must prevent any further transfers of data to that country[65] but the Commission may negotiate to remedy this position.[66] The Commission may recognise that a third country has an adequate level of protection by reason of its domestic law or international agreements it has made or as a result of its negotiations with the Commission. In such a situation, Member States must allow data transfers to go ahead.[67]

[59.] Recital 56.
[60.] Article 25(1).
[61.] Article 25(2).
[62.] Recital 60 and Article 8.
[63.] Article 25(3).
[64.] See Article 31 at para [22.25].
[65.] Article 25(4).
[66.] Article 25(5)
[67.] Article 25(6).

Derogations

[**22.35**] Member States must allow transfers to a third country which do not have adequate data protection in the following situations:

    (a) where the data subject has given his unambiguous consent to the transfer;[68] or

    (b) where the transfer is necessary for the performance of a contract between the data subject and the controller or the implementation of pre-contractual measures taken in response to the data subject's request;[69] or

    (c) where the transfer is necessary for the conclusion or performance of a contract concluded in the interest of the data subject between the controller and a third party;[70] or

    (d) where the transfer is necessary or legally required on important public interest grounds or for the establishment, exercise or defence of legal claims.[71]; or

    (e) where the transfer is necessary in order to protect the vital interest of the data subject;[72] or

    (f) where the transfer is made from a register which according to law is intended to provide information to the public and which is open to public consultation or by any person who can demonstrate a legitimate interest, provided that conditions laid down in law for consultation are fulfilled.[73] Transfers should not involve the entirety of the data or entire categories of the data contained in the register and where the register is intended for consultation by persons having legitimate interest, the transfer should only be made at the request of those persons or if they are to be the recipients.[74]

[**22.36**] Transfers may be authorised to third countries which do not have adequate levels of protection if the controller has adequate safeguards for the protection of privacy and the fundamental rights and freedoms of individuals. These safeguards may, in particular, be provided by appropriate

---

68. Article 26(1)(a).
69. Article 26(1)(b).
70. Article 26(1)(c).
71. Article 26(1)(d). An example of an important public interest is the international transfers of data between tax, customs or social security administrators. In this case, the transfer should not involve the entirety of the data or data categories contained in the register: Recital 58.
72. Article 26(1)(e).
73. Article 26(1)(f).
74. Recital 58.

contracts[75] and the Member States must inform the Commission and other Member States of any such authorisations. If a Member State or the Commission objects to such transfers, on justified grounds, the Commission must take appropriate measures. Member States must comply with the Commission's decision on this matter.[76] If the Commission decides that certain standard contractual clauses do offer sufficient safeguards, then Member States must comply with their decision and allow transfers.[77]

[22.37] The use of contracts to ensure data protection in countries which do not have adequate safeguards has proven its worth in a number of cases which involved transfers of data within Europe. In 1986, the Spanish archives requested a copy of a list of Spanish refugees who had fled to France during the Spanish Civil War but at the time, Spain did not have sufficient data protection safeguards. The French data protection body, the Commission Nationale de L'Informatique et des Libertes (CNIL) insisted that the list be put into anonymous form before transfer.

[22.38] In 1989, the Fiat motor company wished to transfer personnel data from its Paris office to Turin, Italy. Again, Italy had no adequate data protection legislation, however, as Italy was a member of the EU, the French could not interfere with the right of the Italians to free movement of goods. To deal with this situation the CNIL insisted that the Turin office of Fiat contract with its Paris office that it would respect the rights contained of the French data subjects. This would allow French employees of Fiat to assert their rights of access and rectification in the Italian office.[78] In another case a network called Eurocode was established by the European Organisation for the Research and Treatment of Cancer, in Brussels. This network would allow medical practitioners to access information on the network from anywhere in Europe. The CNIL was concerned that medical data concerning French cancer patients might be entered into the network where it would not be guaranteed the same protections as were available in France. The CNIL decided that a contractual solution was appropriate as in the Fiat case. The relevant French cancer research body was required to enter into a contract with the European organisation to ensure that data protection would be guaranteed. In particular, the CNIL required that identification codes for patients be used which would make it more difficult to identify the individuals from the data.[79]

[75.] Article 26(2).
[76.] Article 26(3) and Article 31(2).
[77.] Article 26(4).
[78.] Deliberation No 89-78, 11 July 1989, CNIL.
[79.] Deliberation No 89-98, 16 September 1989, CNIL.

[22.39] The contractual approach relies essentially on trust. The difficulty with a contractual solution is that it may be difficult to enforce, it may only be enforceable if the company in the third country which receives the data has a subsidiary in the country from which the data is sent, which can be sued. The supervisory authority will have to ensure compliance with the contracts which may prove difficult as third countries may not appreciate outside public bodies inspecting and assessing the performance of companies within their borders.[80]

[80.] For a discussion of transborder data flows and similar cases throughout Europe and elsewhere, see OECD, *Privacy and Data Protection* (1994).

Chapter 23

The Reality of Data Protection

INTRODUCTION

[23.01] The rationale behind data protection is to ensure that information about any individual is not abused. The Data Protection Act 1988 attempts to do this by giving individuals some control over their personal data. The Act ensures that any responsible body will have to go to the expense of registering any data it holds. Unfortunately, the greatest threat to individuals' privacy is likely to be posed by irresponsible organisations who are unlikely to register in any event. Knowledge of data protection would appear to be patchy amongst data controllers. The Price Waterhouse Survey found a 'poor understanding' of the legislation. Only 20% of financial institutions rated themselves as having a good knowledge of this law and a further 4% rated themselves as having a poor knowledge. In the top 200 Irish companies, 12% gave themselves a poor rating.[1]

[23.02] The 1988 Act may have created a very impressive set of rights but they have yet to be exercised in practice to any significant degree. The Act may be seen as a product of the 1980s and, in particular, a fear that information technology would allow the State to develop control over individuals' lives analogous to that of 'Big Brother' in George Orwell's novel *1984*. Although the Act may have been created to allay these fears, the State has granted itself exemptions from the Act. The Act provides that the State, health boards and local authorities do not have to allow access to data or ensure that data is obtained and processed fairly where the data is kept for the purpose of assessing or collecting any tax, duty or other moneys owed.[2] Obviously, the State must be able to ensure that it is paid what it is owed and that it can protect itself against fraud. Private sector companies have similar objectives and there is no good reason why these companies should have to allow access to their data while the State does not. The Directive will not remedy matters, as Member States may exempt the application of the principles relating to data quality,[3] the requirement that information be given

---

[1.] Price Waterhouse, *Priority Data Systems Computer Virus and Security Survey*, February 1995, p 13.
[2.] Data Protection Act 1988, s 4.
[3.] Article 6(1).

to data subjects,[4] the subject's right of access[5] and the requirement that processing be publicised.[6] This exemption may be granted where it is necessary for the economic or financial interests of the State.[7]

[23.03] The State has a wide variety of powers and information-gathering functions which cannot be described in detail here. However, one important example is the Central Statistics Office ('CSO') which has extensive powers to gather information about citizens on behalf of the State. The main method of gathering such information is through the census. Failure to co-operate with the census officials is made a criminal offence by the Statistics Act 1993. Any person who fails or refuses to provide information will be guilty of an offence[8] as will any person who prevents an officer of the CSO from entering their premises.[9] The officers of the CSO have a limited right of entry to any premises for the purposes of carrying out the census[10] and any person who obstructs an officer of the CSO will be guilty of an offence.[11] Anyone who furnishes false information to the CSO will be guilty of an offence[12] as will any person who willingly destroys, damages or falsifies a document issued for the census.[13] Public authorities must supply the CSO with access to their records free of charge[14] and the CSO may request a public authority to consult and co-operate with them for the purposes of improving their records for statistical purposes.[15] The justification for these wide ranging powers is a fear that individuals might disrupt the census by withdrawing their co-operation.

[23.04] While the CSO has extensive powers to gather information it is limited in the uses to which it can put that information. All information furnished to it, under the Act, may only be used for statistical purposes.[16] No information obtained under the Act which can be related to an identifiable person or undertaking can be disseminated, shown or communicated to anyone unless the subject of the information consents, it is necessary to

---

4. Articles 10 and 11(1).
5. Article 12.
6. Article 21.
7. Article 13.
8. Statistics Act 1993, s 36.
9. Statistics Act 1993, s 37.
10. Statistics Act 1993, s 29.
11. Statistics Act 1993, s 40.
12. Statistics Act 1993, s 43.
13. Statistics Act 1993, s 42.
14. Statistics Act 1993, s 30.
15. Statistics Act 1993, s 31.
16. Statistics Act 1993, s 32.

prosecute an offence under the Act or it is necessary for the administration of the census or the CSO.[17] The CSO may provide for statistical purposes only information gathered under the Act in such a form that it cannot be directly or indirectly related to an identifiable person or undertaking.[18]

[23.05] The confidentiality of this information is protected by the creation of criminal offences for any disclosure of any information which is not permitted by the 1993 Act. Any person who uses or discloses information furnished under the census will be guilty of an offence[19] as will any officer of the CSO who, in the pretended performance of his functions, obtains any information which he is not entitled to.[20] This means that the CSO's powers to gather information, some of which are quite draconian, are balanced by statutory protections which should ensure that the information remains confidential.

THE CRIMINAL JUSTICE ACT 1994

[23.06] Unfortunately, the same controls on information which is gathered or disclosed to the State is not replicated in other Acts. The Criminal Justice Act 1994 greatly increased the State's power to investigate the banking affairs of individuals. This increase has been justified by the obvious need to combat drug trafficking and, in particular, to make it more difficult to launder the proceeds of that trafficking. The 1994 Act implements the EU Directive on the Prevention of the Use of the Financial System for the Purpose of Money Laundering.[21] This Act effectively forces banks and other financial institutions to act as information gatherers on behalf of the State. Section 32 of the Act compels banks, building societies, life assurance companies and other designated bodies to take reasonable measures to establish the identity of anyone it provides a service for.[22] These measures must be taken on a continuing basis or where the transactions amount to at least £10,000 or where it is suspected that money laundering is occurring.[23] If the financial institution suspects that someone is acting on behalf of a third party, then it must take reasonable measures to establish the identity of the third party.[24] Once a person has established their identity, the financial

---

17. Statistics Act 1993, s 33.
18. Statistics Act 1993, s 34.
19. Statistics Act 1993, s 38.
20. Statistics Act 1993, s 39.
21. Council Directive 91/308, OJ 1991 L166/77.
22. Designated bodies is defined in s 32(1). The services to which the Act applies are defined in s 32(2) which are services specified in the annex to Council Directive 89/646/EEC and other activities as specified in Council Directive 79/267/EEC or in Regulations.
23. Criminal Justice Act 1994, s 32(3).
24. Criminal Justice Act 1994, s 32(5).

institution must retain a copy of all identification documents for at least five years after the relationship with that person has ended. Materials relating to transactions must also be retained for at least five years after the transaction.[25] Failing to uphold this section will be a criminal offence.

[23.07] Section 57 of the 1994 Act requires that any person to whom s 32 of the Act applies must report to the gardaí where they suspect that a money laundering offence has occurred.[26] A person who supervises another person or body must report to the gardaí where they suspect that that person or body is committing an offence under s 31[27] or s 32 of the Act.[28] It is an offence not to comply with this reporting requirement.[29] Where a person or body discloses information in compliance with this requirement, that disclosure will not be treated as a breach of any restriction on disclosure imposed by statute or otherwise and will not attach the person or body making the disclosure with liability of any kind.[30] Unlike the Statistics Act 1993, the Criminal Justice Act 1994 does not in any way attempt to control that information once it is disclosed to the State authorities. This may be justified by the threat which drug trafficking and other similar crimes present to the State. It might have been wise to have at least provided some controls in the 1994 Act so as to ensure that information gathered under the Act would not be abused by individuals for their own ends. In the long term, the success of this legislation may be affected by the advent of digital cash.[31] Once money can be moved around in an electronic form it has been suggested that the authorities will lose all control as it moves through computer networks, bypassing the banks and other bodies.[32] The lack of controls in the Criminal Justice Act 1994 may be unfavourably compared with the Europol Convention which contains extensive provisions to control the use of personal data and in particular to ensure that it is not accessed for illegitimate purposes.[33]

[25.] Criminal Justice Act 1994, s 32(9).

[26.] Criminal Justice Act 1994, s 57(1).

[27.] Criminal Justice Act 1994, s 31 makes it an offence to conceal or disguise any property or to convert, transfer or remove that property from the state if the property represents the proceeds of drug trafficking or other criminal activity on ones own behalf or on behalf of another. It is also an offence to handle such property.

[28.] Criminal Justice Act 1994, s 57(2).

[29.] Criminal Justice Act 1994, s 57(5) states that a person who is summarily convicted of an offence under this section is liable to a fine not exceeding £1,000 or to imprisonment for a term not exceeding 12 months or to both. On indictment, a person will be liable to a fine or to imprisonment for a term not exceeding 5 years or to both.

[30.] Criminal Justice Act 1994, s 57(7).

[31.] See para **[27.02]** on electronic money.

[32.] *The Economist*, 'Survey of the World Economy', 7 October 1995.

[33.] See generally Magliveras, 'Defeating the Money Launderer', Journal of Business Law, 1992, p 161.

THE EUROPOL CONVENTION

[23.08] As the European Union develops, it is finding it necessary to create information collection and distribution systems which operate throughout Europe. The creation of these huge systems may fuel fears that authorities will abuse this information to manipulate and control individuals. The Europol Convention establishes a European Police Office (Europol).[34] The purpose of this to improve police co-operation in the fields of terrorism, drug trafficking and other serious forms of international crime. This will be done through a constant, confidential and intensive exchange of information between Europol and Member States' national units. To do this the Convention will set up an information system so that information may be accessed throughout Europe.[35] The system will contain data relating to persons who are suspected criminals or persons who is it suspected will commit offences in the future. This information may only include the surname, maiden name, given names and any aliases, date and place of birth, nationality, sex and other identifying characteristics of any individual. The system may also store details about their suspected crimes and the locations where they were committed, their means of committing crimes, the departments handling the case, suspected membership of a criminal organisations and criminal convictions. Additional information may be communicated by Europol or other national organisations.[36] Europol may request information from other public, international organisations and third countries.[37]

[23.09] Such a system could be open to abuse as has occurred in the UK,[38] therefore the Convention lays down extensive safeguards. Only national units and officers of Europol will have the right to enter and extract data from the system. Only the unit which initially entered particular data may modify it.[39] The Convention acknowledges that particular attention must be paid to the rights of individuals and the protection of their personal data. Each Member State must ensure that the standard of data protection is at least that of the Strasbourg Convention, which is implemented in Ireland by the Data Protection Act 1988. The difficulty with this is that the Data

---

[34.] The Convention based on Article 3 of the Treaty on European Union on the Establishment of a European Police Office (Europol Convention); OJ No C316 p 2, 27 November 1995. See also Joint Action on 10 March 1995 adopted by the Council on the basis of Article k3 of the Treaty on European Union concerning the Europol Drugs Unit. OJ L 62, 20/3/95, p 1.
[35.] Title II, Articles 7, 8 and 9.
[36.] Article 8.
[37.] Article 10(4).
[38.] *R v Brown* [1996] 1 All ER 545.
[39.] Article 9.

Protection Act contains extensive exceptions for law enforcement activities. However, the communication of personal data may not begin until such data protection is in place. Europol must also observe the principles of data protection with respect to non-automated data or paper files.[40] To ensure that data is not accessed for inappropriate purposes, Europol must draw up reports for at least 10% of all retrievals of personal data.[41] Personal data may only transmitted or utilised in order to prevent and combat serious crimes.[42] Europol may also transmit data to States and bodies which are not part of Europol provided it is necessary to prevent or combat crime and an adequate level of data protection is assured.[43] Individuals have a right of access to data relating to themselves which is stored with Europol but this request may be refused if it is necessary to enable Europol to fulfil its duties. They may also have their data checked[44] and Europol must correct and delete any inaccurate data.[45] Data may only be held by Europol for as long as is necessary for the performance of its tasks. The need to retain data must be reviewed after three years. Some types of data such as data relating to the victims of crime or witnesses must be deleted after three years However, every addition or other access to the data will cause time to run afresh. The need for continued storage of the data must be reviewed annually.[46]

[23.10] Member States must appoint a national supervisory body to monitor the application of data protection to Europol within the Member State.[47] There will also be a joint supervisory authority to monitor the activities of Europol as a whole.[48] There are strict provisions to ensure the security of data. Measures must be implemented to ensure the following:

1. Denial of unauthorised access to data processing equipment used for processing personal data.

2. Prevention of unauthorised reading, copying, modification or removal of data media.

3. Prevention of unauthorised input of data and the unauthorised inspection, modification or deletion of stored personal data.

4. Prevention of the use of automated data processing systems by unauthorised persons using data communication equipment.

[40.] Article 14.
[41.] Article 16.
[42.] Article 17.
[43.] Article 18.
[44.] Article 19
[45.] Article 20.
[46.] Article 21.
[47.] Article 23.
[48.] Article 24.

5. Persons authorised to use an automated data processing system only have access to the data covered by their access authorisation.

6. It is possible to verify and establish to which bodies personal data may be transmitted using data communication equipment.

7. It is subsequently possible to verify and establish which personal data have been input into automated data or processing systems and when and by whom the data were input.

8. Prevention of unauthorised reading, copying, modification, or deletion of personal data during transfers of personal data or during transportation of data media.

9. Installed systems may in case of interruption be immediately restored.

10. The functions of the system perform without fault, that the appearance of faults in the functions is immediately reported and that stored data cannot be corrupted by means of a malfunctioning of the system.[49]

These provisions should ensure that access to the data is carefully controlled. One of the difficulties with this extensive control is that some States might find it preferable to withhold data from the Europol system because they do not want it to be subject to scrutiny in this way.

THE CUSTOMS INFORMATION SYSTEM

[23.11] Any effective campaign against drug trafficking and cross-border terrorism will have to utilise the facilities of Europe's custom services. To make this more efficient, the EU will set up a customs information system.[50] The aim of this system will be to assist in preventing, investigating and prosecuting serious contraventions of the law by increasing the effectiveness of co-operation and control between customs services by the rapid dissemination of information.[51] This system will consist of a central database which may be accessed from terminals in each Member State. It will include data relating to commodities, means of transport, businesses, persons, fraud trends and availability of expertise. The items of personal data will comprise no more than the name, maiden name, forename and aliases, date and place of birth, nationality, sex, any identifying characteristics reason for inclusion of data, suggested action, and a warning code to indicate if the person is armed, violent or a fugitive.[52] This Convention contains similar data protection safeguards to the Europol Convention.

[49.] Article 25.
[50.] Convention drawn up on the basis of Article k3 of the Treaty on European Union, on the Use Of Information Technology For Customs Purposes. OJ LC 316 27/11/95, p 34.
[51.] Article 2.
[52.] Article 4.

CONCLUSION

[23.12] Although the State is capable of gathering considerable amounts of information about its citizens, Irish people find it difficult to obtain any information about the State. This is in spite of the fact that the Constitution provides that the power of government derives from the people.[53] If Irish citizens are ultimately in control of the State it would seem logical that they should be able to get access to reasonable amounts of information about it. The Ombudsman in his annual report has highlighted the difficulties of getting information from government departments and other organs of the State.[54] He stated:

> "Information is at the centre of the citizens' dealings with public bodies and in its absence he or she cannot even begin to ask how and why decisions were made. There is no doubt that information is fundamental to transparency and accountability in the way Government and public bodies operate. Increasing the availability of official information enables the public to become more involved in the making and administration of laws and policies of central government and in the actions and decisions of local government and other state bodies."

In order to remedy these difficulties the Freedom of Information Bill 1996 has been introduced. The Bill proposes to give every person a right of access to any record held by a public body.[55] Public bodies must give assistance to anyone searching for such information and a request for the information must be made in writing. However the Bill contains extensive exemptions which allow the right of access to be denied. One of these exemptions is that access may be refused if it would involve the disclosure of personal information unless the person requesting the information is the subject of it or that person has consented to its release or the information is available to the general public or it is necessary in order to avoid imminent danger to the life or health of an individual.[56] Section 17 of the Bill provides for the correction of personal records held by a public body. The public body should have been doing this anyway where the data is held in a computer under s 6 of the Data Protection Act 1988. The Bill seeks to extend this right of rectification to all records.

[53.] Article 6 of the Constitution provides "All powers of government, legislative, executive and judicial, derive, under God, from the people, whose right it is to designate the rulers of the State and, in final appeal, to decide all questions of national policy, according to the requirements of the common good".

[54.] Annual Report of the Ombudsman 1996.

[55.] Freedom of Information Bill 1996, s 6.

[56.] Freedom of Information Bill 1996, s 28.

Chapter 24

Evidence

[24.01] Computers generate two different types of evidence. First, calculations or analyses which are generated by the computer itself and are real evidence. Secondly, there are documents and records which are held on computer and are be treated as hearsay. The Criminal Evidence Act 1992 has greatly simplified the rules for the admission of such evidence in criminal matters while evidence in civil cases continues to be admissible under the normal rules of evidence.

REAL EVIDENCE

[24.02] Examples of real evidence are murder weapons, the clothes a victim was wearing or drugs alleged to have been found in the possession of an accused. Computers can also generate real evidence and this will be admissible in court.

> "Where information is recorded by mechanical means without the intervention of a human mind, the record made by the machine is admissible in evidence, provided of course, it is accepted that the machine is reliable."[1]

[24.03] An early case which dealt with this question concerned a record of radar readings showing the locations of two ships involved in a collision. This recording was made by a machine without human interference. In *The Statue of Liberty*[2] Simon P held that such a recording would be admissible as real evidence. He referred to *R v Maqsud Ali*[3] which dealt with the admissibility of tape recordings:

> "if tape recordings are admissible, it seems equally a photograph of radar reception is admissible - as indeed, any other type of photograph. It would be an absurd distinction that a photograph should be admissible if the camera were operated manually by a photographer, but not if it were operated by a trip or clock mechanism. Similarly, if evidence of weather conditions were relevant, the law would affront common sense if they were

---

1. Smith, 'The Admissibility of Statements by Computer', (1981) Crim LR 390, quoted with approval by the Court of Appeal in *R v Spiby* (1990) 91 Cr App Rep 186.
2. [1968] 1 WLR 739.
3. [1966] 1 QB 688.

to say that those could be proved by a person who looked at a barometer from time to time but not by producing a barograph record ... The law is bound these days to take cognisance of the fact that mechanical means replace human effort."

This case was followed in *R v Wood*,[4] which concerned the theft of certain metals which had been found in the accused's possession. An analysis of the stolen metals and those found in the accused's possession was carried out. Computer print-outs were held admissible as real evidence as the computer was used as a calculator:

"This computer was rightly described as a tool. It did not contribute its own knowledge. It merely did a sophisticated calculation which could have been done manually by the chemist."[5]

In *R v Spiby*[6] the appellant had been convicted of being knowingly involved in the unlawful importation of cannabis. The prosecution used telephone print-outs from a hotel's computer to show that a particular guest at that hotel had called the appellant at his home and club. The appellant was convicted and appealed unsuccessfully. The Court of Criminal Appeal held that the print-outs were real evidence. All that had happened was that when a guest in the hotel lifted the phone receiver, the computer recorded what had occurred and printed it out. It would have been different if a telephone operator had gathered the information and typed it into the computer bank before it was printed. If this had been done then the evidence would have been hearsay.

[24.04] If evidence is to be admitted as real evidence, there is a requirement that the computer be working properly. In *Spiby* the hotel manager stated that the machine was working satisfactorily and that no-one had complained about their bills. An appeal was taken on the basis that a computer engineer should have been called to prove this point. However, the Court of Appeal applied the principle that if the instrument (or computer) was one of a kind which, to common knowledge, are more often than not in working order, then in the absence of evidence to the contrary, the courts will presume that the machine was in working order at the material time.[7] This would

---

4. (1982) 76 Cr App R 23.
5. *Ibid*, at 27.
6. *R v Spiby* (1990) 91 Cr App Rep 186.
7. The court followed *Castle v Cross* [1985] 1 All ER 87: "The working accuracy of mechanical agents and scientific instruments eg watches, speedometers may be presumed. (*Prima facie*, the instrument is presumed correct although no evidence as to its accuracy has been given)". See *Phipson on Evidence*, 14th ed, (Sweet & Maxwell, 1990), para 17-57.

effectively transfer the burden of proving that the machine was not working properly onto the defendant, which is a heavy burden, as is discussed below.

[24.05] In *R v Blackburn*[8] the Court of Appeal made it clear that they would be extremely reluctant to accept a document produced on a word processor rather than on a typewriter or using a quill as the product of the computer as opposed to the human writer.

The Reliability of Computers

[24.06] It is highly questionable that it is common knowledge that computers are more often than not in working order since there have been numerous examples of computers failing to work as intended. For example, a computer error caused Telecom Éireann to overcharge approximately two-thirds of its mobile phone users.[9] Apparently, the Telecom computer was wrongly programmed to register the standard rate during the reduced rate period.[10] The computer used for generating customer bills by Telecom would have had a broadly similar function to that of the hotel computer in *Spiby*.[11] Another example of computer error occurred between 1985 and 1987 when at least four Americans died after being exposed to lethal doses of radiation from Therac-25-linear accelerator machines used for the radiation treatment of cancer. Software errors caused the machines to incorrectly calculate the amount of radiation being delivered to the patients.[12]

[24.07] The question of computer reliability is contentious. Although computer hardware has a very good reputation for reliability,[13] software does not.[14] The English Law Commission was willing to accept that view of

---

8. *The Times*, 1 December 1992.
9. *The Irish Times*, 3 April 1995.
10. *The Sunday Business Post*, 2 April 1995. Telecom Éireann stated that the overcharging "was not due to a computer fault but was a result of human error".
11. A more dramatic example of a telecommunications company's computers failing occurred on 15 January 1990 when some of the computers used by AT&T in the USA to switch or direct calls failed due to a software error. As a result some 74,000,000 calls were not completed. Computers can also malfunction due to malicious actions: On 13 June 1989 anyone making a phone call to the Palm Beach County Probation Department in Florida USA, would have found themselves talking to 'Tina' on a phone-sex line in New York. This was the result of hackers, allegedly members of the so-called 'Legion of Doom', interfering with the computer which managed the local telephone system. See, Sterling, *The Hacker Crackdown*, (Bantam, 1992) pp 35 & 98.
12. BYTE September 1995, p 125. See also Lee 'The Day the Phones Stopped', Primus 1992.
13. In *King v State ex rel Murdoch Acceptance Corporation* 222 So 2d 393 (Miss 1969) the court stated that "the scientific reliability of such machines, electronic computing equipment, in the light of their general use and the general reliance of the business world on them can scarcely be questioned". It might be better to state that while computer hardware rarely breaks down completely, it can malfunction.

Tapper that "most computer error is either immediately detectable or results from errors in the data entered into the machine".[15] However, in view of the frequent and often dramatic occasions where computer software fails to work correctly, the courts should be cautious before presuming that computers are working correctly, particularly in criminal trials.

HEARSAY EVIDENCE

[24.08] It is well established by the common law that hearsay evidence is not admissible in court. This rule was stated by *Cross* as follows:

> "An assertion other than one made by a person while giving oral evidence in the proceedings is inadmissible as evidence of any fact or opinion asserted."[16]

The exact scope of the rule is unclear. However, the above quotation is a reasonably accurate definition. While computers have proven their value as calculators and analytical tools for scientists, they are also used to store data. Businesses, governments and other institutions all rely on computers for this purpose. In many cases, records will only exist on computer and will not have any paper counterpart. These records may be produced in court but they must be proved and while a witness may refer to such records in the course of giving evidence, it is only in very limited circumstances that the records may be treated as evidence in themselves. In criminal cases, records held on a computer may be admissible under the Criminal Evidence Act 1992. This will only occur where the records were "compiled in the ordinary course of business". In all other situations and in civil cases,[17] the records will only be admitted if they fall within one of the exceptions to the rule at common law.

---

14. See Gibbs, 'Software's Chronic Crisis', Scientific American, September 1994, p 72. The difficulties of proving the reliability of computers in court is dealt with at para **[24.27]**.
15. Tapper, 'Discovery in Modern Times: A Voyage Around The Common Law World' (1991) 67 Chicago-Kent Law Review 217, 248. Quoted in the Law Commission Consultation Paper 'Evidence in Criminal Proceedings' No 138 1995, para 14.17.
16. *Cross on Evidence*, 7th ed, (Butterworths, 1990) p 42. This definition is that preferred by the English Law Commission in its Consultation Paper "Evidence in Criminal Proceedings" No 138, p 13, 1995, and was approved of by the House of Lords in *R v Sharp* [1988] 1 WLR 7. *Phipson on Evidence* defines hearsay as "Former statements of any persons whether or not he is a witness in the proceedings, may not be given in evidence if the purpose is to tender them as evidence of the truth of the matters asserted in them": *Phipson on Evidence*, 14th ed, (Sweet & Maxwell, 1990), para 21.02.
17. In general, civil courts will not apply the rules of evidence as strictly as those engaged in criminal trials.

Common Law Exceptions to the Rule against Hearsay

[24.09] At present, the rule against hearsay is very firmly established at common law. However, a number of exceptions to the rule have developed. The following is a brief list of exceptions to the rule:

(i)   Admissions and confessions of parties.

(ii)   Where a person has died, statements made may be admissible. These statements or declarations must fall into one of the following categories: declarations against interest; declarations in the course of duty; declarations as to public or general rights; declarations as to pedigree; dying declarations in cases of murder; and finally, declarations by testators as to their wills.

(iii)   Documents or statements which are in the possession of a party will be admissible as original evidence against that party to show his knowledge of their contents, his connection with the transactions to which they relate or a state of mind.[18]

(iv)   Public documents.

(v)   *Res Gestae* - oral or written statements which are made during an event.

(vi)   Hearsay statements may be admitted to prove the character, pedigree or marriage of an individual, to prove the existence of a public or general right or to identify any party.

A witness may refresh his memory by referring to notes made by him at the time of the event provided that he had personal knowledge of the facts recorded. However, if the person who created the note or record cannot be called as a witness, whether because he cannot be identified or because he is unable or unwilling to be called, then the evidence contained in those records or notes will not be admissible. The difficulty with computer records is that it is often difficult to show who the author actually is or even how many authors created a document. As many computer records are now held on computer networks, the documents may have hundreds of potential authors. In *Myers v DPP*,[19] the accused was alleged to have substituted the registration numbers and other numbers of wrecked cars for those of stolen cars. The prosecution called an employee of the manufacturer of the stolen cars who produced microfilm records purporting to show that the engine block numbers of the stolen cars corresponded with the engine block

---

18. In *R v Madden* (1986) Crim LR 804 the defendant was charged with the possession of cannabis which was contained in a trunk delivered to her home. Letters from the father of her children containing a promise to send drugs to her were admissible to rebut her defence that she had no knowledge of the contents of the trunk and had not asked for the drugs.

19. [1965] AC 1001, House of Lords.

numbers of the cars found in the possession of the accused. The microfilm contained images of cards which were compiled by various workmen during the manufacture of the cars. The witness was not involved in the compilation of this record. The defendant appealed against the admission of these records and was unsuccessful in the Court of Criminal Appeal. However, the House of Lords ruled that this evidence was hearsay and as such was inadmissible:

> "The entries on the cards were assertions by the unidentifiable men who made them that they had entered numbers which they had seen on the cars."[20]

The House of Lords refused to create a new exception to the rule against hearsay and stated that the rule could only be changed by legislation.

[24.10] The decision of the House of Lords in *Myers v DPP* caused obvious difficulties for the English courts, however, the problem was swiftly dealt with by the enactment of the Criminal Evidence Act 1965 and the Civil Evidence Act 1968. The equivalent criminal legislation was not enacted in Ireland until 1992 with the Criminal Evidence Act. There is still no legislation to deal with civil cases. As there has been no Irish case on a point equivalent to *Myers*, it is difficult to say what the Irish law is in this area. The Law Reform Commission has suggested that the Irish courts might not follow the House of Lords in this regard[21] and might instead follow the Canadian courts in the case of *Ares v Venner*.[22] In that case the Canadian Supreme Court expressly declined to follow *Myers* and stated that:

> "hospital records including nurses' notes made contemporaneously by someone having personal knowledge of the matters then being recorded and under a duty to make the entry or record should be received in evidence as *prima facie* proof of the facts stated therein."

The Canadian Supreme Court has been willing to take a flexible approach to the admission of hearsay in two recent judgments, *Khan*[23] and *Smith*.[24]

---

20. *Ibid* at 1022, Lord Reid.
21. The Law Reform Commission, 'The Rule against Hearsay', Working Paper No 9-1980.
22. [1970] SCR 608.
23. *Khan* (1990) 59 CCC (3d) 92. In this case the Canadian Supreme Court admitted hearsay evidence of a statement made by a child about sexual abuse. The court made it explicitly clear that its decision was not to be seen as turning on its facts. Instead, it "signalled an end to the old categorical approach to the admission of hearsay evidence. Hearsay evidence is now admissible on a principled basis, the governing principles being the reliability of the evidence and its necessity."
24. *Smith* (1992) 75 CCC (3d) 257. Smith was accused of the murder of Ms King. Evidence of two telephone calls made by the deceased to her mother were admissible to prove that she wanted to return home but not to prove that she had been abandoned by the accused.

[24.11] Furthermore, the English Court of Appeal has had difficulty following the rule in *Myers*. In *R v Shone*,[25] the accused was charged with the theft of certain vehicle springs. It was held that evidence could be given of the absence of any entries on a stock record card for the springs. If the springs had been sold or used, there would have been an entry stating this. As there was none, the prosecution used this absence to prove that the springs were stolen. In *R v Muir*[26] the accused was charged with the theft of a video recorder. His defence was that it had been repossessed. The prosecution called the manager of the video hiring company to give evidence to state that there was no documentary evidence of this at his head office. The manager knew this because he had telephoned the office and asked for the information. This was held admissible even though it involved a form of 'double hearsay'. The records at head office would have been hearsay under *Myers* and as the manager never looked at them but only rang up and asked about them.

[24.12] It is open to the Irish courts to create new exceptions to the rule against hearsay evidence. However, even if this is done, computer records may not be sufficiently reliable to be admissible. The question of how reliable computer records must be in order to be admitted is dealt with below.

THE CRIMINAL EVIDENCE ACT 1992

[24.13] The Criminal Evidence Act 1992 regulates the admissibility of business and computerised records into evidence.

Definitions

[24.14] 'Document' is defined as including a map, plan, graph, drawing or photograph, or a reproduction in a permanent legible form, by a computer or other means (including enlarging) of information in non-legible form.[27] Information in a non-legible form is defined as including information on microfilm, microfiche, magnetic tape or disk. Information is defined as any representation of fact, whether in words or otherwise.[28]

[25.] (1983) 76 Cr App R 72 (CA).
[26.] (1984) 79 Cr App R 153 (CA).
[27.] Section 2.
[28.] Section 2.

[24.15] 'Business' is defined as including:

> any trade, profession or other occupation carried on, for reward or otherwise, whether within or outside the State and includes also the performance of functions by or on behalf of -
>
> (a)   any person or body remunerated or financed wholly or partly out moneys provided by the Oireachtas;
>
> (b)   any institution of the European Communities;
>
> (c)   any national or local authority in a jurisdiction outside the State; or
>
> (d)   any international organisation.[29]

The Admissibility of Evidence

[24.16] Section 5(1) of the Criminal Evidence Act 1992 provides that:

> information contained in a document shall be admissible in any criminal proceedings as evidence of any fact therein of which direct oral evidence would be admissible if the information -
>
> (a)   was compiled in the ordinary course of a business,
>
> (b)   was supplied by a person (whether or not he so compiled it and is identifiable) who had, or may reasonably be supposed to have had, personal knowledge of the matters dealt with, and
>
> (c)   in the case of information in non-legible form that has been reproduced in permanent legible form, was reproduced in the course of the normal operation of the reproduction system concerned.

This subsection will apply whether or not the information was supplied directly or indirectly but if it was supplied indirectly, only if each person (whether or not he is identifiable) through whom it was supplied received it in the ordinary course of a business.[30]

[24.17] Section 5(1) does not apply to information that is privileged from disclosure in criminal proceedings or information supplied by a person who could not be compelled to give evidence at the instance of the party wishing to give the information in evidence. Documents containing information compiled for the purposes or in contemplation of any criminal investigation, investigations or inquiries carried out pursuant to or under any enactment, cannot be produced in court pursuant to s 5(1). Neither can documents containing information complied for the purposes or in contemplation of civil or criminal proceedings or proceedings of a disciplinary nature.[31]

[29.]   Section 4.
[30.]   Section 5(2).
[31.]   Section 5(3).

[24.18] However, where the document concerned is a deposition made on oath in the District Court by a person who is alleged to have committed an offence and who is ordinarily resident abroad, or where s 14 of the Criminal Procedure Act 1967 (which deals with the taking of depositions) could not be invoked or where the accused has died or has fled the jurisdiction, then documents compiled in the course of an investigation or other proceeding may be produced in court.[32] Where the document containing the information is a map, plan, drawing or photograph (including any explanatory material in or accompanying the document concerned), a record of a direction given by a member of the Garda Síochána pursuant to any enactment, a record of the receipt, handling, transmission, examination or analysis of any thing by any person acting on behalf of any party to the proceedings or a record by a registered medical practitioner of an examination of a living or dead person, then it will be admissible under s 5(1) regardless of whether it was compiled in the course of an investigation or other court proceeding.[33]

[24.19] Where the document contains information which the average person would not understand without explanation, then an explanation will be admissible if it is given in court, orally, by a competent person or it is contained in a document which is signed by such a competent person.[34]

Evidence of Admissibility

[24.20] Where a document is given in evidence by any party to criminal proceedings, then a certificate may also be given in evidence. This certificate must be signed by a person who occupies a management position in the business which compiled the information or else must be signed by a person who is competent to give the requisite information. If the certificate is given, it will be evidence of any matter stated or specified within it. The certificate must contain the following:

(1) a statement that the information was compiled in the ordinary course of business;

(2) a statement that the information is not privileged or given by a person who would not be compellable to give evidence;

(3) a statement that the information was not compiled for any investigation or other proceeding, or if it was compiled in such circumstances, which exception applies to it;[35]

[32.] Section 5(4)(a).
[33.] Section 5(4)(b).
[34.] Section 5(6).
[35.] See s 5(3)(c) and s 5(4).

(4) a statement that the information was supplied, either directly or indirectly through intermediaries (who received the information in the ordinary course of a specified business), by a person who had or may reasonably be supposed to have had, personal knowledge of the matters dealt with in the information;[36]

(5) where the information has been printed out, then it should be stated that this was done in the course of the normal operation of a specified system;

(6) if appropriate, it should state that the person who supplied the information cannot reasonably be expected to have any recollection of the contents of the information having regard to the lapse of time since the information was compiled or any other specified circumstance;

(7) unless there is a date on the information then a statement should be included of when the information was compiled; and

(8) a statement of any other matter which is relevant to the admissibility in evidence of the information.[37]

The requirement that the supplier of information have a personal knowledge of the information contained in the document has led to problems in the UK. In *R v Pettigrew*,[38] the defendant was accused of stealing bank notes. A computer print-out from the Bank of England was used to prove that the notes in the defendant's possession had previously been in the possession of the victim of the theft. The Court of Appeal ruled that the print-out was inadmissible as an exception to the hearsay rule under the Criminal Evidence Act 1965 because for the record to be admissible, it must derive from a person who had personal knowledge of the matter. As no human had any knowledge of the numbers of the notes, the print-out could not be admitted into court.[39]

[24.21] The Irish Act states that it is sufficient that any statement be made to the best of the knowledge and belief of the person stating it.[40] If a statement

---

[36.] If the intermediaries can be identified, then they must be specified in the certificate.

[37.] Section 6(1).

[38.] (1980) 71 Cr App R 39.

[39.] This decision was criticised at the time because the evidence should have been admissible as real evidence. The confusion arose because the computer had a dual purpose. It performed an automated task, that of sorting bank notes and the evidence derived from this task would have been admissible as real evidence. However, it also had a recording function of recording the numbers of the bank notes which it sorted. It was this record which was sought to be admitted as hearsay.

[40.] Section 6(2).

is made in the certificate which the author knows to be false or does not believe to be true, then he will be guilty of an offence and liable to a fine not exceeding £500 or imprisonment for a term not exceeding six months on summary conviction. On conviction on indictment, the author may be liable to a fine or imprisonment for a term not exceeding two years or both.[41]

[24.22] It is not compulsory to give a certificate, but if one were not given, then the appropriate manager or other person would have to give evidence in person. Even if a certificate is given, the court may require oral evidence to be given of any matter stated in the certificate, where an objection has been made to the admissibility of the evidence or in any other case.[42]

Notice of Documentary Evidence

[24.23] If it is proposed to admit information contained in a document into court, then a copy of the document and the certificate (if appropriate) must be served on the accused.[43] Where any party to the proceedings wishes to tender the information contained in the document in evidence, then a copy of the document and a copy of the certificate must be served on every other party to the proceedings not later than 21 days before the commencement of the trial. If this is not done, then the information contained in the document will not be admissible without the leave of the court.[44] Once the document has been served on a party to the proceedings, that party may not object to the admissibility of that document without the leave of the court unless a notice has been served on the other parties to the proceedings objecting to the admission of the document not later than seven days before the commencement of the trial.[45]

[24.24] Service may be effected on any party to proceedings: by delivering the material to him; by addressing it to him and leaving it at his usual or last known residence or place of a business or by addressing it to his solicitor's office; by sending it by registered post to him at his usual or last known residence or place of business or to his solicitor's office; or in the case of a body corporate, by delivering it to the secretary or clerk of the body at its registered or principal office or sending it by registered post to the secretary or clerk of that body at that office.[46] If an accused person is not represented by a solicitor, notice must be served on him in person.[47]

[41.] Section 6(4).
[42.] Section 6(3).
[43.] This service must be made pursuant to s 6(1) of the Criminal Procedure Act 1967.
[44.] Section 7(1).
[45.] Section 7(2).
[46.] Section 7(3).
[47.] Section 7(4)

Weight of Documentary Evidence

[24.25] The admission of evidence contained in a document is totally at the discretion of the court. Information contained in a document will not be admitted if the court is of the opinion that in the interests of justice the information ought not to be admitted.[48] In considering whether to admit evidence, the court must have regard to all the circumstances including:

(1) whether or not having regard to the contents and source of the information and the circumstances in which it was compiled, it is reasonable to infer that the information is reliable;

(2) whether or not, having regard to the nature and source of the document containing the information and to any other circumstances that appear to the court to be relevant, it is reasonable to assume that the document is authentic; and

(3) any risk that the admission or exclusion of the information will be unfair to the accused, particularly if the supplier of the information does not attend the court to give oral evidence.[49]

In weighing the evidence, the court must have regard to all the circumstances from which the accuracy of the document may be reasonably inferred.[50] Where computers are used to store records or databases, they are probably as reliable as other forms of record keeping. Although there is a danger that files may become damaged, it may be easier to recover lost information from such a system. Computer systems can also offer more complete files than other systems, as all files on a computer system may be interlinked. Records on a computer may become unreliable in different ways. First, there may be errors in entering the data into the computer system. Secondly, the data may become corrupted or damaged while stored in the computer system. Finally, a third party may remove or alter the data.

[24.26] In *R v Sinha*,[51] the defendant, a doctor, was convicted of perverting the course of justice. A patient had consulted him, complaining of palpitations and the defendant prescribed a course of beta blockers without ascertaining from her medical records that she was an asthmatic. It was accepted at the trial that it is dangerous to prescribe beta blockers to asthmatics. On the following day, the patient took one of the beta blockers and later died as a result of an acute asthma attack. The defendant admitted that on three occasions, following the patient's death, he had altered her

---

48. Section 8(1)
49. Section 8(2).
50. Section 8(3).
51. [1995] Crim LR 68.

computerised therapy records which had previously contained four separate references to her asthmatic condition. The coroner requested that the senior partner at the defendant's practice supply him with the patient's records. The senior partner could not find the written records, so he sent the computerised version which included the alterations. A later analysis revealed that the records had been altered and the defendant was sentenced to six months imprisonment. Although most programs have a function which allows them to delete files, this process does not mean that the files are actually destroyed. All that occurs is that the computer will 'flag' the deleted files so that it can write other files on top of the deleted files. This means that an expert can recover deleted files from a computer.

The Reliability of Computer Information

[24.27] The assessment of the reliability of information contained in a computer has given rise to a considerable amount of caselaw in the UK.[52] This is a result of s 69 of the Police and Criminal Evidence Act 1984 which provides that:

> In any proceedings, a statement contained in a document produced by a computer shall not be admissible as evidence of any fact stated therein unless it is shown:
>
> (a) that there are no reasonable grounds for believing that the statement is inaccurate because of improper use of the computer;
>
> (b) that at all material times the computer was operating properly or if not, that any respect in which it was not operating properly or was out of operation was not such as to affect the production of the document or the accuracy of its contents.

This section has caused considerable difficulties in the UK. In *R v Newbury and Teal*,[53] between fifteen and twenty hours of a five week trial were spent satisfying the requirements of s 69. The UK Law Commission has provisionally proposed the abolition of this section without replacement. However, the caselaw on this section gives a useful guide to how the reliability of computer evidence may be ascertained in Ireland.

[24.28] When the defendant in *R v Hilda Shephard*[54] was arrested, her car was found to contain goods from Marks & Spencers which were not packed into the store's bags and for which she had no receipt. A store detective

---

52. See Tapper, 'Reform of the Law of Evidence in Relation to the Output from Computers', International Journal of Law and Information Technology, Vol 3 No 1, 1995, p 79. Ockelton, 'Documentary Hearsay in Criminal Cases' Crim Law Rev, January 1992, p 15.

53. Isleworth Crown Court, 1995, referred to by the Law Commission in its Consultation Paper 'Evidence in Criminal Proceedings' No 138, p 204, 1995,

54. *R v Shephard* [1991] Cr App R 139.

checked the till rolls at the appropriate store for payments matching the goods which were found but found no payments for the goods found in the defendant's car. At trial, the detective gave evidence as to the proper functioning of the cash register. An appeal was taken on the basis that the detective was not qualified to do this. It was held by the Court of Appeal that she was qualified, as she was familiar with the operation of the computer.

[24.29] The court distinguished a previous decision of the Court of Appeal that of *R v Minors and Harper*[55] where the second defendant had been convicted of stealing a stolen transport card. The serial numbers of stolen cards had been entered into a computer and evidence of this was given at the trial by a Revenue Protection Official for London Regional Transport:

> "She was not a computer technologist. She said that she had no reason to doubt the reliability of the London Regional Transport computer and she said that she regularly relied on printouts from it."[56]

The Court of Appeal ruled that her evidence should not have been admitted as she could not from her own knowledge testify as to the reliability of the computer. In *Shephard*, the Court of Appeal stated that the store detective had a greater familiarity with the operation of the computer than the Revenue Protection Official in *R v Minors and Harper*. However, the Court did not offer any test to determine what the appropriate level of familiarity should be before a witness can give evidence. The court stated that the store detective in *Shephard* had the same level of familiarity with the computer system as did the hotel manager in *R v Spiby*.[57] This might suggest that witnesses would need to have a day to day familiarity with the computer system, although they will not need any technical expertise.

[24.30] In *R v Cochrane*[58] a building society incorrectly debited the defendant's account with a sum of money. A number of withdrawals were made in quick succession from his account and the defendant was convicted of theft. He appealed on the basis that the prosecution had not proved that these transactions had actually occurred. The withdrawals were made from automatic teller machines (ATM). These contained computers which were linked to a mainframe computer located elsewhere. None of the witnesses at the trial even knew in which town the mainframe was located and no evidence of its functioning was given. The mainframe had to verify that the card and the personal identification number entered into the ATM were

---

[55.] (1989) 89 Cr App R 102.
[56.] *Ibid*, at 111.
[57.] See para **[24.03]** above.
[58.] [1993] Crim LR 48.

correct. The Court of Appeal ruled that none of the evidence from the ATMs were admissible as evidence and the defendant's conviction was quashed.

[24.31] The appellant in *McKeown v DPP*,[59] was convicted of driving while in excess of the legal alcohol limit. She was tested using an intoximeter, the clock on which was thirteen minutes slow. She appealed on the grounds that as the clock was inaccurate, documents produced by the intoximeter which was a computer, were inadmissible. The prosecution had called a director of the firm which supplied the intoximeter, at the trial to give evidence that the clock had no bearing on the accuracy of the intoximeter. He was not an electronics expert and did not understand the circuitry of the clock. Although the court accepted that the director had the qualifications and experience to give expert evidence, the appellant's conviction was quashed.

[24.32] Section 8(2) of the Irish Criminal Evidence Act 1992 only requires that the Irish courts consider whether or not it is a reasonable inference that the information which is to be admitted is reliable. The court must also decide whether or not the document containing the information is reliable. This is not as strict a standard as that contained in s 69 of the UK Police and Criminal Evidence Act 1984. The Irish courts have more discretion than the UK and it is unlikely that a decision similar to *McKeown* would be made here. The Irish courts would probably apply a standard similar to that applied in *R v Shephard*.

Evidence as to the credibility of supplier of information

[24.33] As it is possible that the supplier of the information may not attend court, the 1992 Act allows the accused to attack the credibility of the supplier as a witness even though he is not present. Any evidence which would have been admissible as relevant to the credibility of the supplier will be admissible where he does not attend court. Evidence which could have been put to the supplier in cross-examination as relevant to his credibility may be given with the leave of the court even though the evidence could not have been adduced by the cross-examining party. Evidence that the supplier has made a statement, whether orally or otherwise, which is inconsistent with the information supplied is admissible for the purpose of showing that he has contradicted himself.[60]

Computer Animated Re-enactments

[24.34] Computer animated re-enactments (CARS) on video or CD-ROM are becoming popular in American courts. Modern software allows

---

[59] [1995] Crim LR 69.
[60] Section 9.

remarkable creation and manipulation of moving images as any large budget Hollywood movie will demonstrate. On a smaller scale this technology may be used to create an animation which depicts events central to a criminal or civil case. The limitations of the technology and cost mean that the depiction will be closer in quality to a cartoon than to a film of live people. Obviously, it is only a matter of time before it is cheap and easy to create images on a computer which are indistinguishable from a film of participants in an event or actors depicting that event. This technology has its advantages. A complex sequence of events may be summarised and clearly described on screen. On the other hand, it is expensive and this may give one side an unfair advantage. A computer animated re-enactment was used *In re Aircrash at Dallas/Fortworth Airport*.[61] That case involved complex and highly technical issues concerning a Delta Airlines crash which killed 137 people. The US government spent over two years preparing a fifty-five minute computer animated re-enactment which depicted the aircraft, a storm cloud and the airport from a number of different angles and at different times. It also gave a view from the cockpit of the plane. The use of the re-enactment was successful.[62]

[24.35] It is unlikely that computer re-enactments will become as popular in the Irish courts as they have in the American courts. This is because in general juries are not generally used for civil cases in Irish courts. Although the English courts appear willing to admit evidence of computer re-enactments they have indicated that limitations will be placed upon their use. Computer re-enactments were used in an English Admiralty case: *The Golden Polydinamos*[63] which concerned a collision between two ships off the entrance to the Panama Canal. The plaintiffs called an expert witness who gave evidence as to the tracks of the two ships by means of a reconstruction created by a computer program called 'Mathman'. The trial judge said of the reconstruction that it was:

> "... of great assistance, although it is I think important to recognise the limitations of any exercise in reconstruction. In particular every reconstruction involves making a number of assumptions of fact."

The plaintiffs were unsuccessful at first instance and appealed. One of their grounds was that they sought to introduce further evidence of reconstructions of the course of the vessels. This was not successful,

---

[61.] 720 F Supp 1258 (ND Tex 1989), *affirmed,* 919 F 2d 1079 (5th Circuit 1991), *Cert denied* 112 S Ct 276 (1991).

[62.] Simmons and Lounsbery, 'Demonstrative Evidence', Trial, September, 1994.

[63.] (1995) 1 Lloyds Law Reports 589 quoted by Glidwell LJ at 592. The initial judgment is reported at (1993) 2 Lloyds Law Reports 464.

however, the Court of Appeal referred approvingly to the use of the computer program and stated:

> "We would not wish to discourage the use of a program like Mathman which is obviously capable of saving the effort of a good deal of manual calculation. But we think that a party who proposes to use such a program should disclose it at an early stage, so that the experts on both sides can have the opportunity to agree on its validity or to formulate any criticisms. It should then be possible for both sides to check the consequences of the assumptions for which they are contending against the results produced by the program. The Judge too, if he is considering a finding which neither side has supported in full, may also wish to have the opportunity to check it against the program."[64]

[24.36] The Court of Appeal suggested that full disclosure of a program be made. This disclosure would appear to go beyond merely announcing the intention to use a specified program. The side seeking to use the program must allow the other side to test the program against their assumptions. Presumably, if they find that the program exhibits a bias or does not reflect their view of events they may object to the use of the program. How far they must go is unclear. In non-contentious cases it may be sufficient to allow the other side see the program and how it works. In other cases it may be necessary to reveal the models and concepts which underlie the workings of the program. If one party to a case intends to use such a presentation, other parties should not be complacent. Whilst a computer cannot be inherently biased, its programmer can.

[24.37] It is unclear how the Irish courts would react to the use of such re-enactments. In legal terms, the re-enactments are hearsay. To create the re-enactment a computer animator will have to be given an account of the events to be depicted which he will then interpret this information by programming a computer. The computer software and hardware will impose their own constraints and these will inevitably affect the animators interpretations of the event. Furthermore, the animator may rely on several different accounts of the events. It would have to be shown that the probative value of introducing a re-enactment is greater than its prejudicial effect. Evidence on video is admissible under the Criminal Evidence Act 1992, where evidence may also be given through an intermediary. This evidence is only admissible in cases involving sexual or violent offences.[65] It is difficult to see how its admission would have been allowed without statutory intervention.

---

64. At 596.
65. Part III.

INSPECTION AND DISCOVERY OF COMPUTER DATA

[24.38] Commercial firms and financial institutions now hold much, if not all, of their records on computers or in other electronic storage devices. In litigation proceedings it is not uncommon for one party to wish to obtain access to the records of another. This is usually done in the case of paper records by means of an application for an order for discovery of documents. Computerised records have caused some confusion in this regard. The contents of a computer may be regarded as documents and so suitable material for an order of discovery, a computer may be regarded as an object, the contents of which need to be examined by means of an order of inspection.

[24.39] In view of the Supreme Court decision in *McCarthy v O'Flynn*[66] where the Court considered that X-ray photographs were documents for the purposes of discovery under Order 31 r 12 of the Rules of the Superior Courts,[67] it is hard to believe that the Irish courts would have any difficulty in ordering the discovery of documents held on a computer.

[24.40] The examination of computerised data was the subject of *Dun & Bradstreet v Typesetting Facilities*[68] which concerned a computerised database. The plaintiffs wished to examine the database held by the defendants which they alleged had been copied from theirs. The plaintiffs brought a motion for inspection, which is limited to physical things. Harman J stated that although he could make an order which would allow one to look at the hard disk or floppy disks which contained the database, this would be a "fairly useless sort of order to make". The examination of the contents of the computer was not inspection of a chattel but disclosure of its contents. He felt that the contents of the disks were analogous to a document. In this case the appropriate order was held to be one of discovery.[69]

[24.41] In *C v PBP*[70] the court held that what was important was the information to be disclosed and not the form in which it was held. The court found that it was able to deal with lacuna in the Rules of the Superior Courts which had arisen because the rules had not anticipated modern computer technology. In that case it was alleged by the plaintiff that the defendant had copied information from the plaintiff's computer database into its own. The plaintiff applied for disclosure of the defendant's computer files containing information relating to the identity, requirements and purchases of the

---

66. [1979] IR 127.
67. See para **[18.11]** *et seq.*
68. [1992] FSR 320.
69. RSC Order 31, r 12.

defendant's potential and actual customers so that they might be inspected by an independent expert in information technology (with suitable safeguards to protect confidentiality) for the purposes of comparing them with the plaintiff's database to see if there had been copying. The defendant objected on the basis that the database was not property (so it could not be the subject of an order for inspection) nor was it a document (so it could not be discovered). The court held that computer files and the information they contain were relevant documents so they could be discovered or alternatively they were property that could be inspected. The issue was not what the information was but whether it had been copied. The court stated that it would be strange if the court had an inherent power to order disclosure by way of an Anton Piller order but not on the hearing of an interlocutory summons seeking this relief.

[24.42] The difficulty with allowing discovery of the contents of a database or a computer hard disk is that applicant may not be willing merely to receive the documents which the defendant downloads from the hard disk. It is easy to alter documents held on computer. However, traces of these alterations may remain and so the applicant may wish to receive the entirety of the contents of a computer. Of course, this means that considerable information may be made available, much of which may not be relevant or may be privileged. This question was examined in *Derby & Co Ltd v Weldon*.[71] The defendants applied for discovery of a computerised database held by the plaintiff which contained details of various transactions which were the subject of the litigation. Vinelott J held that a computer database which forms part of the business records of a company is, in so far as it contains information capable of being retrieved and converted into readable form, a 'document' for purposes of the making discovery. However, the

---

[70.] The English High Court, unrep, 31 October 1995, Lee J Current Law Digest December 1995, 448. Some right holders may go to extraordinary lengths in order to gather evidence about copying as is illustrated by the facts which led to litigation in *Filmlab Systems International Ltd & anor v Pennington & Others* [1994] 4 All ER 673. The first named defendant was employed by the plaintiff, he was suspected of setting up a company which was to compete with his employers. In a discussion with the first named defendant, one of the directors of the plaintiff company learned that the hard drive on the plaintiff's computer had been faulty and had been replaced, he also learnt the name of the service company which had carried out this work. The plaintiff subsequently bought the faulty disk from the service company and sent it to another company which specialised in the recovery of data from faulty disks. As a result of the analysis of the data, the plaintiff came to the conclusion that the defendant was infringing the copyright in their software and that the source code used by the defendants in their competing products would contain substantial sections copied from the plaintiff's works.

[71.] [1991] 2 All ER 901.

party seeking discovery is not entitled to unrestricted access to the database and the court will only permit discovery in the light of expert evidence as to the extent to which the relevant information was available on line or from back-up systems. The court allowed the defendants to access the database subject to agreement or expert evidence as to what information was or could be made available, to what extent inspection was necessary and whether the provision of print-outs would be sufficient.[72]

ANTON PILLER ORDERS

[24.43] It is relatively easy to alter records, programs or data held on a computer or other electronic storage device. Although such an action may sometimes be detectable, often no traces will be left. This may be contrasted with evidence written or printed on paper where any alterations will leave marks or other signs. It is essential that an aggrieved party obtain access to all the available evidence as soon as possible. In *Ibcos Computers v Barclays Mercantile Highland Finance Ltd*,[73] the plaintiffs obtained an *ex parte* order, sometimes called a 'door step' Anton Piller order which requires the defendant to deliver up all relevant material. This type of order is appropriate where it is desirable that the evidence be frozen and there is a real danger that without the order it may disappear or be modified. More extensive orders may be made which require the defendant to allow the plaintiff to enter his premises, inspect documents or other articles and remove any which belong to the plaintiff. These latter are particularly effective in intellectual property cases. The Anton Piller order[74] is usually granted *ex parte* and the proceedings are held *in camera* to prevent the defendant getting a warning of the order and destroying incriminating material. The order will not allow the plaintiff to enter the defendant's premises but it does require that the defendant let the plaintiff in. If the defendant does not do so or tries to hinder the plaintiff this will amount to a contempt of court. An Anton Piller order was granted in *Orion Pictures Corporation v Patrick Hickey (t/a Ace Video Club)*.[75] Representatives of the plaintiff sought to enforce the order but the defendant assaulted one of the representatives and tried to frustrate the operation of the order. As a result, the defendant was sentenced to one month in jail for contempt of court.

[72.] In general, printouts will not be sufficient as a computer hard disk and floppy disks may contain evidence or attempts to alter or erase evidence. See *R v Sinha* [1995] Crim LR 68.

[73.] [1994] FSR 275.

[74.] *Anton Piller KG v Manufacturing Processes Ltd* [1976] 1 All ER 779.

[75.] High Court, unrep, 18 January 1991, Costello J.

[24.44] In order to get an Anton Piller order the plaintiff must establish three things. First, he must have an extremely strong case. Secondly, he must show actual or potential damage of a serious nature and finally, he must have clear evidence that the defendant is in possession of incriminating evidence and that there is a real danger of its destruction before a normal application such as discovery could be made. Denning MR suggested that the inspection should not do any real harm to the defendant or his case. The order should not be used as a fishing expedition.[76] These principles were upheld by the House of Lords in *Rank Films v Video Information*.[77] However, the Court also held that the defendant could rely on the privilege against self-incrimination and so refuse to comply with the order.

[24.45] In *Dun & Bradstreet Ltd v Typesetting Facilities Ltd*[78] once the plaintiffs suspected that their database had been copied, they brought a motion before Ferris J who accepted an undertaking from the defendants that they would make a copy of the data contained in any file, in any computer in the custody or in control of that defendant and any floppy disk or other means of storing computer characters in its possession, being data to which the defendant had unrestricted access, excluding certain specific data. The defendants further undertook to deliver that copy to their own solicitors within ten days and not to delete data to be copied from those sources or to amend it. The defendant's solicitors undertook to retain the copy in safe custody and not to permit any access to it. The purpose of this undertaking was to preserve the status quo of the computer records until the full hearing of the motion. The necessity for measures as extreme as these is illustrated by the case of *MS Associates v Power*[79] where the plaintiffs had entered into negotiations with the defendant as they were interested in buying his program. When the plaintiffs inspected the program, they found very great similarities between their own program and that of the defendant. The plaintiffs successfully applied for an interim injunction. On their application for an interlocutory injunction, one of the crucial witnesses for the plaintiff was forced to change his affidavit as he realised that some of his statements in his initial affidavit were inaccurate. The changes resulted from a second inspection of the defendant's program following the *ex parte* injunction. At the second inspection some of the similarities between the programs seen at the first inspection were no longer present, at least in the copy of the program which they were allowed to inspect. The defendant's evidence was

---

76. *High Track v Conveyers* [1983] 1 WLR 44.
77. [1982] AC 380.
78. [1992] FSR 320.
79. [1988] FSR 246.

that no alterations had been made so as to exclude certain similarities which had been seen initially. Falconer J stated that this was a question that might have to be gone into and resolved at the full trial of the action.

[24.46] In *Alliance and Leicester Building Society v Ghahremani*[80] the court made an order of discovery allowing the plaintiffs to inspect and retrieve information contained on a computer in a solicitor's office. The action concerned an allegation of mortgage fraud. Once the order was made the plaintiff's solicitor went to the office and a Mr Chopra accessed various files on the computer. One contained a two page document, the first page of which detailed a £6,000,000 transaction and the second referred to various disbursements. Later the same day the plaintiff's solicitor returned with a computer expert. When he accessed the same document the first page was missing. The computer's directory showed that the file had been saved at a time when it was proven that Mr Chopra was operating the computer. It was contended that there had been no breach of the order as the order applied to documents which did not include information stored on a computer. However, Hoffman J applied *Derby v Weldon*[81] to the effect that the order for discovery did apply to the contents of the computer. As a result, Mr Chopra, who was himself a solicitor, was committed for contempt of court and fined £1,000.

Confidential Information

[24.47] If an action is based on a claim that one party has copied or plagiarised another's program, then the case will turn on how similar the parties' respective programs are. This can only be done by examining each party's source code for comparison.[82] The party which is alleging plagiarism will have to get a copy of the defendant's code. One way of doing this is to decompile a copy of the defendant's program, however, this may involve breaching the defendant's copyright. It is preferable to apply to court for an order allowing the examination of the appropriate codes. However, examining the codes in such detail may involve the revelation of other commercially sensitive or secret information. One solution is to have the court order that the codes be examined by a third party who will be required by the court to keep any information he may receive secret. This may not necessarily be acceptable to the courts. In *Atari v Philips*,[83] the plaintiff

---

[80.] The Times Law Reports, 19 March 1992.

[81.] [1991] 2 All ER 901.

[82.] See para **[3.16]** *et seq*. Source code is a computer program in its original form which can be read and understood by humans. Most programs sold commercially are only sold in object code form which, realistically, can only be understood by computers.

[83.] [1988] FSR 416.

alleged that the defendant had copied its 'pac-man' computer game in order to produce a game called 'munchkin'. The 'munchkin' game had been created by a Mr Averett and the defendant wished to have him examine the source codes of the 'pac-man' program. The plaintiff instead suggested that the examination be carried out by an independent expert. This latter suggestion was not taken up by the court. Whitford J made an order requiring that a copy of the source code be delivered to the defendant's solicitors who would have to make undertakings as to its safe keeping. He was of the view that Mr Averett should be able to inspect them. Although he understood the plaintiff's hesitation at allowing this, since they were alleging that Mr Averett was the man responsible for the copying, he pointed out that it was they who had decided to bring proceedings. The courts might be more amenable to the suggestion that an agreed independent third party alone inspect confidential documents, if it were the plaintiff who sought the examination, in order to protect the position of the defendant. However, employing expert witnesses in this way is close to allowing them to decide substantive matters of fact and not just to give their expert opinions.

[24.48] Parties may wish to keep certain information secret for reasons other than commerce. Copying may be an offence under the Copyright Act 1963 and other offences may be revealed. In *Process Development v Hogg*,[84] the plaintiff alleged that the defendant had stolen confidential information and physical parts from it in order to manufacture his own products. The plaintiff had got an *Anton Piller* order against the defendant and wished to report to the police admissions made by the defendant and recorded in the supervising solicitor's report, as well as property recovered from his house. The Court of Appeal held that the ordinary rule of discovery that documents disclosed in litigation may not be used for any other purpose without leave of the court did not apply as what was in issue was not the defendant's own property but rather goods alleged to have been stolen from the plaintiff. The disclosure of this information to the police would not be a breach of the rule that a person may not be required to testify against himself. Although there was no reason why the disclosure to the police should not be made, it was on the whole undesirable to allow disclosure of the supervising solicitor's report unless some obviously useful purpose was served by it. The Court of Appeal therefore allowed all material to be disclosed to the police except the report of the supervising solicitor.

---

[84] [1996] FSR 45.

EVIDENCE ON AFFIDAVIT FROM OUTSIDE THE STATE

[24.49] It may be necessary to acquire evidence from outside the State, particularly in cases of software or other piracy where the owner of copyright may reside outside the State. In *Roche v District Judge Martin and the DPP*,[85] Roche was convicted of ten offences of 'video piracy' under s 27 of the Copyright Act 1963. Roche sought judicial review of his conviction on the grounds, *inter alia,* that there was no evidence that any person owned the copyright in the works which had been copied and that there was no evidence that the copyright owner had not consented to the copying of the work. It was accepted in the High Court that the alleged owners of the work, 20th Century Fox Film Corporation, had not given any evidence in the District Court. However, a representative of the Irish National Federation Against Copyright Theft gave evidence as to why he believed the videos were copies. The High Court refused to overturn the finding of fact by the District Judge that copying had occurred, particularly, as there was no stenographer's record of the evidence given in the District Court.

[24.50] As the conviction had been challenged by way of judicial review, the court would have found it very difficult to overturn the decision of the District Judge because of insufficient evidence. If this case had been appealed to the Circuit Court then the lack of evidence of ownership might well have been fatal to the prosecution. Obviously, to fly representatives of American film companies or software companies to attend the District Court in Ireland would be prohibitively expensive. Therefore, where it is necessary to get such evidence, affidavits may be procured.

[24.51] The requirements for evidence given on affidavit, under Order 39, rule 1 of the Rules of the Superior Courts was examined in *Phonographic Performances (Ireland) Ltd v William Cody and Princes Investments Ltd*.[86] The plaintiffs, collectors of performance fees for record companies, alleged that the defendants were playing music in their nightclub without paying fees. In their defence, the defendants put in issue the question of whether or not the plaintiffs were the owners of copyright or the exclusive licensees. The plaintiffs argued that "tens of thousands of new sound recordings affected by their licence schemes are made each year and issued to the public and that proof of these matters in every case by oral evidence is wholly impractical".[87] They wrote to the defendants indicating that they would prove these matters by affidavits from the relevant persons. The defendants

---

[85.] [1993] ILRM 651.
[86.] [1994] 2 ILRM 241.
[87.] *Ibid,* at 249.

refused to agree to this. The plaintiffs then brought a notice of motion applying, *inter alia,* for an order pursuant to Order 39 rule 1. Keane J held that the order was discretionary and it could only be made where sufficient reason was shown and where justice required that it should be made.

He stated that the requirements for making such an order were:

1. The facts sought to be proved do not relate to issues significantly in dispute between the parties;

2. The court is not satisfied that the other party *bona fide* requires the production of the deponent for cross-examination;

3. The difficulty or expense of producing the deponent in court is such that there is a serious risk of injustice to the party seeking to adduce the evidence on affidavit;

4. The application is made as a preliminary application before the trial of the action.

In this case Keane J held that the plaintiffs had fulfilled the requirements and made the order. If such an order is not made then it may be necessary to receive evidence on commission.[88]

EXPERT WITNESSES

[24.52] Irish courts are increasingly reliant on the evidence of expert witnesses[89] and the categories of expert evidence which can be admitted are ever expanding. The English Court of Appeal has recently ruled that evidence of facial mapping by video superimposition can be given and supplemented by expert evidence.[90] In cases such as road traffic accidents, this does not pose any particular problem for the court because judges, lawyers and litigants are usually able to understand and interpret evidence relating to physical injuries and the location of an accident. In a case concerning the copying of software or damaging data, the evidence may be complex and difficult to understand. The modern computer industry only dates back a little over 15 years to the first sale of the IBM PC.[91] As a result, their workings are unfamiliar to many people involved in the courts. This means that judges, lawyers and litigants will have to rely on experts to analyse and explain complex technology. Unlike a personal injury action, they will not be able to apply their own experience and knowledge to assess

---

88. RSC, Order 39, r 4.
89. For a detailed examination of expert witnesses, see Kelleher, 'Expert Evidence in Ireland', ILT, February 1996, p 42.
90. *R v Clarke*, (1995) 2 Cr App R 425.
91. Others might take their starting point as the sale of the first Apple computer in the 1970s.

the value and accuracy of the evidence given by this witness. This problem might be solved by appointing an expert as a judge in a particular case. However, it is not possible to empanel twelve computer experts on a jury for criminal trials. As knowledge of information technology becomes more common this will cease to be such a problem.

[24.53] If litigation concerns technology as complex as that of computers, it is essential that experts should try to be as objective as possible. This is not always attained. In *News Datacom v Lyons*,[92] it was alleged that the defendant had infringed the plaintiff's copyright. The plaintiff's claim rested on its assertion that to produce the goods sold by the defendant (decoder cards for satellite dishes) the defendant must have infringed its copyright. However, Flood J described the evidence of the plaintiff's computer expert as partisan and noted that the plaintiff had offered no scientific basis for this claim. Furthermore, one of the affidavits supporting the plaintiff's claim was that of a computer scientist and software engineer who contradicted the claim of his own side. This illustrates the pressures to which expert witnesses may be subject. Although, an expert witness is expected to give his honest opinion to the court, the side which employs and pays him will anticipate that his evidence will be favourable to it.

Admissibility

[24.54] The judge in an individual case must decide whether an individual's credentials entitle him to give evidence as an expert.[93] There is no guarantee that the courts will be consistent in this regard. Where a case involves medical evidence it is relatively easy to assess the expertise of a particular witness as doctors must pass various examinations which determine their status. This is not possible in information technology, where there are no formal, recognised professional standards. Some highly capable computer professionals may never have gone to university, others such as Bill Gates, the founder of Microsoft, may have dropped out. If an expert's credentials are to be questioned, it should be done in the absence of the jury.[94] The English Court of Appeal has held that if there is no need for expert evidence the court should have but does not have the power to limit the number of experts or prevent such evidence being called.[95]

---

92. [1994] 1 ILRM 450.
93. *R v Silverlock* [1894] 2 QB 766 and also see *Archbold*, (Sweet & Maxwell, 1995) Vol 1, pp 1500-1506, and *Phipson on Evidence,* 14th ed, (Sweet & Maxwell, 1990) pp 804-842, for a full review of the English law in this area.
94. *R v Deakin, The Times,* 3 May 1994.
95. *Rawlinson v Westbrook, The Times,* 25 January 1995.

[24.55] An individual judge has a wide discretion in deciding as to the reliability of an expert's opinion. In *R v Robb*[96] expert evidence of voice identification was admitted at trial. The technique used by the prosecution expert was considered unreliable by the majority of professionals if used alone. The defendant did not call evidence to rebut the expert evidence. Instead the defence counsel sought to demonstrate in cross-examination that the evidence was unsound. The defendant was convicted and an appeal was taken. The Court of Appeal held that while the expert's view was that of a minority, he had good reasons for holding to it. On the facts of the case, the expert could not be shown to be wrong and his evidence was rightly admitted.

Duties

[24.56] The duties and responsibilities of an expert witness were recently considered by Cresswell J in *The Ikarian Reefer*:[97]

(1) The expert's evidence should be, and should be seen to be, the independent product of the expert uninfluenced as to form or content by the exigencies of litigation;

(2) The witness should provide expert, unbiased opinion in relation to matters within his expertise and should never assume the role of advocate;

(3) An expert should state the facts or assumptions upon which his opinion is based. He should not omit to consider material facts which detract from his concluded opinion. In the Irish case of *Flanagan v UCD*[98] the applicant was accused of plagiarism and was brought before a disciplinary committee. An outside expert was appointed by the committee to examine the applicant's work and to decide whether the applicant had engaged in plagiarism. His report was duly submitted and sent to the applicant. It suggested that the applicant had in fact plagiarised the work of others. A second paragraph, suggesting that this was an aberration and that the applicant should be allowed to re-sit her exams was deleted. The applicant applied to the High Court and on this and other grounds was successful in obtaining an injunction quashing the decision of the disciplinary committee;

[96.] 93 Cr App R 161.
[97.] *National Justice Compania Naviera SA v Prudential Assurance Co. Ltd* [1993] 2 Lloyd's Rep 68.
[98.] [1988] IR 724.

(4) The expert should make it clear when a question falls outside his own expertise;

(5) If the expert has insufficient data, his opinion should state if it is provisional only, or subject to any qualification;

(6) If, after exchange of reports, the expert changes his view, this should be communicated to the other side and the court without delay; and

(7) Where the expert evidence refers to photographs, plans, calculations, analyses, measurements, survey reports or other similar documents, these must be provided to the other party at the same time as reports are exchanged.

The status of expert evidence

[24.57] The expert witness should only give an unbiased opinion. The judge or the jury must ultimately decide what the facts in a particular case are. To give an expert opinion without offering any scientific basis may not be sufficient. In *News Datacom v Lyons,* the plaintiff relied solely on the opinion of its experts, it could have carried out scientific tests to prove the claim, but did not. As a result, Flood J clearly felt the assertions of the plaintiff's expert witness lacked weight.

[24.58] In *DPP v Kehoe*[99] the accused was charged with murder, to which he had confessed. His only defence was one of provocation. To buttress this defence the accused called a psychiatrist, who was not called to establish insanity or any other form of mental illness or derangement but only to give evidence on what effect jealousy would have on the accused and the plausibility of the defence put forward. The jury convicted the accused and the case was taken to the Court of Criminal Appeal on the basis that the trial judge was 'scathing' in relation to the evidence of the psychiatrist. The appeal was rejected by the Court of Criminal Appeal which stated that the defence should have been considered by the jury without interference from the psychiatrist.

[24.59] In a case of copyright infringement, where one party is alleging that another party has copied its computer program, expert witnesses might be called to establish points of similarity between the two programs. However, they should not attempt to establish a causal connection between the two programs (unless they have a particular knowledge of the facts in the case). Nor should they try to establish that there is a substantial similarity between

---

[99.] Court of Criminal Appeal, unrep, 6 November 1991, O'Flaherty J delivering judgment.

the programs taken as a whole. These are questions which must be ultimately decided by the trial judge.

[24.60] The case of *Aro Road and Land Vehicles Limited v Insurance Corporation of Ireland*[100] concerned a contract for insurance. The managing director of the plaintiff company, the insured, had failed to inform the defendant that in 1962 he had been convicted of receiving stolen motor parts and had been sentenced to 21 months imprisonment. In the High Court, Carroll J considered that the conviction could not be material to the plaintiff's claim. An underwriter gave evidence on behalf of the defendant that the opposite was in fact the case. Carroll J felt compelled to concur with his view once she was satisfied that he was a reasonable and prudent underwriter, even though it was at variance with her own. The Supreme Court held that she was incorrect to do so, as trial judge she herself was "the sole and final arbiter". However, in cases involving advanced and complex technology, judicial reliance on expert testimony will be considerable if not total. The extent of judicial reliance on expert evidence in computer cases was summed up by Jacob J in *Ibcos Computers Ltd v Barclays Finance Ltd*[101] where he stated:

> "In a computer program case ... the court cannot so readily assess the question of substantial part unaided by expert evidence. I believe I should therefore be largely guided by such evidence."

Differences of opinion

[24.61] Experts may often give evidence in court which directly contradicts the evidence of other experts, invariably those engaged by the opposing side. In the case of *Best v Welcome*[102] it was alleged on behalf of the plaintiff that he had been seriously injured as a result of a vaccination against whooping cough. There was a considerable difference of opinion between the plaintiff's expert witnesses and those of the defendant as to the link between the potency and the toxicity of the vaccine. In the Supreme Court Finlay CJ stated:

> "It is not possible either for a judge of trial or for an appellate court to take upon itself the role of a determining scientific authority resolving disputes between distinguished scientists in any particular line of technical expertise. The function which a court must perform in the trial of a case in order to achieve a just result is to apply common sense and a careful

---

[100.] [1986] 1 IR 403.
[101.] [1994] FSR 275.
[102.] [1993] 3 IR 421.

understanding of the logic and likelihood of events to conflicting opinions and conflicting theories concerning a matter of this kind."

The court should consider all the expert evidence available to it. In *Kelly v St Laurence's Hospital*[103] the trial judge repeated the expert evidence called by the plaintiff in his summing up but failed to mention that called by the defendant. The Supreme Court held that he should have done so.

Facts upon which the expert bases his opinion

[24.62] In a criminal trial the prosecution must make exhibits available for examination by the defence experts. This is one of the reasons why it is so hard to bring computer crime cases before the courts. If an institution wishes to show that an individual has overcome its security, then it will have to reveal intimate details of that security to the defence. Obviously, it will fear that this information may be abused. In *Murphy v DPP*[104] the accused was charged with various offences relating to the driving of a motor vehicle. The accused's lawyers informed the gardaí at an early stage that they wished to have the vehicle forensically examined. Subsequently, a fingerprint expert was retained to examine the car. However, by then the vehicle had been disposed of and the examination was impossible. The conduct amounted to a breach of fair procedures and the applicant was granted an injunction preventing the DPP from bringing charges relating to the driving of the car.

Bias

[24.63] In *Ibcos Computers v Barclays*,[105] Jacob J could not understand how the experts employed by the defendant failed to see that certain resemblances were 'overwhelming indicia of copying'. In the USA, 'hired gun' expert witnesses are common and frequent use of partisan and biased evidence is bringing the court process into disrepute. One American study found that 57% of judges questioned felt that expert witnesses were 'hired guns' who would give biased testimony and 79% of them felt that expert witnesses could not be relied upon to be impartial.[106] An examination of claims for compensation against the Workers' Compensation Board of New York found that while 99.5% of doctors consulted by claimants found that the claimant was suffering a disability, only 24% of doctors used by insurance companies made a similar finding. In only 0.5% of cases did the doctor consulted by the claimant find no evidence of disability, while 75% of

---

[103.] [1988] IR 402.

[104.] [1989] ILRM 71.

[105.] [1994] FSR 275.

[106.] Shuman, Whitaker, Champagne, 'An Empirical Examination of the Use of Expert Witnesses in the Courts', Jurimetrics Journal, Vol 34, Winter 1994, p 193.

insurance company doctors stated there was no evidence of disability.[107] In one UK case three forensic scientists used by the prosecution saw their role as being one of helping the police. They suppressed evidence which could have proved the defendant's innocence. The Court of Appeal held that where an expert has carried out tests which tend to disprove or cast doubts upon the opinion which he is expressing, the party calling him must also disclose the results of such tests. The English courts now accept the existence of biased experts as a matter of reality. If a defendant wishes to adjourn a case to allow him seek expert evidence, his application cannot be rejected on the basis that the prosecution expert is neutral.[108] As a result of the dangers of biased evidence, the current system of all parties to a case being able to call their own expert witnesses has been criticised. Instead, it has been suggested that the courts should appoint a single 'independent' expert to deliberate upon the evidence and give his own expert conclusions to the court. Unfortunately, there is no guarantee that allowing a judge to appoint a single expert will necessarily ensure that the expert is any more independent than those who are appointed by the parties. It has been pointed out that judges will most likely appoint experts whose views and prejudices are similar to their own, thus reducing the independence of that evidence.[109]

---

[107] Haddad, 'Analysis of 2932 Workers' Compensation back injury cases', Spine, Vol 12(8), p 765, (1987).

[108] *R v Sunderland Justices, ex parte Dryden, The Times*, 18 May 1994.

[109] Katz, 'The Fallacy of the Impartial Expert, Revisited', Bulletin of the American Academy of Psychiatry and Law, Vol 20, No 2, 1992, p 141 at 143.

Chapter 25

Control of Content on the Internet

INTRODUCTION

[25.01] Freedom of expression is protected by Article 40.6.1°(i) which states:

> The State guarantees liberty for the exercise, subject to public order and morality, of ...
> The right of the citizens to express freely their convictions and opinions.

This right is limited as the State must ensure that the organs of public opinion such as radio, the press and the cinema may not be used to undermine public order, morality or the authority of the State. Furthermore, the publication or utterance of blasphemous, seditious or indecent matter is an offence. This means that the right of freedom of expression is an equivocal right and this uncertainty is increased by the fact that the extent of the right has never been fully defined.

[25.02] The Irish State has sought to control public expression in a number of ways. In general, this control has been exerted over two types of publication. First, publications which are associated with subversive activities may be restricted by the Offences Against the State Act 1939. This Act prohibits the publication of treasonable or seditious material. Secondly, indecent or obscene activities are subject to the Censorship of Publications Acts 1929-1967 and the Censorship of Films Acts 1923-1992. Controlling expression is easy so long as that expression can only be made public through the medium of books, film, or the press. The Censorship of Publications Act 1946 requires the Censorship of Publications Board to examine every book which is referred to them by customs officers or in respect of which a complaint is made.[1] The Censorship of Films Act prohibits the showing of any films in Ireland which have not been certified by the Censor as being fit for public exhibition.[2] The European Union has also tried to exert some control over the content of television broadcasts.[3]

---

1. Censorship of Publications Act 1946 , s 6.
2. Censorship of Films Act, s 5.
3. The Council Directive on the Co-Ordination of Certain Provisions Laid Down By Law, Regulation or Administrative Action in Member States Concerning the Pursuit of Television Broadcasting Activities: OJ L 298, 17/10/89 p 23.

The Directive on the regulation of television requires Member States to ensure that television programs do not seriously impair the physical, mental or moral development of children and in particular to avoid programs that involve pornography or gratuitous violence.[4] The distribution of these types of materials is easily controlled and so enforcing the legislation has not been difficult. This legislation may be ill-suited to dealing with the modern problem of computer pornography.

PORNOGRAPHY ON THE INTERNET

[25.03] The Internet allows anyone to express their opinions in a wide variety of fora. The rapid dissemination of information and opinions which is facilitated by such networks makes traditional control of these activities impossible. For example, details of a pre-trial hearing of Rosemary West were available in the UK over the Internet although any newspaper which published them would have been in contempt of court.[5] Pornographic material is available to users of the Internet and this causes concern particularly as it may be accessed by children. One survey found nearly one million sexually explicit computer files. It is impossible to monitor every electronic message or file transmitted into Ireland. Child pornography is a particularly serious problem. Images can be downloaded from the Internet, printed out and sold. Such activity has been reported in Dublin and Belfast.[6] A Bill to deal with pornography on the Internet (and elsewhere) was introduced in the Dáil in late 1996. The Child Pornography Bill 1996 will make it an offence to take, distribute, show, possess or advertise indecent photographs of a child. 'Photograph' is widely defined as including "data stored on a computer disk by other electronic means which is capable of conversion into a photograph", the definition will also encompass images made using computer graphics which appear to be photographs. The Bill provides for a defence that they had not seen the indecent photographs and did not know or suspect that they were indecent. It appears, at the time of writing, that this bill will not proceed and that instead amendments will be introduced to the Childrens Bill 1996 to deal with the problem of child pornography. All manifestations of pornography whether on the Internet, in films, videos, photographs, written or sound recordings will be subject to the

---

4. Article 22.
5. Arthur, New Scientist, 11 March 1995.
6. *The Irish Times*, 17 May 1996. Where pornography is printed out and sold on the streets it might be prosecuted under s 72 of the Towns Improvement Act 1854. This makes it an offence to publicly offer for sale an profane, indecent or obscene book, paper, print, drawing, painting or representation. However, the penalty on conviction is a fine not exceeding 40 shillings.

Bill. The production, printing, publishing, exporting, importing, selling or distributing of child pornography will also be an offence and maximum sentences will range from three years to life.[7]

The Video Recordings Act 1989

[25.04] The Video Recordings Act 1989 regulates the sale and distribution of videos in Ireland. In essence, the Act makes it an offence to supply videos unless the Official Censor of Films has certified that they are suitable for viewing. However, the definition of video in the Act is sufficiently broad to allow for the interpretation that it also applies to computer disks. A video recording is defined as "any disk or magnetic tape containing information by the use of which the whole or a part of a video work may be produced". A video work is defined as:

> any series of visual images (whether with or without sound) -
>
> (a) produced, whether electronically or by other means, by the use of information contained on any disk or magnetic tape, and
>
> (b) shown as a moving picture.[8]

The possibility that the Video Recordings Act 1989 may be used to combat computer pornography is increased as a result of the English High Court decision in *Meechie v Multi-Media Marketing*.[9] The respondents organised a club which supplied pornographic material on computer disks. The applicants were trading standards officers who had recovered 23 such disks from the respondents. The respondents were prosecuted under the UK Video Recordings Act 1984 which contains provisions similar to those found in the Irish Act[10]

[25.05] At first instance it had been concluded that the images created by the disks were not 'moving pictures' within the definition of video works. This was decided because while it was clear that the visual image was produced electronically from information contained on a disk, the image was only

---

7. *The Irish Times,* 12 February 1997.
8. Video Recordings Act 1989, s 1(1).
9. *The Times* 9 May 1995.
10. Section 1(2) of the UK Video Recordings Act 1984 provides:
    Video work means any series of visual images (with or without sound)
    (a) produced electronically by the use of information contained on any disk or magnetic tape, and
    (b) shown as a moving picture.
    Section 1(3) defines Video Recording as "any disk or magnetic tape containing information by the use of which the whole or part of a video work may be produced".

produced for a short time (thirty seconds). On appeal it was held that this decision was erroneous and that the UK Act did apply to these computer disks. It may be concluded that if computer pornography is supplied on disk, then the supplier may be prosecuted under the Video Recordings Act 1989. If this decision is applied in Ireland it means that every CD-ROM and computer disk which contains a moving image must be submitted to the Official Censor of Films. The decision does not mean that there is a law which can deal effectively with the problem of computer pornography. To come within the provisions of the Act, an image must be moving, so still pictures will be outside the scope of the Act. It is also probable that many suppliers of the pornography would be outside the jurisdiction of the State. The Act is only effective against suppliers and not the individuals who receive pornography, which would reduce its effectiveness unless it was held that a provider of Internet access was held to be the supplier for the purposes of the Act. It is a defence to charges under the Act to claim that the accused reasonably believed that the works concerned did not infringe the Act.[11] Internet providers might be able to use this as a defence. To hold otherwise would put an impossible burden on Internet providers as it would force them to control what their subscribers were accessing over the Internet or close down.

[25.06] The Official Censor of Films must supply a certificate declaring that a video is fit for viewing unless the viewing of it, in his opinion, would be likely to cause persons to commit crimes, either by incitement or by suggesting methods of doing so, would be likely to stir up hatred against a group of persons in the State or elsewhere on account of their race, colour, religion, nationality, ethnic or national origins, membership of the travelling community or sexual orientation; or would tend to deprave or corrupt persons who might view obscene or indecent material included in the video. The Censor may also refuse a certificate if the video depicts acts of gross violence or cruelty towards humans or animals.[12] There are a number of types of works which are exempted from the Act such as recordings which are not supplied for reward.[13] Any person who supplies or offers to supply a video recording which does not have a certificate will be guilty of an offence.[14] Possession of a video without a certificate with intent to supply is also an offence.[15] If the Censor has viewed a video and decides that the work is unfit for viewing, he may make a prohibition order[16] which will make the

---

11. Video Recordings Act 1989, s 5 & 6.
12. Video Recordings Act 1989, s 3(1).
13. Video Recordings Act 1989, s 2(1)(a).
14. Video Recordings Act 1989, s 5.
15. Video Recordings Act 1989, s 6.

supply[17] or possession with intent to supply of such a video an offence.[18] It is an offence to allow the viewing of a prohibited video or one which does not have a certificate in a private dwelling, for reward or before others.[19] The importation of prohibited videos is banned[20] and customs officials may refer any video to the Censor for examination.[21] The Censor must retain a register of certificates[22] and of prohibited videos.[23] Warrants for the search of premises and for the seizure of videos may be granted by the District Court or a Peace Commissioner[24] and the gardaí have a power of arrest.[25] If a person is convicted of an offence under the Act, any infringing videos may be forfeited or destroyed.[26]

The Post Office (Amendment) Act 1951

[25.07] The sending of obscene messages using the telephone system is made a criminal offence by s 13 of the Post Office (Amendment) Act 1951, as amended by s 8(1) of the Postal and Telecommunications Act 1951, which provides that any person who:

(a) sends by means of the telecommunications system operated by Bord Telecom Eireann, any message or other matter which is grossly offensive or of an indecent, obscene or menacing character, whether addressed to an operator or any other person, or,

(b) sends by those means, for the purpose of causing annoyance, inconvenience or needless anxiety to another, a message which he knows to be false or persistently makes use of those means for that purpose, shall be guilty of an offence.

Unfortunately, the effect of this section is limited by the requirement that the message be sent using the telecommunications system operated by Telecom Eireann. Sending offensive messages on a private network or on systems run by competitors to Telecom Eireann is not an offence. Although there is no definition given of what constitutes a 'message' there is no reason to believe that e-mail would not be included within this definition. Under s 13(2) an offence will be prosecuted under the terms of the Post Office Act 1908. On

---

16. Video Recordings Act 1989, s 7.
17. Video Recordings Act 1989, s 8.
18. Video Recordings Act 1989, s 9.
19. Video Recordings Act 1989, s 11.
20. Video Recordings Act 1989, s 16.
21. Video Recordings Act 1989, s 17.
22. Video Recordings Act 1989, s 14.
23. Video Recordings Act 1989, s 15.
24. Video Recordings Act 1989, s 25.
25. Video Recordings Act 1989, s 26.
26. Video Recordings Act 1989, s 28.

summary conviction a penalty of a fine not exceeding £800 or imprisonment not exceeding twelve months or both may be imposed. On conviction upon indictment, a fine not exceeding £50,000 or at the discretion of the court, a term of imprisonment not exceeding five years or both may be imposed. On conviction on indictment for this offence, the court may also order the forfeiture of any apparatus, equipment or other thing used to commit the offence.[27] Summary offences may be prosecuted by Telecom Éireann.[28]

The Common Law

[25.08] The common law offers a more flexible method of prosecuting obscenity. It is an indictable offence at common law to publish obscene matter. Section 13 of the Defamation Act 1961 makes it an offence to publish an 'obscene libel'. There is no statutory definition of what constitutes obscenity, however, the common law test is:

> "whether the tendency of the matter charged as obscene was to deprave or corrupt those whose minds are open to such immoral influences and into whose hands a publication of this sort may fall".[29]

Prosecutions at common law for obscenity are rare. A notorious Irish example is *The Attorney General v Simpson*[30] which concerned a play entitled 'The Rose Tattoo' by Tennessee Williams. It was alleged that this play was obscene because of undue dwelling on matrimony and sex. However, the District Justice held that the play did not tend to corrupt or deprave and that no jury would reasonably convict on the charges and so charges were dismissed against the defendant. Extending such venerable law to the Internet may be difficult.[31] The possession of obscene material is not an offence, only publication, which may be difficult to prove. In particular, does placing pornography on a bulletin board amount to publication? This gives rise to problems akin to those encountered in suing for breach of copyright on the Internet.[32] Problems with jurisdiction may also occur. If an Irishman sends pornography to a Dutch bulletin board, does the publication

---

27. Postal and Telecommunications Services Act 1983, s 4.
28. Postal and Telecommunications Services Act 1983, s 5(5).
29. *R v Hicklin* (1868) LR 3 QB 360.
30. (1959) 93 ILTR 33.
31. However the willingness of the courts to combat pornography should not be underestimated. In an English case *R v Fellowes and Arnold,* High Court, unrep, 2 April 1996, the Crown Court had little difficulty in extending the definition of 'copy of a photograph' in the English Protection of Children Act 1978, to include copies of photographs which are saved on a computer disk: see Manchester, 'More about Computer Pornography', (1996) Crim LR 645.
32. See para **[25.32]** below.

take place when it is sent or when it arrives? This last question is important as an item which is unlawful in Ireland may be lawful in Holland.[33]

[25.09] The first defendant in *R v Fellows & Arnold*[34] was an employee of Birmingham University. He used his employer's computer to store data which enabled it to display indecent pictures of children on a computer screen and to produce print-outs. The data was created by scanning a photograph to create a digital image which was then transmitted to the Birmingham computer. It was accepted by the Court that there was no difference between the screen image, a computer print-out and the original photograph, except that the digitised image had a reference number superimposed on it. Fellows accumulated an archive over twelve months, which consisted of about 11,650 pictures stored in numerous sub-directories. One of these directories entitled 'Young/Minors' contained 1,875 pictures depicting various sexual acts or poses. There were also hundreds of pornographic photographs which had been obtained from computer bulletin boards in Denmark and the USA. Fellows made the pictures available on the Internet, he established a password system so that it could only be accessed by those who were vouched for by existing users or those who were willing to augment his archive. The second named defendant, Arnold, was responsible for transmitting data relating to 20-30 photographs to the first appellant.

[25.10] The defendants were convicted of offences under the Protection of Children Act 1978 and the Obscene Publications Acts 1958 & 1964, and they appealed to the Court of Appeal. The UK Obscene Publications Acts make it an offence to publish an obscene article.[35] The definition of 'article' in s 1 of the Obscene Publications Act 1959 states that it means:

> ... any description of article containing or embodying matter to be read or looked at or both, any sound record, and any film or other record of a picture or pictures.[36]

The definition of 'publish' sets out as follows:

> ... a person publishes an article who:
>
> (a) distributes, circulates, sells, lets on hire, gives or lends it, or who offers it for sale or for letting on hire; or
>
> (b) in the case of an article containing or embodying matter to be looked at ... shows, plays or projects it.[37]

[33.] See Ch 15.
[34.] *The Times* 3 October 1996.
[35.] Section 2(1).
[36.] Section 1(2).

This was amended by s 9 of the Criminal Justice and Public Order Act 1994 which extends the definition of publication to include "or where the matter is stored electronically, transmits that data". The Court of Appeal found that the offending 'article' was the computer disk. Counsel for Fellows argued that 'publication' required some active conduct and that providing access to a computer was passive conduct only. This was rejected by the Court. It also rejected the submission that the data on the disk was not 'shown, played or projected' to those who accessed the computer, as it found that this was within the ordinary meaning of these words. The defendants submitted that the Obscene Publications Act 1957 did not apply to them since the Parliament of the day would hardly have anticipated the development of computers and computer pornography and that as such their actions were outside the scope of this legislation. This was rejected by the Court of Appeal.

[25.11] The majority of the deliberations of the Court focused on the application of the UK Protection of Children Act 1978. Section 1 of this Act provides that:

> It is an offence for a person:
>
> (a) to take or permit to be taken any indecent photograph of a child (meaning a person under the age of 16) or;
>
> (b) to have in his possession such indecent photographs, with a view to their being distributed or shown by himself or another.

Under s 1(2) a person would be regarded as distributing an indecent photograph if he "parts with possession of it to, or exposes or offers it for acquisition by another person". 'Indecent photograph' is defined as including "an indecent film, a copy of an indecent photograph comprised in a film".[38] Section 84 of the UK Criminal Justice and Public Order Act 1994 inserts the term 'pseudo-photographs' after the word 'photograph' where it occurs in the Protection of Children Act 1978. A 'pseudo-photograph' is defined as meaning an "image whether made by computer-graphics or otherwise howsoever which appears to be a photograph".[39] References to photographs are redefined as including "the negative as well as the positive version; and data stored on a computer disk or by other electronic means which is capable of conversion into a photograph".[40] The Court of Appeal had to decide whether the disk which contained Fellow's archive was an

---

[37.] Section 1(3).
[38.] UK Protection of Children Act 1978, s 7(2).
[39.] UK Criminal Justice and Public Order Act 1994, s 84(7).
[40.] UK Criminal Justice and Public Order Act 1994, 84(3)(b).

indecent photograph. It found that the disk did not come within the dictionary definition of photograph as that required "a picture or other image obtained by the chemical action of light or other radiation on specially sensitised material such as film or glass"[41] as there was no picture or image on or in the disk which could be seen. However, the Court was willing to find that the disk was a copy of a photograph and so the legislation applied to the defendants.

[25.12] The UK legislation which applies to computer pornography is far from perfect. In particular, it may be difficult to apply the concept of 'possession' to a situation where images are stored on a network. Here the images will not be in the physical possession of one person, rather they will be stored on computers controlled by the network.[42] Whether possession could be inferred from the knowledge of a password or other means of accessing such data is unclear. For this reason, any pornography legislation will have to focus on the distribution and sale of such material. The main effect of these convictions may simply be to ensure that such archives are held in more welcoming or less vigilant jurisdictions in future.

Conspiracy to Corrupt Public Morals

[25.13] Another venerable common law offence which may prove useful in prosecuting the modern problem of computer pornography is the offence of conspiracy to corrupt public morals.[43] The difficulty with this offence is that if it is not an offence to publish or distribute computer pornography then how can a conspiracy to do so be an offence? This question was addressed in *AG (SPUC) v Open Door Counselling*[44] where the defendants were involved in the referral of women to the UK for abortions. The plaintiff objected to this on the basis of the Eighth Amendment to the Constitution which outlawed abortion. Although abortion is legal in the UK (in certain circumstances) Hamilton P held that the supply of information could be an offence. He cited with approval the decision of the House of Lords in *Knuller (Publishing, Printing & Promotions) Ltd & Ors v DPP*.[45] In that case the defendants had published a magazine which contained

---

41. No reference given in the text of the judgment but this definition corresponds to that given in the *Concise Oxford Dictionary*, 8th edition.
42. This fact should encourage network controllers, at least in the UK, to keep their networks free of pornography.
43. In *AG (SPUC) v Open Door Counselling* [1988] IR 593 Hamilton P accepted the decision of the House of Lords in *Knuller v DPP* [1973] AC 45 that "conspiracy to corrupt public morals is a common law misdemeanour and is indictable at common law" at p 611.
44. [1988] IR 593.
45. [1973] AC 435.

advertisements inviting readers to meet others in order to engage in homosexual acts which were legal in the UK. The House of Lords held that they were convicted of conspiring to corrupt public morals. Reid LJ stated that "there is a material difference between merely exempting certain conduct from criminal penalties and making it lawful in the full sense, prostitution and gaming are examples of this".[46] Hamilton P noted that the defendants were reputable organisations providing needed services to women. He stated that a finding that such activities or conduct is liable to corrupt public morals is one not to be reached lightly. He quoted with approval Simon LJ:

> "The words 'corrupt public morals' suggest conduct which a jury might find to be destructive of the very fabric of society."[47]

In *AG (SPUC) v Open Door Counselling* Hamilton P was unwilling to find that the defendants were engaged in a criminal conspiracy to corrupt public morals as this was a question which should be left to the jury in a criminal trial. It is quite possible therefore that a jury would find that a conspiracy to supply pornography would amount to a conspiracy to corrupt public morals.

Outraging Public Decency

[25.14] Distributing or publishing pornography may also amount to outraging public decency. In *DPP v Knuller* a majority of the House of Lords[48] held that there is an offence of outraging public decency and therefore also an offence of conspiring to outrage public decency. Public decency may be outraged in a number of ways, for example by indecent exposure,[49] indecent words[50] or exhibiting pictures.[51] The act must be committed in public[52] this means that:

> "The substantive offence (and therefore the conduct the subject of the conspiracy) must be committed in public, in the sense that the circumstances must be such that the alleged outrageously indecent matter could have been seen by more than one person, even though in fact no more than one did see it. If it is capable of being seen by one person only, no offence is committed."[53]

---

46. *Ibid* at 457.
47. Page 491 of *Knuller,* quoted at p 613 of *AG (SPUC) v Open Door Counselling.*
48. Diplock LJ and Reid LJ dissenting.
49. *R v Runden* (1809) 2 Comp 89.
50. *R v Saunders* (1875) 1 QBD 75.
51. *R v Grey* (1864) 4 F & F 73.
52. *R v Mayling* (1963) 2 QB 717; [1963] 1 All ER 687.
53. *Per* Simon LJ in *DPP v Knuller* at 494.

[25.15] A bulletin board or other site on the Internet would probably come within this definition, as it makes material available to the public. The fact that passwords or other systems may limit access to a sub-section of the public would appear to be irrelevant. The fact that material is only available to those who have a computer, a modem, access to the Internet and know where to look, would not be an defence. In *DPP v Knuller* Morris LJ found that the fact that indecent material was available only between the innocuous covers of a magazine was not defence.[54] Since an offence will not be committed when one person only can view it, holding material in private collections will not be an offence. The offence appears to be flexible enough to extend to modern technology such as computer systems. In dealing with the question of whether the offence could be committed by publication in a book or newspaper, Simon LJ held that although the authorities cited before the House of Lords showed no such application of the offence to publication in a magazine this did not mean that the offence could not be applied "provided there are circumstances which are fairly within the rule".[55] However he noted that:

> "It should be emphasised that 'outrage' like 'corrupt' is a very strong word. 'Outraging public decency' goes considerably beyond offending the susceptibilities of, or even shocking resonable people. Moreover the offence is, in my view, concerned with recognised minimum standards of decency, which are likely to vary from time to time ... notwithstanding that 'public' in the offence is used in a locative sense, public decency must be viewed as a whole; and I think the jury should be invited, where appropriate, to remember that they live in a plural society, with a tradition of tolerance towards minorities and that this atmosphere of toleration is itself part of public decency."[56]

The Importation of Pornography

[25.16] The decentralised structure of the Internet makes controlling the content available on it very difficult, if not impossible. The Internet is a global network and this makes it impossible to set a standard which will be acceptable to all. What is acceptable in The Netherlands may be offensive in Ireland. These differing standards may be used by the authorities to their advantage. In one US case, the operators of a bulletin board whose activities might have been acceptable in their home State of California were instead successfully prosecuted in conservative Tennessee for distributing obscene pictures.[57] Another tactic used in the US is to prosecute the distributors of

---

54. *Ibid* at 467.
55. *Ibid* at 494.
56. *Ibid* at 495.
57. *United States v Thomas* No 94-CR-20019 (WD Tenn 28 July 1994).

pornographic materials in several conservative States simultaneously. Although this tactic did not prove popular with the US judiciary, it had the effect of bankrupting the distributors.[58] There are two features of the Internet which make it difficult to prohibit the importation of pornography. First, the Internet in general will not distinguish between countries and locations. Users in any part of the world have access to the same material. This means that countries with a liberal attitude towards pornography will allow domestic suppliers to distribute their wares over the Internet and there is nothing that a more conservative country can do to prevent this distribution. Secondly, even if a prohibition against the importation of pornography is imposed, it will be impossible to police. It is impossible to discern the content of electronic messages without processing. Such a prohibition would necessitate the examination of every electronic message imported into Ireland. This task would be made more difficult by the fact that many such pornographic images are encrypted to avoid detection. Attempting to exert any control in this way would be very costly and have the effect of inhibiting Irish access to the Internet.

[25.17] One of the primary ambitions of the European Union is to create an internal market with a free flow of goods between Member States,[59] this applies to pornography as much as any other goods. Governments within the European Union may find their ability to restrict the importation of pornography from other EU countries limited, at least until the EU decides on a common strategy for dealing with computer pornography. It would appear to be possible for Ireland to restrict the importation of pornography on grounds of public immorality.[60] However, if the Irish Government sought to prohibit or restrict the importation of pornography while not enacting legislation to control or prohibit the manufacture and distribution of such material within Ireland, then its importation restrictions will be prohibited by European law.[61] Attempts to control television broadcasts from other European States on satellite channels have already failed, for example in

---

58. Rose, *Netlaw*, (Addisson-Wellsley, 1995).
59. Article 3 of the Treaty of Rome: "... The activities of the community shall include ... (c) an internal market characterised by the abolition as between Member States of obstacles to the free movement of goods, persons services and capital".
60. *B v Henn & Darby* Case 34/79 [1979] ECB 3796; (1980) 1 CMLB 246. The defendants were convicted of importing a consignment of magazines and pornographic films contrary to s 42 of the Customs Consolidation Act 1876 which provides that the importation of indecent or obscene prints, paintings, photographs, books, cards, lithographic or other engravings or any other indecent or obscene articles may be prohibited and if they are imported they may be forfeited and destroyed. The prohibition was held to be justified by Article 36 of the Treaty of Rome which provides that such restrictions may be justified on grounds of public morality.

Commission v United Kingdom[62] where the European Court of Justice dealt with a complaint that the United Kingdom was attempting to exert control over satellite broadcasts from other Member States contrary to a Council Directive on television broadcasts.[63] The complaint was upheld.[64]

The US Response to Computer Pornography

[25.18] The principal American legislation dealing with computer pornography is the Federal Child Pornography Statute.[65] Under this statute any person who knowingly transports, by any means including by computer, any visual depiction showing a minor engaging in sexually explicit conduct is guilty of an offence. The reception, reproduction or distribution of such pornography is also made an offence.

[25.19] The Communications Decency Act 1996 prohibited the transmission of sexually offensive or indecent material which might be accessible to children on the Internet. This was challenged in the courts in *American Civil Liberties Union v Reno*[66] and was found to infringe the right to freedom of speech protected by the First Amendment of the American Constitution. Section 223(a) of the Act provides that an offence will be committed by any person who:

    (1) in interstate or other foreign communications ...

        (b) by means of a telecommunications device[67] knowingly,

            (i) makes, creates or solicits, and

            (ii) initiates the transmission of, any comment, request, suggestion, proposal, image, or other communication which is obscene or indecent, knowing that the recipient of the communication is under 18 years of age regardless of whether the maker of such communication placed the call or initiated the communication.

[61.] *Conegate v HM Customs and Excise* Case No 121/85 [1986] ECB 1007; (1986) 1 CMLB 739. In that case a similar restriction was not held to be justified as the goods prohibited from importation could be manufactured and distributed within the UK. See generally, Oliver, *Free Movement of Goods in The European Community* (Sweet and Maxwell, 1996).

[62.] Case C-222/94, Judgment of the ECJ 10 September 1996.

[63.] Council Directive 89/552/EEC of 3 October 1989 on the co-ordination of certain provisions laid down by law, regulation or administrative action in Member States concerning the pursuit of television broadcasting activities. OJ 1989 L 298 p 23.

[64.] See also: *Collectieve Antennevoorziening Gouda v Commissariaat voor de Media*, Case C-288/89 (1991) 1 ECR 4007; *Federacion de Distribuidores Cinematagraficos v Spain*, Case C-17/92 (1993) 1 ECR 2239; *TV10 SA v Commissariaat Voor de Media*, Case C-23/93 (1995) CMLR 284.

[65.] 18 USC s 2252 (1991).

[66.] 969 F Supp 824, 64 USLW 2794,

[67.] 'Telecommunications device' is specifically defined not to include "the use of an interactive computer service" which is covered by s 223(d).

(2) knowingly permits any telecommunications facility under his control to be used for any activity prohibited by paragraph (1) with the intent that it be used for such activity.

The second impugned section was s 223(d), referred to as the 'patently offensive' provision, which provided that an offence will be committed by any person who:

(1) in interstate or foreign communications knowingly ...

    (b) uses an interactive computer service to send to a specific person or persons under 18 years of age or

    (c) uses any interactive computer service to display in a manner available to a person under 18 years of age, any comment, request, suggestion, proposal, image or other communication that, in context, depicts or describes, in terms patently offensive as measured by contemporary community standards, sexual or excretory activities or organs, regardless of whether the user of such service placed the call or initiated the communication; or,

(2) knowingly permits any telecommunications facility under such person's control to be used for an activity prohibited by paragraph (1) with the intent that it be used for such activity.

These offences made it a crime to send obscene, indecent or patently offensive material to any person under the age of 18. The Act also provided for several defences. These provided that:

(1) No person shall be held to have violated subsection (a) or (d) of this section solely for providing access or connection to or from a facility, system, or network now under that person's control, including transmission, downloading, intermediate storage, access software, or other related capabilities that are incidental to providing such access or connection that does not include the creation of the content of the communication.

(2) The defences provided by paragraph (1) of this sub-section shall not be applicable to a person who is a conspirator with an entity actively involved in the creation or knowing distribution of communications that violate this section, or who knowingly advertises the availability of such communications.

(3) The defences provided in paragraph (1) of this subsection shall not be applicable to a person who provides access or connection to a facility, system or network engaged in the violation of this section that is owned or controlled by such person.

(4) No employer shall be held liable under this section for the actions of an employer agent unless the employee's or agent's conduct is within the scope of his or her employment or agency and the employer (a) having knowledge of such conduct, authorizes or ratifies such conduct, or (b) recklessly disregards such conduct.

    (5) It is a defence to a prosecution ... that a person:

        (a) has taken in good faith, reasonable, effective, and appropriate actions under the circumstances to restrict or prevent access by minors to a communication specified in such subsections, which may involve any appropriate measures to restrict minors from such communications, including any method which is feasible under available technology; or

        (b) has restricted access to such communication by requiring use of a verified credit card, debit account, adult access code or adult personal identification number.

[25.20] The difficulty for the court in *American Civil Liberties Union v Reno* was that it is impossible on the Internet to ascertain the age of users. An e-mail address will provide no authoritative information about the user as he may use an alias or an anonymous re-mailer. For similar reasons, anyone posting a message to an Internet chat-room cannot be sure that everyone else is an adult. Even if minors could be blocked, it may be impossible to prevent them accessing indecent material without also preventing them from viewing material which is not indecent. Age verification could be introduced but this would be expensive, prone to abuse and difficult to implement. The American government has proposed a 'tagging' system where indecent material would be tagged by inserting a string of characters in the code. This could be recognised by a computer program which if installed would prevent the material being viewed by the user. This was rejected by the parties in *American Civil Liberties Union v Reno* as being impractical. The parties were able to agree on 'parental empowerment' software which allows parents to limit the availability of material on the Internet which parents may consider inappropriate for their children. A program has been launched by the World Wide Web Consortium known as PICS (Program for Internet Content Selection). The object of this program is to develop technical standards that will support parents' ability to filter and screen material that their children will see on the World Wide Web. Some programs are available which endeavour to allow parents block their children's access to sites on the Internet. Cyber Patrol, sorts sites into twelve categories ranging from violence and profanity, to alcohol, beer and wine. Parents may block sites in some or all of these categories. Although parents have some prospect of control, there is no technology in prospect which would realistically allow suppliers to control who accesses their material.[68]

[25.21] The decision is under appeal to the American Supreme Court.[69] Assessing the implications of this judgment for Ireland is difficult. The

---

[68.] *Ibid* p 838-849. See also *The Economist* 18 May 1996.
[69.] 117 S Ct 554; 65 USLW 3414.

Court noted that 40% of the content on the Internet comes from outside the USA.[70] While that proportion is growing, the USA will remain the dominant provider of content for a long time to come. This means that it is America which may ultimately need to set standards of content on the Internet, in the same way as American firms influence technical standards.

DEFAMATION

[25.22] Article 40.3.2° of the Constitution provides:

> The State shall, in particular, by its laws protect as best as it may from unjust attack and, in the case of injustice done, vindicate the life, person, good name ... of every citizen.

This is done by means of the tort of defamation which attempts to balance freedom of expression with every citizen's right to his good name.[71] Defamation is committed when a false statement is wrongfully published about a person and which lowers the standing of that person in the eyes of right thinking members of society. In order for a statement to be published it must be communicated to a third party. This may be by means of newspapers, magazines or television programs amongst others. Posting messages to bulletin boards on the Internet allows statements to be read by large numbers of people, distributed around the world and would amount to publication for the purposes of defamation.[72]

[25.23] Libel is a statement which is published in permanent form such as in a newspaper, whereas slander is a statement which is published in a transient form, such as speech. This distinction is important because libel is actionable *per se,* whereas in an action for slander, the plaintiff must establish that he has suffered special damage. It seems likely that defamatory statements made on the Internet constitute libel since these statements are at least as permanent as radio and television broadcasts, which are treated as publication in permanent form by s 15 of the Defamation Act 1961.

[25.24] In general, the author of a statement will be the primary defendant in an action for defamation. In *Rindos v Hardwick*[73] the plaintiff, who was an

---

70. *Ibid* p 848.
71. See generally McMahon and Binchy, *Irish Law of Torts*, 2nd Ed (Butterworths, 1990) and McDonald, *Irish Law of Defamation*, (Round Hall Press, 1989).
72. In a recent case, the UK supermarket chain ASDA paid several thousand pounds to settle an action brought by a customer who had allegedly been defamed on ASDA's electronic mail system: *The Sunday Times*, 23 April 1995. See also allegations that an Irishman was included on the International Child Molester Database which makes information available about the identities of paedophiles: *The Irish Times*, 9 July 1996.
73. Supreme Court of Western Australia, 31 March 1994.

anthropologist, claimed that he had been defamed in an entry placed on a bulletin board by another anthropologist. He sued successfully, the judge holding that the author of the original defamatory message was liable. This may be more difficult where a statement is published by sending it to a bulletin board or discussion group on the Internet. There are several reasons for this. First, it may be impossible to identify the original author of the statement. Anonymous re-mailers are available which remove anything which might identify the author of a particular statement.[74] Secondly, the person making the defamatory statement may reside in a foreign jurisdiction where defamation laws are different, such as the USA. Finally, they may have insufficient funds to pay any likely award of damages. For all of these reasons, plaintiffs may prefer to sue the operator of the bulletin board or the system on which the defamatory statement was made.

[25.25] The operators of a bulletin board may be analogous to distributors of publications such as newsagents or book shops.[75] Many bulletin boards will receive thousands of messages every day and it is obviously impossible for an operator to monitor the content of each one. In *Cubby Inc v CompuServe Inc*,[76] the defendants, providers of computer services in the USA, administered various special interest fora which comprised electronic bulletin boards, on-line conferences and databases. One such forum also made available a daily computer newsletter called *Rumorville USA* which contained gossip about journalists. The plaintiffs established a database called *Skuttlebut* to carry similar information and to compete for the same market. On several occasions *Rumorville* carried items about the plaintiff, which the plaintiff claimed were defamatory. The plaintiff sued CompuServe which did not dispute the defamatory nature of the statements but rather claimed that it was a distributor and not a publisher of the material and had no reason to know of the statements. The plaintiff's action was dismissed on the basis that CompuServe had no editorial control over the contents of *Rumorville*. This decision has been questioned as CompuServe may have had as long as two days in which to review a publication prior to distribution. Furthermore, the operators usually run a virus detection program and an obscenity program which searches for specific offensive words.[77] However, a program to search for defamatory statements is far beyond the capability of modern technology.

---

74. Arthur, New Scientist, 11 March 1995.
75. *Fitzgibbon v Eason & Son* (1910) 45 ILTR 91.
76. 776 F Supp 135 (SDNY 1991).
77. See Cutrera, 'Computer Networks, Libel and the First Amendment', Computer Law Journal, 1992, p 555.

[25.26] The subsequent case of *Stratton Oakmont Inc v Prodigy Services Company*[78] appears to have widened the scope of liability. The defendant was a bulletin board operator. Defamatory statements were made about the plaintiff on the defendant's bulletin board by an anonymous user. The defendant was held to be responsible for the defamatory statement because they had considerable control over the content of their bulletin boards. They employed personnel to monitor the contents of bulletin boards and to delete unacceptable messages. They also used software to screen out obscenities and other undesirable statements. Although Prodigy pointed out that they received 60,000 messages per day and could not be expected to check all of them, the fact that Prodigy held itself out to be in control of the content of its services was held to be sufficient to make them liable.

[25.27] If cases such as these are brought in Ireland the service provider may try to argue that they are innocent disseminators as opposed to publishers of the work. If the defendant can prove that it was an innocent disseminator then it may escape liability.[79] Innocent disseminators such as newspaper vendors or booksellers will not be found to be publishers if they can show that did not know and were not negligent in failing to know, that a newspaper or book sold by him contained the relevant libel.[80] It is arguable that service providers who receive thousands of messages a day are in this category and not that of publishers.

[25.28] In the USA, the Communications Decency Act 1996 protects service providers such as Prodigy from actions such as this. Section 509 of the Act[81] provides that:

[78.] 23 Media Law Reports 1794, NY Supreme Court 24 May 1995.

[79.] See *FitzGibbon v Eason* 45 ILTR 91; *Ross v Eason* [1911] 2 IR 459; *O'Brien v Eason* 47 ILTR 266; *McDermott v Eanson* 48 ILTR 1; see also *Vizetelly v Mudie's Select Library* [1900] 2 QB 170.

[80.] "As regards a person, who is not the printer or first or main publisher of a work which contains a libel, but has only taken a subordinate part in disseminating it, in considering whether there has been a publication of it by him, the particular circumstances under which he disseminated the work must be considered. If he did it in the ordinary way of his business, the nature of the business and way in which it was conducted must be looked at; and if he succeeds in showing (1) that he was innocent of any knowledge of the libel contained in the work disseminated by him, (2) that there was nothing in the work or the circumstances under which it came to him or was disseminated by him which ought to have led him to suppose that it contained a libel, and (3) that, when the work was disseminated by him, it was not by any negligence on his part that he did not know that it contained the libel, then although the dissemination of the work by him was prima facie publication of it, he may nevertheless, on proof of the before-mentioned facts be held not to have published it." *per* Romer LJ in *Vizetelly v Mudie's Select Library* [1900] 2 QB 170 at 180. Quoted in *Clerk & Lindsell on Torts*, Seventeenth edition, (1995, Sweet & Maxwell) para 21-69.

[81.] 47 USC s 203(c)(1).

no provider or user of an interactive computer service shall be treated as the publisher or speaker of any information provided by another information content provider.

It also provided that no provider of an interactive computer service shall be held liable on account of any voluntary action:

taken in good faith to restrict access to or availability of material that the provider or user considers to be obscene, lewd, lascivious, filthy, excessively violent, harassing or otherwise objectionable.

These sections have not been affected by the decision in *American Civil Liberties Union v Reno*.[82] However it remains to be seen how the American courts will interpret these sections.[83]

Defences

[25.29] There are several defences to a claim of defamation. First, there is justification, which requires the defendant to prove the truth of the statement. Secondly, a defendant may claim that the statement was fair comment on a matter of public interest. To avail of this defence it must be shown that the statement was not an assertion of fact but rather was one of opinion. Thirdly, there is the defence of privilege which may be absolute or qualified. Fourthly, it may be a defence if it can be shown that the plaintiff has consented to the publication of the statement.

[25.30] The defendant may make an apology which will be admissible as evidence in mitigation of damages.[84] The defendant may also make an offer of amends in a case of unintentional defamation.[85]

Vulgar Abuse and 'Flaming'

[25.31] 'Flaming' is abuse contained in e-mail which is often sent in response to real or imagined breaches of on-line etiquette (sometimes referred to as 'netiquette'). Two lawyers from Arizona who decided to advertise their services on the Internet created a program which placed their advertisement on almost every bulletin board connected to the Internet. This incensed other users who responded by sending abusive messages in their thousands to the lawyers. These messages ultimately overloaded their connection to the Internet and they were disconnected from the service.[86] Usually vulgar abuse of this kind will not be actionable.[87] Even if

---

82. 969 F Supp 824; 64 USLW 2794.
83. See Smedinghoff, *Online Law*, Addison Wesley Developers Press, 1996, p 344.
84. Defamation Act 1961, s 17.
85. Defamation Act 1961, s 21.
86. *Time*, 25 July 1994, p 50.
87. See *Crawford v Vance* [1908] 2 IR 521.

defamatory statements are made, if they are only sent to the person who is the subject of the defamation, there may have been no publication and so the statements may not be actionable but the sender of the statement must consider the likelihood of it being read by a third party.

International Jurisdiction

[25.32] Under the Brussels Convention, which is implemented in Ireland by the Jurisdiction of Courts and Enforcement of Judgments (European Communities) Act 1988, the Irish courts have jurisdiction in tort cases provided that the 'harmful event' complained of occurred in Ireland.[88] The application of this to defamation law was examined in *Jay Murray v Times Newspapers Ltd.*[89] The plaintiff claimed damages in the Irish courts for losses suffered by it in the UK as well as Ireland as a result of alleged defamatory statements published by it. Barron J accepted that:

> "before courts of this State have jurisdiction in relation to tort involving a defendant who is not domiciled within this jurisdiction it is necessary to show that the harmful event upon which the cause of action is based occurred within the jurisdiction".[90]

He referred to a decision of the European Court of Justice in *Sheville and others v Presse Alliance SA.*[91] In that case the claim related to an alleged libel published in *France Soir*, copies of which were distributed in the UK. Proceedings were commenced in the UK and the question arose whether the English courts had jurisdiction to deal with the alleged libel.[92] The court held that:

> "On a proper construction of the expression 'place where the harmful event occurred' in Article 5(3) of the Convention, the victim of a libel by a newspaper article distributed in several contracting states may bring an

---

[88.] Article 5(3) of the Convention. See *James Casey v Ingersoll Rand* [1996] 2 ILRM 456. See also *Short & Others v Ireland, the Attorney General and British Nuclear Fuels Ltd (BNFL)* Supreme Court, unrep, 24 October 1996, the plaintiffs all lived in County Louth where they claimed to be suffering damage as a result of the activities of BNFL at Sellafield and its Thorp project in particular. Under Order 11 of the Rules of the Superior Courts they sought and received from Barrington J a High Court order which permitted them to serve BNFL in the UK with a plenary summons. The Supreme Court was willing to accept that the plaintiff might have a cause of action as a result the alleged harmful effect of BNFL's activities in Ireland and not the activities themselves.

[89.] High Court, unrep, 12 December 1995, Barron J.

[90.] Page 5 of the Judgment.

[91.] Judgment given on 7 March 1995.

[92.] See s 4 of The Jurisdiction of Courts and Enforcement of Judgments (European Communities) Act 1988 "Judicial Notice shall be taken of any ruling or decision of or expression of opinion by the European Court on any Question as to the meaning or effect of any provision of the Conventions"

action for damages against the publisher either before the courts of the contracting state of the place where the publisher of the defamatory publication is established which have jurisdiction to award damages for all the harm caused by the defamation or before the courts of each contracting state in which publication was distributed and where the victim claims to have suffered injury to his reputation which have jurisdiction to rule solely in respect of the harm caused in the state of the court seised".[93]

[25.33] If this rule is to be applied to cases of defamation on the Internet (and other such networks), as it would be in the courts of Contracting States to the Brussels Convention, it would mean that if a defamatory statement was published on a UK system or Web site then an action could be brought in the UK. An action could also be brought in Ireland and any other Contracting State to the Brussels Convention if it could be shown that the statement was distributed there, which might prove problematic. Barron J also noted the ECJ's finding that:

> "The criteria for assessing whether the event in question is harmful and the evidence required of the existence and extent of the harm alleged by the victim of the defamation are not governed by the Convention but by the substantive law determined by the national conflict of law rules of the Court seised provided that the effectiveness of the convention is not thereby impaired."[94]

Barron J found that having regard to this decision, the claim to damages arising in the UK was not one which came within Article 5(3) of the Brussels Convention.

[25.34] In tort cases the value of awards notoriously vary from jurisdiction to jurisdiction which may encourage some potential litigants to 'forum shop' for the legal system which offers the greatest potential rewards. Legal rights and standards also vary between jurisdictions, for example, France has extremely strict rules protecting the privacy of individuals. However, it should be recalled that courts and juries are usually dubious about forum shopping, particularly on an international level. If the tort involves a conflict of laws between Ireland and a state outside the Brussels Convention then the question becomes more complex.[95]

---

93. Para 33 of the judgment of the ECJ, quoted on p 6 of the judgment of Barron J.
94. Para 41 of the judgment of the ECJ, quoted on pp 6-7 of the judgment of Barron J.
95. See *James Casey v Ingersoll Rand* [1996] 2 ILRM 456. See also *Short & Others v Ireland, the Attorney General and British Nuclear Fuels Ltd* Supreme Court, unrep, 24 October 1996.

The Right to Information

[25.35] One important aspect of the Internet and other such networks is that they act as immense information retrieval systems. There is much information on the Internet which many people find objectionable such as information on how to make bombs.[96] Governments may at times attempt to restrict access to this information, for example it is an offence for South Koreans to access North Korea's home page on the Internet.[97] The status of the right to information is unclear in Ireland. In *AG (SPUC) v Open Door Counselling*[98] the Supreme Court held that access to information on abortion in the UK could be restricted.[99] What is clear is that the Internet will make it more difficult, if not impossible, to impose such restrictions in the future. The imposition of restrictions on the access to information on the Internet creates a dilemma for governments, restrictions which protect citizens from terrorist information or pornography may appear justified but such restrictions may also have the effect of turning one's country into a boreen running alongside the Information Superhighway. Stringent restrictions are very difficult, if not impossible, to police, they would require the monitoring of every computer connected to the Internet in Ireland and the material downloaded by it. This would make providing access to the Internet prohibitively expensive. Such monitoring would be made even more difficult by the fact that it is now commonplace to encrypt communications on the Internet. Lax restrictions such as restricting access to certain Internet sites may be by-passed and in any event the objectionable information may simply appear elsewhere.

---

96. *Irish Times*, 10 February 1997.
97. *The Economist*, 18 January 1997, p 60.
98. [1988] IR 593.
99. See also *Open Door Counselling and Dublin Well Woman Ltd. v Ireland* Series A, No 246, 1993, 15 EHRR 244 and *AG v X* [1992] 1 IR 1.

Chapter 26

Privacy

INTRODUCTION

[26.01] Personal data is at its most vulnerable when it is being transmitted across networks. The advent of the 'network computer' means that some individual computers will be replaced by machines which are fully integrated into these networks. Digital phone networks record and correlate information about the use of a person's phone such as the destination, time and length of calls. Modern phone systems may be tapped using a minimum of physical equipment. More importantly, it may be possible to access the computers which regulate a telephone network and examine information being transmitted across that network without ever interfering with the phone system. No offence may be committed by doing so, if the perpetrator has a right of access to the computer which is regulating the network. The Internet and other such systems are not necessarily less private than other fora in which to conduct a person's public or private life. The difference is that if someone breaks into a person's home or office and rummages through their letters and records, they will probably notice it very quickly. However, if someone accesses another's computer without authorisation and copies every piece of information on it you may never find out. Computers have the ability to record millions of trivial pieces of information about a person, they also have the ability to analyse that information to give a picture of what that person purchases, who they talk to and any other habits which give rise to an electronic record. Data held on computers is currently regulated by the Data Protection Act 1988. The Act and the Data Protection Directive[1] do attempt to limit the transmission of data across borders but it is questionable whether these provisions are enforceable when huge amounts of data may be transmitted at high speed across long distances for little cost.

[26.02] The Law Reform Commission Consultation Paper on Privacy has suggested that it should be an offence for a person to access data without permission which amounts to making the theft of information a crime.[2] At present, the theft of information is not a crime so long as it is not

---

[1.] OJ L 281, 23/11/95, p 31. See Ch 19-23.
[2.] Para 12.23, p 277.

permanently removed.[3] There are good reasons for distinguishing between the removal of information and the removal, for example, of a television set. It is possible to copy information without damaging the usefulness of the information to the person who owns it. In certain situations the law allows the owner to claim damages where the act of copying has caused him loss such as actions for breach of copyright, infringement of patent rights or for breach of confidence. In general, however, it is possible to copy information while leaving the original intact. If damage is done to the original or it is permanently removed then a criminal offence will be committed. Hence it is not an offence to copy data under the Criminal Damage Act 1991 (although it is an offence to move it) but it is an offence to damage it.[4] In contrast, it is impossible to steal a television set without depriving the owner of it. The Consultation Paper does not offer any persuasive reasons for implementing this change. We are frequently told that we live in an age of information, changes such as this may act to reduce the flow of information to Irish citizens.

[26.03] Any law which is enacted to protect privacy and property on the Internet and other networks will be very difficult to implement and enforce. As a result, the ability to encrypt or encode data will become crucial. Encryption is defined as the conversion of data into code in order to prevent unauthorised access,[5] or in other words a method of protecting privacy. The law may ultimately have to decide that if data is not encrypted or otherwise protected it is obviously not worth that much to the owner and does not require the protection of the criminal law. In the future it may be simpler to criminalise only the accessing of encrypted or otherwise protected data and to treat unprotected data as a form of electronic commonage. The question of how strong encryption should be is also an important question. Encryption programs threaten to make the use of phone-taps irrelevant since they can at present resist all unauthorised efforts to decrypt information encrypted using them. If telecommunications operators are required to provide an encryption service to their subscribers then a debate will begin about how strong that encryption should be.[6] The State will want weak encryption which it can overcome but which will defy casual interceptors of communications. Obviously subscribers will prefer the strongest encryption possible, particularly as it is unlikely to be any more expensive.

[3.] See para **[18.02]**.
[4.] Section 2.
[5.] Collins *Concise English Dictionary*, (8th ed).
[6.] Para 12.30, p 280.

Encryption

[26.04] Some commercially available encryption programs are so secure that they are suitable for use by the military and other users who require extreme levels of security. This has obvious benefits for legitimate users who do not relish the thoughts of strangers reading their electronic mail. However, terrorists and criminals may use encryption to ensure that communications made in the preparation or commission of illegal actions may be kept secret. Encryption may effectively end the usefulness of phone tapping to the authorities.

Public key cryptography

[26.05] A popular encryption system is that of *public key cryptography*. In this system a program is used to generate two paired standard keys (a key is a long string of text). One of these keys is the public key which the user will give to every person with whom the user intends to communicate. The other is a private key which the user then uses to decrypt the messages which are sent to him encrypted by the public key. The private key will only be known to the user. The system also works in reverse. The most popular version of the system is PGP (Pretty Good Privacy).[7] The difficulty with this system is that it is important to be sure of the authenticity of a public key. This problem may be avoided by transmitting the public key through a trusted administrator who can vouch for its authenticity or by handing it over in person. Concerns over the lack of security afforded to messages on the Internet has also led to the redesign of the Internet Protocol (the rules which determine how messages may be sent on the Internet) to make it more secure and ensure that e-mail remains confidential and secure.[8]

Clipper Chip

[26.06] The usefulness of encryption to criminals has caused the US government to ban the export of encryption technology. This was done by classifying this technology as munitions which allowed the US government to control its export. This decision has been heavily criticised on commercial grounds.[9] However, this prohibition has now been made redundant as similar encryption technology has now been developed in Japan, beyond the reach of the American authorities.[10] The US government has also tried to promote

---

[7.] For a discussion of PGP see BYTE, July 1994, p 193.
[8.] See: Stallings, 'Internet Armor', BYTE, December 1996, p 127; and 'The New and Improved Internet Protocol', BYTE, September 1996.
[9.] Evans, 'US Export Control of Encryption Software', NCJ Int'l Law and Communications Reg, Vol 19, 1994, p 469. See also Aley, *Fortune*, 16 May 1994, p 66.
[10.] *The Economist*, 8 June 1996, p 75.

its *Clipper Chip*, an encryption program held on a silicon chip which can be bypassed if necessary by government authorities. This system was also criticised in the USA on the grounds that it would involve excessive cost[11] and would breach privacy.[12] The clipper chip system involves using the chip to encrypt messages. In general these messages would be secure, however, if necessary the authorities could gain access to a special key which would allow them to read all messages encrypted with that individual chip. This special key would be held in two pieces by the US Justice Department and the National Institute of Standards and Technology. Americans never believed that this system would be secure and they also thought that it was aimed at citizens carrying out their normal business as opposed to criminals and terrorists. This is because such people would obviously never use an encryption system to which the US government has access.[13] The development of the Japanese encryption systems has also made the clipper chip redundant. The Irish government does not appear to have any policy on encryption although other European governments such as the French are trying to restrict its use.

Anonymity

[26.07] Many persons who use the Internet do not wish others to know their real names. It is common to use a *handle* or pseudonym to protect one's identity but this is not sufficient for some. Anonymous re-mailers have been developed which receive electronic mail, remove anything which might identify its source and then send it to its ultimate destination. These pose an obvious problem for law enforcement authorities as they may make it impossible to trace the source of a message. Re-mailers have legitimate uses, for example, support groups for victims of abuse may benefit from them, however, fears that they may be abused by criminals may outweigh the possible benefits of these systems.[14]

PRIVACY AND TELECOMMUNICATIONS

[26.08] The right of privacy was first successfully asserted in *Kennedy v Ireland*[15] where the plaintiffs, who were journalists, complained that their

---

11. Wayner, 'Clipped Wings? Encryption chip draws fire', BYTE, July 1994, p 36. See also 'Clipping Clipper's Wings', *Newsweek*, 13 June 1994, p 43.
12. Lennon, 'The Fourth Amendments Prohibition on Encryption Limitations', Albany Law Review, 1994, p 467. Also Freeman, 'When Technology and Privacy Collide', Information Systems Management, Spring 1995, p 43.
13. *The Economist*, 11 June 1994.
14. Arthur, New Scientist, 11 March 1995.
15. [1987] IR 587; [1988] ILRM 472.

telephones had been tapped by the State and sought damages in respect of this breach of their privacy.[16] Hamilton P held that:

> "the right of privacy is one of the fundamental personal rights of the citizen ... it is not an unqualified right ... The nature of the right to privacy must be such as to ensure the dignity and freedom of an individual in the type of society envisaged by the Constitution, namely, a sovereign, independent and democratic society. The dignity and freedom of an individual in a democratic society cannot be ensured if his communications of a private nature, be they written or telephonic are deliberately conscientiously and unjustifiably intruded upon and interfered with. I emphasise the words 'deliberately, consciously and unjustifiably' because an individual must accept the risk of accidental interference with his communications and the fact that in certain circumstances the exigencies of the common good may require and justify such intrusion and interference. No such circumstances exist in this case".

However, the Irish courts appear to have an ambiguous attitude towards privacy. The courts seem willing to enforce a right of privacy where technology is used to breach an individual's privacy as occurred in the *Kennedy* case.[17] This may stem from the surreptitious nature of the surveillance. If a garda had followed Geraldine Kennedy and tried to listen to her conversations, then she would probably have noticed the garda presence and altered her activities accordingly. Phone taps and other technological means of surveillance may not be so obvious. Ireland, as a modern society, places ever increasing reliance on modern

---

16. The right to privacy is explicitly recognised by the European Convention on Human Rights. Article 8(1) of the Convention provides: "Everyone has the right to respect for his private and family life, his home and his correspondence." However the right may be limited under s 8(2) if it is necessary in the interests of "national security, public safety or the economic well being of the country, for the prevention of disorder or crime, for the protection of health or morals, or for the protection of the rights or freedoms of others". The interception of communications and the infringement of privacy was considered by the European Court of Justice in *Malone,* Court Judgment, 2 August 1984, Series A, No 82, 7 EHRR 14; *Klass,* Court Judgment, 6 September 1978, Series A No 28, 2 EHRR 214; *Huvig* 24 April 1990, Series A, No 176-B, 12 EHRR 528; *Kruslin* 24 April 1990, Series A, No 176-B, 12 EHRR 547; and, *Ludi v Switzerland* Court Judgment, 15 June 1992, Series A No 238, 15 EHRR 197.

17. In general invoking the right to privacy in an Irish courtroom is no guarantee of success. The plaintiff succeeded in *McGee v Ireland* [1974] IR 284, but she also invoked the right of the family under Article 41 of the Constitution. The Irish courts failed to hold that the right to privacy had been breached in *Norris v Ireland* [1984] IR 36, *DPP v Kenny* [1992] 2 IR 141 and in *Desmond v Glackin,* High Court, unrep, 25 February 1992. At present the Irish courts clearly do not regard the right to privacy as absolute, the contrasting decisions in *McGee* and *Norris* would appear to suggest that the constitutional protection given to privacy *per se* may be quite weak. The decision in *Kane* would appear to support this view.

telecommunications technology. If the privacy of the users of such technology is subject to arbitrary interference then users may lose confidence in these systems. This is one explanation for the judgment of the Supreme Court in *Kane v The Governor of Mountjoy*[18] where the Supreme Court made it clear that the gardaí could conduct surveillance of an individual which was remarkably intense provided that they could show "a specific adequate justification for it". This decision has its limitations. In particular the *Kane* case was remarkable because of the obtrusive and obvious nature of the surveillance. The applicant was followed by as many as eleven gardaí and three patrol cars,[19] when he entered a solicitor's office gardaí remained on the landing and stairs outside the office.[20] The Supreme Court accepted that "overt surveillance may under certain circumstances be more onerous than covert surveillance"[21] but what caused concern for the Supreme Court in this case was that an individual's reputation and peace of mind could be badly damaged by such surveillance. Whether the Court would have been as concerned if the surveillance had been surreptitious is not clear. The right to privacy is not clearly enunciated by the Constitution and it is difficult to decide what forms of conduct future courts will hold as breaching that right.[22]

The Interception of Telecommunications Messages

[26.09] The interception of telecommunications is prohibited under s 98 of the Postal and Telecommunications Services Act 1983 where interception is defined as the listening to or recording of a telecommunications message.[23] Section 98(1) provides:

> A person who (a) intercepts or attempts to intercept, or (b) authorises, suffers or permits another person to intercept, or (c) does anything that will enable him or another person to intercept, telecommunications being

---

18. [1988] IR 757.
19. *Ibid* p 770.
20. *Ibid* p 765.
21. *Per* Finlay CJ, at p 769.
22. The Law Reform Commission has suggested that the gardaí might have to get ministerial permission before engaging in video surveillance of a person or premises Consultation paper on Privacy. para 10.56-10.66, p 238-242. This would still be a lower standard of protection than that required by the Telecommunications Act 1993 for intercepting telecommunications messages.
23. Intercept is defined as "listen to, or record by any means, in the course of its transmission, a telecommunications message but does not include such listening or recording where either person on whose behalf the message is transmitted or the person intended to receive the message has consented to the recording", Section 9(6) of the Postal and Telecommunications Services Act 1983, as amended by s 13(3) of the Interception of Postal Packets and Telecommunications Act 1993.

transmitted by the company or who discloses the existence, substance or purport of any such message which has been intercepted or uses for any purpose any information obtained from any such message shall be guilty of an offence.

On summary conviction for this offence a penalty of a fine not exceeding £800 or imprisonment not exceeding 12 months or both may be imposed. On conviction upon indictment a fine not exceeding £50,000 or at the discretion of the court a term of imprisonment not exceeding 5 years or both may be imposed. On conviction on indictment for this offence the court may also order the forfeiture of any apparatus, equipment or other thing used to commit the offence.[24] Summary offences may be prosecuted by Telecom Éireann.[25]

[26.10] The section will not apply where the interception is carried out by the gardaí in response to a complaint of offensive phone calls, it is authorised by the Minister for Justice or other lawful authority or it is necessary for the maintenance of the phone system.[26] There is no definition of the term 'telecommunications message', the Law Reform Commission has suggested that the term may not cover all telegraphic messages, such as telegrams although it will cover messages sent by telephone.[27] The provision will cover e-mail and other such communications while they are being transmitted on the Telecom Éireann network. The main defect with this provision is that it only applies to messages transmitted by Telecom Éireann but not when they are being processed by a computer or being transmitted over a private network. Messages transmitted on services provided by companies other than Telecom Éireann are presumably not covered by this provision. Since the supply of telecommunications services by operators other than Telecom Éireann will become common place, this defect will need to remedied soon.[28]

Interception of telecommunications messages by the State

[26.11] As a result of the *Kennedy v Ireland* case, the Interception of Postal Packets and Telecommunications Messages (Regulation) Act 1993 was enacted. Under the 1993 Act the Minister for Justice may authorise the

---

[24.] Postal and Telecommunications Services Act 1983, s 4.

[25.] Section 5(5), *ibid*.

[26.] Section 98(2).

[27.] Law Reform Commission Report on Privacy, 1996, para. 5.64, p 111. The Commission also suggests that the terms 'telecommunications message' and 'postal packet' be replaced by the term 'communication', para 12.18, p 275.

[28.] This has been suggested by the Law Reform Commission Consultation Paper on Privacy, see para 12.8 p 286.

interception of telecommunications messages but only for the purposes of criminal investigation or in the interests of the security of the State. The authorisation must be given by warrant, although if required urgently it may be given orally.[29] The interception of telecommunications will be authorised if the following conditions are satisfied:

(1) Investigations are being carried out by the gardaí or other public authority into a serious offence or to prevent a serious offence.

(2) Investigations not involving interception have failed or are likely to fail to produce information to show whether the offence has been committed or evidence for the purpose of criminal proceedings or to prevent a serious offence.

(3) There is a reasonable prospect that the interception of telecommunications messages would be of material assistance in providing information or evidence for the above purposes.

(4) The importance of obtaining the information or evidence is sufficient to justify the interception having regard to all the circumstances and to the importance of preserving the privacy of telecommunication messages.[30]

A serious offence is an offence for which a person may be punished by imprisonment for a term of five years or more and is an offence that involves loss of human life, serious personal injury or serious loss of or damage to property or a serious risk of any such loss, injury or damage, that results in substantial gain or the facts of which make it an especially serious case. This definition includes an act or an omission done outside the State which would be a serious offence if done within the State.[31]

[26.12] The interception of telecommunication messages may be authorised in the interests of State security in the following circumstances:

(1) There are reasonable grounds for believing that particular activities that are endangering or are likely to endanger State security are being carried on or proposed.

(2) Investigations are being carried out by the person applying for authorisation to ascertain whether these types of activities are being carried on and by whom.

(3) Investigations not involving interception have failed to provide sufficient information.

[29.] Section 2.
[30.] Section 4.
[31.] Section 1.

(4) There is a reasonable prospect that the interception of telecommunications will be of material assistance and the importance of obtaining information is sufficient to justify the interception having regard to all the circumstances and the importance of preserving privacy.[32]

A High Court judge is appointed under the Act to review its application and to report to the Taoiseach.[33] A complaints referee is also appointed under the Act who has the power to investigate complaints relating to the interception of telecommunications messages.[34]

[26.13] Although, the 1988 and 1993 Acts clearly protect voice transmissions over telecommunications networks, it is not explicitly clear that this protection would also apply to transmissions of e-mail and other electronic data over the same or similar networks. The Acts apply to the listening or recording of a telecommunications message which would suggest that they only apply to spoken messages and not messages which contain text. It is possible that a court might extend this protection to e-mail since it would seem anomalous that one set of electronic data which, when processed would become a voice message should be protected while another indistinguishable set of electronic data should not merely because it would become text when it is processed.

THE TORT OF 'BREACH OF PRIVACY'

[26.14] The title of this section is a misnomer as it is clear at this stage that there is no such thing as a tort of breaching another's privacy at common law. However several means have been suggested which might be used to establish this tort. Claims might be made based on the torts of: trespass to land,[35] goods or to the person; private nuisance; defamation,[36] malicious falsehood; passing off; and breach of statutory duty. The use of the equitable doctrine of confidentiality has also been suggested.[37]

[26.15] In the English case of *Kaye v Robertson*[38] an attempt was made to protect the privacy of a popular actor who had suffered extensive head injuries. The defendants were the editor and publisher of the *Sunday Sport*,

---

[32.] Section 5.

[33.] Section 8.

[34.] Section 9.

[35.] See *Bernstein v Skyviews* (1978) 1 QB 479.

[36.] See Law Reform Commission Consultation Paper on Defamation 1991.

[37.] See the Law Reform Commission Consultation Paper on Privacy 1996, Ch 4. See Also McMahon & Binchy *Irish Law of Torts* (2nd ed, 1990).

[38.] [1991] FSR 62.

an English tabloid newspaper. While the plaintiff was recuperating in hospital, journalists from the paper gained access to his room, ignoring notices which prohibited such entry. They interviewed the plaintiff and took photographs of him lying in his hospital bed. The plaintiff sought an injunction to prevent the publication of an article in the *Sunday Sport* based on the interview and containing at least one of the photographs. However he was unable to base his claim on a breach of his right to privacy as "It is well-known that in English law there is no right to privacy, and accordingly there is no right of action for breach of a person's privacy".[39] Therefore the plaintiff was forced to make out his claim on the basis of an action for libel, malicious falsehood, trespass to the person and passing off. All of these claims effectively failed to prevent publication of the article. However the plaintiff did succeed in getting an order preventing the paper from alleging that he had consented to the interview or to the taking of photographs. In spite of the depredations of the English tabloid press the House of Commons has shyed away from strengthening the protection of privacy. This is not to everyone's satisfaction, the Lord Chancellor of England and Wales, Lord Bingham,[40] has indicated that:

> "... if ... legislation is not forthcoming, I think it almost inevitable that cases will arise in the courts in which the need to give relief is obvious and pressing; and when such cases do arise, I do not think the courts will be found wanting".[41]

[26.16] The Irish Law Reform Commission Consultation Paper on Privacy suggests the creation of a tort of privacy. It has also suggested that those who feared a breach of their privacy should be able to prevent the breach by applying for a 'Privacy Order'.[42] Individual privacy would further be protected by the imposition of criminal penalties on those who breached it.[43] There are many defects in the view which the Commission perhaps the most basic is that it is unable to cite examples of the Irish media invading the private life of individuals in an objectionable manner. Furthermore, the reforms suggested in the Consultation Paper would create protections for privacy equivalent, if not superior to explicitly recognising and protecting that right in the Constitution. This would appear to be Constitutional reform by the back door and may offend against the principle that the Constitution

---

[39.] *Per* Glidewell LJ, at p 66.
[40.] Who heard the *Kaye v Robertson* case in the Court of Appeal. Lord Bingham did not think that the plaintiff would have succeeded if he had brought his case based on trespass to the grounds of the hospital or breach of confidence. See, Bingham 'Opinion: Should there be a law to protect rights of personal privacy', [1996] EHRLR Issue 5, p 450 at p 457.
[41.] *Ibid,* at 462.
[42.] The Law Reform Commission Consultation Paper on Privacy, para. 9.18-9.62, p 200-212.
[43.] *Ibid,* para 11.27-11.31, p 255-256.

can only be amended by a referendum. If privacy is to be protected, then the appropriate route is to put the matter before the people in the form of a referendum.

THE PROTECTION OF PERSONAL DATA ON DIGITAL NETWORKS

[26.17] Digital networks generate large volumes of data such as destinations of calls, frequency and lengths of those calls, as a matter of course. This data is used for legitimate purposes such as billing but there is also a danger that it may be abused. This information may be protected by s 98(2A) of the Postal and Telecommunications Services Act 1983[44] which provides that an employee of Telecom Éireann will commit an offence if he discloses any information concerning the use made of telecommunications equipment provided to another person by Telecom Éireann save where the disclosure is made:

(a) at the request or with the consent of (that) other person,

(b) for the prevention or detection of crime or for the purpose of any criminal proceedings,

(c) in the interests of the security of the State,

(d) in pursuance of an order of a court,

(e) for the purpose of civil proceedings in any court, or

(f) to another person to whom (the employee) is required, in the course of his duty as such an employee, to make such disclosure.

The obvious disadvantage with this provision is that it only applies to employees of Telecom Éireann. Traditionally the phone systems of most countries have been closely controlled by the State. At present the European Union is making considerable efforts to liberalise the European telecommunications market. Obviously this will give rise to fears that new operators in the market will not protect their subscribers' privacy. To allay these fears the draft Directive on the Protection of Personal Data and privacy in the context of digital telecommunications networks, in particular the integrated services digital network (ISDN) and digital mobile networks was submitted by the Commission on 14 June 1994.[45] The purpose of this draft Directive is to try to balance the rights of individuals to data protection[46] with new advanced digital public telecommunications networks which are emerging within the Community.[47] The draft Directive is an

---

[44.] As amended by s 13 of The Interception of Postal Packets and Telecommunications Messages (Regulations) Act 1993.

[45.] OJ 94/C 200/04.

[46.] Recital 1.

[47.] Recital 2.

acknowledgement of the increasing risks connected with computerised storage and the processing of personal data in such networks and that specific legal, regulatory and technical provisions must be made in order to protect personal data and the privacy of users.[48] There is a danger that as Member States adopt diverging provisions to regulate this area, the internal market for telecommunications will be hindered.[49]

Objective of the Directive

[26.18] The Directive provides for the harmonisation of data protection and for the free movement of telecommunication equipment and services within the European Union. The Directive applies to the processing of personal data by telecommunications organisations[50] in connection with the provision of public telecommunications services[51] in public digital telecommunications networks[52] in the Community, particularly via the integrated services digital network (ISDN) and public digital mobile networks.[53] Member States must endeavour to ensure that this Directive will also be applied to analogue networks[54] which are the older type of phone system.

Security

[26.19] If there is a particular risk of a breach of security, the telephone company must inform subscribers[55] of these risks and offer them encryption facilities. This is particularly relevant to mobile phone calls[56] which in the past have been prone to interception.[57]

---

[48]. Recital 6. A user is any person using a telecommunications service for private or business purposes without necessarily having subscribed to this service. Article 2.

[49]. Recital 8.

[50]. Article 2(1) defines this as a public or privacy body to which a Member States grants special or exclusive rights for the provision of a public telecommunications network and where applicable public telecommunications services.

[51]. Article 2(6) defines public telecommunications service as a telecommunications service whose supply Member States have specifically entrusted *inter alia* to one or more telecommunications organisations eg Telecom Éireann.

[52]. Article 2(5) defines this as public telecommunications infrastructure which permits the conveyance of signals between defined network termination points by wire, microwave or optical means or by other electromagnetic means.

[53]. Article 3.

[54]. Article 3(3).

[55]. A subscriber is defined as any natural or legal person having subscribed to a telecommunications service of a telecommunications organisation or another service provider. A service provider is a natural or legal person providing services whose provision consists of the transmission and routing of signals in a public telecommunications network, with the exception of radio broadcasting and television. Article 2.

[56]. Article 4.

[57]. Telecom.

Billing data

[26.20] Processing of the number and identification of the subscriber, his address, the number of units used, details of phone calls made by the subscriber and other information such as payments by instalments, disconnection and reminders will be permitted for the purposes of billing. Access to this information must be restricted to the persons responsible for billing. This data may only be stored until the end of the statutory period in which the bill may be challenged.[58] The Statute of Limitations 1957 prescribes a period of six years in which an action for breach of contract may be brought. Personal data used by the switching gear of a telecommunications system to process calls must be erased as soon as it is no longer needed.[59] If an itemised bill is produced, Member States must ensure that the privacy of those who make and receive calls is preserved.[60] Calls may only be forwarded from one subscriber to another if the recipient has agreed.[61]

[26.21] If 'call-line identification' is offered by a telecommunications company, the caller must have the option of preventing the transmission of their identification with each call or from all outgoing or incoming calls. Subscribers must also be given the option of only receiving incoming calls whose callers have not removed their identification. These provisions will apply to all calls made to and from third countries. These services must be offered free of charge.[62] In some exceptional circumstances, the telecommunications company may disregard a caller's elimination of his identification. This will occur where a subscriber wishes to trace malicious calls. In this situation the data must be stored by the telecommunications company and made available to the appropriate authority. It will also occur where a specific court order is made to prevent or pursue serious criminal offences. A permanent facility may be made available to fire brigades and emergency phone services. This facility must be available on a national and community wide basis.[63]

Directories

[26.22] Entries in a telephone directory must be limited to what is necessary for identification unless the subscriber has consented to the entry of additional information. The subscriber must be able to prevent the

---

[58.] Article 5.
[59.] Article 6.
[60.] Article 7.
[61.] Article 10.
[62.] Article 8.
[63.] Article 9.

identification of his or her sex and be omitted from the directory free of charge.[64]

Surveillance of communications

[26.23] Member States must ensure that eavesdropping equipment will only be used when authorised by the appropriate judicial or other authorities. The content of telephone calls may only be recorded or broadcast via loud speakers with the consent of the parties to the phone call. This last provision will not apply if the call is malicious or if it is the subject of an investigation to prevent or pursue serious criminal offences.[65]

Unsolicited calls

[26.24] Appropriate measures to prohibit unsolicited calls for promotional advertising or research purposes must be made by Member States, if subscribers do not wish to receive them. Automatic call devices for transmitting pre-recorded messages may only be used in respect of subscribers who have given their consent. These provisions will also apply to fax messages.[66]

Technical features and standardisation

[26.25] In implementing the Directive, Member States must ensure that no technical features are imposed on equipment which could impede the free circulation of such equipment within the EU. If such features are necessary, the Commission must be informed. If necessary the Commission will ensure the drawing of common European standards.[67] If the Directive has to be adapted to meet changing technology, the Commission will determine how it is to be modified.[68]

Judicial Remedies

[26.26] If the rights guaranteed by the Directive are breached, every person has the right to a judicial remedy. The Member State must impose sanctions to dissuade any individual from breaching the Directive.[69] The Working Party and the Committee established by the Data Protection Directive[70] will also be responsible for data protection under this Directive.[71]

---

64. Article 11.
65. Article 12.
66. Article 13.
67. Article 14.
68. Article 15.
69. Article 16.
70. OJ L 281, 23/11/95, p 31.
71. Articles 17 and 18.

Chapter 27

Electronic Commerce

INTRODUCTION

[27.01] At present, enormous sums of money are transferred every day by means of electronic networks. Banks, financial services companies and other institutions all rely on networks to facilitate the transfer of cash and the performance of contracts. Electronic data interchange (EDI) and other similar services all enable commercial transactions to be carried out electronically. However, the Internet presents the opportunity to sell goods and services directly to consumers 24 hours a day throughout the year regardless of the remoteness of the supplier and consumer from one another. At present, 11 million people search for holidays on the Internet[1] and German companies have complained of increased competition as customers search for rival suppliers on the Internet.[2] In some cases, such as transmission of a video or a program over the Internet may be new types of goods or services. Groceries and consumer durables may also be ordered over the Internet and delivery arranged. The Internet will make considerable sums of money for the first company or person to work out how to sell products on it successfully. At present, the growth of this type of activity is restrained by insufficient capacity on most telecommunications systems and an absence of proper methods of payment. Only $200m worth of goods are sold on the Internet at present. Estimates suggest however that up to $30 billion of goods may be sold in this way by the end of this century.[3] Credit card numbers may be used for payment over the Internet but fears about the insecurity of networks has led to an unwillingness to use them. The development of the Internet as an emporium for sales to the public will have to wait until a suitable form of electronic money or method of payment is developed.

ELECTRONIC MONEY

[27.02] Although electronic money has the potential to create an international currency and redefine how business is carried out, at present there is no suitable form of electronic money and there are several problems

---

1. *The Economist*, 3 August 1996.
2. *The Financial Times*, April 1996.
3. *The Economist*, 27 July 1996.

which must be overcome. First, the Internet is insecure without suitable software and it would be difficult to transfer electronic money securely and guard against forgery. Secondly, because of the danger of forgery, buyers and sellers must be able to authenticate the money which they receive. Thirdly, some buyers and sellers will prefer to use money which cannot be traced to them in the same way as cash may be used anonymously. Finally, electronic money must be divisible which would mean that one unit of electronic money could be divided into much smaller units. Any electronic currency will have to be international since the Internet is international. It is likely that the currency will be denominated in terms of dollars or Euros. One of the most enthusiastic advocates of this type of cash is the EU which sees it as part of monetary union. However, much of the research has concentrated on electronic smart cards.[4]

[27.03] Once commercial activities become common on the Internet, they will cause a myriad of problems for the established law. Gamblers will be able to place bets with casinos and other operations in remote countries. Taxation will be a major problem since it will be very difficult to control and police the millions of transactions which may occur every day. If a company is established in a tax haven for the purpose of trading on the Internet, it will argue that it is subject to the lenient tax regime of that jurisdiction. Some US States have tried to overcome this by claiming that the local service provider is in fact the point of sale and not a computer based in the Cayman Islands[5] or another State with a low tax regime.

DIGITAL SIGNATURES

[27.04] One of the major problems with the Internet is that it is impossible to be sure that everybody is who they say they are.[6] The standard e-mail screen can be easily faked,[7] but even without such technical trickery communications can be easily counterfeited. Messages on the Internet come in a string of nondescript code which deprive humans of the visual and aural clues which allow them to be sure that people are who they say they are. Encryption may solve this problem simply and cheaply. Public key systems create digital signatures by encrypting a block of text with the private key. Anyone can use the public key to decrypt the message but no one can create such a file without knowing the private key.[8] Encryption based systems have been developed which are specifically designed to authenticate users and

---

4. BYTE, June 1996, p 80.
5. *The Economist,* July 1996.
6. See generally, Wright, 'Alternatives for Signing Electronic Documents', (1995) 11 (May-June), CLSR 136.
7. Wallich, 'Wire Pirates', Scientific American, March 1994
8. Stallings, 'Pretty Good Privacy' BYTE, July 1994, pp 193-196.

network connections.[9] However, authenticating large numbers of users is very difficult and may need to be handled by specialist companies.

[27.05] A digital signature is an electronic substitute for a manual signature. To use a digital signature the user must have created a public and private key pair.[10] The signature will be a code will be encrypted before it is sent using the sender's private key. The recipient will be able to determine whether the communication was sent by the person who claims to have sent it by decoding it using the public key. Since the signature is a summary of what is contained in the document he will also be able to determine whether the whether the message has been altered after it was signed by comparing the two. The main difficulty with this system is that it all depends on being certain that the individual using a certain public key is who they say they are. This could be verified by receiving the public key from an individual in person, but this is often not practical. As a result 'certification authorities' have sprung up; these are trusted persons or institutions who ascertain the identity of a person and certify that the public key of a public-private key pair used to create digital signatures belongs to that person. If the certification authority is satisfied that a subscriber to their service is genuine, they will issue a certificate, this is a computerised record that certifies that an identified individual uses a certain public key. This certificate will usually then be held on a database controlled by the authority where anyone who wishes to communicate with the individual may verify the authenticity of their public key. To protect the authenticity of digital signatures they may be altered periodically.

MAKING CONTRACTS ON NETWORKS

[27.06] There should be no great legal difference between buying a product from a vendor who operates a sales service using e-mail than buying one from a vendor who uses the phone system. The problems which may arise particular to contracts formed on-line may arise from difficulties verifying the identity of the parties. Where contracts are made on-line they will follow the normal rules of offer and acceptance. In general, where a advertisement is placed on the World Wide Web or similar system, it will be regarded as an invitation to treat and not an actual offer.[11] If the courts are to find that a contract has been created then they must find that a definite offer has been made[12] which must have been accepted by the other. The point of interest

---

9. Kay, 'Distributed and secure', BYTE, June 1994, p 170.
10. See para **[26.05]**.
11. See *Minister for Industry and Commerce v Pim* [1966] IR 154; see also *Partridge v Crittenden* [1968] 2 All ER 421; [1968] 1 WLR 1204; *Pharmaceutical Society of Great Britain v Boots Cash Chemists* [1952] 2 QB 795; [1952] 2 All ER 456, [1953] 1 QB 401; [1953] 1 All ER 482.
12. See *Carlill v Carbolic Smoke Ball Co* [1892] 2 QB 484; [1893] 1 QB 256.

here is how that acceptance is communicated. Mere silence will not indicate consent,[13] there must be some act done or message sent which the law can regard as a communication of acceptance. Where an on-line contract is made, the parties may never meet face to face and they may well eschew the use of paper, relying instead exclusively on the use of e-mail and other electronic documents to communicate their intentions. If acceptance is communicated by e-mail, then logically it should be treated the same as a communication which is made by telex. In *Entores v Miles Far East Corporation*[14] the plaintiffs were based in the UK and the defendant's agents were based in Amsterdam. The plaintiffs offered to buy goods from the defendants and they dully accepted. The offer and the acceptance were made using telex machinery. The Court of Appeal ruled that the parties were in effect in each other's presence and that the contract was made when it was accepted by the plaintiffs in London.[15]

International Jurisdiction

[27.07] International computer networks such as the Internet will obviously cause problems of international jurisdiction. The most serious difficulties may be found to be evidential and procedural, it is possible that the greatest difficulty will be the logistical problems of dealing with a large increase in the number of cases involving questions relating to conflicts of law. It is now common for companies to invite competitive tenders, on the Internet, from suppliers situated anywhere in the world.[16] The Brussels Convention on Jurisdiction and the Enforcement of Judgments in Civil and Commercial matters is implemented in Ireland as The Jurisdiction of Courts and Enforcement of Judgments (European Communities) Act 1988. Article 2 of the Convention provides that a "person domiciled in a contracting state shall, whatever their nationality by sued in the Courts of that state". However, Article 5(1) of the Convention provides that "A person domiciled in a contracting state may in another contracting state be sued in matters relating to a contracts in the courts for the place of performance of the obligation in question". Reconciling these two provisions caused problems in *Hanbridge Services Ltd v Aerospace Communications Ltd.*[17] The plaintiff contended that it had agreed to manufacture and the defendant had agreed to buy 8,000 computers. The plaintiff was registered and domiciled in Ireland and the

---

13. See *Russell & Baird v Hoban* [1922] 2 IR 159; *Felthouse v Bindley* (1862) 11 CBNS 869; *Miller* 35 MLR 489.
14. [1955] 2 QB 327; [1955] 2 All ER 493.
15. See also *Brinkibon v Stahag Stahl und Stahlwarenhandelsgesellschaft GmbH* [1983] 2 AC 34; [1982] 1 All ER 293.
16. For example Japan Airlines has a special procurement section on the its Web-site (WWW.jal.co.jp) which lists items that it wishes foreign firms to bid for. *The Economist*, 8 February 1997.
17. [1994] ILRM 39.

defendant was registered and domiciled in the UK. In the Supreme Court Finlay CJ applied the principles set out by that court in *Unidare Plc v James Scott Ltd*[18] and *Gannon & Co v B & I Steampacket Co*,[19] he also referred to the judgment of the European Court of Justice in *Athanasios Kalfelis v Bankhaus Shroder Munchmeyer Hengst & Co*.[20] He came to following conclusions:

> "(1) The onus is on the plaintiff who seeks to have his claim tried in the jurisdiction of a contracting state other than the contracting state in which the defendant is domiciled to establish that such claim unequivocally comes within the relevant exception.
>
> (2) In a case of a claim for breach of contract, therefore, what he must prove is that the obligation in question in that claim is by virtue of the terms of the contract or by some generally applicable principle of Irish law an obligation which must be performed in Ireland.
>
> (3) It would follow from this that where the evidence adduced by a plaintiff seeking to have a claim for breach of contract tried within the jurisdiction of a contracting state other than the state of domicile of the defendant amounts to no greater standard of proof than establishing that the obligation which it is claimed was breached *could*[21] have been performed in such a state he would have failed to satisfy his entitlement to sue pursuant to Article 5(1), the necessary proof being that the obligation which it is claimed has been broken by the defendant according to the contract or according to some general principle of Irish law *must*[22] be performed in the state concerned."[23]

No appeal had been taken against the conclusion of the High Court that actual delivery was to take place in England. However, the breach was alleged to have been the defendant's failure to place orders with the plaintiff in Shannon. The Court could find no evidence to support this conclusion and could not unambiguously state that the obligation to place the order in Shannon was an act to be performed or not. The Supreme Court made an order striking out the plaintiff's proceedings on the grounds that they were not maintainable in the Irish courts. As more commercial transactions are carried out on networks such as the Internet, disputes of this kind will become more common. If an Irish person places an order with a German based firm which supplies software from a UK company, is the place of

---

18. [1991] 2 IR 88.

19. [1993] 2 IR 359.

20. Case 189/87 [1988 ECR] 5565. See s 4 of The Jurisdiction of Courts and Enforcement of Judgments (European Communities) Act 1988 "Judicial Notice shall be taken of any ruling or decision of or expression of opinion by the European Court on any Question as to the meaning or effect of any provision of the Conventions"

21. Finlay CJ's emphasis.

22. Finlay CJ's emphasis.

23. Page 45 of the judgment.

performance of the obligation Germany (where the order is received), the UK (from whence the software is dispatched) or Ireland (from where the order is dispatched and where the software is received)?[24]

[27.08] The Brussels Convention also confers special rights on consumers, if they make a contract with another party they may bring a claim against the other party in their own State or that of the other party.[25] In contrast, the other party may only bring proceedings in the State in which the consumer is divided, although this does not affect the right to bring a counter-claim.[26] In proceedings relating to patents, trademarks and designs the courts of the State in which registration has been applied for will have exclusive jurisdiction.[27] If parties to a contract, one of whom is residing in a contracting state, agree that the courts of another state are to have jurisdiction to settle any disputes which may arise with regard to a particular legal relationship then that court will exclusive jurisdiction.[28] One of the most important features of the Convention is that it provides for judgments of the courts of contracting states to be recognised and enforceable in each others' jurisdictions.[29]

ELECTRONIC DATA INTERCHANGE CONTRACTS

[27.09] Electronic Data Interchange ('EDI') is frequently used by large companies and institutions for conducting commercial transactions over telecommunications networks. Product specifications, pricing and other commercial information may be transferred using EDI and as a result contracts will be made. Funds may also be transferred by banks and other financial institutions using this system.[30] The European Commission

---

24. See *Carl Stuart v Biotrace Ltd* [1993] ILRM 633; *Ferndale Films v Granada Television Ltd* [1993] 3 IR 368 and decisions of the ECJ in *de Bloos v Bouyer* [1976] ECR 1497; *Shenavai v Kreischer* [1987] ECR 239.
25. Article 13.
26. Article 14. Although this may be departed from if agreements were made - Article 15.
27. Article 16(4)
28. Article 17.
29. Sections 3 & 5 of the Act and Articles 26 and 31 of the Convention. See also *Barnaby (London) Ltd v Mullen* [1996] ILRM 24; *Paper Properties v Power Corporation* High Court unrep, 26 October 1995 Carroll J; *Elwyn (Cottons) Ltd v Pearle Designs Ltd* [1989] IR 9; [1989] ILRM 162; *Rhatigan v Textiles Y Confecciones Europeas SA* [1990] 1 IR 126; [1990] ILRM 825; *Westpac Banking Corporation v Dempsey* [1993] 3 IR 331; *Fraser v Buckle* [1991] 1 IR 1.
30. See generally, Carr and Williams (Eds) *Computers and Law*, (Intellect Books, 1995). Walden, 'Contractual Harmonisation in the EU', Computer Law & Practice, Vol 11, No 1, 1995; Maduegbuna, 'The effects of electronic banking techniques on the use of paper based payment mechanisms in international trade', JBL 1994, p 338; McKeon, 'EDI: uses and legal aspects in the commercial arena', Journal of Computer & Information Law, Vol XII, 1994, p 511.

Recommendation[31] relating to the legal aspects of EDI promotes a model or standard EDI agreement in order to promote consistency of agreements within the EU. EDI is defined as the electronic transfer from computer to computer of commercial and administrative data using an agreed standard to structure EDI messages. These messages are prepared in a computer readable format and are capable of being automatically and unambiguously processed.[32] The importance of EDI standards is that they ensure the compatibility of electronic messages. The Commission Recommendation tries to take this process a step further by promoting contracts which are standard throughout the EU.

[27.10] The standard form contract requires that parties expressly waive any rights to contest the validity of a contract solely because it was effected by EDI. Each party must ensure that the content of the EDI message is not inconsistent with the law of its country. Any contract effected by EDI is concluded at the time and place where the EDI message constituting acceptance of an offer reaches the computer system of the offeror.[33] The parties must agree that in the event of a dispute the records of EDI messages will be admissible before the court and will constitute evidence of the facts contained within unless evidence to the contrary is produced.[34] These articles try to make it easier to enforce EDI contracts through the courts.

[27.11] The parties must agree that messages will be processed as soon as possible after receipt. An acknowledgement of receipt will not be required unless requested. If such an acknowledgement is requested, it must be sent within one business day of the time of the receipt of the message. If the acknowledgement is not received, the sender may treat the EDI message as null and void.[35] The parties must undertake to implement and maintain security procedures in order to ensure that the EDI messages are protected against unauthorised access, alteration, delay, destruction or loss. Security procedures must ensure the verification of origin and integrity, the non-repudiation of origin, and receipt and confidentiality of EDI messages. The verification of origin and integrity which identifies the sender of a message and ensures that any message received is complete and uncorrupted are mandatory for all EDI messages. If EDI messages are rejected or errors are detected in such a message, the sender must be informed. The receiver of the message may not act upon it until proper instructions are received from the sender.[36]

[31.] 19 October 1994 OJ L 338, 28/12/94, p 98.
[32.] Article 2.
[33.] Article 3.
[34.] Article 4.
[35.] Article 5.
[36.] Article 6.

[27.12] The parties must ensure that EDI messages containing confidential information are maintained in confidence and are not disclosed or transmitted to other parties. If information is in the public domain it cannot be regarded as confidential. The parties may use encryption to ensure confidentiality. If the EDI message includes personal data and it is sent to a country with no data protection law, each party must agree to respect provisions relating to the automatic processing of personal data.[37] A complete and chronological record of all EDI messages must be maintained by the parties unaltered and securely for three years following the completion of the particular transaction to which the messages relate. This time period is only a minimum and longer periods may be required by legislation. The Criminal Justice Act 1994 (which deals with money laundering) requires records of bank transactions to be kept for five years.[38] EDI messages must be stored by the sender in the transmitted format and by the receiver in the format in which they were received. Parties must ensure that computer records of the EDI messages are readily accessible and are capable of being reproduced and printed in a human readable form.[39]

[27.13] The parties must undertake to implement and maintain the environment in which EDI operates. This means providing and maintaining the equipment, software and services necessary to transmit, receive, translate, record and store EDI messages. The parties may determine the means of communication and must ensure that messages are transmitted in accordance with the UN/EDIFACT standards.[40] The contract must include a technical annex which will give the technical, organisational and procedural specifications which will allow EDI to be operated according to the terms of the agreement.[41]

[27.14] No party to the agreement will be liable for any special, indirect or consequential damages caused by failure to perform its obligations under the agreement. Parties to the agreement will not be liable for loss or damage caused by delay or failure to implement the agreement where that delay is caused by an impediment beyond that party's control. Many companies will not have the expertise to use EDI and so they may engage the services of intermediaries to do this for them. If an intermediary is engaged by one party to operate EDI, that party will be liable for damages arising from the intermediary acts, failures or omissions. If one party requires the other to use the services of an intermediary, then the party who required the use of the intermediary will be liable for the intermediary's acts, failures or

---

37. Article 7.
38. Criminal Justice Act 1994, s 32(9).
39. Article 8.
40. Article 9.
41. Article 10.

omissions.[42] The draft agreement has two alternatives for dispute resolution. The parties may either agree to arbitration or else that the courts of a specified State will have sole jurisdiction.[43] They must agree which country's law will apply to the agreement.[44] The agreement will be effective from the date on which it was signed. Modifications may be made to it and any party may terminate the agreement by giving one month's notice. If any article is found to be invalid, all other articles will remain in full force and effect.[45]

DISTANCE SELLING AND THE PROTECTION OF CONSUMERS

[27.15] The telephone has already been used and abused for the purposes of marketing. As a result, rules are already being enacted to deal with this problem. The European Union is now in the final stages of enacting a directive which will deal directly with this problem and will be directly applicable to e-mail.[46]

Distance Selling Directive

[27.16] The draft Council Directive on the Protection of Consumers in Respect of Contracts Negotiated at a Distance (distance selling)[47] regulates the relationship between suppliers and consumers where contracts of sale are not negotiated in person.[48] The Directive applies to the following means of communication: printed matter, standard letters, press advertising or catalogues with an order form, small advertisements, telesales whether automated or otherwise, radio, video phone or video text, electronic mail, fax machines, teleshopping and video cassettes.[49]

[27.17] Member States must take effective measures to ensure that those who do not wish to be solicited may avoid such solicitation. These measures should be without prejudice to other legislation concerning the protection of personal data and privacy. Fax machines, electronic mail, telephones and automatic calling machines may only be used with the prior consent of the consumer.[50] These provisions will seriously hamper the organisation of

---

[42.] Article 11.

[43.] Article 12.

[44.] Article 13.

[45.] Criminal Justice Act 1994, s 14.

[46.] See also a decision of the European Court of Justice, *Alpine Investments BV v Minister van Financien* (Case C-384/93) 10 May 1995; [1995] All ER (EC) 543.

[47.] COM (93) 396 Final - SYN 411. 1993/C 308/18.

[48.] The Directive has no application to automatic vending machines, automated commercial premises, contracts for the supply of foodstuffs, beverages or other goods for current consumption in the household.

[49.] Annex 1.

[50.] Article 4.

distance selling operations since it will be necessary to get the consent of every potential customer before contacting them on the phone, presumably by means such as the post. All contracts should be designed and presented in such a way to comply with the principles of good faith in commercial transactions and to ensure the protection of minors and others who are unable to give their consent. All solicitations should make their commercial purpose clear, preventing commercial operations from masquerading as charities, sports clubs or other non-commercial bodies. The solicitation should state without ambiguity whether the cost of communication to place the order is borne by the consumer.[51]

[27.18] When a consumer is approached he must be given clear and unambiguous information, in particular about the identity of the supplier; the main characteristics of the product or service; the price and quantity of any transport charges and VAT charges if not included; the payment, delivery and performance arrangements; the right of withdrawal; and the period for which the solicitation remains valid.[52]

Solicitation by teleshopping

[27.19] Where consumers are solicited by television advertisements and shopping channels, presentations must comply with the provisions of Directive 89/552/EEC.[53] If the full contents of any contract are not displayed on the television screen, the consumer may request that this information be conveyed in writing.[54]

Inertia Selling

[27.20] Member States must ensure that consumers are not supplied with products or services which they have not ordered beforehand and asked either to purchase them or to return them, even at no cost. If products or services are so supplied, the consumer will have the right to do with them as he pleases without making any payment unless there has been an obvious mistake. This means that the consumer need never return the goods and this should ensure that this type of sale will never be used. If there has been a mistake, then the consumer may merely hold them at the disposal of the supplier for a reasonable period provided that no inconvenience is caused to the consumer. Failure to reply does not constitute consent. The provisions do not apply to free samples or promotional gifts provided it is made clear that they are completely free of charge and that the consumer is not under any obligation. If a supplier cannot supply the exact product or service specified

---

[51.] Article 5.
[52.] Article 6.
[53.] The Council Directive on the co-ordination of certain provisions laid down by law, regulation or administrative action in Member States concerning the pursuit of television broadcasting activities. OJ L 298, 17/10/89.
[54.] Article 7.

in a contract, but instead supplies a similar product, this will not constitute inertia selling provided that the consumer may return the substitute product if dissatisfied.[55]

The Right of Withdrawal

[27.21] Where a contract is negotiated at a distance, the consumer must have at least seven days in which to cancel the order without cost. The period of seven days will begin for products from the receipt of the product and for services, on the date when the consumer receives documentation informing him that the contract has been concluded. The consumer must be able to provide a document as evidence of return, which presumably is a receipt of posting. If the product or service is purchased on credit, then the consumer must be able to cancel the credit where it has been supplied directly by the supplier or where it has been provided by a lender on the basis of a prior agreement with the supplier. This right will not apply *inter alia* to services performed within seven days, personalised goods or hotel, catering or transport reservations. This right is without prejudice to other rights such as those relating to defective products.[56]

Content of the Contract

[27.22] Not later than the time of delivery, the consumer must receive at least the following information in writing and in the language used in the contract solicitation:

-   the information referred to in para **[27.18]** above;
-   the name and address of the supplier's most appropriate place of business for the consumer;
-   payment arrangements, including credit terms or terms for payment by instalments;
-   arrangements for exercising the right of withdrawal;
-   other contractual conditions such as those relating to guarantees.

If the contract is open-ended, the conditions under which it can be rescinded must be indicated. These provisions have no application to services supplied by means of telecommunications such as long distance telephone calls, however, the supplier must nevertheless indicate his most appropriate place of business and the amount of costs incurred by the service on demand.[57] The consumer cannot be required to make a payment before delivery of the product or performance of a service.[58] If no time limit is stipulated in the contract, performance must begin not more than 30 days after the order is

---

55. Article 9.
56. Article 12.
57. Article 11.
58. Article 8.

received by the supplier.[59] The consumer may not waive any rights conferred on him by this Directive.

[27.23] If a non-EU country is chosen as the country whose laws are applicable to the contract, then Member States must ensure that the rights under this Directive will not be prejudiced.[60] Member States must also ensure that consumers are informed of the provisions of this Directive and of relevant codes of conduct.[61] They should also ensure that adequate and effective means exist to enforce compliance with this Directive. This should involve enabling trade and consumer organisations to take legal action. Courts should be able to demand from suppliers proof of the existence of a request, the consumer's consent and compliance with time limits. The courts must also be able to order discontinuation of solicitation.[62]

Credit Cards

[27.24] If the holder of a credit card questions the validity of any operation in which the number of the credit card has been recorded without identification of the means of payment, the operation must be cancelled. The supplier's bank account must be debited and the consumer's bank account must be credited as soon as possible.[63]

Codes of Practice

[27.25] The European Commission has recommended that trade associations of suppliers should adopt codes of practice to regulate distance selling.[64] The trade associations should ensure that their members comply with the code. A code of practice should at least contain the following: consumers should not be approached if they have made it clear that they do not want such approaches, ethical principles (especially respect for human dignity and religious or political beliefs) to be respected, fair competition to be upheld with regard to sales promotions such as reductions, rebates, gifts lotteries and competitions, consumers are to receive clear information and provision should be made for reimbursements of payments if required and a right of withdrawal. This is provided for in the Irish code of practice for advertising standards.

---

59. Article 10.
60. Article 16.
61. Article 15.
62. Article 14.
63. Article 13.
64. Commission Recommendation of 7 April 1992 on codes of practice for the protection of consumers in respect of contracts negotiated at a distance. 92/295/EEC, OJ L 156/21, 10 June 1992.

Chapter 28

Liability for Defective Computer Products and Services

CONTRACTUAL LIABILITY

[28.01] The normal rules of contract and commerce apply to computer software and hardware as they do to any other product or service. Providers of these products or services will be liable for defects, non-compliance, misrepresentation and all other normal contractual liabilities. Standards are different for computer products than for other goods. It is not unusual for programs to contain several errors or 'bugs' which are usually regarded by customers as a normal feature of buying or commissioning new computer software.

THE SALE OF GOODS LEGISLATION

[28.02] Sales of goods and services are regulated by the Sale of Goods Act 1893 as amended by the Sale of Goods and Supply of Services Act 1980. This legislation will imply a condition of sale into every contract of sale that the goods supplied must be of merchantable quality and reasonably fit for any purpose for which they are supplied.[1] It would seem likely that computer software will be regarded as 'goods' for the purposes of the Act. The Sale of Goods Act itself defines goods as:

> including all chattels personal other than things in action and money (and also) emblements, industrial growing crops and things attached to or forming part of the land which are agreed to be severed before sale or under the contract of sale.[2]

In an Australian case of *Toby Constructions Products Ltd v Computer Bar Sales Pty Ltd*,[3] the court held that a sale of a computer system, comprising both hardware and software constituted a sale of goods. However the court left open the question of whether software alone was goods. This question was addressed by the English High Court in *St Albans City Council v*

---

[1]. Sale of Goods Act 1893, s 14 as amended by s 10 of the Sale of Goods Act 1980.
[2]. Section 62.
[3]. [1983] 2 NSWLR 48; 50 ALR 684.

International Computers Ltd.[4] The definition of goods in the UK Sale of Goods Act 1979 is similar to that in the Irish legislation. Although Scott-Baker J did not believe that it was necessary to decide the point, he was of the view "that software probably is goods within the Act". He pointed out that if the supply of software was not a supply of goods it would be difficult to see what it could be, other than something to which no statutory rules apply. This would leave the purchaser unprotected in the absence of an express agreement. The decision was appealed and in the Court of Appeal, Glidewell J examined the question of whether or not software was goods. He felt that a computer disk containing a program came within the definition of goods in the UK Sale of Goods Act 1979 but that equally clearly a program of itself did not. He declined to hold that this contract was subject to the sale of goods legislation because the plaintiff was never supplied with computer disks or any other tangible thing on which the program was encoded, an employee of the defendant had installed the particular program onto the plaintiff's computer, removing the disk when he left. This is difficult to reconcile with the decision of the Court of Appeal in *R v Whiteley*[5] where the court held that the magnetic particles which held computer data on a disk were tangible enough to be damaged under the terms of the UK Criminal Damage Act 1971. The creation of a set of magnetic particles which held the program on the plaintiff's computer could amount to the delivery of goods.

[28.03] An alternative analysis is that the act of creation of the program on the plaintiff's computer is a service. However, the more practical approach to the sale of a program, or more usually the sale of a licence to use a program, is to treat it as a sale of goods. Most programs are sold and used in a manner similar to typewriters or televisions. Where services are supplied, such as advice and maintenance, these are usually ancillary to the sale of the program. The main difficulty with regarding software as goods is that software is rarely sold, rather a licence is granted allowing the buyer to use the program. Whether a licence to use a program can be a sale of goods for the purposes of the legislation is unclear. The Copyright Act 1963 may lessen the uncertainty in this regard as s 47 states that:

> ... copyright shall be transmissible by assignment, by testamentary disposition or by operation of law, as personal or movable property.

[4.] [1995] FSR 686. Subsequently upheld by the Court of Appeal, see *The Times* 14 August 1996.

[5.] (1991) 93 Cr App Rep 25.

Merchantable Quality

[28.04] Usually, contracts will contain terms relating to the description and quality of the goods to be provided. Terms may also be implied by the Sale of Goods and Supply of Services Acts 1893-1980. Section 14 of the 1893 Act provides that where a seller sells goods in the course of a business, there is an implied condition that they are of merchantable quality. This will not apply if the defects are specifically drawn to the buyer's attention or if an examination is made prior to contract by which the defect should have been revealed. Goods are of 'merchantable quality' if:

> they are as fit for the purpose or purposes for which goods of that kind are commonly bought and are as durable as it is reasonable to expect having regard to any description applied to them, the price (if relevant) and all the other relevant circumstances.

Since it may be widely accepted that programs are frequently sold with minor faults and bugs contained in them, only exceptionally bad programs will breach the standard of 'merchantable quality'. In *Saphena Computing Ltd v Allied Collection Agencies Ltd*,[6] the plaintiff company agreed to supply the defendant with a computer system for use in the defendant's debt collection business. A dispute arose and the plaintiff sued for monies owed and to vindicate its intellectual property rights. The defendant counterclaimed, *inter alia*, for the supplier's failure to supply software which was reasonably fit for the purpose for which it was required. In the Court of Appeal, Staughton LJ accepted that:

> "software is not necessarily a commodity which is handed over or delivered once and for all at one time. It may well have to be tested and modified as necessary. It would not be a breach of contract at all to deliver software in the first instance with a defect in it."

He accepted that in this case the supplier should have the right and the duty to test and modify as necessary the software they supplied. This would have to have been done within a reasonable time.[7]

Supply of Services

[28.05] Contracts for computer software and hardware may also contain agreements to maintain and service the system supplied. The Act includes terms which are to be implied into contracts for the supply of services where the supplier is acting in the course of business. These terms imply:

[6.] [1995] FSR 616.

[7.] See also *Virgin Interactive Entertainment Ltd v Bluewall Ltd* Ch Div, Masons Computer Law Reports, 27 January 1995, p 4.

(a)   that the supplier has the necessary skill to render the service;

(b)   that he will supply the service with due skill, care and diligence;

(c)   that where materials are used, they will be sound and reasonably fit for the purpose for which they are required; and

(d)   that where goods are supplied under the contract, they will be of merchantable quality within the meaning of s 14(3) of the Act.[8]

In *Irish Telephone Rentals v Irish Civil Service Building Society*,[9] the plaintiff agreed to install and maintain the defendant's telephone system. At first the system worked well but after a few years it was unable to cope with an increased volume of calls as the defendant's business expanded. The system was supposed to be able to cope with this expansion and Costello J held that under s 39 the contract contained an implied term that goods supplied pursuant to the contract would be of merchantable quality. As the telephone system did not work, the plaintiff was in breach of this term.

[28.06] In *Stephenson Blake (Holdings) Ltd v Streets Heaver Ltd*,[10] the plaintiff engaged the defendant as a consultant to advise it on the purchase and installation of a new computer system for its business. The defendant was commissioned to advise on various issues, including a review of the existing system, selection of suppliers, implementation of the new system and assessment of the need for training and other requirements. The defendant was also to advise on whether it would be better to order a packaged software system or commission a new one. It was accepted by the court that the plaintiff had very little knowledge of computers and that the plaintiff relied entirely on the defendant's expertise and advice. The defendant accepted that it was an implied term of the contract that it would at all material times exercise a reasonable degree of care and skill. The defendant recommended that the plaintiff acquire a package called Management 2000 and the plaintiff duly purchased this. This package was inadequate. Only two elements of it were suitable, the rest of the package was either incomplete or unproved in commercial use. At the time it was recommended to the plaintiff, the system was unacceptably deficient in its capacity to carry out the functions for which it was required and contained an excessive number of faults. However, there was no evidence of actual knowledge of the defects by the defendant and the plaintiff failed to show that the defendant should have carried out the tests which would have

---

8.   Section 39.
9.   [1991] ILRM 880.
10. Judgment of Hicks QC on the Queen's Bench, 2 March 1994. Masons Computer Law Reports, p 17.

enabled the defendant to learn of the defects. The defendant also advised on the installation of hardware and this was hopelessly inadequate. The defendant had passed on a quote from a supplier who had an obvious incentive to under-specify in order to undercut prices without any independent calculation of its own. The court therefore held that the defendant knew or should have known that the hardware was inadequate for the plaintiff's purposes.

[28.07] The court accepted that a suitable system for the plaintiff would have been more expensive than that acquired on the advice of the defendant. Competent advice from the defendant would not have protected the plaintiff against all defects and it must be assumed that the plaintiff would not have enjoyed a totally trouble-free period of implementation and use but rather would have had to endure the normal difficulties encountered when setting up a new computer system. Hicks J held that the defendant's fees were not recoverable for the work done in setting up the Management 2000 system. However, assessing damages and fees recoverable for advice given on how to minimise the damage done by the installation of the inadequate system was complicated by the fact that the plaintiff had acquired a new simpler system which replaced the Management 2000 system and which worked well. Hicks J therefore ordered a further trial to assess what damages would be payable as a result.[11]

[28.08] The plaintiff in *Simpson Nash Wharton v Barco Graphics Ltd*[12] had the misfortune to be used as a 'guinea pig' when it bought a computerised design system, including both software and hardware, from the defendant. The system with which it was supplied was a brand new update of the defendant's successful product and failed to work at all. The plaintiff's employees were not trained in the use of the system (nor were the people training them), there were no manuals with the system and the software was littered with faults. After spending considerable time trying to get the system to work, the plaintiff rescinded the contract and successfully sued for the return of monies paid and consequential loss. One question before the court was at what time should the plaintiff have rescinded the contract. The defendant suggested that recission should have occurred within three weeks of the supply of the system but the plaintiff did not in fact rescind until the fortieth week. The defendant sought to show that as a result of the lapse of time and the plaintiff's continued use of the system, the plaintiff had accepted the system. The court held that the plaintiff was justified to wait this long as it had made a considerable investment in the product and the

---

11. The parties later settled the action out of court.
12. Queen's Bench, unrep, 1 July 1991.

defendant continued to make representations to the plaintiff that the system could be made to work.

[28.09] It is not unusual for exalted claims to be made about the usefulness and quality of commercial products but this is a particular problem in the computer industry since highly complex and expensive products may be bought by people with little or no expertise in the use or application of computers. In *MacKenzie, Patten and Co v British Olivetti Ltd*[13] the plaintiffs were a two-man firm of solicitors who knew nothing about computers but believing that one might be helpful with their office administration invited a representative of the defendant to call and discuss matters. As a result the plaintiffs bought a computer which nine months later they asked the defendant to remove, having never used it. The difficulty which the plaintiffs faced was that as they had acquired the computer on lease from a third party finance company, they could not sue under the Sale of Goods Act. Instead they sued, alleging breach of a common law warranty in a collateral contract, misrepresentation and negligence. The plaintiffs were successful and the court effectively ordered recission of the contract of sale. The case is interesting because there was considerable difference between the parties as to the capabilities of the computer the plaintiffs thought they were buying. One of the partners was enthusiastic about the purchase since he erroneously believed that the computer would connect him to a database in the Central Criminal Court and show the progress of trials in which they were involved. There was no such database in existence and there was no way for the computer to communicate with the database even if it did exist.

EXCLUSION CLAUSES

[28.10] Most suppliers of software and hardware will anticipate possible problems by inserting exclusion clauses in contracts for their products. These will usually be contained in standard form contracts which consumers and other customers may not be able to negotiate. An exclusion clause is a contractual term which purports to limit or exclude liability for breach of contractual terms. A common example is a clause which places a limitation on the damages which may be claimed for such a breach. However there are several routes by which the application of such clauses may be limited.

[13.] See Staines 'Computer Sales "Caveat Distributor"' (1985) MLR 344.

Fundamental Breach

[28.11] If one party seeks to rely on an exclusion clause, the other party may rely on the doctrine of fundamental breach which will not allow one party to evade liability for breach of one of the fundamental elements of the contract. This was accepted by the Supreme Court in *Clayton Love & Sons (Dublin) v British and Irish Steam Packet Co Ltd.*[14] The defendant had agreed to carry frozen scampi to the UK. The plaintiff had made it clear to the defendant that the cargo would have to be shipped frozen, however, it was loaded into holds at atmospheric temperature and it took seven hours before freezing point was reached. The scampi was destroyed. When the plaintiff sued, the defendant sought to rely on two exclusion terms, one purporting to exclude all liability in respect of any loss or damage whatsoever and the other requiring any claims for damages to be made in writing within three days of the cargo arriving. The Supreme Court held that the exclusion clauses were unenforceable as the failure to keep the scampi below freezing point was a breach of a fundamental term.

Commercial Sales and the Sale of Goods Act

[28.12] If a sale is a commercial one, exclusion clauses which purport to exclude or limit liability for breach of terms implied by the Sale of Goods Act relating to the quality of the goods will be unenforceable unless they are shown to be fair and reasonable.[15] The schedule to the 1980 Act sets out the criteria which are taken into account in determining what is fair and reasonable:

1. If a term is fair and reasonable the test is that it shall be a fair and reasonable one to be included having regard to the circumstances which were or ought reasonably to have been known to or in the contemplation of the parties when the contract was made.

2. Regard is to be had in particular to any of the following which appear to be relevant:

    (a) The strength of the bargaining positions of the parties relative to each other taking into account (among other things) alternative means by which the customer's requirement could have been met;

    (b) whether the customer received an inducement to agree to the term or in accepting it had an opportunity of entering

---

14. (1970) 104 ILTR 157.
15. Section 55(4).

into a similar contract with other persons but without having to accept a similar term;

(c) whether the customer knew or ought reasonably to have known of the existence and extent of the term (having regard, among other things, to the custom of the trade and any previous course of dealing between the parties);

(d) where the term excludes or restricts any relevant liability if some condition is not complied with, whether it was reasonable at the time of the contract to expect that compliance with that condition would be practicable; and

(e) whether any goods involved were manufactured, processed or adapted to the special order of the customer.

'Fair and reasonable'

[28.13] The question of whether a term was fair and reasonable was examined in *The Salvage Association v CAP Financial Services*.[16] The plaintiff had contracted with the defendant for the design, development and supply of computer accounting software. The defendant was unable to complete the software and that which it had completed contained numerous errors. The plaintiff terminated the contract, rejected the software and dismissed the defendant. The plaintiff sued for breach of contract and claimed for the repayment of the contract price and damages for wasted expenditure. The contract contained a clause which limited the defendant's liability to £25,000. The court had to decide whether this term was fair and reasonable under the UK Unfair Contract Terms Act 1977 which has requirements similar, though not identical, to the Irish Sale of Goods Acts. Forbes J accepted that both parties were of equal bargaining power, the contract was freely negotiated and that there were companies other than the defendant with whom the plaintiff could have negotiated. The plaintiff did not feel disadvantaged while negotiating the contracts and had received professional advice relating to them. However, Forbes J felt there were other circumstances which led him to the conclusion that the limited liability term was not fair and reasonable. First, the defendant offered no evidence to justify the figure of £25,000 or show how it had been calculated. The figure had no relationship to the defendant's turnover, insurance cover, the value of the contract and the financial risk to which the plaintiff was exposed. Secondly, the inadequacy of this figure had been accepted by the defendant's management who had decided to increase it to £1,000,000 for other contracts, however, this increase was not included in this contract.

[16.] [1995] FSR 654.

Therefore, Forbes J held that the figure of £25,000 was far too low to be reasonable, considering the defendant's standing, resources and turnover. In addition, there were other factors which reinforced Forbes J's decision. The defendant had never suggested that there was any risk of failure and it appeared that the work required was quite straightforward. The plaintiff reasonably believed that the system would be satisfactorily completed within an acceptable time scale. It was not possible for the plaintiff to obtain insurance against the failure of the defendant and indeed, the plaintiff would not have had any good reason to seek out such insurance. Finally, the defendant had the resources to meet a substantial claim for damages. The defendant was insured in respect of the plaintiff's claim for £5,000,000. In any event, the defendant could have met claims of up to £1,000,000 from its own resources. He awarded damages of over £600,000 for monies paid under the contract, items of wasted expenditure and wasted management time.

[28.14] The question of fairness and reasonableness of terms in computer contracts was also considered in *St Albans City Council v International Computers Ltd*[17] where the plaintiff, a local authority, entered into a contract with the defendant for a computer system which was to be used in administering the council's collection of the community charge. The contract for the system was signed in haste as the council was under pressure to have the system up and running as soon as possible. The system included a database which contained the details of every charge-payer in the council's area. In order to set the charge, the council extracted the number of charge-payers from the database. Due to an error in the software, the population was overstated by 2,966 resulting in an underestimate of the sum which each individual charge-payer had to pay. The extraction of the population figures from the database was an extremely complex process which took about 40 hours, however, when completed, the print-out of the results just contained a series of zeros. The plaintiff assumed that this meant that there was a problem with the part of the program that produced print-outs. Therefore the plaintiff copied the figures from the display screen which a representative of the defendant had assured it was safe to do. In reality, the representative of the defendant did not have the necessary technical knowledge of the system to give such an assurance and he did not check the facts with his company's technical staff. These figures were erroneous because of a defect in the software. The loss to the plaintiff as a result of the error was £1,314,846. However, the contract signed by the defendant limited its liability to £100,000. In his judgment, Scott-Baker J noted the serious time restrictions which had been placed on the plaintiff. Although the plaintiff's agents had

17. [1995] FSR 686.

queried this clause, they were told that any divergence from the defendant's standards terms and conditions would result in delays and might affect its ability to supply the software in time. Scott-Baker J was satisfied that the defendant fully exploited the plaintiff's concern to obtain a prompt agreement and that the plaintiff had no realistic option other than to accept the defendant's limited liability term. He also noted that all of the firms, including IBM, which had tendered for the contract included a limited liability term in their standard contracts.

[28.15] Although the defendant sought to rely on the limited liability clause, under s 3 of the Unfair Contract Terms Act 1977, they could only rely on the clause to the extent to which it was reasonable. In deciding that the clause was unreasonable, Scott-Baker J first examined the defendant's resources. He noted that in 1988 the defendant had issued a press release which stated that it was a subsidiary of a communications and information systems group with a worth of £2 billion and before-tax-profits of £100.2 million on a turnover of £1,109 million for the first half of 1988. Secondly, the defendant held product liability insurance for an aggregate sum of £50 million world-wide. The defendant called no evidence to show that it was fair and reasonable to limit its liability to £100,000. Thirdly, the defendant was in a very strong bargaining position. There was only a very limited number of companies who could meet the plaintiff's requirements and the plaintiff was "over a barrel because of the tight time scale". Fourthly, the plaintiff received no inducement to accept the clause and had it entered into a contract with anyone else they would have met a similar clause. Finally, Scott-Baker J concluded that all of these factors outweighed the fact that the plaintiff knew about the exemption clause and had made representations about it.

[28.16] The decision was appealed by the defendant. The first ground of appeal was that the defendant had agreed to supply a system which was to be fully operational by the end of February 1990, until that date the contract between the parties recognised that it would be a system which was still being developed. In particular, the defendant claimed that it was not contractually bound to provide software which would enable the correct figure to be extracted in December. This submission was rejected by the Court of Appeal. Nourse LJ stated that parties who agree to supply and acquire a system recognising that it is still in the course of development cannot be taken, merely by virtue of that recognition, to intend that the supplier shall be at liberty to supply software which cannot perform the function expected of it at that stage of development.[18] The *St Albans* case

---

[18.] The appellant did succeed in getting the damages reduced as the amount which was not claimed from the taxpayers could still be claimed.

illustrates the difficulties which may be encountered when buying software which is still in development.

Consumer Sales and the Sale of Goods Acts

[28.17] The Sale of Goods Acts contain provisions to protect consumers from exclusion clauses. If a purchaser buys software or hardware as a consumer, any term which purports to exclude or diminish his rights relating to the implied terms as to the quality of the goods is declared void.[19] Consumer sales are defined as follows:

> A party to a contract is said to deal as consumer in relation to another party if:
>
> > (a) he neither makes the contract in the course of a business nor holds himself out as doing so, and
> >
> > (b) the other party does make the contract in the course of a business, and
> >
> > (c) the goods ... supplied under or in pursuance of the contract are of a type ordinarily supplied for private use or consumption.[20]

All three conditions must be met before the sale can be regarded as a consumer sale. Computers and software will often be bought for the dual purposes of both private and business use. This may not prevent the sale from being regarded as a consumer purchase. For example in *R & B Customs Brokers Co v United Dominions Trust Ltd*,[21] the purchase of a car by a company and used privately by the owners of the company was still held to be a consumer purchase as the car was ordinarily used for private purposes.

The Unfair Terms in Consumer Contracts Regulation 1995

[28.18] The Unfair Terms in Consumer Contracts Directive[22] was implemented in Ireland as the European Communities (Unfair Terms in Consumer Contracts) Regulations 1995[23] and has the objective of counteracting unfair terms in consumer contracts. The Regulations apply to any term in a contract concluded between a seller of goods or supplier of services and a consumer which has not been individually negotiated.[24] This refers to standard form contracts. Even if one specific term has been individually negotiated, this will not prevent the application of the

---

19. Section 55(4).
20. Section 3(1) of the 1980 Act.
21. [1988] 1 WLR 321.
22. OJ L 95/29. Council Directive 93/13 of 5 April 1993.
23. SI 27/1995.
24. Regulation 3(1).

Regulations to the rest of the contract.[25] A consumer is any natural person who is acting for purposes which are outside his business, trade or profession.[26] If a term is found to be unfair, it will not be binding on a consumer but if the contract is capable of continuing in existence without the unfair term, it will continue otherwise to bind the parties.[27]

[28.19] A contractual term will be regarded as unfair if it causes a significant imbalance in the parties' rights and obligations under the contract to the detriment of the consumer and contrary to the requirements of good faith. This must take into account the nature of the goods or services for which the contract was concluded and all circumstances surrounding the conclusion of the contract and all other terms of the contract or of another contract on which it is dependent.[28] In determining whether a term is in good faith or not, regard must be had to the following: the strength of the bargaining positions of the parties; whether the consumer was induced into agreeing to any term; whether the goods or services were sold or supplied to the special order of the consumer and finally, the extent to which the seller or supplier has dealt fairly and equitably with the consumer whose legitimate interests he has to take into account.[29]

[28.20] The Regulations suggest that the following terms are unfair, however this list is only indicative and not exhaustive. These terms are those which have the effect of:

(1) Excluding or limited the legal liability of the vendor in the event of the customer dying or suffering personal injury as a result of an act or omission or the vendor.

(2) Inappropriately excluding or limiting legal rights of the consumer against the vendor in the event of the non-performance or inadequate performance of the contract. This might apply to suppliers of software who claim to exclude liability for errors, bugs and faults in the software.

[25.] The burden of showing that a term was individually negotiated is placed on the person claiming that it was: Regulation 3(6).

[26.] Regulation 2. The Regulations will not apply to employment contracts, those relating to succession rights or rights under family law, any contract relating to the incorporation and organisation of companies or partnerships and any contracts which reflect legal obligations: Schedule 1.

[27.] Section 6.

[28.] Regulation 3(2).

[29.] Schedule 2.

(3) Making an agreement binding on the consumer whilst making the vendor's obligations dependant on the fulfilment of a condition which can only be fulfilled by the vendor.

(4) Allowing the vendor to retain monies paid by the consumer if he does not fulfil the contract without providing for the consumer to receive equivalent compensation if the vendor does not fulfil the contract.

(5) Requiring any consumer who fails to fulfil his obligation to pay a disproportionately high sum in compensation.

(6) Allowing the vendor to dissolve the contract on a discretionary basis if the same facility is not granted to the consumer or allowing the vendor to retain monies paid for services not yet supplied if the vendor dissolves the contract.

(7) Allowing the vendor to terminate the contract of indeterminate duration without reasonable notice except where there are serious grounds for doing so.

(8) Automatically extending a contract of fixed duration, if the consumer does not otherwise indicate by a fixed deadline, if this deadline is unreasonably early.

(9) Irrevocably binding the consumer to terms with which he had no real opportunity of becoming acquainted before the conclusion of the contract.

(10) Enabling the vendor to unilaterally alter the terms of the contract without a valid reason specified in the contract unless the consumer is given reasonable notice of the change and is free to dissolve the contract.

(11) Enabling the vendor to unilaterally alter any characteristics of the products or services to be provided.

(12) Providing that the prices are to be determined at the time of delivery or allowing the vendor to increase prices without giving the consumer a right of cancellation if the price is too high.

(13) Giving the vendor the right to determine whether goods or services are in conformity with he contract or giving him the exclusive right to interpret any term of the contract.

(14) Limiting the vendor's obligation to respect commitments undertaken by his agents.

(15) Obliging the consumer to fulfil all his obligations even if the vendor does not perform his.

(16) Giving the vendor the possibility of transferring his rights and obligations under the contract to another without his consent.

(17) Excluding or limiting the consumer's right to take legal action or exercise any other legal remedy particularly by requiring the consumer to take disputes exclusively to arbitration not covered by legal provisions or unduly restricting the evidence available to the consumer or imposing on him a burden of proof which would normally lie with another party to the contract.[30]

A term will not be regarded as unfair in relation to the definition of the main subject matter of the contract or to the adequacy of the price or remuneration provided these terms are in plain, intelligible language.[31] Where the terms of the contract are in writing, the vendor must ensure that they are drafted in plain and intelligible language. If there is a doubt about the meaning of a term, then the interpretation most favourable to the consumer must prevail.[32] The Director of Consumer Affairs may apply to the High Court for an order prohibiting the use of unfair terms in contracts.[33]

[28.21] Retention of title clauses are a normal part of many commercial contracts. Such a clause will usually provide that property or title in specific goods will not pass to the purchaser until the full purchase price of those goods has been paid to the vendor.[34] There is no reason why title in intellectual property cannot be retained by the vendor in much the same way as property in other forms of property. The Sale of Goods Acts 1893-1980 also contain potential remedies for the unpaid vendor:[35] the vendor will have a lien or a right of retention over the relevant goods; if the purchaser is insolvent then the vendor has the right to stop the goods in transit; the vendor has a right of resale, and if property in the goods has not passed, then the vendor may withhold delivery to the purchaser.[36] In any contract for the supply of information technology it is essential that the rights and duties of the parties in the event of a breakdown of the contract are clearly set out. Many companies may find that if they cannot use their computers they effectively will be forced to cease trading, at least until they can restart their

---

[30.] Section 3(7), Schedule 3.

[31.] Section 4.

[32.] Section 5.

[33.] Section 8.

[34.] See, for example, *Re Stokes and McKiernan* [1978] ILRM 240; *Frigoscandia (Contracting) Ltd v Continental Irish Meats Ltd* [1982] ILRM 396; *Uniake v Cassidy Electrical Supply Co Ltd* [1988] IR 126.

[35.] Part IV of the Act, ss 38-48.

[36.] Section 39.

systems. Users should ensure that any contracts which they sign for the supply of information technology services state that in the event of a dispute arising between the parties they will still be able to use the relevant programs or other material at least until they can find a replacement. Contracts might state that all such disputes be referred to arbitration, they should also clearly and unambiguously specify who is the owner of any software supplied. If software is supplied under licence from a third party then the contract should specify who is the licensee and who is responsible for maintaining the licence.

CONTRACTS AND COMPUTER CRIMES

[28.22] The Criminal Damage Act 1991 is a broadly worded piece of legislation and as a result criminal offences may be unwittingly committed by those involved in commercial transactions. Contracts for the sale, maintenance and service of computer software should be specific about the circumstances in which software and other computer components may be repossessed, removed or disabled. If a dispute arises as to payment during a commercial transaction, it is not unusual for the vendor to repossess his property or otherwise assert what he perceives to be his rights. This may give rise to problems in a dispute over computer software since by repossessing or disabling the software, the vendor may be committing a number of offences under the Criminal Damage Act 1991. He may gain unauthorised access to the buyer's computer system and in repossessing the software he may intentionally or otherwise damage the buyer's data. Confusion over commercial contracts such as these has led to criminal prosecutions in the UK. In *R v Goulden*[37] the defendant installed security software on his client's computer system. The software had a facility which prevented use of the system if the password was not entered. The defendant utilised this facility in an effort to secure payment of his fees for £2,275. He prevented the client from using his computer for several days. The client claimed to have lost business worth £35,000 and to have paid £1,000 to an expert to override the password system. The defendant was charged with unauthorised modification of computer material, pursuant to s 3 of the UK Computer Misuse Act 1990. On conviction, the court imposed a two year conditional discharge and £1,650 fine on the defendant.

[28.23] In *R v Whitaker*,[38] the defendant was a software developer who was contracted to develop software for a client. A dispute developed over

---

[37.] Southwark Crown Court, unrep, 1992.
[38.] Scunthorpe Magistrates Court, unrep, 1993.

payment. He initiated a small program which prevented use of the software by his client in an effort to force his client to pay. He argued that he was entitled to modify the software under his contract since under the contract, he had retained all intellectual property rights in the software until payment. However, he was charged with unauthorised modification of computer material, pursuant to s 3 of the UK Computer Misuse Act 1990. In spite of his contract, he was convicted as the court held that the contract limited the exercise of these rights. It was noted by the court that had a clause been inserted in the contract which specifically allowed for this action, then the defendant would not have been convicted. Similarly, clauses should be inserted into contracts for the writing, sale and maintenance of software stating that where data is damaged as a result of the normal operation of that software, whether by bugs in the program or other technical problems, that damage is not actionable.

TORTIOUS LIABILITY

[28.24] Where computer software and hardware fail to work as required, then those who suffer damage as a result may be able to sue for damages or compensation in tort. The essence of a tort action is that if one person has a duty of care to another and fails to take reasonable steps to vindicate that duty and as a result of which the other party suffers injury, he may be liable for his negligence. This is a much wider cause of action than are based on contract. If defective software or hardware is bought, only the parties to the contract of sale will be able to sue for damages caused by the defect under contract law. The duty of care extends to persons who are not necessarily parties to a contract. Indeed, there may not even be any contract.

[28.25] In *Donoghue v Stevenson*[39] the duty of care was stated to be that:

> "you must take reasonable care to avoid acts or omissions which you can reasonably foresee would be liable to injure your neighbour. Who then in law is my neighbour? The answer seems to be - persons who are so closely and directly affected by my act that I ought reasonably to have them in contemplation as being so affected when I am directing my mind to the acts or omissions which are called in question."

There are two types of tort action which are currently viewed as having particular application to information technology. These are the torts of breach of privacy and defamation. These are dealt with elsewhere in the book.[40]

[39.] [1932] AC 562, accepted in Ireland in numerous judgments, eg *Keane v ESB* [1981] IR 44.
[40.] See Chs 25 & 26.

LIABILITY FOR COMPUTER VIRUSES

[28.26] In theory, it should be possible to recover damages from an individual who places a virus on another's computer. The usual scenario is that one person's computer is infected with a virus which unknowingly and inadvertently, they pass on to another. The most obvious defendant in this situation is the author of the virus but it is unlikely that this person will be identifiable. Therefore the most likely action to be taken is against the person responsible for placing the virus on the computer. If this was done, while doing other work such as maintenance or servicing, there may be a contractual clause which will regulate the liability. Viruses have at times been included in packaged software and in such a case purchasers will have a remedy against the retailer under the Sale of Goods Act 1893 and the Sale of Goods and Supply of Services Act 1980. If the virus is placed on a computer in a non-commercial situation, in the absence of a contract or user agreement, the only remedy may be in tort. This might occur, for example, where one person gives another a disk containing a computer game which also contains a virus. In this situation it may be difficult to show that the defendant owed a duty of care to the plaintiff not to place a virus on his computer or rather not to use virus-infected disks.

[28.27] The difficulty here is that it may not be possible to take an action directly for the damage caused by the virus unless it can be shown that the defendant wrote the virus or deliberately placed it on the computer. Instead, the action will have to be taken for the negligence involved in allowing a virus to be placed on a computer which then causes damage. It may be very difficult to show a causal connection between the defendant's actions and injury to the plaintiff. Although the defendant may have been negligent in using an infected disk, the plaintiff may also have been negligent by not having a virus scanning program installed on his computer to check that disk. Since the only way that the defendant could have avoided infecting the plaintiff's computer would have been to have such a program installed on his own computer, the plaintiff's contributory negligence would arguably be equal to that of the defendant. Furthermore, the damage caused by the virus may be too remote to be linked to the defendant's actions. Some viruses may not cause damage for long periods of time[41] and when they do, users may take action which exacerbates the problem, such as reformatting their hard disk unnecessarily. Finally, even if it can be shown that someone placed a virus on a computer, and data was damaged on that computer, proving a connection between these two facts may be extremely difficult.

---

[41] See paras **[13.05]-[13.14]**.

LIABILITY FOR BREACHES OF COMPUTER SECURITY

[28.28] Where an individual or a company is employed to maintain the computer systems of another and there is a breach of security on that system, the liability for that breach might be regulated by contract. However, if somebody's privacy is compromised as a result of such a breach, such a person may wish to seek damages. There may be no contractual relationship between the parties. However, the Data Protection Act 1988 gives individuals a right of action in these circumstances. Under s 2 of the Act, the data controller must take appropriate security measures to prevent unauthorised access to, or alteration, disclosure or destruction of the data. Section 7 provides that for the purposes of the law of torts, data controllers and processors have a duty of care to the data subject in respect of their dealing with personal data. Alternatively, an action might be brought for a breach of the constitutional right to privacy, breach of confidence or nuisance.

[28.29] It would be very difficult to prove quantum damages in a case such as this unless it could be shown that the plaintiff was deprived of some direct benefit or suffered particularly adverse consequences. The courts may find it difficult to assess the appropriate sum of damages to be awarded in cases of embarrassment or annoyance unless it could be shown that the plaintiff had suffered a real (ie, medically accepted) trauma.

PROFESSIONAL NEGLIGENCE AND STANDARDS

[28.30] Any computer programmer or other person working with computers will be expected to exercise care and skill in his work. The application of standards of professional negligence to computer programmers is problematic. Unlike other professions, computer programming and other computer work does not have clear standards which are laid down by established authorities and applied throughout the computer industry. This is probably due to the fact that the computer industry is in its infancy and the rapid pace of change in the industry ensures that any agreed standards may be obsolete before they are published. As a result, consumers and others are forced to rely mainly on the representations of computer professionals that they are in fact competent to do their work.

[28.31] If a computer consultant or programmer holds himself out as having an expertise in a particular field, then he must attain the ordinary level of skill held by those who specialise in the same field. He will not be required to be any better than that standard.[42] The difficulty in computer cases is that the standard may be quite low.

[42.] *O'Donovan v Cork County Council* [1967] IR 173.

Standards for computer programming

[28.32] International standards exist for the documentation which should accompany computer software packages.[43] There is also an international standard for software quality.[44] This identifies six characteristics to be applied in determining software quality. These are functionality, reliability, utility, efficiency, maintainability and portability.

Standards for computer security

[28.33] There are also a wide variety of standards for computer security.[45] The British Computer Society and the Council of European Professional Informatics Societies have published security guidelines for computer professionals. These require that such professionals carry out an analysis of the risks to security of a particular computer system and establish security policies.

LIABILITY FOR DEFECTIVE PRODUCTS

[28.34] The Defective Products Act 1991 implements a European Directive concerning defective products.[46] Under this legislation a producer will be held liable in tort for damage caused wholly or partly by a defect in his product.[47] 'Product' is defined as movables and this includes movables incorporated into another product, or electricity, where damage is caused as a result of a failure of electricity generation. It is likely that a computer program will be included within this definition as a movable product. The EU Commission has confirmed in the European Parliament that the Directive does apply to software. However, this confirmation is not binding on a national court.[48] In any event, the use of the term 'movables' would suggest that the Act applies to everything except land and buildings.

[28.35] Damage means death, personal injury, or damage or destruction of property other than the defective product itself. The item of property destroyed or damaged must be of a type normally intended for private use and used by the injured person for his own private use.[49] Although defective software may do considerable damage, this damage is often in the form of

---

43. ISO (International Organisation for Standardisation) 9127.
44. ISO 9126.
45. For example, ISO 11131 which deals with sign-on authentication.
46. OJ L 210, 7/8/85, p 29.
47. Section 2(1).
48. Triaille, 'The EEC Directive of July 25th on Liability for Defective Products', Computer Law and Security Report, 1993, Vol 9, p 214.
49. Section 1.

time spent in order to rectify the defect in the software and the time for which the injured party must do without the services of the computer system. However, if damage is caused to other property by use of a defective computer program, then this damage would be recoverable. Since the Act only applies to property intended for private use, the damages recoverable will be limited since the most valuable forms of data or information will be those which may be exploited commercially. Nevertheless, computers are used in increasing numbers of toys, cars and domestic appliances. If these products are defective, they may cause injuries or damage which are actionable under the Act.

[28.36] A product will be defective if it fails to provide the safety which a person is entitled to expect. Account must be taken of factors such as the presentation of the product, its anticipated use and when the product was put into circulation. A product may not be considered defective solely because a better product is put into circulation subsequently.[50] The onus is on the injured party to prove the damage, the defect and the causal relationship between the defect and the damage.[51] An action for the recovery of damages under the Act may not be brought after the expiration of three years from the date of the cause of action arising or the date on which the plaintiff became aware of the damage, the defect and the identity of the producer. The right of action will be extinguished ten years after the actual product which caused the damage was put into circulation.[52] The Act does not affect any other rights of an injured person.[53] The liability of the producer may not be limited or excluded by contractual terms, notices or any other provisions.[54]

[28.37] The term 'producer' is defined very broadly. He may be the manufacturer or producer of a finished product or the manufacturer or producer of any raw material or component part used in a product. He may also be any person who holds himself out to be the producer of a product by placing his name, trade mark or other distinguishing feature on the product. He may be the person who imported the product into the State. If the producer cannot be identified, then the person who supplied the product will be liable provided that the injured person requests the supplier to identify the producer within a reasonable time and the producer fails to do so.[55]

[50.] Section 5.
[51.] Section 4.
[52.] Section 7.
[53.] Section 11.
[54.] Section 10.
[55.] Section 2.

[28.38] If damages to be awarded in respect of loss or damage caused by a defective product would not exceed £350, no damages will be awarded and where damages exceeding £350 would be awarded, only the sum in excess can be awarded.[56]

DEFENCES

[28.39] A producer will not be liable if he can show that:

(1) He did not put the product into circulation;

(2) It is probable that the defect which caused the damage did not exist at the time he put the product into circulation;

(3) The product was not manufactured or distributed by him for an economic purpose or in the course of business;

(4) The defect is due to compliance with any legal requirements including those imposed by the European Union;

(5) The defect could not have been discovered given the state of scientific and technical knowledge at the time the product was put into circulation; or

(6) In the case of a producer of a raw material or component, he can show that the defect is entirely attributable to the design of a product in which the component has been fitted.[57]

Quantum of damages

[28.40] The purpose of awarding damages or compensation is to ensure that the person who has suffered damage will be placed in the position which he was in before the actions of the defendant. The difficulty in computer cases is that it may be difficult to assess the quantum of this damage. Most prudent computer users will back-up data regularly, so that if data is lost on a computer due to the negligence of one party, then the user will be able to remedy the defect easily and cheaply. Provided the user has been prudent in this manner and has become aware of the problem at an early stage and is so able to remedy it, damage may be minimised and indeed problems of this type are considered normal. However, damages will be considerable if the defendant does not realise the difficulty and his data becomes corrupted without his knowledge. In *St Albans City Council v International Computers Ltd*,[58] the plaintiff suffered losses of £1,314,846 as a result of an incorrect assessment by a program supplied by the defendant of the number of

---

56. Section 3.
57. Section 6.
58. [1995] FSR 686; see para **[28.11]** *ante.*

potential tax payers within the plaintiff's borough. This figure was arrived at purely on the basis of the income lost by the plaintiff and interest payable on that income. However this sum was subsequently reduced by the Court of Appeal which held that the amount of tax which was not collected as a result of the program malfunction could still be collected from those who should have paid it at the time. Damages may also have to take into account the steps taken by the plaintiff to remedy the damage.[59] In *The Salvage Association v CAP Financial Services*[60] damages were awarded for items of expenditure which were wasted as a result of the defendant's failure to provide suitable computer software. These included payments for provision of computer services, wasted computer stationary, payments to consultants and testers and wasted management time. However, it would appear that a plaintiff can only claim for wasted expenditure or loss of profits. He cannot combine a claim for both.[61] The assessment of damages may be complicated by the fact that the plaintiff may have taken steps to minimise his loss. In some situations the plaintiff may simply dispose of defective software and hardware as occurred in *Stephenson Blake (Holdings) Ltd v Streets Heaver Ltd*.[62] Even if the defendant can show that defective software might be repaired and rendered usable, disposing of it may be justified if the plaintiff reasonably believed that the system was not reliable.

[59.] 15 Tr L 444, *The Times* 14 August 1996.

[60.] [1995] FSR 654.

[61.] See *Waterford Harbour Commissioners v British Rail* Supreme Court, unrep, 18 February 1981 and *Anglia Television Ltd v Reed* [1972] QB 60; [1972] 3 All ER 690.

[62.] Judgment of Hicks QC on the Queen's Bench, 2 March 1994. Masons Computer Law Reports, p 17.

Chapter 29

Computers in the Workplace

[29.01] Computers are now commonplace in every aspect of industry and commerce. They bring their own risks and dangers to the workers who use them. One of the most controversial injuries is that of repetitive strain injury which may affect users of computer keyboards. If a computer does cause injury, the victim may be able to claim damages through the tort process. Medical opinion on this injury is divided. The plaintiff's claim for 'tennis elbow' failed in *Sammon v Flemming GmbH*[1] where she claimed to have been engaged screwing caps on phials of drugs for eight hours a day. The expert opinion differed on the matter, the plaintiff's expert said that the plaintiff's condition was caused by her work but the defendant's expert disagreed. Barron J dismissed the claim as the defendant had acted reasonably and could not have been expected to anticipate the onset of this problem. However repetitive strain injury has become a "frequent feature of personal injury litigation in the UK".[2] In *Smith v Baker & Mckenzie*[3] the plaintiff was a legal secretary who claimed to have been given no breaks from her keyboard work. She found that high pressure typing caused her left hand to become stiff, painful and difficult to move and she was unable to perform certain household tasks. Ultimately, the plaintiff had to abandon audio-typing and was dismissed by the defendants. The court found in favour of the plaintiff and awarded her £7,250 in general damages, an award which totalled £35,313 once loss of earnings was included.

HEALTH & SAFETY LEGISLATION

[29.02] The Safety, Health and Welfare at Work Regulations[4] give effect to the Council Directive on Display Screen Equipment[5] which sets out both the minimum safety and health requirements for work with display screen

---

[1.] High Court, unrep, 23 November 1993 Barron J. See *Personal Injury Reports from Doyle Court Reporters*, Trinity and Michaelmas Terms 1993, p 158.

[2.] Kemp & Kemp *The Quantum of Damages,* Sweet & Maxwell, 1996 Vol 3 H8-001.

[3.] Unreported Judgment of HH Judge Callman, Mayors and City of London Court 11 April 1994, See Generally Kemp & Kemp, *The Quantum of Damages,* Sweet & Maxwell, 1996 Vol 3 H8-002-100.

[4.] SI 44/1993.

[5.] OJ L 156/14, 21/6/90.

equipment and provisions to ensure that those working with computers will have their eye sight adequately protected. Display screen equipment is defined as "an alphanumeric or graphic display screen regardless of the display process employed".[6] The Directive recognised that compliance with the minimum requirements for ensuring a better level of safety at workstations with display screens was essential for ensuring the safety and health of workers. It does however, try to avoid imposing administrative, financial and legal constraints in a way which might hold back the creation and development of small and medium sized undertakings. Employers are obliged to keep themselves informed of the latest advances in technology and scientific findings concerning workstation design so that they can make any changes necessary so as to be able to guarantee a better level of protection of workers' safety and health.[7]

[29.03] The Regulation has no application to control cabs or vehicles or machinery, computer systems on board a means of transport, or computer systems mainly intended for public use. Neither does it apply to portable systems which are not in prolonged use at a workstation, calculators, cash registers and any equipment having a small display and it does not apply to typewriters of traditional design.[8]

EMPLOYERS' DUTIES

[29.04] Employers are obliged to analyse their workstations in order to evaluate the health and safety environment of their employees. An employee is defined as anyone who habitually uses display screen equipment as a significant part of his normal work.[9] In particular, as regards possible risks to eyesight, physical problems and problems of mental stress, employers must take appropriate measures to remedy the risks found on the basis of this evaluation, taking account the combined effects of these risks.[10] A workstation is defined as an assembly comprising display screen equipment which may be provided with a keyboard or input device and/or software determining the operator/machine interface, optional accessories, peripherals including the disk drive, telephone, modem, printer, document holder, work chair and work desk or work surface and the immediate work environment of the display screen equipment.[11]

6. Regulation 29.
7. Recitals to the Directive.
8. Regulation 30.
9. Regulation 29.
10. Regulation 31(1)(b).
11. Regulation 29.

[29.05] Employers must also ensure that all workstations put into service after 31 December 1992 meet with the minimum requirements of the Regulations. There are lower standards for workstations put into service before that date but all workstations regardless of when they entered service must comply with all of the minimum requirements by 31 December 1996. The minimum requirement is generally that the use of computer equipment must not be a source of risk for employees. These requirements may be adapted to take account of technical progress, developments in international regulations and specifications and knowledge in the field of display screen equipment.[12]

The Working Environment for Computers[13]

(1) Equipment

[29.06] The characters on the computer screen must be well defined and clearly formed, of adequate size and with adequate spacing between the characters and lines. The image on the screen should be stable, with no flickering or other forms of instability and the screen must be free of reflective glare and reflections which might be liable to cause discomfort to the user. The brightness and/or contrast between the characters and the background must be easily adjustable by the operator and also be easily adjustable to ambient conditions. The screen must swivel and tilt easily and freely to suit the needs of the operator and it must be possible to use a separate base for the screen or an adjustable table.

[29.07] The keyboard must be tiltable and separate from the screen so as to allow the worker to find a comfortable working position avoiding fatigue in the arms or hands. The space in front of the keyboard must be sufficient to provide support for the hands and arms of the operator. The keyboard must have a matt surface to avoid reflective glare. The arrangement of the keyboard and the characteristics of the keys must be such as to facilitate the use of the keyboard. The symbols on the keys must be adequately contrasted and legible from the design working position.

[29.08] The work desk or surface must have a sufficiently large, low reflectance surface and allow a flexible arrangement of the screen, keyboard, documents and related equipment. The document holder must be stable and adjustable and positioned so as to minimise the need for uncomfortable head and eye movement. There must be adequate space for employees to find a comfortable position.

---

12. Article 10 of the Directive.
13. Schedule 10 and 11.

[29.09] The work chair must be stable and allow the operator easy freedom of movement and a comfortable position. The seat must be adjustable in height and the seat back must be adjustable in both height and tilt. A foot rest should be made available to anyone who wishes to use one. Alternative suitable seating may be provided.[14]

(2) The Environment

[29.10] The workstation must be dimensioned and designed so as to provide sufficient space for the user to change his position and vary his movements. The room lighting must ensure satisfactory lighting conditions and an appropriate contrast between the screen and the background environment, taking into account the type of work and the user's vision requirements. Any disturbing glare and reflections on the screen or other equipment must be prevented by co-ordinating the workplace and workstation layout with the positioning and technical characteristics of the artificial light sources. Workstations must be designed so that sources of light, such as windows and other openings, transparent or translucent walls, and brightly coloured fixtures or walls cause no direct glare and as far as possible no reflections on the screen. Windows should be fitted with a suitable system of adjustable covering to attenuate the daylight that falls on the workstation.

[29.11] When the workstation is being equipped, noise emitted by the equipment must be taken into account so as not to distract attention or disturb speech. The equipment belonging to the workstation must not produce excess heat which could cause discomfort to employees.

[29.12] All radiation with the exception of the visible part of the electromagnetic spectrum must be reduced to negligible levels from the point of view of the protection of employees' safety and health. An adequate level of humidity must be established and maintained.

(3) Operator/Computer Interface

[29.13] In designing, selecting, commissioning and modifying software and in designing tasks using display screen equipment, the employer must take into account the following principles:

  (i)   software must be suitable for the task;

  (ii)   software must be easy to use and where appropriate, adaptable to the operator's level of knowledge or experience. No quantitative or qualitative checking facility may be used without the knowledge of the employees;

[14.] Regulation 31(3).

(iii)   systems must provide feedback to employees on their performance;

(iv)   systems must display information in a format and at a pace which are adapted to operators;

(v)   the principles of software ergonomics must be applied, in particular to human data processing.

The requirements for software selection are self-evident. All employers will try to buy software which is suitable for their employees' work and will normally endeavour to buy the software which is easiest to use. The days when employers could autocratically decree how their employees should do their work and what tools they should use would seem to be at an end in some areas. One of the main reasons for the success of *WordPerfect* and then *Word for Windows* is that employers found it easier to buy the type of software which their employees were most familiar with and which they found easiest to use.

The training of employees

[29.14] Employees are entitled to receive information on all aspects of safety and health in relation to their workstation, in particular, information on measures which are implemented under the Regulations. Before the commencement of work, every worker should receive training in use of the workstation.[15] The employer must structure worker activities so that daily work on the display screen is periodically interrupted by breaks or changes so as to reduce the workload at the display screen.[16]

Protection of employees' eyes and eyesight

[29.15] All employers must ensure that all employees have access to an appropriate eye and eyesight test carried out by an optician. This should be available before commencing display screen work, at regular intervals afterwards and if they experience visual difficulties which may be due to working with display screens. If the results of the eye test suggest that it is necessary, an ophthalmological examination should be made available to the worker. If normal glasses or other corrective appliances are not suitable, then special corrective appliances must be made available.[17]

[15.]   Regulation 31(1)(g).
[16.]   Regulation 31(1)(f).
[17.]   Regulation 32.

Index